T0298957

# MACRO
# SOCIO-
# ECONOMICS

# MACRO SOCIO-ECONOMICS

## From Theory to Activism

David Sciulli

Editor

Routledge
Taylor & Francis Group

LONDON AND NEW YORK

First published 1996 by M.E. Sharpe

Published 2015 by Routledge
2 Park Square, Milton Park, Abingdon, Oxon OX14 4RN
711 Third Avenue, New York, NY 10017, USA

*Routledge is an imprint of the Taylor & Francis Group, an informa business*

Macro socio-economics : from theory to activism / David Sciulli, editor
p.    cm.
Festschrift for Amitai Etzioni.
Includes index.
ISBN 1-56324-650-3 (hardcover : alk. paper).
ISBN 1-56324-651-1 (pbk. : alk. paper).
1. Economics—Sociological aspects.   2. Macrosociology.
3. Social action.   4. Etzioni, Amitai.
I. Sciulli, David.   II. Etzioni, Amitai.
HM35.M35       1995
306.3—dc20       95-17028
CIP

ISBN 13: 9781563246517 (pbk)
ISBN 13: 9781563246500 (hbk)

# Contents

# Tables and Figures

# Acknowledgments

My first debt is to the contributors to this volume, all of whom worked hard in meeting our deadline—and also, I daresay, in putting up with my "suggestions for improvement" and other forms of abuse that editors mete out once they assume their position. Then, very quickly, I thank Amitai for asking me to put this collection together back in June 1993, in the midst of the Thirty-first Congress of the International Institute of Sociology in Paris. Sitting at a small table outdoors in the Place de Sorbonne on a warm, sunny day—quite literally in front of the statue of August Comte—Amitai assured me that I would have free rein over this collection. He wanted papers in his honor, but he did not want either the contributors or me looking over our shoulders for his approval. His ideas were fair game, and criticisms were to be tolerated, even encouraged. As always, Amitai has kept his word: He has not seen a single sentence of this collection in draft.

One more word. The norm for collections is that they are notoriously unwieldy contributions to scholarship. This is the case because an editor cannot know in advance who will come on board and who will beg off, and who later will deliver and who will falter for one reason or another. Even more, an editor cannot really know what the final contribution of any of the writers will look like, either in form or in substance, let alone whether and how they might relate to each other. An editor cannot really know, in short, whether the text that results will contain a coherent scholarly position or will instead fly off in four directions (or more!). In my view an identifiable tapestry of ideas runs through this volume, and I confess that this is not a product of my own doing. The contributors to this collection are talking to each other. Yet, none of them saw the work of the others at any stage in this collection's evolution. The reason that a tapestry has emerged is that all of us are operating within, through, and around Amitai Etzioni's ideas, and the richness of his own contribution to the discipline over four decades has brought us into dialogue. As editor, I arranged the chapter parts, but the dialogue that emerged is Amitai's doing.

# MACRO
# SOCIO-
# ECONOMICS

# Introduction

## By Etzioni: Theory, Research, and Policy

*David Sciulli*

Amitai Etzioni has been as prolific a sociologist across his career as any classic or contemporary social theorist. Like the discipline's other major social theorists, his writings, too, have fostered conceptual debate by theorists, empirical study by researchers, and policy proposals by decision makers and observers of the political scene. Indeed, of all sociologists in the world born since 1900, Etzioni ranks ninth in total citations in social science journals (Coughlin 1994). In addition, Etzioni has founded a research center (the Center for Policy Research at Columbia University), a new professional association (the Society for the Advancement of Socio-Economics), a new journal (*The Responsive Community*), and a new social movement (the Communitarian Network). It is important, I think, to stand back and place these accomplishments into context, both historical and contemporary.

In historical context, Etzioni's spanning of theory, research, and policy reminds one of the discipline's classic social theorists. Marx, Weber, and Durkheim all worked in these three areas (we tend to forget that all three were lively polemicists), and their writings also influenced others who worked in each area. More recently, Talcott Parsons may be remembered best as a grand theorist, and yet his effort to escape relativism at a conceptual level influenced three generations of prominent theorists and researchers. Much of Etzioni's own early work contains direct and indirect responses to Parsons's ideas. We cannot forget, moreover, that Parsons was actively engaged in formulating American policy

---

I have benefited greatly in writing this introductory statement from lengthy, lively conversations with Gideon Sjoberg in Austin, TX.

toward postwar Germany (Gerhardt 1993) and that he founded Harvard's inter-disciplinary Department of Social Relations (which he chaired until 1956).

In contemporary context, three American social theorists have been particularly courageous in entering the postwar domestic policy domain, spanning the 1950s, the 1960s, and now the 1980s and 1990s. Robert Merton dedicated himself to providing theoretical frameworks for empirical research. Yet, his engagement in the policy domain includes not only the development of policy toward the sciences but also a courageous resistance to McCarthyism at a moment most dire (Schrecker 1986 offers reminders for those who may have forgotten how dire). Merton was one of the first academicians in the country to protest the California loyalty oaths. Closer to home, he and other prominent Columbia professors publicly supported a leftist colleague on the campus—one who lacked tenure and other means of support—who had come to the attention of a New York State McCarthy committee. It is difficult to name a single other instance of this happening during the entire McCarthy period (and there were few instances indeed of university presidents coming to the support of self-proclaimed leftist colleagues).

James Coleman also is unique in publishing seminal works in theory, research, and the policy domain—plus Coleman in 1989 initiated a new scholarly journal, *Rationality and Society*. Coleman's contributions to educational policy in the 1960s stand as a model of courage, not only in the public policy domain but in the discipline of sociology itself. Just as Merton faced unthinking attacks by upstate New York farmers who wished to rid Columbia of leftist faculty, Coleman had to persevere in the face of unthinking colleagues in the discipline who were more interested in shouting him down in hallways at annual meetings than in engaging him in reasoned debate.

Today, Etzioni is bringing into the public domain controversial ideas regarding the relationship between the community and the individual, between the language of responsibility and the language of rights. He is presenting his ideas courageously in the face of those who prefer to label his ideas rather than to debate them.[1] (Readers of this volume will see that David Popenoe also is not particularly reticent about bringing controversial issues into today's scholarly and popular debate over the future of the family.)

### Grounded Critique and Practicable Policy Options

With one exception, theorists who effectively criticize current or historical social arrangements establish, and then defend with reasons, the standard of comparison they are using. Put more technically, these theorists "ground" their critique and thereby "elevate" their own positions above personal opinions, group preferences, or the fashions of the day in the academic world. The exception to this strategy of grounding for theorists who are critics of existing arrangements is to launch an absolutist critique. Social theorists turn to absolutism, for instance, when they adopt concepts that define any and all exercises of collective power in contemporary societies as inherently oppressive, as manifestations of a seamless "domination" or "hegemony." Foucault comes to mind as a skillful proponent of such absolutism, but so does Marcuse earlier and many postmodernists and literary critics today. Ironically, to move down the road of absolutism is, eventually, to arrive at a radical relativism, one culminating in outright nihilism (as Arendt demonstrated so eloquently in 1951). After all, if all exercises of collective power are pernicious, why exactly are SS agents more threatening than British bobbies?

By contrast, to move down the road of grounded critique is to keep open the possibility of renascence, of posing credible alternatives to existing social arrangements, alternatives that are reasoned, prudent, and practicable. Across his career, Amitai Etzioni has moved down this second road, at first lightly in his work on organizations, and even in his major theoretical work *The Active Society*, but then more forcefully in his more recent contributions to socioeconomics and communitarianism.

Let me stand back for a moment. If one excludes Etzioni's writings on international relations, his scholarly writings fall into four periods—even as the overarching concern that I mentioned above cuts across all four. What is remarkable about each period is that not only the substance of his concerns shifts but also his mode of presentation. The first period is marked by Etzioni's work on organizations (local, national, and international), and in particular his efforts to ground "guidance theory"—a theory of guided social change—on the distinction between utilitarian, coercive, and normative incentives. His mode of presentation is marked by a combination of middle-range concepts and reports of empirical research and case studies. The second period is marked by *The Active Society*, Etzioni's most elaborate and rigorous theoretical statement. His mode of presentation in this work reminds one of Parsons's, namely, thick, ponderous, and abstract. This work is developed methodically, claiming both internal consistency at a conceptual level and empirical suggestiveness. The third period is marked by a combination of policy-oriented statements (from *Genetic Fix* in 1973 to *Capital Corruption* in 1984) and the launching of socioeconomics in 1989, which was an effort to identify the "capsule" of norms and social bonds within which beneficial economic activity takes place. The mode of presentation here is a combination of scholarly reporting of others' research findings and a journalistic use of individual illustrations and hypothetical possibilities. The fourth period is Etzioni's synthetic reaction to signs of disintegration in America's major cities (including the nation's capitol), a reaction that he aptly calls communitarianism. Here the mode of presentation is both journalistic and moralistic, a mode designed to draw the attention and then active participation of the broad reading public.

Overall, Etzioni's work is significant not only for its intrinsic merits as a body of scholarly work developed across an impressive career but also as a tempered reflection of the direction of change of postwar America and of the West more generally. Signs of social disintegration are much more prominent on the contemporary landscape than they were even at the height of the antiwar protests in 1970. In retrospect, the oil embargo and recession of 1973 proved to be far more important for American and Western domestic policy than anything that happened in the 1960s.

Accordingly, Etzioni has become more critical, and at times even skeptical. Yet, there is another significant quality in his work: It has always been and remains today quintessentially American in its criticisms of existing social arrangements and public policies. (I stand by this statement even as I acknowledge, of course, that Etzioni was born in Germany and raised in Israel.) Contemporary Americans remain optimists, albeit somewhat frayed optimists of late. They continue to believe in "progress." They believe that problems are solvable, particularly those springing from faulty institutional design. Name a single major American theorist who has shared Weber's pathos, or the Frankfurt school's disillusionment. Not even Alvin Gouldner would quality. On the other hand, it is easy to name European-born social theorists who moved intellectually from pathos to greater optimism as they moved physically to the United States. Hannah Arendt in particular became as enthralled by the handiwork of this country's founders and framers as any constitutional scholar or American historian.

At the same time, it was only at the turn of the century that Americans themselves, led by the pragmatists, abandoned the founders' and framers' greater guardedness, their sense that a republic's institutional design rests ultimately on citizens' remaining vigilant in keeping government limited and otherwise responding to "abuse." The founders and framers were certain that the interrelationship between limited government and a social order congenial to such citizens is never an automatic outcome of strictly self-interested behavior in the market. By contrast, during the first decades of this century American pragmatists questioned the value or merit of deferring to any inherited rules and principles. They elevated the quest for "results" above "timeless principles." This questioning and this concern with immediate results resulted, eventually, in liberal complacency over institutional design utterly replacing the founders' and framers' earlier republican vigilance as this country's very ethos. Today, Americans believe that a limited government and a benign social order are somehow automatic outcomes of the equilibrium of supply and demand that accompanies individuals' decentralized efforts to maximize their own private wealth. Americans adopt the complacency of producers and consumers, forgetting that they are also citizens whose ultimate responsibility is to remain vigilant concerning the abuse or arbitrariness of state power and of exercises of collective power by "private" intermediate associations such as corporations.

The 1980s and 1990s have reminded Americans, however much they prefer to ignore the reminder, of what the founders and framers always sensed: The "hidden hand" of the market might well automatically balance supply and demand for producers and consumers and advance private wealth, but it does not some-how automatically yield an acceptable institutional design, one that interrelates limited government and a benign social order—a social order that institutional-izes normative mediations on abuse. All of Etzioni's works across his career can be read as updating and reformulating this reminder. In addition, when I said above that Etzioni's criticisms are quintessentially American, I meant that he has always linked his observations of existing social arrangements and public policies to positively stated, practicable alternatives and options. Far more than most other American social theorists, Etzioni has then actually pursued these alternatives and options into the public domain of politics and social movements.

**The Volume at Hand**

In the opening chapter of this volume, Richard Coughlin provides an overview of the contributions of four of Etzioni's major works, rightly arguing that Etzioni's focus has been on the normative factors in social action. In addition, Coughlin follows the trail of citations of Etzioni's first major work, *A Comparative Analysis of Complex Organizations* (1961), and explores three lines of criticism of his most recent major work, *The Moral Dimension* (1988). Coughlin's appendix, an important contribution in itself, contains a cluster map of cocitations with other prominent social scientists; with this, we can literally see where Etzioni's works "fit" in relationship to those of classics and contemporaries alike.

The two contributions in Part I address and use concepts from *The Active Society*. Hans Joas notes that while Etzioni's general prominence both in the United States and internationally is unquestioned, his major contribution to theory, *The Active Society*, has not generated much exegesis or commentary. What little it has received has been both superficial and critical. Joas's explanation for this state of affairs is that Etzioni's theory offered a synthetic alternative to Parsons's structural functionalism, but by the late 1960s the discipline became more interested in thoroughgoing criticisms of this then-reigning "paradigm." Ever since, the discipline has had difficulty categorizing this particular work, finding its place in relationship to contemporary schools of sociological theory. Joas remedies this situation by offering a new way of thinking about *The Active Society*, namely, that in 1968 it anticipated where the various criticisms of the Parsonian "paradigm" would end up. With this approach to Etzioni's work as a backdrop, Joas also provides a context in classical social theory for Etzioni's more recent treatments of rationality and morality, and also for how he portrays the relationship between theory and action.

Etzioni's view of an "active society" revolves around how knowledge is developed and transmitted across society, and yet he has said very little about the news media. Edward and Ethna Lehman fill this gap by employing an Etzionian-inspired approach, namely, exploring the relationship between news media and political participation. They point out that the news media are integral to the political system and yet differentiated from it. Being differentiated, the news media develop along three lines: internal concentration, bureaucratization, and professionalization. These three simultaneous processes may not yield the scope or quality of political participation that political elites prefer or expect, even as political elites clearly influence news story selection and content. The news media have already "altered the morphology of political participation" by helping to undermine the power and influence of political parties in particular.

The four contributions in Part II explore the theoretical underpinnings of socioeconomics and communitarianism. Uta Gerhardt sets up this section by methodically reviewing Etzioni's argument in *The Moral Dimension* and then connecting this discussion to Etzioni's views of community. To this end, she explores the analytical concepts underlying Etzioni's socioeconomics and then compares them to Parsons's analytical approach to morality and community. Theorists reading her chapter will also appreciate that Gerhardt establishes in her endnotes numerous other linkages to an earlier generation of theorists and researchers (e.g., Kurt Lewin, Max Wertheimer, Karl Mannheim). In the body of the text she proposes in particular that the "common ground" on which these contemporary theorists meet was first laid by Hegel in his philosophy of bourgeois society. Indeed, it may be that in a post–Cold War world Hegel's *Philosophy of Right* needs to be worked much more explicitly into contemporary sociological theory generally. Gerhardt's position is that Hegel offers an opening beyond both utilitarianism and social conservatism, and that today this is one of Etzioni's goals in socioeconomics.

Deborah DeMott, a legal scholar, shows that the American courts have always enforced moral codes in corporate law by imposing "fiduciary duties" on corporate managers. The significance of her discussion for sociologists is that this behavior by the courts is *normative* behavior. The courts as an institution do not simply approach corporations by seeking the most efficient means to maximize corporate profits. Rather, they also uphold existing relationships of trust. As behavior in the world, the courts' actions are as amenable to methodical empirical study as any other set of actions, including individuals' strictly rational-normative behavior in the marketplace. As normative behavior in the world, however, the courts' actions elude neoclassical approaches, including those offered by rational-choice theory in sociology and the law-and-economics movement in legal scholarship. Yet, developments in legal theory, and then in judicial practice, nonetheless affect commercial and corporate behavior. This means that current developments in law-and-economics are hardly neutral or purely descriptive. Rather, they are inadvertently—or, worse, purposefully—undermining corporate law's existing moral codes. These developments rest on a vision of a future, "better" corporate law, one that runs counter to existing corporate law and current judicial practice.

At first glance Göran Therborn's contribution to this volume seems cut from a different cloth than his many contributions to *New Left Review* and other publications on the left. Yet, Therborn is proposing an ecumenical approach to normative action akin to that developed by Etzioni in *The Moral Dimension*. Such an approach not only can reconcile Therborn's own scholarly contributions but also, in principle, can synthesize the work of others irrespective of whether it rests on material approaches or cultural approaches to normative action.

With an acknowledgement to Merton, Therborn partitions the notion of "theories of the middle range" by making a case for "theories of middle height." The latter are theories that draw upon a wide range of data but that operate at a modest "height," that is, a modest level of abstraction. Theories of normative action, of institutions, and of networks fit the bill well, and Therborn makes the case for the first type just mentioned. He calls on sociologists to describe and explain the normative action of actors in the world (for instance, the American judiciary's normative action that DeMott discusses). He does not call on sociologists, however, to bring their own normative prescriptions for change to these descriptions and explanations. Therborn wants "theoretical work on sociological articles of wide-ranging everyday use" in an effort to secure the "widest possible range of application." Still, he acknowledges that the success of his call rests on some prior reform in the discipline itself, since the "usefulness of such work tends [now] to be inversely correlated with the best way of making a theoretical career."

This author shows in chapter 7 that Etzioni's later conceptual decisions, when he turned to socioeconomics and communitarianism, may be traced to decisions he made at a conceptual level in his first major work, *A Comparative Analysis of Complex Organizations*. His later works contain criticisms of existing social arrangements and prescriptions for reform, and Etzioni appreciates that in order for his position to be warranted it must rest on some conceptual "grounding"; it must not be reducible to his own subjective impressions or preferences. Eventually, Etzioni chose a concept of human nature as a grounding. I demonstrate, however, that this step became necessary because Etzioni failed to secure a grounding at an institutional level of analysis earlier in his career. Specifically, he failed to distinguish between organizations that are possibly integrative and organizations that are demonstrably controlling. I discuss this distinction and then examine Etzioni's later work against this backdrop.

The three contributions in Part III present findings from empirical research (both the authors' and others') that bear on Etzioni's positions on socioeconomics and communitarianism. Since the publication of his comparative study of the Swedish and the American family, *Disturbing the Nest* (1988), David Popenoe has been engaged in a great debate over the present condition and future prospects of the American family. His contribution here is the latest salvo, and yet it is more than that. Popenoe is interested in grappling directly with what cumulative research findings are telling us rather than in adapting their message to the current policy preferences of either liberals or conservatives. For specialists on the family, Popenoe's positions on homosexuality, premarital sex, pornography, and abortion will be eye-opening, possibly startling; for nonspecialists, his review of the literature will bring them into the thick of current research and debate.

Wolfgang Streeck has contributed his ideas on worker–management relations to President Clinton's Dunlop Commission, which released its report in January 1995. His chapter here builds on that contribution, arguing that the new positive integration of workers who accept responsibility can be read as an exercise in community building. Still, Streeck acknowledges that formal rules—"constitutionalization"—are also likely to be needed in American (as opposed to Japanese) workplaces. Two central issues that Streeck explores are: First, how finely tuned can any legislative changes in this area be, and what, instead, must be left to work councils to negotiate among their members? And, second, what role are unions actually to play in all of this, or have work councils rendered them obsolete? Streeck's answer, that work councils work best when coupled with strong unions, raises all sorts of policy problems for the Clinton administration and American legislators because such a small percentage of the American workforce is currently unionized (let alone organized in strong unions).

Calvin Morrill brings to bear a rich set of findings from his own scores of ethnographies of corporate managers (two cases of which he employs here) on one of Etzioni's central theoretical concerns, namely, how do these individuals actually balance self-interest and moral commitment in decision making? One of Morrill's findings is that the corporate context itself typically sets this balance. Individual managers, in turn, consciously or purposely adapt to this context—as opposed to being oversocialized automatons. In Morrill's view, then, the substantive corporate culture, including the types of linguistic codes that it institutionalizes, is the critical factor to study, and only ethnographic approaches can adequately describe and explain this factor.

The three contributions to Part IV raise questions, in one way or another, about the prospects for "community" in both the United States and advanced societies generally. Paula England and Linda Markowitz open with a clear, cogent presentation of "comparable worth," and then their chapter moves on to even grander theoretical issues. The policy issue of comparable worth comes to the fore when, for instance, city maintenance workers who lack educational credentials nonetheless receive a higher wage—even when they perform menial tasks (such as washing cars)—than city secretaries, nurses, or legal secretaries who possess credentials and perform more complicated tasks. England and Markowitz see the source of inequity in the fact that certain types of jobs are traditionally perceived as male-dominated, whereas other types are traditionally perceived as female-dominated. The characteristics of the jobs themselves fail to warrant the inequity. With this, England and Markowitz challenge those who turn immediately to the purportedly shared substantive norms—or shared meanings—of a "community" as a whole. Radical cultural feminists in particular call all sorts of existing arrangements into question, not only pay inequity. They are concerned that references to "community" are essentially references to a "monolithic morality" that, as such, inherently disadvantages women.

This author points out in chapter 12 that if community is to be promoted today, the stratum of society that will bear the brunt of the effort will be the middle class. Yet, the literature devoted to the beliefs and practices of the contemporary middle class, both American and French, is more portentous than promising. Most of the middle class has already withdrawn from public affairs and is engaged in utilitarian or affective pursuits. The most prominent stratum, the bourgeoisie, or more specifically the upper middle class and cultivated elite, treats even the basic procedural norms unique to modern democracy as if they are as negotiable and as available for innovative alterations as the substantive qualities of music appreciation, art collection, or architectural design. With this, I identify instances of the "discrete nihilism of the bourgeoisie," that is, instances where the bourgeoisie encroaches on these basic procedural norms and thereby relativizes modern democracy itself.

Communitarians promote a language of community responsibilities as a counterbalance to today's language of individual rights. Still, both languages compete within the confines of the nation-state. Gideon Sjoberg argues that if we move beyond these confines, then a concern for human rights speaks to broader concerns than the language of community responsibilities. He points out that when communitarians themselves refer to a "higher law," they likely have in mind some conception of human rights as mediating the demands of communities. With this in mind, Sjoberg introduces the notion of "social triage." In the absence of the mediating force of human rights, it is clearly inefficient to assist the poor either domestically or overseas. It is inefficient, for instance, to lend money to anyone holding a small banking account. Thus, both national and international bureaucracies (such as the International Monetary Fund) treat entire populations—often racial and ethnic minorities—as more of a nuisance than a potential clientele. In Sjoberg's view, "the human rights perspective offers the greatest possibility for building the basis for reasoned moral discourse across the growing differences within and among societies." We can only adequately address atrocities, including genocide, if we "invoke a set of universal standards."

## Note

1. Let me say candidly that I have my own reservations about items that Etzioni and others have placed in the communitarian agenda, and yet I accept at the outset that Etzioni (and Popenoe in this volume) is helping to crystallize the issues in a new public policy debate. This holds out the promise of moving the country, and possibly even the academic world, beyond left and right.

## References

Arendt, Hannah. (1951) 1969. *The Origins of Totalitarianism*. Cleveland: Meridian.
Coughlin, Richard M. 1994. "Amitai Etzioni: The Active Sociologist." *Footnotes* 22 (October): 3.
Gerhardt, Uta, ed. 1993. *Talcott Parsons on National Socialism*. New York: Aldine de Gruyter.
Schrecker, Ellen W. 1986. *No Ivory Tower: McCarthyism and the Universities*. New York: Oxford University Press.

# 1

# Frameworks and Findings: Assessing Etzioni's Contributions to Sociology

*Richard M. Coughlin*

Assessing Etzioni's work using the conventional categories of sociological theory and methodology is difficult for several reasons. First is the sheer volume of his publications, which to date include eighteen books (three since 1991 alone), four edited collections, more than two hundred journal articles and book chapters, and several hundred magazine articles, newspaper columns, and other miscellaneous publications.

Second is the wide variety and breadth of topics Etzioni has addressed, from his well-known early work on complex organizations, to his contributions to macroscopic theory, to his recent work on socioeconomics and communitarianism.

Third, Etzioni has not restricted his attention to topics safely within the domain of sociology as it is conventionally defined. Paralleling his work in mainstream sociology, Etzioni has written extensively on topics normally identified with other disciplines: for example, international relations (*The Hard Way to Peace*, 1962; *Winning Without War*, 1965; *Political Unification*, 1965), the space program (*The Moon-Doggle*, 1964), biotechnological developments (*Genetic Fix*, 1973), and the challenges to contemporary democratic politics (*Demonstration Democracy*, 1971; *An Immodest Agenda*, 1983; *Capital Corruption*, 1984).

Fourth, Etzioni has occupied a dual role as scholar and activist, attempting to connect the theories and empirical findings of academic research to the practical

This chapter draws on subjects addressed by the author in various previous publications (Coughlin 1990; 1994; Lockhart and Coughlin 1992). I am very grateful to Olle Persson and Rickard Danell for their generous donation of time and expertise in performing the cocitation analysis described in the appendix.

concerns of decision makers in the public and private sectors and also to engage the attention of the citizenry at large.[1] This agenda has placed him apart from those academics who hold up pure scholarship as an ideal to be emulated by all. Etzioni himself harbors little sympathy for the claims of disinterested scholarship and value-free social science. In the opening pages of *A Responsive Society,* he recounts a conversation with a professional fund-raiser about the prospects of establishing a new journal (that is, *The Responsive Community*):

> To find out what we would be trying to accomplish with the new publication, she persistently probed: "What slice of the market are you aiming at? How much circulation do you hope to build up the first year? How much profit? What are you trying to achieve?" "None of the above," was my admittedly immodest response. "I want to change the world." (1991, 3)

Etzioni's quest to bring sociology out of the ivory tower and into the wider arena of politics, policy, and social reform has taken many forms, from teach-ins to television appearances, columns in the op-ed pages of the *New York Times* and the *Washington Post,* and literally hundreds of pieces contributed to other newspapers, magazines, and other places where the voices of academic sociologists are seldom heard.

## Plan of This Chapter

An attempt to summarize the entire body of Etzioni's scholarly work, much less to go beyond summary to meaningful analysis, would require a book in itself. The goal of this chapter is much more modest. My purpose is to engage in a critical discussion of major works that are broadly representative of Etzioni's central contributions to sociology. The selection of works examined here is based on both a subjective judgment of which works best represent Etzioni's theoretical perspectives and substantive findings as well as more objective criteria based on the quantitative analysis of bibliographic citations. The citation analysis (described in the appendix to this chapter) helps to place Etzioni's writings in relation to the work of other prominent scholars and also provides some heretofore unpublished empirical data that identify the subareas of intellectual inquiry associated with clusters of authors identified with his work.

## Central Questions and Recurring Themes

Taken as a whole, Etzioni's writings have addressed sociological units of analysis at all levels—whole societies and their constituent formal organizations, communities, and individual persons. Although he has touched on hundreds of specific research questions at various places in his prolific writings, the central questions to which Etzioni has returned again and again, that have driven his work forward, can be reduced to a few fundamental themes: the nature of power and control in social organization; the sources of social cohesion and disintegration in relation to macroscopic social change; and the problem of rationality, broadly defined to include the prospects and limits of informed decision making and the potential of sociological knowledge to guide social and political change. While he has pursued each of these broad themes in different ways in different writings, one or more of them can be found in a prominent position in all of his major works. Etzioni's attention to these themes, furthermore, constitutes his major contributions to three areas in the scholarly literature: (1) the study of complex organizations; (2) general social theory; and (3) socioeconomics. (Empirical evidence identifying these areas in the literature is reported in the appendix.) The specific ways in which he has approached these themes in different works can be best appreciated by examining some of the works themselves, an exercise to which we turn below.

### A Comparative Analysis of Complex Organizations

Etzioni's early work on complex organizations established his reputation as a leading sociological theorist, and his writings in this area have played a pivotal role in shaping the contemporary field of study. *A Comparative Analysis of Complex Organizations* (1961) was one of the ten most often cited books from 1969 to 1977, and it has since earned the designation "citation classic," with over 1,000 citations in the Social Sciences Citation Index.

As his first academic book,[2] it is also the most conventionally sociological of Etzioni's writings and has as its specific aim addressing a critical gap in the sociological literature circa 1960 relevant to complex organizations. Strongly influenced by the framework of Parsonian structural functionalism then dominant in American sociology, Etzioni's analysis nonetheless forges new theoretical territory that serves to improve understanding of how organizations actually function. Drawing on a wide range of empirical studies and examples of different types of organizations, *A Comparative Analysis of Complex Organizations* moves quickly beyond the circular argumentation of Parsonian system maintenance to develop a middle-range theory of organizations that charts a course between the extremes of grand theorizing, on the one hand, and empirical case studies of very limited generality, on the other. Although the analysis ends with a brief discussion of the implications of compliance for different types of political systems, the "comparative" aspect is to be found in the coverage of many different types of organizations rather than a cross-cultural or cross-national mode of comparison.

Etzioni focuses on the use of power in organizations by those in superior positions to control and direct the behavior of subordinates. He uses the term "compliance" to capture the critical aspect of this relationship, and compliance thus is the crucial dependent variable in his subsequent analysis of organizational forms. It is important to note that compliance addresses both the use of power in hierarchical relationships and the response on the part of those over whom those in superior positions are attempting to exert control.

The sources of control Etzioni examines involve, respectively, the use of force or threat of force, the allocation of economic assets, and the manipulation of normative values. These types of control yield a basic typology of organizations as either coercive, utilitarian, or normative in nature. Coercive organizations include prisons, concentration camps, and custodial mental hospitals. Utilitarian organizations include industrial groups and other vehicles of commerce where remuneration is used as a central mechanism of control. Normative organizations, such as religious communities and voluntary organizations, rely on the use of symbolic means to exert control over members.

While a powerful heuristic device, this simple typology requires elaboration to be usefully applied to the full range of organizations. Here Etzioni introduces the idea of "dual structure," in which two modes of control are combined, a primary mode that coexists with and is reinforced by a secondary mode. Principal types of dual structure include normative-coercive organizations (such as educational institutions, where the effort to induce students to "do the right thing" on their own is backed up by various types of punishment if they fail to do so) and normative-utilitarian organizations (such as professional organizations, where voluntary commitment to serve the public good is reinforced by differential economic rewards for different levels and types of service). Other combinations are possible but less frequently observed: A normative-coercive dual structure, for example, characterizes combat units and certain types of labor union organizations; and the coercive-utilitarian structure appears to be restricted to certain archaic cases, such as factory towns and sailing ships.

Having described the types of compliance structures and their main variations, Etzioni's other purpose is to explore the correlates of compliance. Here he develops a threefold classification of organizational goals that parallels the three types of compliance: order (the control of deviant behavior); economics (the production of goods and/or services); and culture (the creation or preservation of cultural products). Although many different combinations of compliance structure and organizational goals are possible (especially if one takes into account the various dual compliance structures in addition to the three basic types), some combinations are clearly more effective and likely to be encountered more frequently than others. So, for example, a coercive compliance structure is more likely to be found in combination with organizational goals of order rather than of economic production or culture; and utilitarian compliance is more likely to coexist with economic goals. Etzioni's position here is a variation on the basic functionalist position: He argues that although many combinations of elements are possible in social life, some are superior to others in terms of effectiveness and therefore enjoy a greater likelihood of success. A similar analytic perspective underlies Etzioni's analysis of the development of cultural integration (that is, consensus, communication, and socialization) and cohesion in different types of organizations. Again he focuses attention on the differential incidence of various patterns and combinations of elements based on the functional considerations of different types of compliance structures in relation to other characteristics of organizations, including the nature of its leadership (e.g., elites' control of expressive versus instrumental activities), variations in recruitment patterns, and the like. There is an implication in this discussion that some combinations of organizational attributes are preferable based on higher-order considerations, such as moral soundness, and not merely "effectiveness," but this theme is left relatively undeveloped in Etzioni's early writings on organizations. As we shall see below, Etzioni's concern with morality as a variable of central importance emerges gradually in his later writings.[3]

In sum, Etzioni's compliance theory finds its enduring value as a seminal statement of middle-range social theory that succeeds in providing useful analytic insights within a framework that is of sufficiently wide scope to encompass a broad range of cases but not so abstract as to lose touch with the need to generate empirically testable hypotheses—and even to produce insights valuable to practitioners seeking to improve organizational performance. While grounded in the structuralist-functionalist tradition, and retaining a certain formal systematic flavor, Etzioni's analysis of organizations ultimately transcends the limitations (ideological as well as theoretical) of its origins. As evidenced by its many citations in the literature, compliance theory has been picked up by literally hundreds of other students of organizational theory. Some have tested pieces of the theory; some have expanded and elaborated upon it; and others have challenged it; but few students of organizations have failed to derive intellectual benefit from it.

### The Active Society

Published in 1968, *The Active Society* builds on and extends Etzioni's concern with organizational control, the nature of social cohesion, and the possibilities for directed change to the broader theoretical question of how and under what circumstances institutions acting and interacting at multiple levels—psychological, social, political, cultural, and historical—can be put to constructive collective purposes (and conversely, how they can fail to do so). More than any of his early writings, *The Active Society* demonstrates Etzioni's ability to weave together a rich and complex social theory with the more universally accessible message that people's lives could be much improved by the systematic application of sociological theory and method to collective problem solving.

*The Active Society* is a bold attempt to lay out the foundations of a theory of macroscopic action. In terms of the scope of analysis, it is arguably the most ambitious of Etzioni's work to date, and at 698 pages it is certainly the longest. Against the backdrop of the sweeping social, economic, and political changes marking the emergence of postmodern society, Etzioni poses the question of how a society can successfully respond by becoming a "master of itself" rather than being pulled along by forces beyond its understanding and control. In tackling this very large question, Etzioni explicitly reaches beyond the borders of sociology as it is conventionally defined (1968, ix) and eschews the role of the disinterested, value-free social scientist (ibid.).

The behavioral underpinnings of Etzioni's conception of the active society are simultaneously social and rational. The image of human beings aspiring toward self-awareness and rational action (despite the formidable obstacles standing in the way) is very much a cornerstone of Etzioni's vision. But self-awareness and rationality are not, in Etzioni's scheme, the attributes of isolated individuals; they are distinctly social in character, just as human beings themselves are social creatures by nature. "To be is to be social" (ibid., 2). This statement prefigures Etzioni's subsequent dialectic in the 1980s and early 1990s with proponents of narrow rational choice, particularly neoclassical economists. But its primary purpose within the theoretical framework of *The Active Society* is to establish the connection between micro- and macro-levels and to suggest that collectivities no less than individuals must overcome the inertia of passivity, whether born of ignorance or alienation, to mobilize the resources at their disposal to achieve the goals that they have defined for themselves. The active society requires an active citizenry—one that is cosmopolitan and postnationalist—but it also must provide the necessary conditions and tools for successful societal guidance. Here the development and application of social science knowledge is, in Etzioni's view, an essential ingredient in a complex process to support and lead collective decision making. It is important to emphasize, however, that Etzioni's conception of the social scientist as expert stops short of advocating technocracy. Social scientists are citizens as well as experts; their appropriate role is to inform and guide processes of change, not dictate them.

The attainment of the active society also depends fundamentally on the nature of the political system. Politics will determine, for example, the manner in which power is exercised in a particular society, how the population perceives and responds to the use of power, and the overall responsiveness of the political system to pressures for change. Here Etzioni is an unabashed advocate of democratic politics, whether in its liberal or social democratic versions, and likewise a critic of authoritarian and totalitarian forms of government. In the analysis of the relationship between political systems and the active society, he draws on compliance theory to argue that control based on normative integration, rather than on coercion or utilitarian principles, offers inherent advantages (but also harbors distinctive risks). The advantages inhere mainly in a greater potential for responsiveness to the will of the people (albeit often expressed in discordant voices), which is a fundamental prerequisite of the active society, compared to systems that are incapable of responding in sufficient time or degree to achieve enduring legitimacy. Indeed, the section titled "Unresponsive Societies and Their Transformation" can be read as a prescient analysis of the sources of instability leading to the collapse of communism in the former Soviet Union and Eastern Europe some twenty years after the publication of *The Active Society*. Similarly,

Etzioni's contrast of tribal systems to true communities, found in a brief preface to part 5 of *The Active Society,* can be lifted and applied virtually intact to understanding the persistent, violent conflicts that have ravaged disintegrating nation-states from the former Yugoslavia to Africa and elsewhere in recent years.

Democratic societies, Etzioni reminds us, have their own set of problems. Chief among these is the affliction resulting from the appearance of responsiveness devoid of substance. Examples of this contradiction are ubiquitous, from vacuous mass entertainment to the growing use of advertising and public relations techniques to sell political candidates and public policies. Etzioni coins the term "inauthenticity" to describe these and other conditions of false responsiveness. In introducing this term, his explicit intent is to differentiate the condition of inauthenticity from the classic sociological concepts of alienation and anomie. Inauthenticity is, in Etzioni's view, not only qualitatively different from alienation and anomie; it is much more widespread and insidious in its effects in modern democratic societies. Inauthenticity is more elusive because it tends to blend into the environment of modern communications technology to the point where it is no longer clear what is genuine, what is fabricated, and where one begins and the other ends.

Authenticity is an analytic concept, to be sure, but it also has an underlying normative dimension. By seeking to draw a distinction between those institutions and arrangements that are truly responsive to the needs of people, compared to those that offer only the illusion of responsiveness, Etzioni is taking an important step toward asserting that there are multiple grounds for preferring certain types of social relations over others. The idea of authenticity, particularly as the basis for moral cohesion in communities, is most highly developed—indeed, it might be argued that it comes to occupy a central role—in Etzioni's recent writings on socioeconomics and communitarianism.

### The Moral Dimension

Etzioni's long-standing concern with the problem of social order is restated in his comprehensive critique of the dominant role the neoclassical paradigm has come to play in economics and other social science disciplines. The debate over neoclassical economics, particularly with respect to utility maximization as the sole explanation of behavior, is hardly new. The novel contribution of *The Moral Dimension* (1988) is to draw together the many scattered threads of theoretical development and empirical findings in the literatures of several academic disciplines and to embark on nothing less than the attempt to establish a new paradigm for analyzing and understanding economic, and more broadly "choice," behavior.

In his critique of neoclassical economics, Etzioni follows Kuhn's (1962) use of the term "paradigm" to describe the broad and pervasive influence that theories exert in shaping how problems are conceived, what is taken for granted, and which questions are regarded as legitimate and which are not. In these terms, both the neoclassical approach and Etzioni's socioeconomics are paradigms in the Kuhnian sense: They do not merely represent alternative hypotheses about how people behave in economic transactions and other areas of social life, but also offer competing conceptions about how the social world is constructed and about the very nature of social reality. This last point is crucial and suggests that evaluating *The Moral Dimension* should proceed along two lines: first, an assessment of how well Etzioni's attempt to synthesize a new paradigm for economic and choice behavior succeeds on its own terms in offering a coherent, theoretically powerful, and empirically verifiable alternative to the neoclassical paradigm; and second, an evaluation of how the new socioeconomic paradigm is likely to fare in the contest with established—and, in economics, clearly dominant—theories.

As Etzioni portrays them, humans still engage in self-interested calculations of material matters that comprise a realm of logical/empirical (L/E) choices. But the essence of human behavior cannot adequately be captured by focusing on this realm alone. Rather, humans respond as well to moral commitments that they acquire through the formation of their social bonds with others; these relationships form a realm of normative/affective (N/A) activity. A cornerstone of Etzioni's socioeconomic thesis is that individual motives arising out of moral commitments and affective ties cannot be reduced to self-interested or pleasure-oriented considerations. Instead, he presents a view of human activity in which preferences grow out of complex interactions of logical, empirical, normative, and emotional factors, with the mixtures themselves varying across individuals and groups. While Etzioni identifies these distinct sources of preference formation, he leaves the details of their interaction in the production of preferences largely unspecified.

The essence of Etzioni's argument is that the mono-utility conception of behavior at the core of conventional rational choice models is simply not tenable. He reasserts the position, earlier articulated in *The Active Society,* that human behavior must be understood in terms of the fusion of individually based and communally based forces and that there is little to be gained (except the false security of theoretical parsimony qua reductionism) in the atomistic assumptions of methodological individualism. Etzioni offers a strong restatement here of Martin Buber's "I" and "Thou," underscoring the fusion of the individual and the social by representing them as a single term, the "I & We." This symbology reflects both an inescapable bond and an underlying tension: The *I* represents the individual acting in his or her own self-interest alongside the *We,* which stands for the obligations and restraints imposed by the collectivity. Etzioni characterizes this conception of behavior as "moderately deontological" in that it views moral commitments as causes. This position stands in marked contrast to the neoclassical preoccupation with self-interest as the sole determinant of behavior, which he rejects as an "undersocialized" conception of man (see Wrong 1961). Self-interest, or the pleasure principle, has its place as a factor shaping human behavior, but this place is alongside the moral forces that bind the individual to the community. Thus, the union of I & We is inevitable and inextricable. At one level, then, socioeconomics offers a restatement of the general problem of social order, and Etzioni succinctly sums up the socioeconomic position as: "The I's need a We to be" (1988, 9).

Etzioni applies this deontological conception of behavior to decision making, arguing that N/A factors play a role at least equal to that of L/E factors. Specifically, although L/E considerations may determine the selection of means to achieve goals, the goals themselves and the range of means that are considered feasible derive directly from N/A considerations. Furthermore, even within L/E zones (that is, areas where decisions are minimally colored by emotion or influenced by social norms) decision making is often less than fully rational due to the limited cognitive capabilities of human beings. In exploring these questions, Etzioni draws on his own earlier work on "mixed scanning" (1967), Simon's ideas on "satisfying behavior," contributions by Kahneman and Tversky (1979) and others associated with the Prospect School, and Lindblom's (1965) notions of "disjointed incrementalism" and "muddling through."

Etzioni goes on to consider the role of the community and power relations in constraining the exercise of individual rationality and the operation of market transactions. Here Etzioni's attack on the neoclassical paradigm is two-pronged. First, he argues that the decisions that economists routinely study are not really individual decisions at all but rather "reflect the society, polity, culture and sub-culture, class . . . and changes in these all" (1988, 181). Using this idea, he explores the thesis that collective rationality as something besides the aggregation of individual decisions is not only possible but in many cases is actually superior, that is, produces qualitatively better decisions. In this context, he reminds us that although the myth of the rugged individualist entrepreneur is a highly cherished one in American culture, most innovation actually occurs within collective structures of action. Second, noting that transactions between individuals in society are virtually never based on conditions of equality and that competition is a form of contained conflict that is always encapsulated within the larger social system, Etzioni takes on yet another central article of neoclassical faith, the play—and even the very existence of—the "free market."

In basic outline, Etzioni's arguments about the inadequacy of "economic man" assumptions are hardly new (see Sen 1977, for a trenchant summary of the literature). Indeed, *The Moral Dimension* is largely a work of synthesis rather than of new evidence. But synthesis does not preclude either well-supported arguments or innovative insights, features with which Etzioni's work is richly endowed. In its breadth of coverage, cogent argumentation, and sheer intellectual energy *The Moral Dimension* is a scholarly tour de force. Not only does it demonstrate Etzioni's panoptic view of the intellectual terrain of the social sciences (the bibliography includes some eight hundred entries drawn from economics, sociology, political science, and psychology); the broad scope of the enterprise and expansive nature of the literature never escape from his control. If the purpose of *The Moral Dimension* is to compel the reader to reconsider conventional assumptions about economic behavior and to reconsider how behavior is shaped and directed by forces outside of narrowly conceived individual self-interest, the book succeeds beyond any measure of doubt.

This is not to say, however, that the questions addressed by *The Moral Dimension* have been laid to rest. In substantive terms, there are at least three possible lines of criticism of Etzioni's socioeconomics. One concerns the possible blurring of radical individualism and more traditional liberal individualism in *The Moral Dimension*. It is undeniably true that Etzioni's critique focuses on the more radical and essentially amoral expressions of individualism found in many contemporary versions of rational choice theory. It might be argued, however, that these do not reflect central tenets of more traditional liberal individualism.

The second criticism centers on the question of plurality in moral values. The morality that Etzioni juxtaposes to neoclassical individualism is broad and not sharply defined. As MacIntyre (1988) notes, there are multiple moralities in various relationships of conflict and coexistence with one another in complex modern societies, and simply juxtaposing morality with individualism is unlikely to carry us very far, unless we are prepared to specify whose morality we are talking about.

Finally, there is the question of the ultimate impact of the argument. It is in the nature of paradigmatic thinking that not all readers will approach a new thesis with an open mind. The paradox, by no means unique to this case, is that those most in need of the message are the ones least likely to be affected by it. *The Moral Dimension* has been enthusiastically received by many sociologists, psychologists, political scientists, anthropologists, philosophers, and those economists already disaffected with neoclassical orthodoxy. This may amount to "preaching to the converted," but that is no small achievement, since the welcome message has had to make itself heard over the powerful voices preaching the theology of unfettered markets and individual utility maximization. Moreover, while *The Moral Dimension* opens up the door for new ways of thinking about choice behavior, there is still an enormous amount of work to be done to "fill in" the fledgling paradigm of socioeconomics.[4]

Ultimately, what chance of success does socioeconomics have in competing with the existing dominant neoclassical paradigm? Etzioni acknowledges the difficulties that are involved in attempting to break the grip of a dominant paradigm. In the preface to *The Moral Dimension* he writes that "We are now in the middle of a paradigmatic struggle" (1988, ix), and goes on to state that several articles that preceded this book

encountered strong reactions of the kind previously faced only when he dealt
with issues such as the . . . war in Vietnam. . . . [T]he author does not expect
that the prevailing neoclassical paradigm will be abandoned; indeed much of
what it has contributed might well be integrated into a more encompassing
paradigm. (ibid., xii)

History teaches that dominant paradigms rarely if ever yield to internal reform
movements, and the reaction thus far of mainstream economists to the challenge
of socioeconomics suggests there is little basis for predicting the present situation will be different. The alternative is to strike out on a separate path in the
hope that others will follow and that the road leads somewhere.

### The Spirit of Community

Etzioni's concern with moral values and social bonds as irreducible sources of
influence on human behavior has emerged even more prominently in his recent
work on communitarianism. His writings and related activities in this area have
elaborated on and explored in greater breadth and depth questions of changing
public and private morality, the social and political implications of these
changes, and the conflicting ideological interpretations and prescriptions that
have emerged in response. Etzioni's communitarian agenda has included the
founding of a new journal (*The Responsive Community*), the organization of a
social movement (the Communitarian Network), and the publication of a best-
selling book (*The Spirit of Community*, 1993). Although aimed at a general
readership rather than an audience of scholars, *The Spirit of Community* nonetheless merits consideration here, since it represents a logical extension of Etzioni's
socioeconomics and provides a clear statement of the direction that his long-
standing interest in social change and normative integration has taken in recent
years.

   *The Spirit of Community* is both sociological analysis and a call for social
action. It is self-consciously a work of social criticism and persuasion aimed at
readers who are not ideologically committed to the political right or left but who
share a sense that American society is experiencing fundamental problems that
require more than superficial palliative action.

   The source of the problem, as Etzioni sees it, is the decay of the sense of
community that binds individuals together, guides and supports their sense of
moral integrity, and provides a stable foundation for the larger society. The main
culprit in the deterioration of community is the elevation of individual rights to
absurd heights while simultaneously ignoring the social responsibilities that go
hand in hand with these rights. As advocated by "radical individualists, such as
libertarians and the American Civil Liberties Union" (1993, 11), the lopsided
concern with rights has not only produced a seemingly endless list of "new
rights," which is a development problematic in and of itself, but has undermined

the capacity of communities to provide for the collective welfare of its members. As a first step toward correcting this situation, Etzioni calls for a moratorium on the creation of any new rights.

Etzioni sees a second threat to healthy community relations coming from the opposite end of the political spectrum, in the form of moral authoritarianism. Moral authoritarians, epitomized by the "religious right," seek to impose their own narrow visions of moral order on the rest of society. From the communitarian standpoint, moral authoritarians suffer from too strong a sense of community, emphasizing only responsibilities to conform to a particular set of norms, with a concomitant lack of concern for individual rights. Thus, while Etzioni is centrally concerned with infusing morality into American social thought, and although some of the subjects he takes on have been claimed by the moral authoritarians as their own (for example, a concern for the welfare of children and the institution of marriage that is sometimes called "family values"), Etzioni's communitarian values are fundamentally distinct from, and ultimately not compatible with, those of the religious right.

In launching the communitarian movement and serving as its leading theoretician, Etzioni is attempting to design a new course in American social thinking: one that engages the moral agenda of the political right (but eschews its reactionary stance and authoritarian prescriptions), addresses libertarian concerns for the freedom and rights of individuals (but not their single-minded insistence on the individual above all else), and seeks to further traditional liberal goals for a more equal and humane society (but does not accept the liberals' tendency to overlook individuals' responsibility for the consequences of their actions). The linking of rights to responsibilities and the attempt to strike a balance between individual and collective interests tap fundamental antagonisms that can be found within all human societies. In attempting to integrate these conflicting elements in the contemporary American context, communitarianism has been all too often mischaracterized and misunderstood. Proponents of existing political, social, religious, and other ideologies have been eager to endorse one part of the communitarian analysis while simultaneously rejecting the other parts. For example, when Etzioni talks about the need to support the institution of the two-parent family, conservatives of various stripes stand up and cheer; but when he goes on to say that in doing so we as a society must be prepared to provide opportunities for parents, men and women equally, to take time off from work to care for their infants and young children, the same conservatives fall silent or object. Traditional liberals, of course, have the opposite problem with the communitarian position: They applaud the idea of parental leave and equal treatment of men and women, but they are loath to concur with the communitarian contention that two-parent families are on average best for children. The task facing communitarianism is to reconcile these and other positions that will inevitably be perceived outside the movement as contradictions.

Whether or not the communitarian movement can succeed in gaining the popular and political support to counteract the powerful forces it has confronted remains to be seen. In more narrowly sociological terms, however, Etzioni's effort to develop and promote communitarianism has delivered a powerful challenge to conventional ideological thinking on both the left and right and, more than any other recent work by a prominent sociologist, departs from the safe path of scientific inquiry and academic debate to attempt to chart new directions for social, economic, and political reform.

**Conclusion**

Etzioni has been a major contributor to social theory in the study of complex organizations and macroscopic social change, the critique of narrow rational choice theories, and, growing out of this critique, the development of socio-economics and communitarianism. A review of his major works reveals the evolution of his theoretical perspective from the early influence of structural functionalism toward a more eclectic orientation in later works, in which he draws on and integrates theories and findings from multiple disciplines. But it is in Etzioni's attitude toward the normative elements of sociological analysis that an even more pronounced change can be observed. Although Etzioni has long been critical of the idea that sociology can be (or should try to be) value free, over time theory and practice have grown ever closer to one another in his work. This pattern is apparent in the comparison of the general prescriptions for guided social change found in *The Active Society* and the more specific reform agenda found in *The Spirit of Community*. This blending of social science and social action has emerged as a mainstay of Etzioni's brand of sociology.

**Appendix**

*Bibliometric Analysis of Etzioni's Work*

Without a lengthy immersion in the various literatures to which Etzioni has contributed, it is difficult to develop anything more than a fragmentary or impressionistic sense of the impact his work has had on other scholars. This is especially true given the voluminous and wide-ranging nature of Etzioni's writings. Fortunately, computer-based bibliographic citation databases and the development of new techniques to analyze them, both of which have emerged in highly developed forms in recent years, can provide some help here.

Bibliometric analysis offers powerful tools for uncovering the often complex and otherwise unobservable interrelationships among scholarly works. One bibliometric technique, cocitation analysis, has been shown to be of particular value in revealing and analyzing the underlying structure of substantive areas of study within and, more importantly, across disciplinary boundaries (White 1990). Briefly, cocitation analysis involves studying patterns of citations in journal articles to (1) identify those authors who are most frequently cited together (i.e., cocited) by other authors who publish articles in scholarly journals; and (2) analyze the patterns of cocitation to reveal possible underlying structures that link pairs or clusters of authors together as major contributors to one or another empirical or theoretical current in the literature. Cocitation analysis is in many ways analogous to social network analysis, only the empirical link between individuals is the citation of a book or article listed in the bibliographic database.

Our cocitation analysis of Etzioni's work uses the methodology for author-based analysis suggested by Persson (1994). We begin by reviewing all citations to Etzioni found in the Social Science Citation Index from 1972 to 1994. This review revealed an average of about one hundred citations per year. From this full list, we decided to focus on the most recent eight years available. The rationale for selecting these years was both practical and theoretical. Practically, each citation to the main author (in this case, Etzioni) yields a geometric increase in the total number of data points (cocitations) for analysis. Thus, the 936 citations to Etzioni from 1986 to 1994 yielded nearly 40,000 total cited references and nearly 90,000 total cocited pairs. Pushing the time frame back before 1986 would have greatly increased all these numbers and brought the analysis to a standstill. On the theoretical side, the focus on recent citations of Etzioni in the literature provides information about the impact of his more recent work as well as an estimate of the enduring value of his earlier writings.

The initial sorting of the cocitation data reveals the sheer magnitude of the diffusion of Etzioni's work throughout the literature of several disciplines. From 1986 to 1994 his work is cocited in five or more journal articles with 1,104 other scholars. The list of authors with at least twenty-five cocitations with Etzioni is found in Table 1.1. The upper end of the distribution includes cocitations with Max Weber (125), Herbert Simon (102), Peter Blau and Talcott Parsons (both 98), and James March (88).

As one moves further down the list, the pattern of cocitations across substantive areas of the social sciences becomes more difficult to discern. Moreover, the cocitation frequencies of authors with Etzioni reveal nothing about the nature of the interrelationships among the authors themselves—linkages related to the underlying structure of different substantive areas of scholarship. To explore these patterns and the deeper structures they represent, we conducted a cluster analysis of the cocited pairs. The plot of coordinates for the fifty-two authors with the highest frequency of cocitation with Etzioni and with each other is shown in Figure 1.1. For purposes of interpretation, we can picture Etzioni at the center of this cluster map, with the distance from the center representing an author's relative proximity to Etzioni in relation to the other authors shown in the table.

Table 1.1

**Names Most Frequently Cocited with Etzioni, 1986–94**

| Author | Citations | Author | Citations |
|--------|-----------|--------|-----------|
| Weber, M. | 125 | Steers, R.M. | 38 |
| Simon, H. | 102 | Galbraith, J.K. | 37 |
| Blau, P. | 98 | Peters, T.J. | 37 |
| Parsons, T. | 98 | Schumpeter, J. | 37 |
| March, J. | 88 | Bacharach, S.B. | 36 |
| Perrow, C. | 82 | Marx, K. | 36 |
| Pfeffer, J. | 82 | Smith, A. | 35 |
| Kanter, R.M. | 81 | Angle, H.L. | 33 |
| Williamson, O. | 76 | Boulding, K.E. | 33 |
| Mintzberg, H. | 62 | Buchanan, J.M. | 33 |
| Coleman, J.S. | 61 | Selznick, P. | 33 |
| Merton, R.K. | 60 | Stinchcombe, A. | 33 |
| Thompson, J.D. | 60 | Bellah, R.N. | 32 |
| Hirschman, A. | 59 | Cohen, J. | 32 |
| Gouldner, A. | 56 | Bell, D. | 31 |
| Becker, G.S. | 55 | Braverman, H. | 31 |
| Elster, J. | 54 | Drucker, P.F. | 31 |
| Lindblom, C. | 54 | Frank, R.H. | 31 |
| Mowday, R.T. | 53 | Arrow, K.J. | 30 |
| Porter, L.W. | 52 | Child, J. | 30 |
| Katz, D. | 51 | Collins, R. | 30 |
| Olson, M. | 51 | Crozier, M. | 30 |
| Sen, A. | 51 | Deutsch, M. | 30 |
| Argyris, C. | 50 | Downs, A. | 30 |
| Ouchi, W. | 50 | Kuhn, T.S. | 30 |
| Weick, K. | 50 | Lawrence, P.R. | 30 |
| Becker, H.S. | 47 | Hannan, M.T. | 29 |
| Granovetter, M. | 46 | Mills, C.W. | 29 |
| Dahl, R.A. | 45 | Pettigrew, A. | 28 |
| Goffman, E. | 45 | Hackman, J.R. | 27 |
| Kahneman, D. | 45 | Meyer, J.W. | 27 |
| Scott, W.R. | 45 | Smelser, N. | 27 |
| Giddens, A. | 44 | Stigler, G.J. | 27 |
| Homans, G. | 44 | Buchanan, B. | 26 |
| Salancik, G.R. | 44 | Cyert, R.M. | 26 |
| Axelrod, R. | 43 | Gamson, W.A. | 26 |
| Durkheim, E. | 43 | Luhmann, N. | 26 |
| Habermas, J. | 43 | Morgan, G. | 26 |
| Barnard, C.I. | 42 | Osgood, C.E. | 26 |
| Schein, E.H. | 42 | Bennis, W.G. | 25 |
| Janis, I.L. | 41 | Coase, R.H. | 25 |
| Hall, R.H. | 40 | Festinger, L. | 25 |
| Wildavsky, A. | 40 | Friedman, M. | 25 |
| Berger, P.L. | 39 | Posner, R.A. | 25 |
| Wilson, J.Q. | 39 | Vroom, V. | 25 |
| French, J.R.P. | 38 | | |

Figure 1.1 **Etzioni Cocitation Cluster Map, 1986–94**

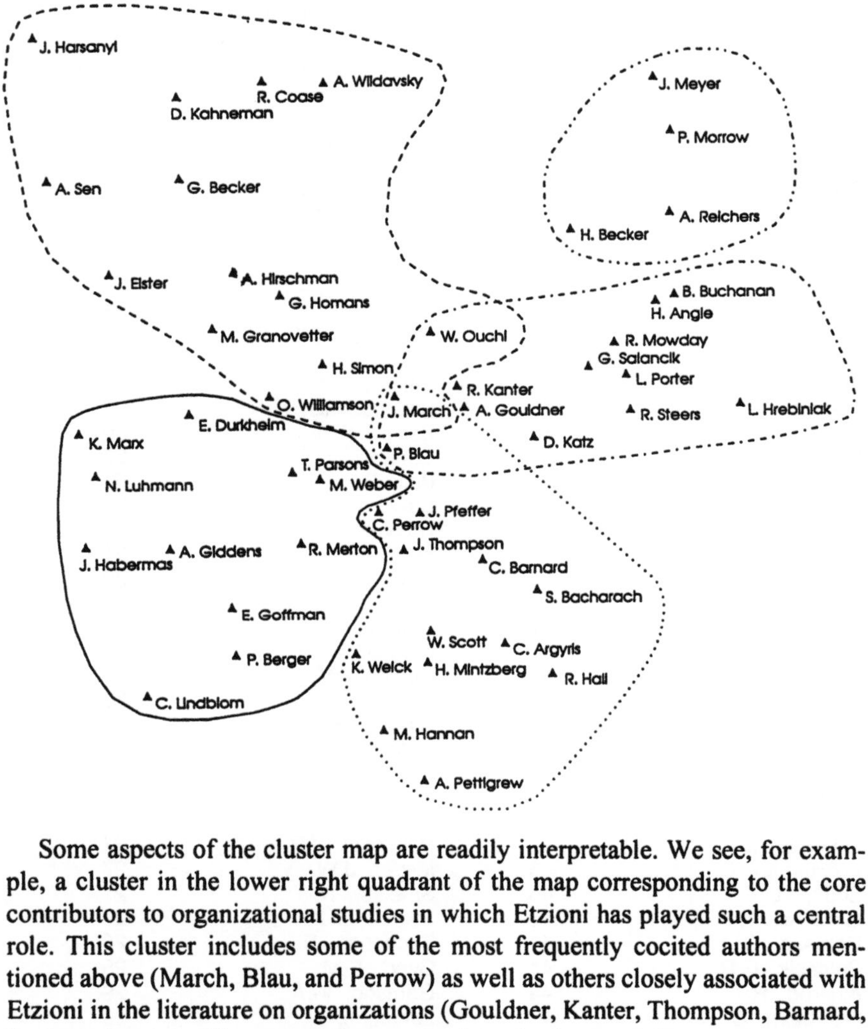

Some aspects of the cluster map are readily interpretable. We see, for example, a cluster in the lower right quadrant of the map corresponding to the core contributors to organizational studies in which Etzioni has played such a central role. This cluster includes some of the most frequently cocited authors mentioned above (March, Blau, and Perrow) as well as others closely associated with Etzioni in the literature on organizations (Gouldner, Kanter, Thompson, Barnard, Bacharach, etc.). The connections extend to the lower right to other authors whose cocitations with Etzioni are less numerous (e.g., Scott, Weick, Argyris, Mintzberg, and Hall), but whose cocitation "network" ties clearly place them in the "organization studies" cluster. In addition, farther to the right and extending upward a bit is a second cluster of authors also related to organizational studies but with a focus on more applied topics such as employee relations, management techniques, and what might be broadly described as the sociology of work.

A third major cluster, spreading from the center into the upper left corner of

Table 1.2

**Citations of Communitarianism in Periodicals**

| Year | Academic[a] | Nonacademic[b] |
|------|------------|----------------|
| 1989 | 8  | 42  |
| 1990 | 9  | 69  |
| 1991 | 5  | 125 |
| 1992 | 9  | 237 |
| 1993 | 29 | 418 |

[a]General Science Index, Humanities Index, Social Science Index, Legal Index.
[b]Business Periodicals Index, Reader's Guide, UMI/Data Courier's Newspaper, Lexis/Nexis Database.

the map, reflects the core of scholars associated with Etzioni's work in socioeconomics. Represented in this cluster are scholars from several disciplines, including economics, political science, philosophy, and sociology. Here we find Herbert Simon (who the cluster map indicates is empirically associated with Etzioni through their respective work in the study of choice behavior, more than through organizational studies), Williamson, Hirschman, Homans, Gary Becker, Elster, Sen, and Harsanyi. In addition to its diversity in terms of disciplinary background, this cluster includes scholars across the full spectrum of theoretical and ideological positions—in other words, encompassing those whose views are consonant with Etzioni's as well as those with whom he has been at odds.

A fourth cluster, extending across the center of the map and down into the lower left quadrant, consists of authors who are identified with Etzioni as core contributors to social theory. We find Parsons, Weber, and Durkheim located so close to the organization studies cluster that they might also be included there. The rest of the "theory" cluster includes Marx, Luhmann, Giddens, Merton, Goffman, Berger, and Lindblom (the lone political scientist in the theory cluster).

Finally, a fifth, loosely grouped cluster is located in the upper right corner of the map and consists of Howard Becker, Reichers, Morrow, and Meyer. This cluster appears to consist of diverse studies in social problems. It is the least structured, least populated, and, relative to the other areas, least important of the clusters.

### A Note on Etzioni's Communitarian Warnings

The citation analysis reported above does not pick up Etzioni's work in communitarianism for two reasons. First, the work is too recent to have accumulated the number of citation frequencies needed to be empirically detectable above the "noise" of the citations of Etzioni's other works. Second, there is evidence that communitarianism has been slower to penetrate the academic literature than the nonacademic literature. As shown in Table 1.2, from 1989 to 1993, references to communitarianism increased tenfold in the nonacademic literature (from 42 to 418 citations). Compare this to the far smaller increase, both in absolute and relative terms, of citations in the academic literature (from 8 to 29) over the same time period. These data suggest that while Etzioni has been highly successful in reaching a broad audience with the communitarian message, the impact among the community of scholars remains uncertain.

## Notes

1. That the roles of scholar and activist have complemented one another in Etzioni's career finds independent support in two studies of journal citations conducted in the 1980s. The first, published in *Current Contents,* ranked him ninth among all sociologists born after 1900 in total citations in social science journals. Perhaps even more significantly, a second study, published in the *Policy Studies Journal,* ranked him first in total citations from 1969 to 1980 among social scientists engaged in public policy analysis.

2. His first book, *A Diary of a Commando Soldier,* was published in Hebrew in 1952.

3. Etzioni's concern with the moral implications of guided change is apparent in much of his earlier work (e.g., the exploration of the implications of biotechnological change in *Genetic Fix,* 1973, which was nominated for a National Book Award). In the 1980s he turned his attention to the moral underpinnings of economic behavior, culminating in the publication of *The Moral Dimension* in 1988.

4. Many others from diverse academic disciplines have joined in support of this effort. The Society for the Advancement of Socio-Economics, which Etzioni founded in 1989 and served as president from 1989 to 1990, has grown into an established organization of about 1,800 members in over forty countries.

## References

Coughlin, Richard M. 1990. "Review of *The Moral Dimension." Journal of Behavioral Economics* 17 (Winter): 295–97.

———. 1994. "Amitai Etzioni: The Active Sociologist." *Footnotes* (October): 3.

Etzioni, Amitai. 1961. *A Comparative Analysis of Complex Organizations: On Power, Involvement, and Their Correlates.* New York: Free Press.

———. 1967. "Mixed Scanning: A 'Third' Approach to Decision-Making." *Public Administration Review* 27 (December): 385–92.

———. 1968. *The Active Society: A Theory of Societal and Political Processes.* New York: Free Press.

———. 1988. *The Moral Dimension: Toward a New Economics.* New York: Free Press.

———. 1991. *A Responsive Society: Collected Essays on Guiding Deliberate Social Change.* San Francisco: Jossey-Bass.

———. 1993. *The Spirit of Community: The Reinvention of American Society.* New York: Simon and Schuster.

Kahneman, Daniel, and Tversky, Amos. 1979. "Prospect Theory: An Analysis of Decision under Risk." *Econometrica* 47 (March): 263–91.

Kuhn, Thomas S. 1962. *The Structure of Scientific Revolutions.* Chicago: University of Chicago Press.

Lindblom, Charles E. 1965. *The Intelligence of Democracy.* New York: Free Press.

———. 1977. *Politics and Markets: The World's Political-Economic Systems.* New York: Basic Books.

Lockhart, Charles, and Coughlin, Richard M. 1992. "Building Better Comparative Social Theory through Alternative Conceptions of Rationality." *Western Political Quarterly* 45 (September): 793–809.

MacIntyre, Alasdair. 1988. *Whose Justice? Which Rationality?* Notre Dame, IN: University of Notre Dame Press.

Persson, Olle. 1994. "The Intellectual Base and Research Fronts of JASIS, 1986–1990." *Journal of the American Society for Information Science* 45: 31–38.

Sen, Amartya K. 1977. "Rational Fools: A Critique of the Behavioral Foundations of Economic Theory." *Philosophy and Public Affairs* 6: 317–44.

Simon, Herbert. 1955. "A Behavioral Model of Rational Choice." *Quarterly Journal of Economics* 69: 99–108.

White, Howard D. 1990. "Author Co-Citation Analysis: Overview and Defense." In *Scholarly Communications and Bibliometrics,* ed. Christine L. Borgman, 84–106. Newbury Park, CA: Sage.

Wrong, Dennis. 1961. "Oversocialized Concept of Man in Sociology." *American Sociological Review* 26: 183–93.

# Part I

## The Active Society

# 2

# Economic Action, Social Action, and the Genesis of Values: An Essay on Amitai Etzioni's Contribution to Social Theory

*Hans Joas*

In spite of the high standing that Amitai Etzioni's work enjoys in the American and international sociological community, his most ambitious and comprehensive contribution to sociological theory has never found an adequate response. When his voluminous study *The Active Society* was originally published in 1968, international attention initially was quite lively.[1] But even then one of the leading scholarly journals published only a very superficial review, the main point of which was a criticism of conceptual work in sociological theory as such from a hyperradical and activist standpoint.[2] After 1968, the book soon fell into almost complete oblivion. A few items may serve as evidence for this assertion. In Jeffrey Alexander's history of sociological theorizing after 1945,[3] Etzioni is not mentioned at all. There is only one booklong study about Etzioni[4]—a ridiculous misproportion compared to the ever-growing literature on, for example, Talcott Parsons—and this book is a rather flat reproduction of his ideas. Even in one of the few later evaluations written in a sympathetic tone,[5] Etzioni's book is called a "fruitful failure" on the way toward a "unified theory of highly differentiated societies," which, given the lack of serious work preparing the ground for such an attempt, "is forced to fall back on eclecticism, bringing in partial theories, empirical propositions, and factual examples taken from various societies and various parts of the social sciences."

This widespread neglect or underestimation of Etzioni's achievement in sociological theory becomes even more spectacular as soon as we take the general development of sociological theory after 1968 into consideration. If Alexander's construction of the development of American sociology is true, we should distinguish three main phases in the post–World War II era. After a relatively stable hegemony of Parsonian structural functionalism, the late sixties brought a concerted effort of various theoretical schools—from symbolic interactionism via conflict sociology to a sort of sociological behaviorism and Marxism—to dethrone Parsons; they were clearly successful in the negative sense, but not in the positive sense of replacing the earlier ruling paradigm with a new one comparable in scope and power. For Alexander and the neofunctionalists in general it took until the 1980s to supersede this age of archaic pluralism and to regain the confidence of new syntheses, "the new theoretical movement," as they called it.[6] Etzioni's 1968 book cannot be easily subsumed to such a description. Etzioni's attempt was clearly synthetic at the outset. *The Active Society* explicitly envisaged a synthesis of the achievements of structural functionalism with cybernetic systems theory and conflict sociology; given its background in Martin Buber's philosophy of intersubjectivity and existentialist reasoning about the authenticity of human life in society, at least some aspects of the interactionist and phenomenological criticisms of Parsons came in, too. I would rather call Etzioni the first dissident from Parsonianism with a full-blown systematic alternative. But it is not only the fact of Etzioni's systematic contribution itself that seems to make him an exception to the general tendencies as they are described by Alexander. More than that it is the fact that Etzioni anticipated a great deal of the substantial innovations contained in the work of the new theoretical attempts at synthesis. This is not the place to present a careful comparison of Etzioni's *Active Society* with the major representatives of contemporary sociological theory like Jürgen Habermas, Anthony Giddens, Alain Touraine, or Niklas Luhmann, and with such schools as neofunctionalism, macrosociologically oriented symbolic interactionism or conflict theory, and macrohistorical sociology.[7] A brief overview of some characteristics of Etzioni's work must be sufficient here.

## A Systematic Alternative to Parsonianism

The most important of these characteristics, in my view, is Etzioni's repudiation of a very frequent conflation. He resolutely denies that the dichotomy of micro and macro in sociology should be identified with the distinction of action and structure. As even the title of his book makes clear, his main interest concerns *macroscopic* actions—actions that are not confined to the immediate lifeworld of everyday actors but that are part of powerful political, economic, or military activities. In the same sense that actions may be macroscopic, systems should not, according to Etzioni, be understood as self-regulating entities that transcend the level of human action. The analytical notion of "system" should not be misunderstood in an essentialist manner but rather applied only in a "realistic," empirically controlled way.

> "Constituting" a system is treated as a proposition subject to empirical test; any two units do not necessarily form a system. When the actors are less related, when there is no feedback effect or only a sporadic and inconsequential one, we shall refer to the relationship as a "situation." Societal units . . . often "behave" as if they were linked in a system fashion. . . . But unlike the analytic system, which is composed of variables, this system is composed of collectivities, organizations, movements, and government agencies.[8]

In the area of social change, Etzioni tried to steer a middle course between the evolutionist assumptions that permeate a large part of the sociological tradition, including modernization theory, and the overly voluntarist bias of political science at that time. The mere fact that Etzioni attempted to clarify the conditions for the possibility of intentional social change made him look to many—when the state-oriented reform euphoria in most Western democracies was over—to be a prototypical representative of the naive belief in the possibilities of state planning and regulation. Again, taking seriously the title of his book would have helped to avoid such a misunderstanding: Etzioni never spoke of "the active state" but rather of "the active society"—emphasizing the increase of agency on the side of individual and collective actors. Like Alain Touraine, who labeled the societies after a dramatic increase in cybernetic capacities "postindustrial," Etzioni chose a new term and spoke, indeed much earlier than Lyotard and his fashionable followers, of "postmodernity." A last element in this brief characterization has to be mentioned. Etzioni's interest in the plurality of collective actors did not entice him to regard the political process in the sense of a free interplay of pluralist forces. His theory of inauthenticity, developed in the long (and clearly normative) epilogue to the book, provided a skeptical distance from mere facades of democratic consensus and the accompanying feelings not of powerlessness, but of manipulation.

It is no wonder that the author of such an ambitious book, after winning so little applause for his achievement, turned his efforts to a different field. For almost two decades Etzioni's work was not directed at the abstract questions of sociological theorizing but mostly at issues of political sociology and political programs.[9] He entered the theoretical arena again with his important proposal for a renewal of the discipline of economics. But *The Moral Dimension*, his startling book of 1988, is less a contribution to sociological theory than a sociological critique of the dominant paradigm in economic theory. As such, it has important predecessors in the sociological tradition, from Émile Durkheim's critique of Spencer in his *Division of Labor* to Talcott Parsons's critique of utilitarianism in his *Structure of Social Action*.[10] Even within the discipline of economics, there have always been countervoices whose intention was similar to Etzioni's, like the German Historical School or American Institutionalism. It is a rather ironic fact that Etzioni's success in founding a movement toward a new "social economics," that is, a new synthesis of sociology, economics, and moral reasoning that supersedes the rational action paradigm within its classic stronghold, takes place simultaneously with the triumphal march of that paradigm across sociology and other social-scientific disciplines. Though Etzioni has astonishingly few remarks to make on the heritage of sociological theory, we can consider his "new economics" as a continuation of this tradition. In all three parts of his study—the insistence on the irreducible character of morality, the elaboration of a new model of decision making, and the emphasis on the role of community and power with respect to markets—Etzioni is clearly part of the normativist Durkheimian and Parsonian tradition. Without simply repeating their lines of reasoning, he establishes himself as one of their contemporary successors. On the basis of his earlier contributions to sociological theory, political reasoning, and economics, Etzioni has recently sketched a booklong manifesto for the communitarian movement. This book goes beyond the confines of normal scholarly work and intends nothing less than "a new progressive movement, a major social effort to energize a package of reforms that will reduce the role of special interests in the government of our local and national communities."[11]

There can be no doubt that these different achievements by a single author add up to an impressive scholarly life's work. But, as is characteristic for scholarly work, some questions always remain open. I would like to address two of them here. The first question is related to the dichotomy between rational action and the existence of morality in Etzioni's argument. The first part of *The Moral Dimension* develops the idea that people pursue at least two utilities, namely pleasure and morality. As convincing as this may be, there is no demonstration of why these should be the only two on the list. The second question concerns the relationship between Etzioni's analyses and his activist impulse. This question should not be misinterpreted to mean that I am interested in the biographical background of Etzioni's work here. What I have in mind is rather the question of whether Etzioni's contributions to social theory contain the conceptual means to analyze the emergence of new values or the revitalization of old ones in a value-oriented social movement such as the one for which Etzioni has delivered the platform.

These two questions seem to be interrelated in a complex fashion. If we want to understand where the ultimate values of human actors come from or how their affective attachment to values can be strengthened, we need a sociological theory of action that allows us to understand the genesis of values. Etzioni himself is very skeptical about the attempts based on the rational action paradigm to come to grips with that problem.[12] Values certainly cannot be produced in a fully rational way, and the attachment to values is not the result of conscious intentions. The evolutionary explanations for the selection of rules have not been very successful either. But a purely normativist standpoint is not a viable alternative to them, since even if the existence of values and norms in general may be beyond doubt, the change of values still needs sociological explanation. As a consequence, this explanatory task may also compel us to revise our ideas about human action.

A full answer to these two questions is certainly beyond the possibilities of a short essay.[13] In order to make the necessity of answering these questions at least plausible, I would like to make a detour and describe how the ideas about rational action and social action are related to each other in the work of the major founders of sociological discourse. On that basis it should become possible to delineate at least the importance of these questions for an integration of the different parts of Etzioni's oeuvre.

## Economic Action and Social Action

In a certain sense, the economic theory of rational action served as a model to be followed by sociology even in the generation of sociology's founders. This proposition has been promulgated in fact for the emergence of sociology as a discipline. In particular, Göran Therborn and Simon Clarke[14] have claimed that the work of the first-generation of classic sociological theorists can be understood only in terms of a tacit acceptance of the model of rational action that had asserted itself in virtually every aspect of economics following the revolutionary impact of the theory of marginal utility on that field in the second half of the nineteenth century. Yet Therborn and Clarke wished to emphasize the degree to which economists as well as sociologists departed from the ideal of Marxist theory, namely, a theory of society based on a critique of political economy. In so doing they simply assumed that economic theory that is informed by the rational model is purely ideological in character. One need not subscribe to this view. The historical substance of their argument remains important even if we assume that any modern theory of society must naturally take account of individual decisions on actions, purchases, and choices and, therefore, cannot dispense with the model of rational action. If the historical proposition is true, this would give us the following picture: Sociology was not constructed on the model of rational action in the way that economics was, yet it accepted the validity of this theory for the purposes of economics. At the same time, it claimed that precisely those tasks and objects of inquiry now fell within the scope of sociology, which the above form of economics had not wished to take on board from earlier economic theory and political philosophy. The intention was thus for sociology to be responsible for analyzing those dimensions of social life that could not be grasped by economic study; and the intention was to analyze them by means of a theory of action that took precisely nonrational forms of action into consideration. Sociology therefore required a fundamental theory of action that was able to define various types of action according to how they differed specifically from rational action. It required a theory of society as an interconnection of actions that was more than merely the unintended linking of actions motivated by self-interest. As a consequence, sociology attached great importance to the normative agreement of the members of the society. Just as a fixation upon an enemy affects an individual as profoundly as does emulation of a role model, so too sociological action theory is permeated with the theory of rational action precisely because it sees types of action only as gradations of deviation from rationality in the full sense of the concept and not as unique phenomena in their own right.

The question is whether this picture actually agrees with the facts. To begin with, there can be no doubt that classical political economy, from Adam Smith onward, had a powerful impact on all avenues of intellectual life. Even those who disputed the accuracy of the concrete contents of the theory nevertheless took it as a yardstick for the theoretical and empirical level at which the question as to the causes for the wealth of nations had to be put. This is not to say that there was in any way a lack of critiques of political economy. The currents of historicism and early attempts to devise a sociology were also, to a greater or lesser extent, a polemic on political economy. They were often not interested in improving the latter but in refuting it, since the tack taken by political economy was often equated with an effort to legitimate a society in which intervention was not allowed to mediate the effects unleashed by market-based activity. Some of Adam Smith's followers were indeed interested in such a legitimation. Both the German historical school of economics and, in France, Auguste Comte's sociological program constituted pragmatic-reformist attempts to limit the legitimation of the principle of laissez-faire in the vulgarized forms in which classical economics had permeated European thought. Comte's main objection was the absence of a moral dimension, while the German school criticized the lack of a political dimension based on the nation-state. Indeed, classical economic theory looked set to fail due to its inability to generate any further insights into either the inescapable social problems raised by a market economy or the national framework of countries that had somehow to come to terms with England's domination of the world market. The weak link in these countercurrents, however, was that they were unable to derive the limits of the principle of laissez-faire from an economic theory of the market economy itself and thus were also unable to calculate in economic terms the benefits of the social reforms and forms of state intervention that they themselves favored. In the middle of the nineteenth century, at least in continental Europe, one could get the impression that classical economic theory was on the retreat again, to the extent that it had ever been on the attack.[15]

In other words, a theory that, for all its flaws, had consistently maintained that human institutions had to be related to the actions and needs of individuals and that refused to recognize the sacrosanct aura of either the state or abstract morality was in jeopardy. The critique of political economy put forward by Marx and Engels preserved this driving force in classical economics more clearly than did the other variants. But their project came up against limits similar to those that classical economic theory had confronted, albeit limits that were located elsewhere. All the different proponents of a theory of objective value since John Locke, and in particular David Ricardo, had been concerned primarily with solving what was essentially a question of social theory, namely, how to uncover the laws by which class-specific revenues were generated, and were less interested in applying their own value-theoretical assumptions to solving the more narrowly economic question of the dynamics of price formation. As the various forms of a market economy asserted themselves, so this omission increasingly came to appear as an intrinsic deficit of economic theory. In this situation, other theorists (who lived, incidentally, in different countries and worked independently of one another) launched an offensive to limit and more closely specify economic theory. I am referring here to the revolution caused by the theory of marginal utility. The marginal utility theorists advocated a reappraisal of value theory, thereby altering the logical status of economics in the hope that this would enable them to answer the question of price formation and the exact nature of the possibilities and limits of state intervention in the economy. Value theory was henceforth not to proceed from the question of how and who created objective values in the production process; rather it was to start from individuals with existing preferences and resources and thus from the issue of how the value of a particular product was constituted subjectively. This point of departure could then lead to the development of a new understanding of private property and the division of labor, as well as of the market and money as means of optimally allocating resources. Needless to say, this involved adopting many of the methods of classical economic theory. But what had often only been implicit in the latter, and inconsistently applied, was now made explicit in the theory and used consistently. Economic theory was no longer to be regarded as a comprehensive theory of society that remained close to political science and moral philosophy but as purely a theory of the actions of individuals with random goals and limited resources that could be applied in different ways. Such a pure theory had to rest inevitably on idealized assumptions and thus had to presume a measure of rational action, competition, and knowledge of conditions such as was not actually encountered in reality. But these idealizations were seen not as an empirical objection to the theory but merely as a methodological detour the theory had to take.

The classic sociologists reacted in various ways to this crisis in classical economic theory and to the "neoclassical" route out of the crisis. The conceptual framework that is best suited to demonstrating the exemplary role played by economic theory and the conception of sociology as a supplement to economics that could grasp nonrational action is to be found in Vilfredo Pareto's work. Pareto termed all rational action in all domains "logical action," and this included even those domains that were not directly economic, such as the military domain and the political and legal spheres. All other action he lumped together under the heading "non-logical action." In other words, to his mind all nonlogical forms of action—and in his opinion they constituted the vast empirical majority of all actions—were encompassed by nothing but a negatively defined residual category. This is not to say that he did not comment on them further. Quite the opposite: what elevates Pareto above all the other economic theorists is the fact that he did not merely treat the issue of a theory of noneconomic spheres of society and nonlogical action summarily. One of the most important motives behind his work was the wish to proceed inductively in this area in order to be able to describe these actions adequately and thus ensure that they did not merely resemble pathological deviations from a normal type. Via this inductive method, however, he arrived at a differentiation of types of action according to the role played by rational considerations in constituting them. "Logical actions are at least for the main the result of a consideration; non-logical actions arise mainly from a particular emotional state, feelings, the sub-consciousness, etc."[16] Pareto wished to show that, both to themselves and to others, individuals portray most of their actions as pseudorational, despite the widely different causes of such actions. Based on this assumption he developed an extensive systematic framework of classes of motives and forms of rationalization, which commentators have regarded as a form of disillusioning ideology critique in the fashion of Nietzsche.[17] Even if what Parsons wrote about Pareto may not be true, namely that the latter defected from economics to sociology, it is most certainly correct that Pareto conceived of sociology as a supplement to an economics that was based on the theory of marginal utility and devised a theory of action to serve this purpose, a theory that has been widely forgotten today.

The position of Max Weber's action theory vis-à-vis economic theory is much more complex in terms of its genesis but quite comparable in its effect. Weber's definitions are certainly the most influential text in the whole of sociological action theory. Weber came up with the well-known definition of sociology as the "science of social action."

> In action is included all human behavior when and insofar as the acting individual attaches a subjective meaning to it. Action in this sense may be either overt or purely inward or subjective, it may consist of positive intervention in a situation, or of deliberately refraining from such intervention or passively acquiescing in the situation. Action is social insofar as, by virtue of the subjective meaning attached to it by the acting individual (or individuals), it takes account of the behavior of others and is thereby oriented in its course.[18]

With this distinction Weber already sets sociology off from economic theory, which is permitted only to focus on rational action as such. There can be no doubt that Weber developed his sociological theory of economic action, which takes up so much of "Economy and Society,"[19] alongside pure economic theory and in part on its basis. The thrust of this assertion cannot be dulled by proving how strongly Weber's thought was influenced by the historical school of economics and in general by German historicism.[20] Although he took on many of the issues raised and solutions found by these schools, he never came out unequivocally in their favor in the controversy between this camp and the theorists of marginal utility. The necessity of distinguishing clearly between the value and factual judgments and the defense of a purely theoretical core matched the thought of Menger much more closely than it did Schmoller. Where Weber expressly criticized the theory of marginal utility and did not express merely his disinterest in the details of that theory—given that any preoccupation with the theory of marginal utility was also subject to the law of declining marginal utility—he criticized both the false understanding Menger and others had of their action theory as well as the possibility of grounding the model of rational action in psychology and anthropology. Weber attempted to create a synthesis of the competing schools of economic theory by viewing the conception of the model of rational action to be an historical ideal type. This, on the one hand, meant accepting the model of classical economic theory and, on the other, subordinating it to the more comprehensive task of overall historical cognition. To Weber's mind, sociology was to be a form of researching both history and the present that was based on a clearer and more systematic clarification of conceptual assumptions than usual in historiography. What became known as Weber's theory of action was his typology of the ways of defining social action, and it is this aspect that has had the greatest influence:

> Social action, like other forms of action, may be classified in the following four types according to its mode of orientation: (1) in terms of rational orientation to a system of discrete individual ends [*zweckrational*], that is, through expectations as to the behavior of objects in the external situation and of other human individuals, making use of these expectations as conditions or means for the successful attainment of the actor's own rationally chosen ends; (2) in terms of rational orientation to an absolute value [*wertrational*]; involving a conscious belief in the absolute value of some ethical, aesthetic, religious and other form of behavior, entirely for its own sake and independently of any prospects of external success; (3) in terms of affectual orientation, especially emotional, determined by the specific affects and states of feeling of the actor; (4) traditionally oriented, through the habituation of long practice.[21]

The interpretation of this proposed typology and the controversial discussions it triggered have shown that the principle underlying Weber's definition is far from transparent. Wolfgang Schluchter has undertaken the clearest attempt to distill what that principle is.[22] He maintains that Weber arranged his types of action along a scale of rationality whereby rational control could be directed toward any or all of the four components of action: means, purpose, value, or consequences. That type of action in which the actor rationally weighed up all the components individually and against one another would thus be highest on the scale and by extension the type of action that was fully rational. Purposive-rational action, which was in this manner charged with a certain ethic of responsibility, would be able to make the strongest claim to being considered an action.

Action oriented toward an absolute value, by contrast, does not include any reflection on the consequences; affectual action jettisons any consideration of values; and traditional action even abandons any thought of purposes. If this interpretation is accurate, then Weber's typology of action, like that of Pareto, is shaped by the fact that types of action that deviate from the norm of rational action are classified predominantly in terms of this deviation, that is, as deficient modes of rational action. Given the multifaceted nature of Weber's concept of rationality, this statement certainly cannot be the last word on Weber's contribution to action theory, but it could present the final judgment on both the typology he put forward and the effect of the model of rational action on Weber's deliberations on action theory.

In other words, from the point of view of action theory, there are distinct similarities between Pareto's and Weber's reactions to the change that the theory of marginal utility brought about in economics. This reaction was shared, albeit a generation later, by Alfred Schütz, so that one could call him a member of the same group. Contrary to widespread assumptions, Schütz's early work was intended not just as an abstract synthesis of the thought of Weber and Husserl but also as the basis for a theory that presented the interaction of the abstract types of action Weber had distinguished in concrete noneconomic actions and was thus meant as a sociological extension of orthodox economic theory.[23]

It was, however, possible to react quite differently to the change, as can be seen in the work of all those thinkers who claim that the model of rational action is of no use even for economic theory. This was a widespread reaction among American theorists at the time. Veblen's critique of the theory of marginal utility and his championing of an evolutionist theory of economics is a particularly famous case. It is a less well-known fact that Charles Cooley's work stems directly from early versions of the institutionalist strand in U.S. economics. He quite clearly believed that his social psychology refuted the individualistic assumptions of the model of rational action.[24]

Of the classical sociologists, it is, above all, Durkheim who belongs in this second group. He had from an early date—since a visit to Germany in 1885–86—been fascinated by the historical school in German economics and jurisprudence. However, he indicated that he distanced himself from the way that school's theories centered on a notion of the state and searched instead for "communitarian" solutions, such as were to be found in the writings of Albert Schäffle.[25] Durkheim differed from Weber in that he did not reject the possibility of grounding the theory of marginal utility in psychology in order to be able to uphold the model of rational action in a limited context by changing the epistemological interpretation of that economic theory. This explains why Durkheim had to concentrate on refuting any hedonist psychology. The sharpness of the distinction he makes between sociology and psychology, and between the social domain and the individual, can only be understood if we bear in mind that he, at least for a time, identified psychology with these hedonist assumptions and that to his mind the individual was synonomous with inclinations that were not subject to normative regulation. If, however, economic theory was not granted validity in a particular sphere, then it was only logical to claim that its subject matter constituted an area best addressed by a subsector of sociology, namely economic sociology. Durkheim admittedly had little chance to actually integrate economics into sociology or subjugate the former to the latter, since economics was a discipline strongly entrenched in French universities. Nevertheless, the school of sociology he founded took the stage with an imperial flourish. Durkheim's crass severing of any link between sociology and an individual's action is clearly the reason that his work initially does not appear to contain any approach for putting sociology on an action-theoretic foundation. This changed during the course of his life to the extent that Durkheim increasingly turned his attention to the question of how the processes of action constitutive for those values were used as a means of orientation and a yardstick in action, explicitly including economic action. Durkheim devised an action-theoretic explanation for the genesis of values but never quite relinquished the idea that economic action, and in particular, production and labor were per se presocial or antisocial. Even in his later theory of religion we still encounter the dualism of individual utilitarian everyday action and collective symbolic-expressive extraordinary action. Durkheim's conception of human nature rests on a notion of anarchic-egocentric impulses. Owing to the dualism underlying his work, Durkheim cannot posit sociality as a dimension in which everyday interpersonal action conflicts are solved. We therefore find that a reconstruction of the tacit assumptions behind the model of rational action is absent from his writings, too. The fact that he rejects this model out of hand leads him initially to counterpose it with a purely mentalistic conception; later he opts instead for a quite different type of action, namely, the ecstasy of collective ritual, which he does not, however, link back to the structure of rational, utilitarian action. In other words, just as there can be no talk of economic theory playing an exemplary role in Durkheim's thought, neither can it be claimed that he succeeded in developing a comprehensive theory of action. His writings pointing in that direction are instead characterized by polemical attacks on the model of rational action and to this extent are still fixated on the latter.

The only form of thought that could lead beyond Durkheim in this respect was one that applied the idea that values are constituted in everyday action and, in particular, one that addressed the question of how the value of rationality itself was constituted. Cooley, Mead, and Dewey all made progress pursuing the first step here.[26] The formulation that values should be considered a social phenomenon and the program put forward for providing social-psychological foundations for value theory both stress that values gained objective validity in social action—thus countering both the old objective doctrine of value per se and the new "subjective" doctrine. This new emphasis demonstrated the intention to invert the relationship between economics and psychology. It was now not economics but rather the newly declared program of social psychology that was to form the point of departure. From this starting point, however, economics could still be accorded a place befitting it.

Georg Simmel's *The Philosophy of Money* was alone in clearly making decisive progress toward the second step. Simmel also attempts to provide a psychological foundation for the objective validity of values—and he succeeds, because he does not construe the value of a good in terms of how it corresponds to a person's impulsive needs but rather as the result of reflective acts of valuation. A conscious act of valuation requires precisely, he claims, that "the native-practical unity of subject and object"[27] first be overcome. "One can therefore say that, although the value of an object rests on its being desired, that desire is no longer purely a matter of instincts."[28]

### Rationalization versus Communitarianism

This change in the psychological presuppositions relating to value judgments also shifts the general focus of attention. Simmel is not interested in economic theory in the narrow sense but in reconstructing those processes that give rise to the distance between individuals and the objects they desire. The reconstructive picture he paints traces both the emergence of a modern money-based economy and the manner in which this goes hand in hand with social processes whereby noneconomic spheres become progressively fragmented and subordinated to rationalization processes based on the rationale of money or analogous structures. The suggestive appeal of Simmel's analysis of the style of modern life is based on his contention that money, law, and intellectuality exhibit parallel structures. Thus, the very economic system that is characterized by its unleashing rational forms of action also rests on principles of valuation that cannot simply be derived from it. It is a well-known fact that Simmel's diagnosis of his time had a strong impact on Weber's own endeavors to analyze the genesis of modern capitalism. Weber, like Simmel, was also intent on showing that all economic action, and therefore in particular rational action as well, was based on cultural values. Whereas, as we have seen above, Weber's action theory itself remained dependent on the model of rational action, Simmel dispensed with trying to provide a more exact action-theoretic account of the assumptions on which his theory of valuation rested. This deficiency led to a profound ambivalence in both men's notions of the way the model of rational action was progressively imposing itself on the reality of the modern age. It remained a moot point whether modern culture should be interpreted as a culture based on the value of rationality or as a culture that, while admittedly exhibiting certain trends toward rationalization, also always contains countercurrents. In the one case, non-rational forms of action are either relics of premodernity or examples of antimodern deviances; in the other, they can lay equal claim to being modern and to being valid in contemporary society. A theory of action that, by virtue of its conceptual structure, considers nonrational action to be a deficient form of rational action provides a hermetic interpretation of modernity that rests on the principles of rationality. In order to generate an alternative diagnosis of contemporary society that does not think of everything in terms of an optimistic or pessimistic account of a linear process of rationalization, we must reconstruct and reintroduce the assumptions on which the model of rational action is based.[29]

Amitai Etzioni is clearly not a proponent of the rationalization approach—neither its optimistic nor its pessimistic version. In the third part of his *Moral Dimension,* he connects the evolution of market economies and the genesis, survival, or destruction of communities in two ways. On the one hand, markets have certain destructive consequences for communities. This is true, above all, in the case of unregulated competition in which not only communities but markets themselves may be destroyed. But even in the case of regulated competition, any extension of markets causes trouble for self-sustained communities. On the other hand, markets presuppose communities and are based on them. For many social theorists and cultural critics, this fact that markets destroy the communities that constituted them leads societies with a market economy into a tragic impasse. In this view, market economies can never be culturally stabilized, since they automatically destroy the cultural resources upon which they live. Etzioni would not jump to such a conclusion. For him it is wrong to neglect the permanent process of a reproduction of moral commitments and even of a genesis of new moral binding forces in societies with market economies. And this view also contains an erroneous understanding of the market. The last sentence of *The Moral Dimension* puts it very bluntly and seemingly paradoxically: "The more people accept the neo-classical paradigm as a guide for their behavior, the more their ability to sustain a market economy is undermined."[30] This sentence severs the affinity between the rational action model and the theory of market economies. If all action were oriented toward the rational action model, market economies indeed could not survive in their social and cultural frameworks. Put the other way round, if we understand markets as embedded in a "societal capsule" (Etzioni), their consequences remain restricted from the same reasons that they work at all. If market economies are undermined by the totalization of rational action, the relativization of rational action is a precondition for the stabilization of market economies.

The communitarian movement is an attempt to achieve the necessary "recommitment to moral values—without puritanical excesses."[31] Its success will depend on the degree of consonance between its goals and the social-structural possibilities for value change. Amitai Etzioni has given us in three books the components of a comprehensive theory. Whereas *The Active Society* delineates the conditions for a self-guiding society, *The Moral Dimension* repudiates the excessive hegemony of a hyperrationalist thinking; and finally, *The Spirit of Community* proclaims the necessity for a moral reorientation and a reawakening of our commitment to the values that are basic to our identity. But the exact relationship between these three books and their topics needs further clarification. What are the possible bases, resources, and opportunities for a mobilization in the communitarian direction; what can self-government mean in a modern society within an increasingly globalized market economy?

## Notes

1. See, e.g., the review symposium in the *American Sociological Review* 33 (1968), which includes such famous contributors as Robert Nisbet, Anatol Rapoport, and others. For Germany, compare the review by Dieter Senghaas and the chapter by Greven.

2. Robert Cook, review of *The Active Society*, pp. 564–65.

3. Jeffrey Alexander, *Twenty Lectures: Sociological Theory Since 1945*.

4. Warren Breed, *The Self-Guiding Society*.

5. Natₐlie Rogoff Ramsoy, *"The Active Society* Revisited."

6. Jeffrey Alexander, "The New Theoretical Movement," pp. 77–101.

7. For recent developments in these schools, compare the excellent collection: *Frontiers in Social Theory: The New Syntheses*, George Ritzer (ed.).

8. Amitai Etzioni, *The Active Society*, p. 125.

9. Amitai Etzioni, *An Immodest Agenda*.

10. Émile Durkheim, *The Division of Labor in Society*; Parsons, *The Structure of Social Action*.

11. Amitai Etzioni, *The Spirit of Community: Rights, Responsibilities and the Communitarian Agenda*, p. 234.

12. Amitai Etzioni, *The Moral Dimension: Toward a New Economics*, pp. 178 ff.

13. For an attempt to elaborate such a theory, compare Joas, *Die Kreativität des Handelns* (English translation, *The Creativity of Action*, in print). In the following part of this essay I take some passages from this book.

14. Göran Therborn, *Science, Class and Society: On the Formation of Sociology and Historical Materialism*; see esp. pp. 240–315; Simon Clarke, *Marx, Marginalism and Modern Sociology: From Adam Smith to Max Weber*.

15. For a convincing new interpretation of these developments, see Peter Wagner, *Sozialwissenschaften und Staat*.

16. Vilfredo Pareto, *Compendium of General Sociology*.

17. Arnold Gehlen, "Vilfredo Pareto und seine 'neue Wissenschaft,' " pp. 149–95.

18. Max Weber, "The Fundamental Concepts of Sociology," p. 88.

19. Ibid., pp. 158–324.

20. Wilhelm Hennis, *Max Weber: Essays in Reconstruction*.

21. Max Weber, "The Fundamental Concepts of Sociology," p. 115.

22. See Wolfgang Schluchter, *The Rise of Western Rationalism*.

23. Christopher Prendergast, "Alfred Schütz and the Austrian School of Economics," pp. 1–26.

24. For example, Charles H. Cooley, "The Institutional Character of Pecuniary Valuation," pp. 543–55.

25. Émile Durkheim, *Ethics and the Sociology of Morals*, pp. 267–343.

26. See, for example, Mead's review of B.M. Anderson Jr.'s *Social Value: A Study in Economic Theory*, pp. 432–36.

27. Georg Simmel, *Philosophy of Money*, p. 66.

28. Ibid., p. 72.

29. With respect to Parsons, Donald Levine and Charles Camic have followed a

strategy similar to the one I pursue here with respect to the sociological classics. See Donald Levine's introduction to his book: *Simmel and Parsons*; Charles Camic, "The Making of a Method: A Historical Reinterpretation of the Early Parsons," pp. 421–39; "'Structure' after 50 Years: The Anatomy of a Charter," pp. 38–107; "Introduction: Talcott Parsons before SSA," pp. ix-lxix. Compare also Joas, "Communitarianism, Pragmatism, Historicism."

30. Amitai Etzioni, *The Moral Dimension: Toward a New Economics*, p. 257.

31. Amitai Etzioni, *The Spirit of Community: Rights, Responsibilities, and the Communitarian Agenda*, p. 1.

# Bibliography

Alexander, Jeffrey. *Twenty Lectures: Sociological Theory Since 1945*. New York: Columbia University Press, 1987.

———. "The New Theoretical Movement." In *Handbook of Sociology*, Neil Smelser (ed), 1988, pp. 77–101. London: Sage.

Breed, Warren. *The Self-Guiding Society*. New York: Free Press, 1972.

Camic, Charles. "The Making of a Method: A Historical Reinterpretation of the Early Parsons." *American Sociological Review* 52 (1987), pp. 421–39.

———. " 'Structure' after 50 Years: The Anatomy of a Charter." *American Journal of Sociology* 95 (1989), pp. 38–107.

———. Introduction: "Talcott Parsons Before SSA." In *Talcott Parsons: The Early Essays*. Chicago: University of Chicago Press, 1991.

Clarke, Simon. *Marx, Marginalism and Modern Sociology: From Adam Smith to Max Weber*. London: Macmillan, 1982.

Cook, Robert. "Review of *The Active Society*." *American Journal of Sociology* 75 (1969–70), pp. 564–65.

Cooley, Charles H. "The Institutional Character of Pecuniary Valuation." *American Journal of Sociology* 18 (1913), pp. 543–55.

Durkheim, Émile. *The Division of Labor in Society*. New York: Macmillan, 1933 (French original: 1893).

———. "La science positive de la morale en Allemagne." In *Écrits*. Vol. 1. Paris: Presses Universitaires de France, 1975.

———. *Ethics and the Sociology of Morals*. Translated and edited by R.T. Hall. Buffalo: Prometheus, 1993.

Etzioni, Amitai. *The Active Society*. New York: Free Press, 1968.

———. *An Immodest Agenda*. New York: McGraw-Hill, 1983.

———. *The Moral Dimension: Toward a New Economics*. New York: Free Press, 1988.

———. *The Spirit of Community: Rights, Responsibilities, and the Communitarian Agenda*. New York: Crown, 1993.

Gehlen, Arnold. "Vilfredo Pareto und seine 'neue Wissenschaft.' " In Gehlen, *Studien zur Anthropologie und Soziologie*, pp. 149–95. Neuweid: Luchterhand, 1963.

Greven, Michael Thomas. *System und Gesellschaftsanalyse. Kritik der Werte und Erkenntnismöglichkeiten in Gesellschaftsmodellen der kybernetischen Systemtheorien*. Darmstadt: Luchterhand, 1974.

Hennis, Wilhelm. *Max Weber: Essays in Reconstruction*. London: Allen and Unwin, 1988.

Joas, Hans. *Die Kreativität des Handelns*. Frankfurt am Main: Suhrkamp, 1992.

———. "Communitarianism, Pragmatism, Historicism." In P. Koslowski, ed., *The Theory of Ethical Economy in the Historical School*, pp. 267–282. Berlin: Springer, 1995.

Levine, Donald. 1980. Simmel and Parsons. New York: Arno Press, 1980.

Mead, George Herbert. "Review of B.M. Anderson Jr.'s *Social Value: A Study in Economic Theory.*" *Psychological Bulletin* 8 (1911), pp. 432–36.

Nisbet, Robert. Review of *The Active Society. American Sociological Review* 33 (1968), pp. 988–90.

Pareto, Vilfredo. *Compendium of General Sociology.* Minneapolis: University of Minnesota Press, 1980.

Parsons, Talcott. *The Structure of Social Action.* New York: McGraw Hill, 1937.

Prendergast, Christopher. "Alfred Schütz and the Austrian School of Economics." *American Journal of Sociology* 92 (1986), pp. 1–26.

Ramsoy, Natalie Rogoff. "*The Active Society* Revisited." *Acta Sociologica* 29 (1986), pp. 337–48.

Rapoport, Anatol. Review of *The Active Society. American Sociological Review* 33 (1968), pp. 978–83.

Ritzer, George, ed., *Frontiers in Social Theory: The New Syntheses.* New York: Columbia University Press, 1990.

Schluchter, Wolfgang. *The Rise of Western Rationalism.* Translated by G. Roth. Berkeley: University of California Press, 1981.

Senghaas, Dieter. "Apathie oder Aktivität. Etzionis Theorie des politischen Handelns." *Politische Vierteljahresschrift* 10 (1969), pp. 118–28.

Simmel, Georg. *The Philosophy of Money.* Translated by T. Bottomore and D. Frisby, 2d enlarged ed. London: Routledge and Kegan Paul, 1978.

Therborn, Göran. *Science, Class and Society: On the Formation of Sociology and Historical Materialism.* London: New Left Books, 1976.

Wagner, Peter. *Sozialwissenschaften und Staat.* Frankfurt am Main: Campus, 1990.

Weber, Max. "The Fundamental Concepts of Sociology." In Weber, *The Theory of Social and Economic Organization.* Translated by A.M. Henderson and T. Parsons. New York: Oxford University Press, 1947.

# 3

# A Theoretical Framework on the Interaction of Politics and News Media: A Dialogue with Etzioni's *The Active Society*

*Edward W. Lehman and Ethna Lehman*

In *The Active Society* (1968), Amitai Etzioni focuses on how societal knowledge converges with state capacities and political participation to foster a more viable democratic polity and a more transformable society. Although *The Active Society* is virtually silent on the role of the news media, its pivotal concerns lead naturally to an inquiry about the relationship between politics and societal knowledge as created by the mass news media. It is now commonplace to blame the news media (particularly television) for many of America's political inadequacies. Neuman (1986), for example, reports:

> It is claimed . . . that television has stimulated the growth of political cynicism and malaise. . . . The media are said to have trivialized politics, depressed voter turnout, led to the decline of the party system, caused dramatic centralization

This chapter is based on a paper presented at the Society for the Advancement of Socio-Economics, Sixth Annual Conference, in Jouy en Josas, France, July 15, 1994. This is a revised version òf a paper presented at the New York University Sociology Department's Workshop in Power, Politics, and Protest on November 5, 1993. Jeff Goodwin and Caitilin Rabbitt were the commentators, and we appreciate their suggestions. Among the participants that day whose comments we also wish to acknowledge are Scott Applerouth, Neva Fernandez, Kelly Moore, Alessandro Pizzorno, and Bruce Western. In addition, Steve Brint, James M. Jasper, Robert Max Jackson, and Richard Maisel provided detailed observations that have been of great assistance in revising this chapter.

of political power, and increased the domination of the executive branch over Congress. . . . (p. 133)

In leveling these charges, critics often treat the news media as either part of the state designed to foster these outcomes or malevolent forces outside ongoing political processes. Here we offer a "social quantum" framework that permits more theoretically comprehensive and empirically open inquiries into the interaction between the news media and politics. This framework asserts first that it is useful to conceptualize the news media both as integral to the political system and differentiated from it (analogous to the formulation in quantum mechanics that says that it is sometimes helpful to see particles as waves and at other times to see waves as particles) and, second, that the news media have an ambivalent location (analogous to the way the duality of particles and waves indicates that they never have only one definite point "but are 'smeared out' with a certain probability distribution" in quantum mechanics [Hawking 1988, 56]).[1]

In this chapter the news media are cast in this social quantum framework to sharpen our appreciation of how political participation operates in modern capitalist democracies, with a particular eye on the United States. In so doing, our focus is less on how other societal forces shape the news media (which they undoubtedly do) and more on fostering theoretically comprehensive and empirically open inquiries into the ways the news media are implicated in how political participation is exerted.

"The mass media," according to Gamson (1992, xi), "are a system in which active agents with specific purposes are constantly engaged in a process of supplying meaning." A more complete definition of mass media demands that one specify both who these active agents are and to whom they are attempting to supply meaning. In today's world, active agents are large corporate actors who control the principal means of mass communication. These media are defined as "mass" by the nature of their targets; that is, not only because they aim at audiences of a large size but because these targets are socially, economically, culturally, and regionally diverse. (For similar definitions, see Ball-Rokeach and Cantor 1986, 10–11; Katz 1960; and Lang and Lang 1992, 1206–7.) The meanings they supply are either entertainment or news (or some combination of these). These two institutionalized components of the media have different objectives, depend on different kinds of resources, at times have distinct organizational bases, and "must be judged according to what are often contradictory criteria of success" (see Alexander 1990, 324–25). This inquiry is limited to the news-supplying role of the media.

This chapter is divided into two parts. The first section treats the first dimension of the news media's ambivalent location, namely, as part of the political system. It elaborates a multilevel model of the political system and locates the news media in a specific zone within it, but it argues that other polity members may also play active news-media roles. The second section introduces the flip side of the news media's ambivalent location, its structural differentiation, the better to ask: (1) How does the ambivalent linkage between the state and the news media affect the orchestration of political participation? (2) How do three historical concomitants of the news media's differentiation—namely, growing internal concentration, bureaucratization, and professionalization—intersect with their polity membership to shape participation? and (3) Have the news media usurped the place of mediating structures that have traditionally stood between state and citizens? Moreover, we argue the social quantum formulation permits a broader array of hypotheses and decisive research questions to be raised about each of the questions.

## The News Media in the Polity

### A Multilevel Polity

The news media, although differentiated from our political system, are at the same time part of it insofar as some of their principal institutionalized activities (although perhaps not their most definitive ones) fall into one of its distinct zones, which we call the "organization level." But what does this mean, and how does it help us to assess how the news media connect with democratic political participation? Let us start by inquiring into how the news media are part of the political system.

We begin by positing, as Etzioni (1968) does, that a satisfactory rendering of contemporary political life requires a multilevel imagery (Lehman 1992). That is, we assume that politics is appreciated and explained more fully when its morphology is thought of as neither strictly horizontal nor two-tiered (as in such formulas as state versus society, public versus private, the autonomy of the state versus the relations of production, etc.). The use of multilevel imagery means society does not determine political life, although it is the supraunit that contains many smaller units such as the political system. While society does limit the forms that political institutions can take, the latter may also shape society.[2] A multilevel imagery also clarifies the relationship of the political system and the state (a matter that remains ambiguous in *The Active Society*). The political system—or polity, for short—is society's overall system of political power. It includes group actors (governments, contenders, and challengers) as well as active and passive individual members. It also includes both downward control processes through which state authorities use political power (the ability to set, pursue, and implement societal goals) to dominate intermember power (other members' ability to set, pursue, and implement particular goals) and upward participation processes through which nonstate actors convert their intermember power into political power. (For additional details, see Etzioni 1968, 94–134.)

Political participation may be thought of as a way nonstate polity members are able to contribute to or try to influence a state's actions as well as a polity's overall configuration (ibid., 387–426). Social scientists tend to classify these contributions or forms of influence as "confidence" and "demands" (see, for example, Easton 1965 and Parsons 1967). Confidence refers to polity members' support for or broad endorsements of incumbents, particularly (although by no means exclusively) the national executive. When widely granted, confidence confers a "zone of acceptability" (Simon 1957) so that officials do not have to deploy resources to insure compliance with each directive. The concept of demands focuses attention on whether and how other polity members channel claims upward to the state and how well they succeed in having their demands converted into policies.[3] The relative efficiency or inefficiency of political participation processes depends on how successfully the partly incompatible exigencies of confidence (delivering support to sitting authorities) and demands (pressing new claims on these leaders) are balanced. (For a fuller discussion of the nature of efficient political participation, see Lehman 1992, 102–7.)

Our model of the polity contains four intrasocietal levels of political control and participation: public, organization, party, and state. They form a hierarchy with the public at the bottom and the state at the top. The more a researcher concentrates on only a single level, the greater the risks of simplistic, one-dimensional analysis.

A theoretically comprehensive examination of political participation must include all four levels. The first three are ever more active creators and processors of influence. While the state has been treated primarily as the target of influence, we shall see that it also generates influence insofar as some state actors attempt to influence the decisions of others. In the past each level has been associated with its own distinctive, and largely self-contained, research tradition—for example, voting and public opinion; social movements and interest group politics; political parties; and government and public administration.

Bureaucratization, political consciousness, and capacity for concerted action increase as one moves from the public to organization to party to state levels, while absolute size tends to decrease (Etzioni 1968, 94–111). The public level is the least bureaucratized, has the least political consciousness and capacity for sustained collective action, and potentially contains all of society's members.[4] It is the tier of the general population. Voting studies and opinion surveys employing explanatory variables taken from social stratification are often used in analyzing it. However, a satisfactory explanatory language ought to take into account a "wide range of local, regional, familial, ethnic, or religious traditions" (Hamilton 1972, 62) and not just economic factors.

The organization level, on which the news media are found, is composed of actors with a bureaucracy at their core. The key actors customarily associated with this level are voluntary associations, interest groups, and social-movement organizations. The web of affiliations spun by voluntary associations increases cohesion within the public's constituencies and helps raise political consciousness and the capacity for collective action. While voluntary associations are part of the organization tier, their most definitive roles are expressive and focus on nonpolitical sectors (as in the case of lodges, fraternal orders, churches, etc.), and consequently they are rarely the decisive political units on this level. Advocacy groups, particularly interest groups and social-movement organizations, are deliberately created formations using significant portions of their assets to exert political influence (that is, to channel confidence and demands), although they may vary in how exclusively political they are. Examples include not only the National Rifle Association, Common Cause, the NAACP, the National Association of Manufacturers, and Right to Life, but most big business corporations and labor unions. Social-movement organizations represent a very visible type of advocacy group in our times. They share with interest groups the bureaucratized core that is a defining feature of the species (although the levels of bureaucratization at the core of social movements are sometimes lower than in more established interest groups). A social movement, however, also includes a periphery of fervent adherents who are not part of a core organization's formal structure but who are capable of mobilization for limited, yet often intense, tasks such as demonstrations, letter-writing campaigns, distributing announcements, and so forth.

The social quantum perspective is particularly suitable for the analysis of the public and organization levels. Most actors on these two tiers have a key characteristic in common: Society's members define and judge both by the roles they play in nonpolitical spheres (for example, the family, the community, the economy, religion, education, entertainment, and the creation of news) as well as political spheres, and the former often looms as more definitive than the latter. The definitive roles of parties and the state, on the other hand, are specified and judged exclusively or primarily in political terms (although these entities routinely interact with other realms).

The modern mass political party is at the interface of the state, the public, and the organization levels. Parties of this type are the prime institutionalized vehicles for converting public and organization expressions of confidence and demands into institutionalized mechanisms for filling state positions and influencing state policies via competitive elections. Only this kind of party falls unequivocally on the third level of the polity.

The fourth level is the state.[5] The hallmark of state agents is the responsibility and capacity to set, pursue, and implement collective goals for a society covering multiple contiguous regions. Access to legitimate means of violence, which is the core of the Weberian definition (Weber [1924] 1968, 56, 65), may serve as the ultimate backing for political power, but it is neither the *differentia specifica* of the state nor the only type of resource needed for its effectiveness.[6] Further, it is never correct to equate the state with the national executive regardless of the latter's power. The state has more than one major branch. It often includes such entities as: the national executive, the administrative branch, the military and police, the judiciary, subcentral government, and the national parliament (Miliband 1969, 49–53).

### The News Media as Organization-Level Actors

The news media as part of the polity are best considered organization-level phenomena. The horizontal, temporal, and geographical dispersion of polity members, and not just their vertical structure, means that news reporting can no longer operate effectively as a locally based cottage industry. Today's principal mass news media actors are the television networks, mass-circulation magazines, and highly influential national newspapers that attempt to inform the citizenry at large rather than speak for circumscribed constituencies. Yet, while the mass news media lie above the public tier, they are not (in democratic systems at least) lodged on the party or state levels. Treatment of the news media as unique organization-tier actors permits a more realistic and sober assessment of their purported negative effects on democratic political participation.

News reporting, in modern polities, plays an essential role in fashioning how citizens shape confidence and demands. In particular, the U.S. news media see themselves as responsible for providing "common knowledge"—"what people think and how they structure ideas" (Neuman, Just, and Crigler 1992, 3)—to make democratic participation more efficient. Ample and credible information entails more than reporting about political events and actions. The news media also regard it as their duty to monitor the conduct of officials and agencies and to act as guardians of democratic institutions and values. Indeed, the *New York Times,* in the midst of the Whitewater scandal, arrogated to the news media such a legally mandated duty when it wrote that "journalists have a constitutionally defined obligation to stick with a story as long as there are unanswered questions of political, legal or moral consequence" (*New York Times* 1994, 18).

Etzioni's (1968, 135–309) emphasis on the diversity and essential nature of societal knowledge makes science (especially in its policy or applied form) the exemplar of the shape such knowledge should take. "All knowledge," he says, "is a simplification—a reduced, schematic abstraction from a richer, less ordered, more concrete reality" (ibid., 148). There are striking similarities between how the news media create common knowledge and the creation of scientific knowledge (beyond the fact that the latter domain is composed of another set of organization-level actors whose political roles warrant fuller explication). Probably the most basic of these is that, although in the business of constructing knowledge, practitioners from both realms engage in reducing and codifying apparently disparate empirical details while framing them using agreed-upon standards, particularly the criterion of objectivity. Students of science recognize that this process is not a neutral one and that "objective" or "value free" can never be equated with "valueless." Like science, the news media must decide about what to do and not to do on the basis of shared rules that inform their communities. Both enterprises, for instance, are also driven by the quest for priority and the pursuit of prizes (either Nobel or Pulitzer). The idea of the news media as a morally neutral, unselective camera passively recording the facts is sociologically nonsensical (Tuchman 1978) in the same way as positivistic views of science that see the latter as driven by facts alone (Alexander 1990; Schudson 1978).

Not only must reporters and editors assign meaning in deciding what appropriate media behavior is, but the creation of news is itself a value-adding process. The mass news media's decisions on what constitutes an event, which events are newsworthy, and what to cover about such phenomena are ongoing processes. The transformation of potential events into actual news stories entails placing raw data onto a kind of social assembly line along which the amount of information is constantly being reduced while meaning or value, or in Gamson's (1988) terms, a "frame," is being added (see also Gans 1979; Gitlin 1980; and Tuchman 1978). While news is being physically condensed, its broader significance and why we should know it are being framed by the news media's staff and managers. Presentation of news in thirty-second television sound bites captures the dilemmas in this process.

### The News-Media Roles of Other Polity Members

Actors on all levels of the polity play multiple roles vis-à-vis the news media. They may be audiences, subjects, sources, or interpreters. In no role are they ever purely passive, although they are inclined to be more active as sources and interpreters than as audiences and subjects. (On the importance of an active dimension for the social sciences, see Etzioni 1968, 1–18.) Further, some actors tend to play more active news-media roles than others, with those on the public level the least active of all. With the exception of the audience role of the public, little systematic research has been done on the diverse news-media roles on different tiers of the polity. Here we offer a preliminary discussion of the ways in which other polity members interact with the news media as a guide for future research.

### Audience Role

Among the more venerable approaches to the place of the news media in political life has been the "hypodermic model of political effects" (see Kraus and Davis 1976 and Tuchman 1978). This tradition focuses on the public viewed as a homogeneous, passive mass of dispersed individuals who unreflectively receive and respond to the same messages from the same sources. However, a significant sociological literature, much of it under either the rubric of "personal influence" (Katz and Lazarsfeld 1955) or "social constructionism" (see especially Gamson 1988; Gamson and Modigliani 1989; and Neuman, Just, and Crigler 1992), has made us aware that the public is both active and interactive in the processing of news-media messages. Members of the public receive, process, and respond in terms of their individual histories and situations (Molotch and Lester 1974) and in concert with their families, friends, neighbors, coworkers, and "political influentials" (Katz 1960).

Recognition of the social nature of the public's reception and processing of and response to news is especially important for understanding voting behavior and public-opinion formation, the two most distinctive aspects of political participation on the public level. This level of the polity is productively seen as heterogeneous and composed of diverse collectivities and subcollectivities (see Etzioni 1968, especially 432–65 on the "morphology of modern and post-modern societies") that do not merely constitute "a vegetative audience, passively absorbing media influences" (Neuman, Just, and Crigler 1992, 8). Yet how active these actors are varies considerably. When, where, why, and how the public's audience role becomes more or less active ought to be a critical topic for media research.

Like the public, actors on the organization, party, even state levels also receive, process, and respond to news-media messages. Despite the dearth of systematic research in this area, enough empirical work exists to illustrate the audience role of such actors. Gitlin (1980), in his iconic study of the transformation of the Students for a Democratic Society (SDS), shows how the SDS as a social-movement organization restructured its leadership and modified its mission in large part as a reaction to how it saw itself portrayed in the news media. In the same study, Gitlin (1980, 223–26) reports how the state itself, in the person of Vice President Spiro Agnew, received news-media coverage on the Vietnam War, reacted negatively, and applied pressure to shape subsequent news-media treatment of the opposition to the war. We know also that American presidents and their staffs now closely monitor the television networks' and major newspapers' daily outputs. But how these outputs have been received, processed, and responded to—and with what political consequences—remains largely unexplored.

*Subject Role*

Polity members from all levels may be the subjects of news-media attention. But some are more likely to be deemed newsworthy than others. According to Molotch and Lester (1974; 1975), the endeavors of political and economic elites—including all branches of the state and their officials, parties, major corporations, and powerful individuals—constitute the predominant focus of the news media's routine activities in the United States. Political actors do not necessarily await the attention of the news media; they actively pursue it. In the case of the two major political parties, for instance, the timing and format of the national nominating conventions have been arranged primarily to suit the preferences of the broadcast networks (Robinson 1977, 19–21).

For political actors outside the establishment, such as challenger social movements, news-media coverage may not be as automatic (see Gamson 1990, 145–51). Molotch (1979) suggests that they actively pursue coverage by staging rallies, marches, sit-ins, and other forms of confrontation. Lipsky (1968) makes the point that coverage of protest is itself a resource for advocacy groups because it allows them to reach strategic third parties from all polity levels whom they could not otherwise contact. Coverage of attacks on civil rights demonstrations, for example, allowed activists to generate support among the public, or what Lipsky (1968, 1145–46) calls "reference publics of protest targets."

The public, too, can be the subject of news-media coverage. This is the realm of "human interest" journalism so widely practiced by the American news media. For example, news accounts of social problems such as single-parent households, health-care costs, crime, AIDS, and so forth, are frequently pegged around poignant stories about "real people with real problems." Here, however, members of the public are often the surrogates for actors and processes more fruitfully analyzed on higher levels of the polity. The result is to turn the political into the personal and to turn attention away from the institutional sources of social problems (Bennett 1988 and Iyengar 1991). As Etzioni (1984) notes:

> *Time* [magazine] is credited with having invented, decades ago, the kind of reporting in which public issues are personalized, treated as they are reflected in the life of one person—not an average person but a "personality." . . . The great success of *Time* has spawned numerous imitators and a very commonly used style of reporting. Often a news story leads off like a personal diary; several personal anecdotes are sure to follow. All this keeps eyes *off* the system. . . . No wonder Americans dwell much more on the integrity of their politicians than the integrity of the American system. (p. 19)

## Sources and Interpreter Roles

When we discuss political actors as sources and interpreters of news, we are moving beyond the matter of mere coverage. Many students of the news media have noted how reliant reporters and commentators are on state agencies and records for "all the news that's fit to print" or broadcast (Sigal 1973; Molotch and Lester 1974; 1975). Government reports on poverty and drug addiction may form the bases for news stories on these topics. Police records may provide the stimulus as well as the evidence for a story about a crime wave in a community. Indeed, news-producing enterprises' organizational (notably economic) needs and the everyday pressures of reporters' jobs are often invoked to explain the news media's ready recourse to official sources and interpretations. Fishman (1980, 43) asserts that there are "no other modes of [news] production in this society that can provide daily newspapers with the scope, variety, dependability, and quantity of information that [government] bureaucracies can deliver—and deliver in a scheduled, predictable way." Of course, political actors outside the state (among them parties, major corporations, and challenger social movements) stand in a similar relationship to the news media as "official" sources. Lipsky (1970, 169–72 and passim), for example, shows how the day-to-day requirements of the pursuit of news brought reporters into close contact with the rank and file and leaders of the Harlem rent strikes of 1963–64 and made journalists more sympathetic to the strikers' aims and conduits for the leaders' messages.

Polity members on all levels are aware of the news media's great dependence on them and are motivated both to cooperate with and manipulate the news media for their own ends. Cooperation may be as simple as scheduling events such as press conferences and ceremonies in ways that satisfy reporters' deadlines. It may involve the establishment of formal structures, such as press offices or public relations consultants, to which journalists can routinely turn for information. "Leaks" or "exclusive interviews" in extraordinary situations are also common practices. But, in any case, it is the political actor who offers, withholds, or distorts the knowledge on which the news media largely rely for their everyday operations. The result, according to Sigal (1973) and Fishman (1980), is that polity members, especially state agents, parties, and leading corporations, exert a major influence over the news media's selection of stories to cover as well as the content of these stories.

One might expect that, in cooperating with the news media, political actors are concerned primarily with advancing their own interests. Paramount among these is the transmission of their messages to others in the polity. Often, the public is the intended target. The President may use a televised address to sway voters to support his programs in the face of opposition from Congress or the judiciary or even his own party. A corporation may well employ newspaper advertisements to appeal directly to the public to stave off legislation or regulation it deems detrimental to its operations.

Yet, in many instances, a political actor may cooperate with the news media in order to influence other polity members above the public level. In the United States, the state, particularly the federal government, is the main source of national and international news (Sigal 1973). Not as well recognized is the extent to which targets of the news are internal to the state itself. The size and complexity of the federal government plus the insulation of officials from one another have made the news media invaluable partners in the transmission of information within the state.[7] But more than information may be at stake. Officials may use the news media to propose new policies ("trial balloons") and to garner or dilute support within the government for existing or emerging policies. Officials may use the news media in their efforts to promote or hinder state actions, to advance their pet programs or agencies, or to mobilize opposition. In any case, the news media can be both a potent weapon in internal struggles of the government as well as the arena in which these struggles are carried out.

Potentially strategic nonstate polity members also have an interest is communicating with polity members above the public. Among these is the political party. Political parties, like state agencies, have press offices and employ media consultants who advise candidates during election campaigns and serve as spokespersons in the newspapers and on television. Of course, the party may command some of the state's capacity to mobilize the news media through members who are themselves in the government, such as the president and members of Congress.

Considerable variation exists in how actors on the organization level attempt to communicate with others above the public tier via the news media. Some powerful corporations such as Mobil and Philip Morris, advocacy groups such as the National Organization for Women, and service organizations like Planned Parenthood or the Catholic Church have press offices and media consultants of their own. Others, including most challenger social-movement organizations, like the Harlem rent strikers of 1963–65 and the SDS, have no such mechanisms. This has reinforced their reliance on unruly or extralegal behaviors to generate news-media attention and thereby to get their messages across to key actors who might influence policy.

As a news source, the public is the least-active tier. Its members' most distinctive political role is voting, and they are unlikely to try to exert influence on higher-tier actors via the news media. "Ordinary citizens" may be portrayed in the news media as pursuing personal political agendas: testifying before Congress about health care or displaying to reporters the deteriorated conditions of their housing. Often these performances are staged events in which one higher-tier actor (e.g., a professional health-care provider association or a welfare-rights organization) selects members of the public to represent its interests in a dramatic fashion to other higher-tier actors whose attention it desires. The public's situation here parallels that of its role as subject.

As sources, political actors on all levels do not necessarily provide "all the facts" or "just the facts." They attempt to tailor the information provided and the news-media outlets to their own needs. Further, they try to affect how information is framed in the news media and read by audiences. That is, they try to interpret the information both before and after it becomes news. Political actors differ in the type and volume of resources they can bring to this interpreter role. As we have noted previously, in the United States, the federal branches of the state have the most-developed apparatus for such news management. Indeed, on this level, specialization has become so great that a distinct category of media personnel has emerged—the "spin doctor," whose task it is to manage the news *after* it has appeared. Parties, major corporations, large labor unions, and established advocacy groups now also have their own versions of spin doctors. Challenger social-movement organizations, we have already seen, tend to lack such institutionalized instruments and depend more on informal access to working journalists to get their "spin" to the news recorded. The public qua public has no organized mechanisms for engaging the news media as interpreters and must rely instead largely on polity members from higher levels to express its viewpoints.

### The News Media as Differentiated and Ambivalently Located

Having made the more controversial point that the news media are part of the American polity, let us return to a seemingly more obvious one: They are also differentiated from it and other societal sectors in ways similar to how the economy, religion, education, politics, and so forth have become distinctive spheres in modern societies (see Alexander 1990). Broadly speaking, the notion of differentiation points to the processes by which particular societal sectors develop specialized definitive roles because they have become increasingly functionally self-sufficient and self-regulating (see Etzioni's [1968, 115–20] instructive comparison of "autonomy" and "autarky" in this regard). The news media are part and parcel of this growing division of labor that is a hallmark of modern industrial development and societal life generally. In the United States, the news media's differentiation from other societal sectors is an ongoing but hardly uniform process (Alexander 1990 and Schudson 1978).

In short, the U.S. news media are not "just" part of the polity and not "in" the state at all; as actors in a differentiated sector, they have their own distinctive historical developments, notably concentration, bureaucratization, and professionalization, and they share key traits with other organization-level actors who are similarly part of the polity yet differentiated from it. When these three factors are cast in a social quantum framework, three critical questions come into clearer focus: (1) How does the ambivalent linkage between the state and the news media affect the orchestration of political participation? (2) How have the news media's concentration, bureaucratization, and professionalization intersected with their polity membership to shape participation? and (3) Have the news media usurped the place of mediating structures that have traditionally stood between state and citizens?

#### Ambivalent Linkages to the State

The close ties between the American state and the mass news media tend to confuse discussions of how the latter's reporting of news has an impact on political influence. In truth, the bond is riddled with incongruities. On the one hand, the entwining is so intimate that some even go so far as to see them as a branch of the state (the "fourth branch," an extension of official tripartite separation-of-powers terms—see, for example, Cater 1965; for a structuralist-Marxist view of the news media as part of the state apparatus, see Althusser 1971). As previously noted, for everyday operations (news gathering) the American news media on all levels rely on official state sources for documents, announcements, press releases, "leaks," and so forth (Sigal 1973). The interpenetration is particularly visible on the national level (Ladd 1987, 554–59).[8] The news media depend on the state for information to do their job; political authorities rely on the news media to transmit their agendas and strive to recruit their cooperation in framing what is truly a national issue (Katz 1989, 495).

Further, in the United States, as in every modern polity, the state exercises some control over the news media (Schudson 1989, 226; for a classic analysis of press–government relations, see Siebert, Peterson, and Schramm 1956). Libel laws, antitrust legislation, and security restrictions (regarding classified materials) are legal curbs that apply to the American news media in all their forms. In the case of the broadcast media, the federal government controls access to the airwaves through licensing procedures. And these media must adhere to the federal fairness doctrine in covering partisan political events.

Still, state control of the news media is more attenuated in the United States than in other democratic polities such as, for example, the United Kingdom, France, Germany, or (nominally democratic, at least) Mexico, to say nothing of overtly nondemocratic systems like China. The American news media are legally separate from the state and, except for the public broadcasting system and enterprises like the Voice of America, privately owned. State financial aid is generally limited to subsidies for the Corporation for Public Broadcasting and preferential postal rates for printed media. This provides the grounds for a measure of self-sufficiency and self-regulation vis-à-vis the state, while making the news media both more profit-oriented (and hence more vulnerable to economic elites and their potential advertising revenues) and more market-driven (and hence more susceptible to popular reactions and tastes) (see Smith 1978).

In sum, there is the paradox of intimacy amid differentiation. Despite virtually total legal separation in the United States, "news organizations have a special relationship with government officials which dominates the day-to-day production of news" (Hallin 1987, 11). The social quantum framework provides a more theoretically comprehensive perspective that permits one to analyze how this paradox shapes the creation and processing of confidence and demands without recourse to one-dimensional formulas that reduce the news media to a branch or tool of the state, or that see the former as merely a wholly autonomous and self-regulating sector of society. Available evidence and subsequent research on the news media and political influence will be better understood when interpreted in light of the assumption that the news media are simultaneously part of, yet differentiated from, the rest of the polity.

## Differentiation and Polity Membership as Sources of News-Media Messages

Since the news media are not simply a branch of the state apparatus, how news-media messages shape confidence and demands remains an open question. Many critics of the news media emphasize their differentiation more and treat their channeling of information as controlled by oligopolies responding to the exigencies of monopoly capitalism. Such concerns obviously spring mainly from the left. Critics on the right also regard the news media as differentiated but more often see them as dominated by a new class of professionalized journalists and (less often) soulless bureaucrats responding simply to organizational needs intent upon fostering an adversary culture. (For an overview of both approaches, see Kellner 1990, 3–6 and passim.) How does the social quantum framework shed light on these assessments?

To begin with, two facts about news-media concentration are incontestable. First, a national news-media complex has emerged that affects both the public and national political elites (Weiss 1974). The vast majority of Americans now draw much of their news information from television. The principal sources are the three major networks and CNN (although local network affiliates also seem to be having a growing impact). The national news magazines (e.g., *Time* and *Newsweek*) remain powerful, however. At the same time a national daily press has emerged (e.g., the *Wall Street Journal,* the *New York Times, USA Today*). This has been accompanied by a greater reliance on the national wire services by purely local press outlets. This national press, in turn, is a major source for television broadcasters (Altehide and Snow 1991).

Second, the concentration of news-media ownership in the hands of a small band of private-sector actors has accelerated over the past three decades (Bagdikian 1990; Gamson et al. 1992; and Schudson 1978). The implications of this development are a matter of contention among news-media analysts. Herman and Chomsky (1988, 2), for instance, argue that "the size, concentrated ownership, owner wealth, and profit orientation of the dominant mass-media firms; . . . [and] advertising as the primary income source of the mass media" are the two most decisive factors that have turned the news media into propaganda machines for economic elites as well as the state. (For a summary and sympathetic critique of this approach, see Goodwin 1994.) In contrast, Alexander (1990, 342–43) suggests that declining economic competition, whatever its adverse effects, may provide the news media with the "financial resources to support their independence from other sectors of society, even from the industrial-corporate one." This leads to what Alexander calls a paradox: "In the period of late capitalism the media became corporatized and their markets oligopolistic. These developments, however, allowed media institutions to save themselves from domination by certain forms of economic power and from a dominant economic class" (ibid., 343).[9]

Two other key historical concomitants of news-media differentiation—namely, their bureaucratization and professionalization—may also encourage diversity in news-media messages. On the one hand, Epstein (1973), Gans (1979), and Tuchman (1978) conclude that organizational factors are decisive in shaping these messages. Pressures to produce a rapid and continuous flow of news means that reporters "must . . . attempt to obtain the most suitable news, from the fewest . . . sources as quickly and easily as possible, and with the least strain on the organization's budget" (Gans 1979, 128). State agencies and powerful corporate actors, with their established press offices, obviously often provide the most expeditious solution to the media's news-gathering problems.

On the other hand, growing professionalization of journalists may serve to brake either state or capitalist domination of news-media messages. We have noted previously that the mass news media share with modern science the fact that they are in the business of making sense of apparently disparate items by reducing, codifying, and adding value to events. But this first point has another critical aspect: As in science, the value that is added by the modern news media is increasingly provided not by external meanings but by cognitive and noncognitive frames created and sustained within a community of professional practitioners. A prime professional ideology common to both domains is objectivity, which constrains how scientists and journalists approach raw data. In the case of the news media, "coverage of issues is preoccupied with covering the who, what, when, where, and (somewhat less often) the why of events. The official discourse of the media tends to be somewhat antiseptic" (Neuman, Just, and Crigler 1992, 76). Yet, in both the news media and science, objectivity could only become determining when that sector became differentiated, that is, not merely functionally specialized but also self-regulating. Of course, journalism's differentiation and concomitant professionalization occurred more slowly than in science, starting only at the end of the nineteenth century (Schudson 1978).

The news media's growing professionalization and use of standards of objectivity have probably reinforced their growing skepticism about state sources since the 1960s and 1970s and, hence, made them even less willing to pass on state-sponsored messages uncritically. Hallin (1987, 11–12) argue that the conflicts in these two decades made journalists "more likely to question official information. They are more likely now to discuss the public relations strategies behind official statements. There has been a diversification of sources. . . . And there is now more 'investigative journalism' involving an active search for information rather than reliance on information released at the government's initiative." This has unquestionably contributed to the growing confidence gap among the general public (Lipset and Schneider 1983).

In sum, news-media passages and how they impact on confidence and demands may be shaped by a variety of forces. Some of these spring from the fact that the news media are polity members without being parts of the state. Others derive from their structural differentiation within American society. However, in the latter instance, news-media concentration, bureaucratization, and professionalization may be producing neither uniform news-media messages nor consistent effects on political influence. Moreover, analysts of how the various historical concomitants of news-media differentiation affect political influence too often make another mistake: They ignore or underestimate the possibility that confidence and demands from organization-, party-, and state-level actors may frequently be major targets of news-media messages. Our social quantum framework encourages us to focus on all of these factors and their possible interactions while keeping their consequences for the packaging of news-media messages and their political consequences an open empirical question and not a matter of theoretical assertion.

## Obliteration of Mediating Structures?

Have the news media's links to the state and their concentration, bureaucratization, and professionalization—singly or in combination—debased the processing of confidence and demands in the American polity? Those who believe they have tend to invoke the so-called "hegemonic" impact of the news media. This notion implies that the news media's societal consequences are both illegitimate and distorting—or, in Etzioni's terms, "inauthentic" (1968, 319–22 and 618–66). Those who maintain that there is news-media hegemony have discussed it along two dimensions: the special interests being served and the political effects. (For overviews of theories of news-media hegemony, see Hallin 1987 and Kellner 1990.) Hegemonic diagnoses of interests have focused on three possible sets of prime beneficiaries: political leaders, economic elites, and the media themselves. Hegemonic diagnoses of political effects have alleged that the news media play an agenda-setting role for individual citizens and that they have had destructive reverberations for the mediating structures that have historically straddled relations between citizens and the state. Here, we focus on the second dimension, the presumed political effects of news-media hegemony.

Analysts of agenda-setting (McCombs and Shaw 1972; Iyengar and Kinder 1987) assert that the news media tell the public what to think by defining the political issues of the day and thereby shaping public opinion and voting behavior. Others, like Lang and Lang (1992, 1210), argue that this view is too simplistic since "the media do not, all on their own, dictate or control the political agenda. . . . Concerns become issues through discussion in which political leaders, government officials, news commentary in the press, and the voices of citizens reciprocally influence one another in a process more aptly characterized as 'agenda-building.'" (See also Lang and Lang 1984.)

Lang and Lang's objection to agenda-setting formulations recalls an older research tradition in media studies, the personal-influence or two-step flow of communications approach (see particularly Katz and Lazarsfeld 1955 and Berelson and Steiner 1964, 546–55). The agenda-setting perspective, with its emphasis on direct media effects on the public, reintroduces a "mass society" model that sees citizens as trapped on an atomized public level unprotected by intervening, mediating groups and hence subject to the manipulations of powerful elites.[10] The personal-influence school claims to have disproved the mass society argument where the news media are concerned. Its proponents found that news-media messages are refracted through people's affiliations: Groups and the most influential figures in them—mainly on the public level—enable the average person to decode what the news media say. However, this approach exaggerates the importance of indigenous influentials and ignores the contributions of other political actors above the public, notably such advocacy groups as interest groups and social-movement organizations. (Two provocative critiques of the personal-influence approach are provided by Etzioni 1968, 451–66, and Gitlin 1978. For a defense of the Katz-Lazarsfeld model, see Wright 1986.)

Thus, while the personal-influence approach sensitizes one to the differences between agenda setting and agenda building, it muddles the multitiered nature of the polity. Recognition of the latter confusion is not a trivial matter for those pursuing more theoretically comprehensive and empirically open inquiries about the political implications of the news media. For one thing, an explicit application of a multilevel model permits a more systematic examination of the contention that the news media, rather than undermining the impact of advocacy groups between citizens and the state, in fact may strengthen their political influence. For example, Robinson (1977, 13), referring to the civil rights marches of the 1960s, argues that television "provided a new and powerful political resource . . . [and] allowed for a previously unattainable level of government access for groups who had few of the traditional resources. *Television became an important means for redistributing power from the haves to the have-nots*" (italics in original; see also Gitlin 1980 and Fishman 1980). The continued and frequently ingenious pursuit of news-media attention by polity members, especially advocacy groups, as subjects, sources, and interpreters (which we discussed previously), may well attest to the sustained vitality of mediating structures in the U.S. polity in this era of advanced communications technology rather than to their destruction.

Nevertheless, in our framework, while the news media may not have destroyed other mediating structures, they are themselves mediating structures. Like many other organization-level actors, they occupy an ambivalent position vis-à-vis the polity because they are outside that system as well as in it. Yet, like other entities on their tier, they self-consciously pursue distinctive roles as polity members who fall between the public, on the one hand, and parties and the state, on the other. As mediating structures they have assumed the following rights and obligations: (1) they provide information about political events, issues, opinions, and personalities to the public as well as to actors on higher levels; (2) they also interpret this information; (3) they see themselves as watchdogs over the conduct of other political actors, including state authorities, and as guardians of the public interest and democratic values; and (4) they define issues and often advocate political positions and promote particular policies. (For a similar enumeration, see Martin 1981, 446–47.)

Of course, as we have suggested at several points, the news media also play a mediating role for other organization-level actors. Our theoretical framework allows us to appreciate more fully that news-media messages do not just flow downward to the general public nor are they just vertical (i.e., upward and downward); news-media messages are horizontal as well. The ambivalent location of many organization-tier actors probably contributes to the (at best) cloudy comprehension of this horizontal mediating role. This role becomes more susceptible to accurate analysis if we use the social quantum perspective, which spotlights both the similarities and differences between the news media and other actors on their level. (For one thing, the news media are more differentiated from public-level groupings than are voluntary associations, interest groups, and social-movement organizations. These other groups seek to mobilize relatively narrow public constituencies and represent their interests to parties and the state. The news media, on the other hand, aim their messages at much broader constituencies on all levels via advanced technology to facilitate so-called "democratic discourse.")

Beclouding matters further is the fact that advocacy groups of many stripes employ in-house newspapers, magazines, radio stations, and television networks to harness the news media's purported power to influence. Although these latter entities are not strictly part of "the mass news media" as we have defined them, they struggle to use media technology and personnel in order to influence strategic constituencies on all levels. Thus, since the line between the news media and other enterprises on the organization tier cannot always be unambiguously drawn, the news media's mediating role among advocacy groups may be more difficult to keep in focus than common sense might make it seem.

While the news media have not destroyed the influence of traditional advocacy groups, and hence ushered in the mass society, they have undoubtedly altered the morphology of political participation. Robinson (1977, 19) asserts that the news media, preeminently television, have caused "fundamental . . . changes in our political institutions, our traditional patterns of voting, our public opinions, and our political life." (See also Lang and Lang 1984.) The party level is one realm that seems particularly to have been affected. Parties' control over selection of candidates and platforms has been eroded. Potential candidates can reach prospective voters and contributors more directly through television than through the parties' traditional electioneering practices. In addition, the personality or character of candidates has become more salient in the election process than specific issues and party loyalty. Increasingly, candidates are turning to media consultants to provide effective media packaging and to run campaigns. These media consultants in turn are becoming more important than party functionaries, causing what Panebianco (1988, 266) calls "an earthquake in party organization: old bureaucratic roles [are] becoming obsolete . . . , new professional roles are gaining ground."

Thus the news media's most significant adverse effects on the processing of influence may be on the party level. They have probably contributed to the other forces accelerating party "decomposition" or "dealignment" (see Burnham 1970; Lehman 1992, 115–19). Television especially may have further contributed to party dealignment through its coverage of reform movements that, beginning in the 1950s, have challenged the party establishments' right and ability to choose candidates. The upshot of these developments has been to shift candidate selection across the country away from party leaders toward "mass-public-participation primaries" (Ladd 1987, 255). In Ladd's view, the parties have become "ancillary structures in the whole process of communication between candidates and elected officials on one side and voters on the other" (ibid., 555).[11]

Yet, however important the news media's position within the polity, they are not confined within its boundaries. Like other corporate actors from the organization tier, they sometimes interact with the political arena merely to pursue their own economic, bureaucratic, and professional interests. These include such concerns as postal rates, station-licensing regulations, libel laws, protection of sources, freedom of the press, and access to state documents. Moreover, as we saw earlier, the news media in the United States are privately owned, legally and structurally separate from the state, with some of their activities taking place outside the political realm (notably news as entertainment). Further, the claims of the *New York Times* notwithstanding, they possess no legal mandate for political action nor any mechanisms for generating such a mandate. Indeed, this ambivalent position may be the grounds for much of the contentiousness surrounding the news media's political role as reflected, for example, in the emergence of such groups as Accuracy in Media and Media Watch as well as alternative broadcast undertakings such as CBN (Christian Broadcasting Network). For these groups, the news media have arrogated to themselves an unwarranted (i.e., illegitimate) role in influencing public opinion, provided a distorted reading of political events, and unabashedly promoted a left–liberal agenda (see Lichter, Rothman, and Lichter [1986] 1990).

## Conclusions

This chapter extends Etzioni's (1968) exploration of how knowledge is essential for societal transformation by providing a theoretical edifice for analyzing the interaction between the news media and democratic political participation. We have introduced a social quantum framework that treats these media's location as ambivalent—as integral to modern multitiered polities, yet, at the same time, differentiated from them—in order to advance judicious assessments of their political impact. This framework permits more theoretically comprehensive and empirically open inquiries about both how the news media's special links to the state and their concentration, bureaucratization, and professionalization affect political influence and whether they have usurped the functions of more traditional advocacy groups and parties in processing confidence and demands in the contemporary United States.

Such a framework also sharpens our sensitivity to the fact that all polity members, including the state, have varied and potentially complex relations with the news media and that the latter are often used to affect the confidence and demands of actors above the public level. Once we recognize this alongside the fact that the news media are also structurally differentiated, we appreciate more fully not only that news-media roles of nonmedia actors occur on all levels but also that these roles are not merely passive or limited to being an audience. In addition, news-media roles include subjects, sources, and interpreters. The last two, in particular, spotlight the activist potential for helping to shape the common knowledge that exists throughout a polity and society.

We have been skeptical about claims that the news media have obliterated the impact of structures that have historically mediated between the state and public. The news media may not wield the hegemony over participation assumed in much contemporary research. Voluntary associations, interest groups, and social-movement organizations are still with us, and at least the most powerful and astute ones seem to have become as adept at manipulating the news media as the latter have in using them. The relationship between parties and the news media deserves closer attention because this bond has probably contributed to protracted party dealignment, but the principal source of this political malaise in all likelihood lies elsewhere (Lehman 1992, 115–19 and 128–37). Of course, it would be incredibly naïve to conclude by ignoring the fact that the mass media provide state actors with enormous opportunities for molding political influence. In the final analysis, however, the precise nature of these opportunities—as well as constraints that may also arise—become more susceptible to open and inclusive scientific inquiry when a multidimensional framework such as the one we have offered here is employed.

**Notes**

1. Our description of quantum physics is drawn entirely from Hawking (1988). For a fuller description of sociological ambivalence, see Merton (1976).

2. Indeed, Giddens (1985) argues that the state via its capacity to create defensible borders and provide internal peace actually brought society as we know it into existence and not vice versa.

3. Electoral participation has been the most commonly studied mechanism for advancing such claims in U.S. social science. But this form of participation is also a statement about confidence. Moreover, demands can be expressed by acceptable and unruly nonelectoral means. Partisans need not be those loyal to the existing rules of the game. They may be, in Tilly's terms, either "contenders" or "challengers" (see, for example, Tilly 1974, 279).

4. It is described by Richard Hamilton (1972, 49–63) in terms of a "theory of group-based politics."

5. This four-level description of the polity is not intended to be a closed model. No intrinsic barriers exist to the addition of more tiers. Transnational levels culminating in a global state system are not precluded. "Nation-states only exist in systemic relations with other nation-states," Giddens reminds us. "The internal administrative coordination of nation-states from their beginnings depends on reflexively monitored conditions of an international nature. 'International relations' is coeval with the origins of nation-states" (Giddens 1985, 4). Thus, while the modern state continues to be the hub of the study of politics, comprehensive analysis requires that larger systems be considered as well. At the very least these exogenous components constrict and channel a state's options; and, in the future, they may become the sites for transnational communities and transformative potential. The European Union seems to have moved into this phase.

6. Our definition incorporates modifications of the Weberian delineation recom-

mended by Etzioni (1968, 107–8, 473–75) as well as ones suggested by Birnbaum (1980), Giddens (1985), Mann (1984), Skowronek (1982, 19–23), Runciman (1969, 35–42), and Tilly (1992). For a slightly different, earlier formulation, see Lehman (1992, 50–52).

7. Although transmitting information among subunits via the news media may be most visible within the national executive branch, the issue goes beyond the need of dispersed federal agencies to communicate with each other. The U.S. system of divided federalism—a federal state with a constitutionally mandated separation of powers on the national level as well as below—may well produce a level of fragmentation that makes national and local officials more reliant on the news media to send signals to other state actors than in other polities.

8. Some analysts (e.g., Paletz, Reichart, and McIntyre 1971) believe that the media's reliance on state sources is greater on the local than on the national level. If this is so, then generalizations about the American press based on the study of local newspapers (e.g., Molotch and Lester 1974; 1975 and Fishman 1980) should be reconsidered.

9. Alexander's essay also illustrates how and why this independence developed further in England and the United States than in France (see Alexander 1990).

10. Hamilton and Wright (1986, 376) conclude: "This theory, we think more than any other, is destined for a retour éternel in intellectual affairs." For a concise critique of mass society theory and the irrationalist tradition of which it is a part, see Rule (1988, 91–118).

11. It should be noted (for the sake of logical closure, at least) that the state actors' interaction with the news media also may affect political influence. We have commented on the fact that some state actors from time to time use the news media to influence the decisions of other state actors. Further, because the media are part of the polity, the state routinely tries to use them to get its message across to nonstate actors on all levels; and because the media are also outside the polity, the state cannot assume the media will process its messages or provide the desired interpretation. This may in part account for the increasing importance of media consultants and spin doctors. The Bush administration's effort to manage the news during the Gulf War is an example of how flagrant the workings of spin doctors have become (MacArthur 1992). President Clinton's recruitment of David Gergen in the spring of 1993 provides stark testimony to how indispensable media specialists now are in the American polity (Kelly 1993).

## References

Alexander, Jeffrey C. 1990. "The Mass News Media in Systemic, Historical, and Comparative Perspective." In *Differentiation Theory and Social Change: Comparative and Historical Perspectives,* eds. Jeffrey C. Alexander and Paul Colomy, 323–66. New York: Columbia University Press.

Altheide, David L., and Snow, Robert P. 1991. *Media Worlds in the Postjournalism Era.* New York: Aldine de Gruyter.

Althusser, Louis. 1971. *Lenin and Philosophy, and Other Essays.* London: New Left Books.

Bagdikian, Ben. 1990. *The Media Monopoly.* 3d ed. Boston: Beacon Press.

Ball-Rokeach, Sandra J., and Cantor, Muriel G. 1986. "Introduction: The Media and the Social Fabric." In *Media, Audience, and Social Structure,* eds. Sandra J. Ball-Rokeach and Muriel G. Cantor, 10–20. Newbury Park, CA: Sage.

Bennett, W. Lance. 1988. *The Politics of Illusion.* 2d ed. New York: Longman.

Berelson, Bernard, and Steiner, Gary A. 1964. *Human Behavior: An Inventory of Findings.* New York: Harcourt, Brace, & World.

Birnbaum, Pierre. 1980. "Central Patterns: States, Ideologies and Collective Action in Western Europe." *International Social Science Journal* 32: 671–86.

Burnham, Walter Dean. 1970. *Critical Elections and the Mainspring of American Politics*. New York: Norton.

Cater, Douglass. 1965. *The Fourth Branch of Government*. New York: Vantage.

Easton, David. 1965. *A Systems Analysis of Political Life*. New York: Wiley.

Epstein, Edward Jay. 1973. *News from Nowhere*. New York: Random House.

Etzioni, Amitai. 1968. *The Active Society: A Theory of Societal and Political Processes*. New York: Free Press.

———. 1984. *Capital Corruption: The New Attack on American Democracy*. New York: Harcourt Brace Jovanovich.

Fishman, Mark. 1980. *Manufacturing the News*. Austin: University of Texas Press.

Gamson, William A. 1988. "A Constructionist Approach to Mass Media and Public Opinion." *Symbolic Interaction* 11: 161–74.

———. 1990. *The Strategy of Social Protest*. 2d ed. Belmont, CA: Wadsworth.

———. 1992. *Talking Politics*. New York: Cambridge University Press.

Gamson, William A.; Croteau, David; Hoynes, William; and Sasson, Theodore. 1992. "Media Images and the Social Construction of Reality." *Annual Review of Sociology* 18: 373–93.

Gamson, William A., and Modigliani, André. 1989. "Media Discourse and Public Opinion on Nuclear Power: A Constructionist Approach." *American Journal of Sociology* 95: 1–37.

Gans, Herbert J. 1979. *Deciding What's News: A Study of CBS Evening News, NBC Nightly News, Newsweek, and Time*. New York: Pantheon.

Giddens, Anthony. 1985. *The Nation-State and Violence*. Vol. 2 of *A Contemporary Critique of Historical Materialism*. Berkeley: University of California Press.

Gitlin, Todd. 1978. "Media Sociology: The Dominant Paradigm." *Theory and Society* 6: 205–53.

———. 1980. *The Whole World Is Watching: Mass Media in the Making and Unmaking of the New Left*. Berkeley: University of California Press.

Goodwin, Jeff. 1994. "What's Right (and Wrong) About Left Media Criticism? Herman and Chomsky's Propaganda Model." *Sociological Forum* 9: 101–11.

Hallin, Daniel C. 1987. "Hegemony: The American News Media from Vietnam to El Salvador, A Study of Ideological Change and Its Limits." In *Political Communications Research: Approaches, Studies, Assessments*, ed. David L. Paletz, pp. 3–25. Norwood, NJ: Ablex.

Hamilton, Richard F. 1972. *Class and Politics in the United States*. New York: Wiley.

Hamilton, Richard F., and Wright, James D. 1986. *The State of the Masses*. New York: Aldine de Gruyter.

Hawking, Stephen W. 1988. *A Brief History of Time: From the Big Bang to Black Holes*. New York: Bantam Books.

Herman, Edwin S., and Chomsky, Noam. 1988. *Manufacturing Consent: The Political Economy of the Mass Media*. New York: Pantheon.

Iyengar, Shanto. 1991. *Is Anyone Responsible?: How Television News Frames Political Issues*. Chicago: University of Chicago Press.

Iyengar, Shanto, and Kinder, Donald R. 1987. *News That Matters: Television and American Opinion*. Chicago: University of Chicago Press.

Katz, Elihu. 1960. "Communication Research and the Image of Society: Convergence of Two Traditions." *American Journal of Sociology* 65: 435–40.

———. 1989. "Mass Media Effects." In *International Encyclopedia of Communications*, vol. 2, ed. Erik Barnouw, 492–97. New York: Oxford University Press.

Katz, Elihu, and Lazarsfeld, Paul F. 1955. *Personal Influence*. New York: Free Press.

Kellner, Douglas. 1990. *Television and the Crisis of Democracy*. Boulder, CO: Westview Press.

Kelly, Michael. 1993. "David Gergen: Master of the Game." *New York Times Magazine* (October 31): 62–71, 80, 94, 97, 103.

Kraus, Sidney, and Davis, Dennis. 1976. *The Effects of Mass Communication on Political Behavior.* University Park: Pennsylvania State University Press.

Ladd, Everett C., Jr. 1987. *The American Polity: The People and Their Government.* 2d ed. New York: Norton.

Lang, Gladys, and Lang, Kurt. 1984. *Politics and Television Re-Viewed.* Beverly Hills, CA: Sage.

———. 1992. "Mass Media Research." In *Encyclopedia of Sociology,* vol. III, eds. Edgar F. Borgatta and Marie L. Borgatta, pp. 1206–11. New York: Macmillan.

Lehman, Edward W. 1992. *The Viable Polity.* Philadelphia: Temple University Press.

Lichter, S. Robert; Rothman, Stanley; and Lichter, Linda S. [1986] 1990. *The Media Elite: America's New Powerbrokers.* New York: Hastings House.

Lipset, Seymour Martin, and Schneider, William. 1983. *The Confidence Gap: Business, Labor, and Government in the Public Mind.* New York: Free Press.

Lipsky, Michael. 1968. "Protest as a Political Resource." *American Political Science Review* 62: 1144–57.

———. 1970. *Protest in City Politics: Rent Strikes, Housing, and the Power of the Poor.* Chicago: Rand McNally.

MacArthur, John R. 1992. *Second Front: Censorship and Propaganda in the Gulf War.* New York: Hill and Wang.

Mann, Michael. 1984. "The Autonomous Power of the State: Its Origins, Mechanisms, and Results." *Archives of European Sociology* 15: 185–213.

Martin, L. John. 1981. "Government and the News Media." In *Handbook of Political Communication,* eds. Dan D. Nimmo and Keith R. Sanders, 445–65. Beverly Hills, CA: Sage.

McCombs, Maxwell, and Shaw, Donald. 1972. "The Agenda-Setting Function of the Mass Media." *Public Opinion Quarterly* 36: 176–87.

Merton, Robert K. 1976. *Sociological Ambivalence and Other Essays.* New York: Free Press.

Miliband, Ralph. 1969. *The State in Capitalist Society.* New York: Basic Books.

Molotch, Harvey. 1979. "Media and Movements." In *The Dynamics of Social Movements,* eds. Mayer Zald and John McCarthy, 71–93. Cambridge, MA: Winthrop.

Molotch, Harvey, and Lester, Marilyn. 1974. "News as Purposive Behavior: On the Strategic Use of Routine Events, Accidents and Scandals." *American Sociological Review* 39: 101–12.

———. 1975. "Accidental News: The Great Oil Spill as Local Occurrence and National Event." *American Journal of Sociology* 81: 235–60.

Neuman, W. Russell. 1986. *The Paradox of Mass Politics: Knowledge and Opinion in the American Electorate.* Cambridge, MA: Harvard University Press.

Neuman, W. Russell; Just, Marion R.; and Crigler, Ann N. 1992. *Common Knowledge: News and the Construction of Political Meaning.* Chicago: University of Chicago Press.

*New York Times.* 1994. "Whitewater and the Press." *Section 4: The Week in Review* (April 10): 18.

Paletz, David L.; Reichart, Peggy; and McIntyre, Barbara. 1971. "How the Media Support Local Government." *Public Opinion Quarterly* 35: 80–92.

Panebianco, Angelo. 1988. *Political Parties: Organization and Power.* New York: Cambridge University Press.

Parsons, Talcott. 1967. *Sociological Theory and Modern Society.* New York: Free Press.

Robinson, Michael J. 1977. "Television and American Politics." *The Public Interest* 48: 3–39.

Rule, James B. 1988. *Theories of Civil Violence.* Berkeley: University of California Press.

Runciman, Walter G. 1969. *Social Science and Political Theory.* 2d ed. New York: Cambridge University Press.

Schudson, Michael. 1978. *Discovering the News: A Social History of American Newspapers.* New York: Basic Books.

———. 1989. "Political Communication—History." In *International Encyclopedia of Communications,* vol. 2, ed. Erik Barnouw, 304–13. New York: Oxford University Press.

Siebert, Fred S.; Peterson, Theodore; and Wilbur Schramm. 1956. *Four Theories of the Press.* Urbana: University of Illinois Press.

Sigal, Leon V. 1973. *Reporters and Officials.* Lexington, MA: Heath.

Simon, Herbert. 1957. *Administrative Behavior.* 2d ed. New York: Macmillan.

Skowronek, Stephen. 1982. *Building a New American State: Expansion of National Administrative Capacities, 1877–1920.* New York: Cambridge University Press.

Smith, Anthony. 1978. *The Politics of Information: Problems of Policy in Modern Media.* London: Macmillan.

Tilly, Charles. 1974. "Town and Country in Revolution." In *Peasant Rebellion and Communist Revolution in Asia,* ed. John Wilson Lewis, 171–302. Stanford, CA: Stanford University Press.

———. 1992. *Coercion, Capital, and European States, A.D. 990–1992.* Revised ed. Cambridge, MA: Blackwell.

Tuchman, Gaye. 1978. *Making News: A Study in the Construction of Reality.* New York: Free Press.

Weber, Max. (1924) 1968. *Economy and Society: An Interpretative Outline of Sociology.* 3 vols. Eds. Guenther Roth and Claus Wittich. New York: Bedminster Press.

Weiss, Carol H. 1974. "What America's Leaders Read." *Public Opinion Quarterly* 38: 1–22.

Wright, Charles R. 1986. "Mass Communications Rediscovered: Its Past and Future in American Sociology." In *Media, Audience, and Social Structure,* eds. Sandra J. Ball-Rokeach and Muriel G. Cantor, 22–33. Newbury Park, CA: Sage.

# Part II

## Socioeconomics and Communitarianism: Theory

# 4

# Community and the Moral Dimension: The Hidden Agenda of Etzioni and Parsons

*Uta Gerhardt*

Amitai Etzioni's work preserves and extends Talcott Parsons's standpoint, which rejects utilitarianism and suggests analysis of society's normative order through the moral principle of interactive reciprocity.

Parsons explained this standpoint in his work in the 1930s and 1940s, giving it a comprehensive gestalt in his seminal treatise *The Social System,* published in 1951. His earlier major opus, *The Structure of Social Action* (1937), had already shown the way to go for a viable sociological theory of community. It overcame utilitarianism as a basis of social action theory and grounded the moral dimension of social life in the idea of interactive reciprocity. Conceptualizing the social actor, Parsons rejected the idea of "economic man" and proposed a notion of nonegoistic activity orientation instead.

This heritage has been most fruitfully preserved and built on by Etzioni's work. In his writings spanning the three decades from the early 1960s until today, Etzioni has combined in an analytical cum political approach the two lines of Parsons's earlier argument.

His socioeconomics, which he has elaborated from a political as well as a more explicitly economic standpoint, reminds sociology that it has a task to

A previous version of this chapter was presented at the session in honor of Amitai Etzioni held at the 1994 SASE Conference in Paris. The chapter's present version benefits greatly from the cogent comments and elaborate suggestions made by David Sciulli, to whom I owe profound thanks.

fulfill in the modern world. Sociology, in this vein, is certainly a social science concerned with collecting, describing, and explaining empirical facts. But, in this endeavor, the sociologist must take into account, even in his or her abstract analyses, that the empirical world encompasses the facts of inequality, injustice, crime, or corruption.

In other words, Etzioni has reintroduced into sociology the sense of humanism that has been present in Parsons's work since the 1930s and 1940s and thereafter, but that has been overlooked frequently by the latter's critics.[1] By reviving the topics that were raised in Parsons's classic, *The Structure of Social Action,* and extending their relevance for sociology in the 1990s, Etzioni rescues for our contemporary analytical perspective a major heritage of the tradition of modern sociological theory.

I wish to draw connections between Etzioni's *The Moral Dimension,* published in 1988, and Parsons's work in the 1930s and early 1940s. First, I reconstruct the argument of *The Moral Dimension* by placing Etzioni's main ideas into an analytical context. Then, I reconstruct Parsons's arguments concerning the moral dimension of community in social life; for this purpose, I focus on various texts written by Parsons in the 1930s and early 1940s in which the topics of morality and community are explicated. I conclude by connecting the various features of the two arguments, thereby revealing what could be called their common ground. I propose, if only tentatively, that the latter lies in the classical program of analysis laid out for the "philosophy of bourgeois society" by Georg Wilhelm Friedrich Hegel in the early nineteenth century.

### Etzioni's *The Moral Dimension*

Etzioni notes at the outset of his work that contemporary sociology is torn by two equally comprehensive but inadequate analytical paradigms. There is, on the one side, utilitarianism and, on the other side, social conservatism. While the former claims that it legitimates democracy, inasmuch as it promotes the principle of individual choice in social life, the latter is related to authority or constraints on individual choice. Both are inadequate in that they fail to relate individual and societal (or institutional) levels of social action. Such a link can be established, Etzioni proposes, by a notion of community linked to a paradigm of reciprocity that he terms "deontological." He writes:

> We are now in the middle of a paradigmatic struggle. Challenged is the entrenched utilitarian, rationalistic-individualistic, neoclassical paradigm which is applied not merely to the economy but also, increasingly, to the full array of social relations from crime to family. One main challenger is a social-conservative paradigm that sees individuals as morally deficient and often irrational, hence requiring a strong authority to control their impulses, direct their endeavors, and maintain order. Out of the dialogue between these two paradigms, a third position arises, which is advanced in this volume. It sees individuals as

able to act rationally and on their own, advancing their self or "*I*," but their ability to do so is deeply affected by how well they are anchored within a sound community and sustained by a firm moral and emotive underpinning—a community they perceive as theirs, as a "*We*," rather than as an imposed, restraining "they." Explicating this new synthesizing paradigm, that of the I & We, and the deontological ethics that are involved, is the subject of this volume. (Etzioni 1988a, ix-x.)

As in many economics works that wish to revise or renew a theory, Etzioni outlines the paradigm of socioeconomics in an introductory chapter that states what he is to argue in detail later in the book. He introduces his own paradigm, then, as a synthesis between the two existing approaches, which might be understood as a thesis and an antithesis.

Whereas the neoclassical paradigm in economics, he suggests, is based on a philosophy of radical individualism and promotes an "undersocialized" view of human nature, the functionalist paradigm frequently adopted in sociology is based on a philosophy of collectivism legitimating power as such and promoting an "oversocialized" view of the human element in society. As a synthesis overcoming both standpoints, socioeconomics realizes that the individual and the collectivity are mediated through each other. Neither can exist except through the other: "The individual and the community make each other and require each other" (ibid., 9). In other words, Etzioni's synthesis is one between the individual and the community, where neither side is primary to the other. Rather, both are equal in a process of social interaction that realizes the principle of reciprocity. And yet, the two sides are equal not necessarily in our empirical world that *is*, but in a community that *ought to be*. In this way, politics comes into the picture. The two sides come together in what Etzioni calls the responsive community, wherein the individual as well as the collective (community) become essential or attain the "same fundamental standing." As Etzioni puts it:

> From this synthesis there results an unavoidable, indeed a deeply productive tension between the two basic elements of the responsive community. Individuals may pull to diminish the community; the community may pull excessively to incorporate individuals. But if neither element gains ascendancy, and if the excesses of one are corrected by shoring up the other, a balanced, responsive community may be sustained. (ibid., 9)

One driving force behind behavioral choices, Etzioni maintains, is pleasure. It refers to satisfaction from bodily or psychological well-being brought about through consumption of goods or services apt to please a person or make him or her attain a goal through means–end rationality. However, such hedonistic and egoistic utility is far from adequate as an explanatory concept. Moreover, its extension into a model of what Etzioni calls interdependent utility lessens its explanatory power. If all social or economic behavior is analyzed in a categorical fashion, as if it is an outflow of subjective utility geared toward pleasure seeking, the concept of pleasure become meaningless. It renders economics' explanatory model tautological.

This situation is unsatisfactory because the duality of utilities that social actors actually use is not taken into account. Not only a sense of pleasure but also a sense of affirmation characterizes social action. Affirmation is related to a person's sense of worth as a member of a community to whose well-being he or she contributes. Moral acts that satisfy this sense of affirmation, Etzioni insists, have four characteristics: imperative quality, generalizability of behavior, symmetry, and expression of a commitment. He elucidates:

> The *imperative* quality of moral acts is reflected in that persons who act morally sense that they "must" behave in the prescribed way, that they are in fact obligated, duty bound. . . . Individuals who act morally are *able to generalize* their behavior—they are able to justify an act to others and to themselves by pointing to general rules, their deontological duties. . . . *Symmetry* is required in that there must be a willingness to accord other comparable people, under comparable circumstances, the same standing or right. . . . Finally, moral acts *affirm or express a commitment*, rather than involve the consumption of a good or a service. Therefore, they are intrinsically motivated and not subject to means–end analysis. (ibid., 42–43)

Etzioni goes on to cite empirical evidence on altruistic behavior that demonstrates that moral obligation is an independent force of motivation. What is clear is that it cannot be squared with a pleasure orientation. Moral duty is often experienced as a burden, not a bonus, despite the fact that its benefit is derived from a feeling of doing right. Altruistic orientations are internalized, becoming a principle of duty beyond the pursuit of individualistic pleasure.[2]

Being internalized, this sense of duty is hardly authoritarian. An authoritarian type of social structure, after all, is based on constraint, not commitment, and it derives its legitimacy from the repressive quality of externally applied social sanctions. It relies on force, not the autonomy of individual members' orientation, in producing social order. Contrasting such undemocratic features of the institutional environment with the principle of individual moral commitment, Etzioni makes it clear that the latter can be based on self-propelling moral preferences. He writes:

> The behavior of a person who feels he/she *ought* to work hard is different from that of one who feels it *pays* to work hard. The difference becomes apparent when the behavioral guidelines are not internalized: (1) when supervision is slack, if opportunities arise from shirking or faking, the person involved will exploit these opportunities; and (2) when persons conform because of constraints, their behavior will be accompanied with resentment or alienation, feelings that are not present when the behavior is based on internalized values, holding constant the degree of pleasure or preference. In short, *moral internalization turns constraints into preferences*. (ibid., 46)

Since the moral and the economic are taken to mean the same thing in economics, moral behavior is falsely subsumed as economic, and economic action is wrongly identified as sufficiently moral. This allows neoclassical economics inadvertently to facilitate immorality in public as well as private behavior. The vices that pervade some arenas of political life, such as corruption, are due to the mistaken assumption that the scope of permissible behavior is what is not punished by the judicial system. Too often in Western as well as non-Western societies, patron–client networks—mafialike organizations or special interest groups—break the rules of solidarity or challenge the system of justice without being sanctioned. Those whose rights are disenfranchised may be too weak or too powerless to assert their warranted claims. But it may also be that not enough emphasis is placed on the mores of solidarity in a given societal community.[3]

But what constitutes moral action in everyday life? How can a sense of affirmation be distinguished from a sense of pleasure and gain? Etzioni sees two issues being central in drawing this distinction, and they may be learned from the answers to the following two questions: (1) What are the driving forces of economic activity in society? and (2) What does rationality mean in everyday life, and what limitations of "ideal-type" means–end rationality can sociological theory recognize?

To begin with, Etzioni reverses the assumption of neoclassical economics that "economic man" acts according to purposive rationality. Rather, he maintains that actors' decisions follow situational expediency. He writes, anticipating an argument that he develops in later chapters, that:

> By this definition, a high level of rationality is quite exceptional. Hence, our *base line* is the concept of a normative-affective, non-rational actor who is inefficient to boot. The special personal and societal factors that move some individuals and communities above the base line, to make them rational to one degree or another, are also explored. (ibid., 91)

Etzioni distinguishes between a normative-affective (N/A) realm of factors that influences the choice of rational behaviors and a logical-empirical (L/E) realm. He explains their relationship on two levels. First, their ratio in any given action situation may range from 100 percent N/A and zero L/E to 100 percent L/E and zero N/A. Actual behavior, however, is typically a mix of both types of factors. Second, social action can take the form of three types of relationships to which the two sets of factors can define zones of *exclusion,* or demarcate zones of *infusion,* or else constitute zones of *indifference.* This distinction is important because, as Etzioni demonstrates, the model of "pure" rationality is rarely followed even in strictly economic affairs. "Cool" calculation is a rare feature of economic behavior. In Etzioni's words: "In other words, L/E considerations are allowed to dominate those choices in which none of the options is N/A-loaded, i.e. when all options have the same or a comparable N/A standing" (ibid., 102).

Even apparently L/E-based knowledge, including science, is far from neutral to N/A considerations. Utilitarians' image of "economic man" may well presuppose that actors are driven by scientifically explicable rationality. Yet, real-life actors rarely refrain from nonrational or frequently inefficient strategies, even when they make seemingly rational choices. Etzioni shows that this is documented by a wide range of evidence from empirical research. As a result, science (L/E knowledge) cannot lead the way out from the conundrum of everyday decision making driven by affectivity and normative considerations. He writes:

> The scientific model, suited for building up analytical knowledge through an endless process (in which the ultimate truth is elusive), is not a suitable model for decision-making and policy-making. It is not only because the actors are highly affective and normative, but their indifference zone is rather small, and their capabilities and resources are limited, but also because of the inner fragmented structure of science. . . . It is not possible to act rationally in complex situations, even when one is backed up with scientific knowledge and methods. (ibid., 126; italics omitted)

This returns us to the question, What is rationality? Etzioni offers an answer in two steps. First, he reviews the criteria of rational behavior discussed in the literature, such as consistency or overdetermination. Second, he proposes to accept as rational any deliberation of an act's purpose that makes sense both to those involved and to a hypothetical "objective observer" (ibid., 145). This yields the idea that rationality is instrumental, inasmuch as behavior serves individuals' situational deliberations. This reintroduces the individual person as the agent of social behavior, but now the individual is no longer portrayed as driven by self-interestedness. It also results in Etzioni's seeing rationality as comprising two distinct types. One is instrumental, but now this type is exposed to normative-affective influences from the personality and the individual's situational deliberations. The other he calls "thoughtless rationality (rules of thumb)." Individuals are thoughtless when they fail to deliberate and instead adopt modes of behavior stemming from their own emotions and values or else from the habits, beliefs, and norms of their social groups.

This leaves us with a new question, namely, How can rationality and freedom best be reconciled in modern society?

Here, as above, Etzioni turns to what he calls the responsive community. The two principles of interaction—cooperation and competition—have different unanticipated consequences. Competition, which is clearly a major principle of social organization of Western societies, is also a latent form of conflict. Like any conflict, it can be costly if it is not contained by collective structures that allow for cooperation.

The paradigm advanced here assumes that if competition is left on its own it will escalate into a destructive, all-out conflict. Hence, those who see virtue in competition must recognize that it is nothing but *contained* conflict, that it can be sustained only within a moral, societal, and governmental context which ensures that conflicts remain confined within prescribed limits. . . . The question hence is how to provide a context that is strong enough to contain competition but not so powerful to undermine it, rather than disregard the role and dynamic of the moral, social, governmental contextualizing factors. (ibid., 182)

But how can collective rationality (as contrasted with individual rationality) and competition be promoted without unduly restricting individual freedom and liberty? Authoritarian organization is clearly not a desirable way for community to overcome radical individualism.[4] Instead, Etzioni proposes a checks-and-balances system of countervailing forces that spurns the economy and the polity. Within this system, the power vested in the structures of interaction (linking together participants in market activities or other subcollectivities of society's members) are of pivotal importance. He clarifies:

The search for socio-economic models of competition draws on a core idea: actors are not necessarily in harmony with one another; and competition is actually a form of conflict—contained conflict. The containing capsule, within which competition is free to range, is composed of normative, social, and governmental mechanisms each working on its own and interacting with the others. Their strength varies from being too weak to discharge their mission, to being too powerful, going beyond limiting conflicts to suppressing competition. The conditions under which the capsule is appropriately potent, without being excessively restrictive, are only beginning to be understood. The internal structure of the system is clearly a key factor. Power relations among the contestants in realms other than those in which the contest takes place—the polity rather than the economy—is the key element of the structure. (ibid., 216)

Such power relations, however, must be based on consensus between the governed and their leaders, and leadership, in turn, must not hesitate to cultivate the voluntary solidarity that allows the population to comply with collective norms. Members' moral education is, in Etzioni's view, in the best interests of a responsive community, one that sets collective objectives and expects voluntary conformity with moral principles. In a community that institutionalizes both commitment and creativity, the individual serves the public interest willingly. He or she does service in the community without being compelled because he or she is convinced that each member is obligated to do his or her share promoting the common good. From this vantage point, Etzioni recommends a strategy of "controlled institutional change"—a Parsonian term—through which the populace might be persuaded to do the right thing. Using "moral education" as well as deliberately noncoercive leadership, the community can move in the direction of better economic and other life circumstances without fostering egoistic self-interest (ibid., 238).[5] Etzioni recommends in particular that public leaders set an example, and in this way appeal to the public to observe certain principles of morally good behavior. They would thereby create a moral climate that would facilitate, among a broad range of worthy goals, a lasting "labor peace" (ibid., 238) and various other citizenship virtues. This, to be sure, underscores the principle of community that could and should be strengthened in a democratic society, namely, a "morality of cooperation" (ibid., 243).

## Some Facets of Parsons's Work in the 1930s and Early 1940s

Like Etzioni, Talcott Parsons believed throughout his scientific sociological analysis that economists often asked the right questions about social behavior but rarely provided satisfactory answers. And, like Etzioni, Parsons believed that this was precisely because economic activities are governed, to some considerable extent, by extraeconomic factors, that is, by normative orientational forces that belong in the realms of sociological and psychological analysis. Actually, Parsons taught economics for four years at Amherst and Harvard before joining the newly formed Department of Ethics and Social Sciences at Harvard in 1931 and then the newly formed Department of Sociology in 1938. Throughout his early work, his training in economics is clearly visible, but so, too, is his training in European social theory. Parsons appreciated that Max Weber had exposed the same limitations in economics a decade and a half earlier.[6]

In particular, Parsons discussed the dichotomy of egoism and altruism as motivational forces in his contribution to a Festschrift for F.W. Taussig, one of his mentors in Harvard's Economics Department. He began by crediting Taussig with transcending the narrow view that scientific economics had to neglect the values of civic society. He wrote:

> It has been doubly fortunate that a voice has been heard which defended economic theory but which was at the same time ethically and politically in the best traditions of a tolerant liberalism, which above all was not deaf to the cry for social justice and the corresponding indictment of certain features of the existing order. (1936, 264)

Parsons saw Taussig introducing insights that exposed the shortcomings of neoclassical economics in two important respects. On one side, that of the economy's environmental context, Taussig assumed that no "invisible hand" organizes economic welfare. He thereby explicitly considered factors that others dismissed as insignificant for economic theory, including force and fraud in economic life and "especially perhaps the fraudulent or semifraudulent abuse of fiduciary positions on the part of directors and officers of corporations" (ibid., 265). On another side, Taussig also noticed that the state's control over economic opportunities tended to be abused by those "acquiring in one way or another influence over the actions of the state, or any political bodies . . . , one of the principal 'illegitimate' means of gaining economic ends." This is illustrated, in Taussig's view as shown by Parsons, by special interest groups "playing a disproportionate role in the determination of tariff policies" (ibid., 265–66).

With regard to economic motivation, Parsons saw two aspects being important. One is that the rational and nonrational elements of economic behavior suggest that economic forces have to be separated from noneconomic ones in the motivation of economic life. He stated:

> In this sense it is possible to abstract the proximate, economic elements of motivation from another, that of ultimate ends, to which the egoistic-altruistic dichotomy, whatever validity it may turn out to possess, properly belongs. (ibid., 276)

The other aspect related to the question of the origin of the altruistic motives. Is it strictly psychological, or can an element of social structure be detected in altruism? Can altruism, or whatever it stands for, be influenced by the degree of liberty, freedom, and justice institutionalized in a social order?

Parsons referred to Weber's notion of "calling" to illustrate this element of altruism. It was " 'disinterested' application to a task for its own sake, apart from any consideration of reward" (ibid., 276). Such disinterestedness may yield interpersonal gratification in behavioral exchanges in the forms of "emulation and social distinction" (ibid., 277). Disinterestedness, as contrasted with self-interestedness, becomes one of the pattern variable polarities that Parsons introduced for the analysis of social structural influences of social action. He held that collectivity orientation and self-orientation constituted one of five alternative action orientations in historical as well as contemporary societies. All five characterize the value structure through which social action takes place.[7]

At this point, a second theme in Parsons's work of the 1930s demands attention. When he invoked "ultimate ends" in referring to altruistic or disinterested behavior, he isolated three types of means–end relationships. He also emphasized that "man is essentially an active, creative, evaluating creature" (1935, 282), thereby establishing that determinism of any kind is alien to sociology, and that sociology has to be scientific when exploring the use of knowledge in "the exercise of will" (ibid., 287). For example, it must find the rationality even in such nonrational practices as magic in primitive societies or ritual in the contemporary world. He cautioned his readers before discussing the nature of ends, particularly the ultimate ends that actors assume as true, that science can never fully encompass reality. He wrote:

> The ultimate reason, then, for the causal independence of ends in action, the fact that they are not determined by the facts of human nature and environ-

ment, is the *fact* that man stands in significant relation to aspects of reality other than those revealed by science. Moreover, the fact that empirical reality can be modified by action shows that this empirical reality, the world of science, is not a closed system but is itself significantly related to the other aspects of reality. (ibid., 290)

From this vantage point, he distinguished between two sociologically import-ant types of means–end relationships, namely, the intrinsic and the symbolic. These types simultaneously represent normative or affective groups for an actor's choice of means *both* in the interest of attaining a given end and as distinct universes of social organization.

The intrinsic means–end relationship suggests a system of ultimate ends that provides a coherent body of interrelated norms, "*moral* norms, not norms of efficiency" (ibid., 299). An institutional structure is integrated by an intrinsic means–end relationship inasmuch as it provides a basis for reciprocity and mutu-ality between actors that, in turn, fend off the danger of "a war of all against all—Hobbes's state of nature:"

> Insofar, then, as action is determined by ultimate ends, the existence of a *system* of such ends common to the members of the community seems to be the only alternative to a state of chaos—a necessary factor in social stability. (ibid., 295)

The symbolic means–end relationship, on the other hand, is illustrated by magic as well as ritual, and it is more typical in primitive societies than in modern ones—although Parsons hastened to remark that ritual was not confined to "so-called 'primitive' societies" (ibid., 301). In fact, ritual is practiced wher-ever actors pursue transcendental ends. He distinguished between two different orientations, however, writing:

> By what means can transcendental ends be pursued? There are two logically possible modes. First they may, by real or supposed logical implication, obli-gate their adherents to pursue certain ultimate empirical ends, which are then capable of attainment by intrinsic means. . . . Then we get complexes of action which, again from the intrinsic point of view, do not serve any (i.e., empirical) end, but are ends in themselves. . . . [Action] is governed by norms which enjoin the *right* selection of means. This action is religious ritual . . . Thus there tends to be a certain moral obligation to employ certain ritual means. (ibid., 302–3)

Drawing the two strands together, Parsons emphasized that ritual constitutes, in fact, a type of rationality that appears irrational when " 'scientific' norms of rationality" are applied to it (ibid., 395). This suggested to him that even modern societies are held together by "value attitudes," that is, comprehensive orienta-tional references that govern all sorts of behavioral choices. These value attitudes are basic to rational as well as ritual behavior, and they influence institutionalized choices of behavior based on the law as well as on religion-like doctrines. He stated:

> Institutes (or) ritual . . . may be direct manifestations of the same ultimate value-attitudes of which ultimate ends are also manifestations. The question of the exact relationships is one which should be left open for empirical determination. (ibid., 307)

From this vantage point, Parsons went on to distinguish between a type of noncontractual gemeinschaft relationship and community that favors personalized, permanent "familistic" (particularistic) preferences, on the one hand, and a type of contractual gesellschaft relationship and community that cultivates nonpersonalized, transitory "external" (universalistic) preferences, on the other.

But why did Parsons emphasize that ritual is a legitimate form of means–end rationality? To be sure, it represents charismatic but also traditional rationality (in Weberian terms). One answer may be that he wished to incorporate into sociological theory the fact that in Germany since 1933 a regime had emerged that epitomized incipient ritualistic traditionalism. This interpretation, no doubt, is borne out by his writings from 1938 onward.[8]

Parsons developed his sociology of antidemocratic society and his theory of the integrated community—which epitomized democratic society—in a memorandum for the Council for Democracy.[9] It was written in 1940 but never published during his lifetime. It anticipates the argument that Etzioni elaborates in the last part of his book under the title "Beyond Radical Individualism."

The memorandum's somewhat bulky title was "The Development of Groups and Organizations Amenable to Use Against American Institutions and Foreign Policy and Possible Measures of Prevention." The memorandum's purpose was to suggest policy measures apt to strengthen the democratic element in American society and thereby also to weaken the effects of any elements that inadvertently or deliberately promoted antidemocratic influence.

In an outline of the "general sociological background," he listed three sources of instability in American society. They were ethnicity, social class, and incomplete realization of universalistic standards in economic life (such as nepotism or "connections"). They were dangerous to social stability, he suggested, since they bred discontent (often due to veritable disenfranchisement) that could be exploited by destructive propaganda. The strains in American society, he knew, had to be seen against the background that democracy was realized more thoroughly here than elsewhere, and yet severe deficiencies and defaults of American democracy could not be denied. He wrote:

> The things which are most important to protect in the present critical situation are perhaps the following: at least our present relative freedom of opportunity for occupational achievement and status; the dominance of universalistic criteria in this field, with favorable conditions for the development of science and

technology; institutional guarantees of individual freedom and liberties; a political system in which authority is subject to law and respect for the rights of the governed, is limited to the powers of constitutionally defined office. These are perhaps more important than "democracy" in the more narrowly technical sense of election of executive and legislature by majority popular vote. (1940, 106)

This led him, in the paper's second part, titled "The Practical Problem," to explain in greater detail what the integrated society is like. Since its integration is based on voluntary commitment, it was radically different from fascism in Germany and elsewhere, where cohesion depended on terror and repression. In other words, the democratic society forms a community inasmuch as it is sufficiently integrated that it can function without force and fraud. These latter elements, Parsons knew, could characterize an entire society such as National Socialism, making it a deviant society. But in a democratic society, deviance is not a prominent feature, the less so if and insofar as integrating characteristics prevail. He explained the integrating and community characteristics under six headings, warning that they represent ideals but also emphasizing that they are necessary ideals. If a sociologically meaningful notion of community is to be introduced, the following six issues will be its main sides. He wrote:

> 1. The "rule of law" or perhaps "constitutionalism." We recognize the necessity of authority in the interest of functional efficiency but no human authority is exercised by any inherent right. It is rather justified only by function on behalf of the community and its goals are limited by relevance to such function. . . .
> 2. What is usually referred to as the system of civil liberties is really a corollary of this. If authority is limited by function its limits must be expressed in the rights of those subject to its potential abuse. The curbing of arbitrary authority *is* the protection of the rights of those affected by it. . . .
> 3. Equality of opportunity. This is of course one of the most fundamental of our historic patterns, imperfectly realized as it is. It follows from the importance of universalistic patterns in the valuation of achievement. It is perhaps the most powerful single solvent of particularistic attachments which might be a source of division in the community. But, as in the case of civil liberties, perhaps here also a shift of emphasis is needed. Too often in the past it has been interpreted as equality of opportunity for personal benefits and advancement rather than for achievement and the performance of function. This is not to say that it is wise to expect or even advocate wholly "altruistic" conduct in the sense of attempting to abolish all differential rewards of achievement in incomes, honors, recognition and the like. But here are very important possible differences of attitude according to the emphasis of different parts of the achievement-reward complex. Perhaps more than many of us realize, "success" gains its meaning from the connection of its achievements with the goals to which the community as a whole is oriented. The standards according to which recognition and rewards are bestowed have a positive content. It is not *only* a question of beating the other fellow for the sake of the prize or of victory for its own sake.

4. Any social system which lays such strong emphasis as does ours on differential achievement and status is faced by a problem as to the situation in which those who, for whatever reason, are relatively "unsuccessful" are placed. . . . The strictures on the ideal of generalized welfare have commonly been put in terms of the potential conflict with productive efficiency. I should like here to bring out a different emphasis. It is dangerous to the sources of high morale in our society to cultivate an egalitarian ideal of common welfare in a direction in which the valuation of high achievement becomes blurred. This does not, however, seem necessary, but there is a rather delicate balance between these elements of our value complex. One important path in reconciliation lies in removing the principal components of the basic standard of living from their present status as symbols of differential achievement. It seems probable that a sense of responsibility can best be symbolized otherwise than by treating loss of economic support as the primary penalty of failing to do one's part. This is particularly true in view of the very large extent to which under modern conditions, actual ability to earn income depends on factors other than ability, achievement and a sense of responsibility in the individual.

5. The rational-critical spirit. . . . It is the basic attitude which underlies the development of science and learning, hence of technology, medicine, law and many other fields of activity. It is here contrasted on the one hand with traditionalism, on the other with the type of anti-intellectualism which glorifies activity and force for their own sake without rational discipline. . . .

6. This last element is of a very general and pervasive character and hence rather difficult in formation. In a very rough way it may be called "activism." (ibid., 120–23).

What Parsons proposed, particularly under numbers 3 and 4, is spectacular. He suggested that sociological theory adopt constitutionalism.[10] He wanted sociological theory to adopt a perspective that is based on the credo of equality of opportunity. He called, too, for the discrepancy between the American creed and the American reality to be narrowed, and he wanted sociology to take this as a conceptual framework. (To be sure, Gunnar Myrdal addressed the same problem in his famous *An American Dilemma,* published in 1944.) Equality of opportunity was to reign supreme in a nonsocialist society, which could only mean that individuals should invariably and consistently have a fair chance for self-realization irrespective of their race, class, or gender. A utopia of socialism comprising propertyless and state-minded comrades was not to be society's way out of the anomalies of modern capitalism. But, he cautioned, a capitalist society should incorporate the principle—and practice—that each individual should find the limits of his own scope of action in those of others. This classical principle of liberalism, as is well known, has also been the classical definition of democracy since John Locke proposed that the limit of a person's freedom be that of the other person (Locke [1690] 1963). But to extend it into the idea that the economy and the polity are to function in a concatenated structure under the humanist principle of respect for the fellow human is, indeed, sociologically innovative. This view proposes an idea of reciprocity as the basic normative feature of social relationships that are governed by a sense of respect for the rights of others.

The society that is being sketched in these broad strokes is the epitome of community as an integrated social system. It functions on the grounds of competence as a principle of stratification. That is, functional instead of repressive authority is to warrant social status and recognition in interpersonal exchange. Esteem as interactional reward is to be derived not so much from one's achievement on the labor market of monetary success in the market economy but from one's responsibility for the function that, in turn, is performed in a disinterested manner for the benefit of others. Such responsibility can relate to comembers in the community, or to the community as a whole, whose values one shares. (This does not mean, however, that a "folk community" ought to be established, as in Nazi Germany; such a situation can be avoided if the society is based on rule of law—constitutionalism—and civil liberties, two features of the integrated society mentioned under numbers 1 and 2 of Parsons's outline.)

Although he does not say much about what responsibility means in detailed terms of interpersonal action, it may be safe to assume that what he had in mind related to his ideas about service. Service, to be sure, is one of the most undervalued categories in Parsons's thinking. In an article for the *Encyclopedia of the Social Sciences* (1934), reprinted in *The Early Essays* (1991), he addressed the problem of service in general terms, linking its modern version to gesellschaft. It denotes reciprocity based on commitment that links individuals and roles to moral incentives and the well-being of the community. Parsons's medical sociology elucidates further what service and responsibility mean for societal community: The physician's intrinsic disinterestedness is the type of responsibility that ought to be emulated by politicians as well as social scientists.[11]

## Dimensions of Community

In order to reveal what the dimensions of community are, and what its thrust as democratic social interchange entails, I reconstructed Etzioni's and Parsons's work above. They should now be drawn together. As a first step, the three levels of community are stated again, in Etzioni's and Parsons's terms. Then their common ground is explored; the common ground is Hegel's idea of *Anerkennung*.[12]

Etzioni's "Beyond Pleasure" introduces the duality of a sense of pleasure and a sense of affirmation as the grounds of motivation of social action (considering economic action as one branch of social action). From this emerges that a duality of motives prevails, egoistic and altruistic, that ought to be recognized by modern economics as distinct from each other. One reason for waste and inefficiency in the nonmarket economy of public services, Etzioni believes, is that both are not taken into account but, rather, only a pleasure motive is acknowledged within a strictly egoistic interpretation.

Parsons also acknowledges that economic activities are frequently governed by other than economic considerations. He identifies them by saying they resemble altruism, and then he describes them more methodically by using the concept of disinterestedness, which he relates to the role of the professions in society. It represents a socioeconomic element that Parsons sees is neither capitalist nor socialist. Disinterestedness as an orientation and the professions as a structural element belong to a third type of society. It might be called constitutionalism or communitarianism.

Etzioni's "Beyond Rationalism" introduces normative and affective elements in social action as sociologically irreducible. These elements supplement rationality, and this means that plans, blueprints, and calculations—including those of science—are only one root of the social process of rational action. The other root is individuals' subjectively instrumental perspectives governing their actions in situations where, at best, an ad hoc rationality may be observed. This emphasizes the importance of actual situations in economic (social) action or interaction. It deemphasizes the role of organizations, and, in fact, authority structures are revealed as being frequently detrimental to individuals' realizing the affective elements of rational action. Etzioni thereby shows that liberal norms need an arena other than that of organizations or institutions, since the latter may be immobilized by vested interests favoring self-serving interest groups.

Parsons shares Etzioni's cautions against authoritarianism that may characterize organizations and institutions. His references to fascism make clear that he sees creativity, freedom of making value choices, and responsible activity as accomplishments of the social system on which individual actors depend in their everyday lives. Authoritarian or closed organizational settings may hinder, if not deny, an individual's responsible use of creativity and freedom of choice of ultimate values. By contrast, open and flexible institutions can be most helpful in facilitating and fostering individuals' autonomous acting out of value orientations. Parsons compares societies, therefore, in terms of how they organize what he calls intrinsic and symbolic means–end relationships. The intrinsic type allows individuals to choose values on moral grounds (following socially available value orientations), and it relies on actors' following their sense of responsibility. The symbolic type emphasizes ritual, and it tends to alienate individuals from their sense of responsibility for their own conduct. Parsons advocates a gesellschaft type of society wherein a community of responsible individual actors is nevertheless linked together through their shared internalization of moral norms.

Etzioni's "Beyond Radical Individualism" introduces the idea of responsive community. Responsive community incorporates competition as a contained structural element. On the one hand, competition is necessary since it offers individuals opportunities to express freely their talents and needs. On the other hand, competition is harmful since it may escalate into conflict that may destroy individuals' sense of achievement and even their socioeconomic status position or basis of livelihood. Etzioni believes that moral education can improve American society's quality as a responsive community. It can strengthen commitment and strengthen individuals' sense of affirmation toward being useful, respected members of families, communities, or the state.

Parsons outlines his idea of community within a war-related initiative to strengthen Americans' democratic beliefs and practices. He distinguishes between an integrated, that is, responsive community type of society, and a deviant society based on force and fraud. For him, American society needs strengthening of certain of its features, and it might benefit from reforms of some of its basic social institutions. Although its democratic aspects may be more developed than in other societies, America should strive to overcome its potentially anti-democratic structural elements, namely, insufficient realization of equality of opportunity and linkage between economic achievement and social appreciation (social affirmation through others).

To this end, Parsons advocates "removing the principal components of the basic standard of living from their present status as symbols of differential achievement." This means that social status is to be decoupled from wealth and power, and he proposes that "doing one's part" in the community become the new criterion of social appreciation and prestige. At the individual level, this new value would be represented through a sense of responsibility and a willingness to commit oneself to non-self-interested means–end relationships. At the structural level, the professions would institutionalize disinterestedness as the now-dominant value orientation. At the level of interaction, individuals would be valued for their commitment to the community—provided that no force is used and that the principle of free will or voluntary commitment is meticulously observed.

For Etzioni as well as Parsons, community epitomizes the better, more humane society at three levels of analysis: the action motive level, the action pattern level, and the societal community level.

At the action motive level, Etzioni introduces the sense of affirmation, and Parsons refers to the value orientation of disinterestedness. At the action pattern level, Etzioni rejects the idea that more science or more organization could improve the dominant type of rationality, suggesting an ad hoc situational type that he calls instrumental rationalism. Parsons introduces two types of action patterning that he calls intrinsic and symbolic, suggesting as much intrinsic rationality as possible due to its affinity to moral standards of intersubjectivity. At the social community level, Etzioni proposes the responsive community that may be strengthened by moral education. Parsons advocates the society where prestige is derived from voluntary service to the community, where equality of opportunity is not limited by particularism or ascription.

Both authors propose a similar conception linking the level of action with that of society, stressing the principle of interaction epitomizing reciprocity. In such interaction, the mutuality of responsiveness to standards of community commitment is decisive. The individuals realize themselves by benefiting others when they act competently in a disinterested manner. In such an interchange, one actor achieves his ends through means that do not disenfranchise others with whom he collaborates or competes and do not seriously disadvantage other groups in society. Each individual derives his sense of worth from his actions' beneficial effects on others. His good feelings are mediated either through the praise or positive reaction of others, the visible benefit to others, or at least the absence of harm or damage done to others.

Hegel's principle of *Anerkennung* means the same type of social relationship as Etzioni's and Parsons's notion of reciprocity. Hegel used *Anerkennung* to formulate succinctly what ought to be the accomplishment of modern economic ("bourgeois") society. He wanted to outline a conception of interpersonal relations that could go beyond and help contain encroaching political control and domination. Allowing for reciprocity as mutual self-realization makes society more human. Etzioni's as well as Parsons's conceptions of community build on this basic philosophical postulate of modern society.

## Notes

1. In this vein, the view on Parsons's work that this chapter adopts abstracts from various interpretive standpoints taken by the secondary literature since the late 1950s and early 1960s. The two main views to which I do not subscribe are the following: (1) Ralf Dahrendorf's criticism mistakes Parsons's system theory as an apology for fascism due to its allegedly monolithic utopia of an integrated society; however, Dahrendorf fails to realize that Parsons's idea of social integration is based on voluntary commitment and is, therefore, different from the hermetic closure of fascist society relying on constraint and compulsive conformity (Dahrendorf 1958); (2) Dennis Wrong's criticism mistakes Parsons's action theory for normative determinism clad into a fiction of rational behavior, whereas empirical action, as Wrong insists, frequently derives from irrational forces releasing antihuman or antisocial action potential; Wrong fails to understand, as Parsons rightly points out in his critical rejoinder, that if sociology aims to be scientific it cannot, at the same time, embrace humanism and advocate revolutionary social change but can only provide an analytical basis for political activism that refuses to adopt a charismatic leader and fights to establish a rational-legal type of legitimation of the social order (Wrong 1961; Parsons 1962).

Rejecting the two well-known criticisms of Parsons's theories of social structure and social action, I go back to Parsons's original writings. Since I wish to emphasize the importance of Etzioni's argument regarding the moral dimension of society by juxtaposing it with that of Parsons, I concentrate on Parsons's work particularly during the period of his *Early Essays* and subsequently to *The Structure of Social Action*, when he first addressed the problems that Etzioni, more than forty years later, revived and elucidated in his *Moral Dimension*.

2. Although Etzioni does not explore tne relationship of his notion of altruistic action with that of Émile Durkheim, a brief comparison may be helpful. Etzioni's, as well as Durkheim's, conception of altruism recognizes it as an opposite of egoism. Yet the two authors use different frames of reference. Etzioni maintains that self-interest defines egoism, whereas concern for the interests and well-being of others constitutes altruism. By contrast, Durkheim perceives egoism as the concern for individual actors' interests or well-being, be they self or others, whereas altruism derives from internalization by

society's members of the collective orientations imperative for the totality of citizens. The level of Etzioni's concept of altruism is, therefore, that of social action's value commitments, whereas the level of Durkheim's concept of altruism is that of society's collective value orientations. In other words, Durkheim's analysis of altruism in his seminal treatise on *Suicide* ([1897] 1952) should not be taken as a forerunner of Etzioni's analysis of altruism. This means that Durkheim's implicit warning against the dangers of altruism should not be mistaken as also applying to altruism as pictured by Etzioni.

3. The issue has been central to various other books of Etzioni's. In *Capital Corruption* (1984), he reveals that lobbyists, special interest groups—PACs, or political action committees—undermine the very principles of American democracy. They convert the essence of rational-legal authority, namely, constitutionalism and *Rechtsstaat,* into de facto structures of apparent patrimonialism.

Whereas Etzioni's work so far focuses on the United States (with some implications for other Western industrialized societies), recent developments in the former Soviet Union might warrant application of Etzioni's categories there. Massive mafialike organizations seem to have spread in the wake of the centralized planned economy, terrorizing local businesses and controlling large parts of the newly privatized industries, often using corruption, force, and fraud liberally. Nothing is known so far about their influence on local and national government, which, however, may be assumed to be most likely high.

4. Among the approaches of the 1940s addressing the issue are two that seem anticipatorily to elucidate Etzioni's views. One is that of Kurt Lewin, the psychologist, distinguishing between three types of group structure, namely, authoritarian, laissez-faire, and democratic social order. Whereas the latter two are often confounded when the democratic is mistaken as some kind of laissez-faire, the former two are in fact more similar to each other than is frequently noted. Lewin shows that authoritarian and laissez-faire structures curtail individuals' sense of independence and security, while they also negate their initiative and responsibility; however, the democratic structure is different on all these accounts. To be sure, the democratic group structure involves leadership that is sensitive to, while also guiding and enhancing, the needs and capabilities of the group participants (Lewin et al. 1939; Lippitt and White 1942). The other approach of the 1940s is that of Max Wertheimer. In a book titled *Productive Thinking* (1945), he proposed a social structure that could mitigate competition on the basis of reciprocity or, to use Etzioni's term, altruism. He illustrated this novel social arrangement by a game of badminton in which the rules did not stipulate that the winner be the one who beats an opponent but where instead the rules required as many successful returns between the two players as could be accomplished. Due to this rule, Wertheimer realized, the better player was no longer the weaker player's competitor, but he or she automatically became the coach or teacherlike partner of his or her coplayer while acting altruistically as well as in his or her own self-interest.

5. One source for further elaboration of the idea of moral education may be Karl Mannheim's notion of "social education" proposed in *Freedom, Power, and Democratic Planning* (1950). Summing up a decade and a half's insights, with which he understood the requirements of a viable democracy that could resist the contemporary attractions of authoritarianism (fascism), Mannheim insisted that the values of fair play were crucially important. He recommended social education as the best way to establish these values through comprehensive internalization. He wrote:

> The primary forms of integration and the corresponding behavior patterns define the basic character of a society. The great alternative is authoritarian organization based upon dominating behavior or democratic co-ordination based upon integrative behav-

ior. . . . The criterion is whether in crucial situations basic cohesion is achieved by dominating or integrative behavior. . . . Social education then has to take stock of the educational impact of social patterns and arrangements and modify them to serve desired ends. . . . The new possibilities of improving the social order—of controlling social groups, institutions, and mechanisms—create the danger of shifting emphasis to their manipulation, thus disregarding the ideal or ethical side of social education. Those who go too far along this path and expect the new social order automatically to change human conduct and character should realize that competition, as recent research has proved, differs not only according to the combination it undergoes with other factors but according to the ideas with which it is associated. The idea of "fair play" is a modifying idea, which does not result automatically from the mechanism of competition, but is derived from the larger culture. Different social situations exert their educative influence; people exposed to them understand their educative meaning. The constant "definition of the situation," the continuous valuation of events makes values an educative power. This re-discovery of their significance in the social context will be welcomed by all who dislike abstract ideas, but are receptive to concrete idealism." (Mannheim 1950, 197–98).

6. In fact, it was around 1910 that Weber agreed to become the editor of a series titled Basic Outline of Social Economics. It was to cover a broad range of topics from "social politics" to an economic analysis of power and the state. Weber was particularly suited to edit this series since he had held chairs in economics and the science of finance (*Finanzwissenschaft*) at the universities of Freiburg and Heidelberg (after having studied history and law at the universities of Heidelberg and Berlin) before engaging in the newly established discipline of sociology on a freelance basis from 1904 onward. When hardly any of the monographs written for the series by colleagues commissioned by Weber satisfied his elaborate expectations, he began to realize that he himself had to write the analytical work that others could not. The outcome was an unfinished volume tentatively titled *Economy and the Social Orders and Powers,* which was to appear as volume 9 of the Basic Outline of Social Economics series. Eventually, it was published posthumously under the title of *Economy and Society.* Its "Conceptual Exposition," written at the end of Weber's life as some kind of abstract of the book's extended analytical chapters, consisted of two parts. One was Weber's clarification of "Basic Sociological Terms," and the other was his outline of "Sociological Categories of Economic Action." (In literal translation from the German original the two fields were called "Basic Sociological Concepts" and "Basic Sociological Categories of Economic Activity.")

7. Regarding pattern variable distinction, in *The Social System* Parsons contrasted the United States and Nazi Germany. Whereas the United States gave ample scope to the liberal professions of law and medicine, whose dominant attitude to their work was disinterestedness, Nazi Germany, similar to other totalitarian systems, denied the liberal professions an autonomous realm of activities. For further detail regarding this distinction and the transformation from one type of system into the other, see Parsons 1945 and, as a recent reconstruction, Gerhardt 1994.

8. It is still a matter of debate whether he did take fascism into account in *The Structure of Social Action* and concomitant theoretical articles, such as that on ultimate values. In "The Place of Ultimate Values in Sociological Theory" he clarified that scientific rationality had to be supplemented by normative as well as affective forces of motivation and that intrinsic rationality in democratic societies was different from symbolic rationality in nondemocratic societies. In *Structure,* one footnote refers to "Nazi methods of control of opinion" as something irreconcilable with "truly moral action" (1937, 395). Furthermore, in *Structure,* Parsons used the issue of religious ritual as the reason why he preferred certain parts of Durkheim's work over some of that of Weber. Durkheim, he

stressed, paid adequate attention to the societal salience of ritual. Since the society of National Socialism depended largely on symbolism ascertaining its so-called Aryan "folk community," it is not unlikely that Parsons's emphasis on ritual denoted his awareness that fascism had to be understood as a contemporary antitype to democratic society. A third piece of proof may be mentioned in favor of the thesis that Parsons's *Structure* was written with the aim of formulating an analytical framework applicable to democratic as well as nondemocratic societies: The text of the advertisement with which the book was announced to its potential readers claimed that it represented "civics in the highest sense."

9. The Council for Democracy was founded by Parsons's Harvard colleague, Carl J. Friedrich, as an agency of voluntary work for social scientists and personalities of public standing who were to strengthen Americans' ability to withstand Nazi propaganda by educating the public through speeches regarding the values inherent in their own democratic way of life. To honor its relentless effort, the Council for Democracy was awarded Variety magazine's Plaque of Patriotic Leadership for 1941; a contemporary article reports that this was given in appreciation of its service to the nation through "successful translation of 'basic values [of American democracy] into understandable everyday terms'" (Larson 1942, 290).

10. As for constitutionalism, it has had two important concretizations as an often neglected type of social structure. One is Carl J. Friedrich's juxtaposition of constitutionalism and plebescitarianism as two distinct forms of modern democracy (Friedrich 1937; 1941). Whereas the former, Friedrich argues, characterized the Anglo-Saxon countries that remained democratic in the face of contemporary totalitarianism, the latter prevailed in the "people's democracy" of Bolshevik Russia and also represented what the Nazis thought was democratic about their state-society, which supposedly had overcome only the negative element of liberalism. The second concretization of what constitutionalism means is more recent. David Sciulli, in a reconstruction of their main arguments, has maintained that the common denominator of Parsons's and Jürgen Habermas's ideas of society is constitutionalism. That is, both authors understand that the individual is essentially a rational and creative being whose needs should be met by the society in which he or she lives. This is desired and even required in the name of humanism to a degree that ensures that the social actor may freely and voluntarily identify with the society that constitutes his lifeworld (Sciulli 1988). In a more recent treatise, Sciulli has elaborated the main features of modern constitutionalism as a distinct type of social order, focusing on the professions as a major social element combining freedom with responsibility and liberal individualism with reciprocity orientation. The theory of societal constitutionalism thus elaborated places central emphasis on the collegial formation of institutions—an element of traditional society that has been preserved and refined in modern society, safeguarding a noncompetitive yet expert-geared form of social organization structured by impersonal yet function-based norms (Sciulli 1992; Frankford 1994).

11. The role model of the physician acting in a disinterested manner sensitive to the sentiments of the other, that is, the patient, but, at the same time, guided by professional standards of technical competence and excellence of practice took shape in Parsons's thinking gradually during the 1930s and 1940s. It was presented in its final form in chapter 10 of *The Social System* (1951). Its original frame of reference was professionalism but also medical economics, as he recollected in a retrospective, written in the 1960s, on how he became a medical sociologist (1964, 326). One aspect that he failed to mention in the 1960s, however, was the political connotation of the role model of the physician that he emphasized in his various writings during the 1940s. To take two examples: (1) In his essay on anti-Semitism (written in 1940–41) he likened the attitude to be adopted by the prospective "re-educator" for Germany to a psychiatrist who helped his patient professionally (1942a, 150–51); and (2) in his most theoretical piece published during World

War II, "Propaganda and Social Control," he epitomized the attitude of the sociologist vis-à-vis the society in which he or she lived and worked using an explication of the physician's role that took up over one-third of the entire article (1942b, 251–72). For further analysis of the link between Parsons's medical sociology and his general sociology (system theory), compare Gerhardt 1990; 1993.

12. Hegel, in his *Phänomenologie des Geistes* (Phenomenology of the Spirit), published in 1807 (here used in a translation from 1977), saw two aspects of the dynamics of development of the human species into a community, one of free, creative, social beings who would live in a world of self-fulfillment but, equally, one of political-social peace and harmony.

## References

Dahrendorf, Ralf. 1958. "Out of Utopia." *American Journal of Sociology* 64: 115–27.

Durkheim, Emile. (1897) 1952. *Suicide: A Study in Sociology.* Translated by John A. Spaulding and George Simpson and edited by George Simpson. London: Routledge and Kegan Paul.

Etzioni, Amitai. 1984. *Capital Corruption: The New Attack on American Democracy.* New York: Harcourt Brace.

———. 1988a. *The Moral Dimension: Toward a New Economics.* New York: Free Press.

Frankford, David M. 1994. "The Critical Potential of the Common Law Tradition." [Review Essay of David Sciulli's *Theory of Societal Constitutionalism*] *Columbia Law Review* 94: 1076–1123.

Friedrich, Carl J. 1937. *Constitutional Government and Politics: Nature and Development.* New York: Harper and Brothers.

———. 1941. *Constitutional Government and Democracy: Theory and Practice in Europe and America.* Boston: Little, Brown

Gerhardt, Uta. 1990. "Models of Illness and the Theory of Society." *International Sociology* 5: 337–55; reprinted in *Talcott Parsons: Critical Assessments,* ed. Peter Hamilton, vol. IV, 77–95. London: Routledge 1992.

———. 1993. "General Theory, German Fascism, and Medical Sociology: Restoring a Neglected Facet of Talcott Parsons's Thought." Paper presented at the Conference of the International Institute of Sociology, Paris.

———. 1994. "Parsons's Systems Theory and the Re-Education of Germany: Classical Theory and Contemporary Society." Paper presented at the Thirteenth World Congress of Sociology, Bielefeld, Germany.

Hegel, Georg Wilhelm Friedrich. (1807) 1977. *Phenomenology of the Spirit.* Translated by A.V. Miller, with analysis of the text and foreword by J.N. Findlay. Oxford: Oxford University Press.

Larson, Cedric. 1942. "The Council for Democracy." *Public Opinion Quarterly* 6: 284–90.

Lewin, Kurt; Lippitt, Ronald; and White, Robert. 1939. "Patterns of Aggressive Behavior in Experimentally Created 'Social Climates.'" *Journal of Social Psychology* 10: 271–99.

Lippitt, Ronald, and White, Robert K.1942. "An Experimental Study of Leadership and Group Life." In *Readings in Social Psychology,* eds. Theodore M. Newcomb and Eugene L. Hartley, 315–30. New York: Henry Holt.

Locke, John. (1690) 1963. *Two Treatises of Government.* A critical edition with an introduction and apparatus criticus by Peter Laslett. Cambridge: Cambridge University Press.

Mannheim, Karl. 1950. *Freedom, Power, and Democratic Planning.* London: Routledge and Kegan Paul.

Myrdal, Gunnar. 1944. *An American Dilemma.* 2 vols. New York: Harper Brothers.

Parsons, Talcott. 1934. "Service." In *Encyclopedia for the Social Sciences.* Reprinted in *The Early Essays,* ed. Charles Camic, 47–50. Chicago: Chicago University Press 1991.

———. 1935. "The Place of Ultimate Values in Sociological Theory." *International Journal of Ethics* 45: 282–316.

———. 1936. "On Certain Sociological Elements in Professor Taussig's Thought." In *Early Essays,* 259–78.

———. 1937. *The Structure of Social Action: A Study in Social Theory with Special Reference to a Group of Recent European Writers.* New York: McGraw-Hill.

———. 1940. "Memorandum: The Development of Groups and Organizations Amenable to Use against American Institutions and Foreign Policy and Possible Measures of Prevention." In *Talcott Parsons on National Socialism,* ed. Uta Gerhardt, 101–30. New York: Aldine de Gruyter, 1993.

———. 1942a. "The Sociology of Anti-Semitism." In *Talcott Parsons on National Socialism,* 131–52.

———. 1942b. "Propaganda and Social Control." In *Talcott Parsons on National Socialism,* 243–74.

———. 1945. "The Problem of Controlled Institutional Change: An Essay in Applied Social Science." In *Talcott Parsons on National Socialism,* 291–324.

———. 1951. *The Social System.* Glencoe, IL: Free Press.

———. 1962. "Individual Autonomy and Social Pressure: An Answer to Dennis Wrong." *Psychoanalysis and Psychoanalytic Review* 49: 70–79.

———. 1964. "Some Theoretical Considerations Bearing on the Field of Medical Sociology." In *Social Structure and Personality,* 325–58. London: Free Press.

Sciulli, David. 1988. "Foundations of Social Constitutionalism: Principles from the Concepts of Communicative Action and Procedural Legality." *British Journal of Sociology* 39: 377–408.

———. 1992. *Theory of Social Constitutionalism: Foundations of a Non-Marxist Critical Theory.* New York: Cambridge University Press.

Weber, Max. (1924) 1968. *Economy and Society: An Outline of Interpretive Sociology.* Edited by Guenther Roth and Claus Wittich. New York: Bedminster Press.

Wertheimer, Max. 1945. *Productive Thinking.* New York: Harper Brothers.

Wrong, Dennis. 1961. "The Oversocialized Conception on Man in Modern Sociology." *American Sociological Review* 26: 183–93; reprinted with changes in *Psychoanalysis and Psychoanalytic Review* 49 (1962): 53–69.

# 5

# Contesting the Fiducial Line: Legal Theory and the Duty to Be Loyal

*Deborah A. DeMott*

## Introduction

To what extent, and in what contexts, are human decisions appropriately as-sumed to be shaped by the actor's rational calculation of self-interest? This question and its corollaries underlie many disputed points not only in contempo-rary social theory but in contemporary legal theory as well. In particular, much work in rational choice theory and in the law-and-economics movement presup-poses that people make decisions in a rationally calculative way in pursuit of self-interest, a presupposition that varies in strength and specificity among au-thors. Amitai Etzioni has explored the limits of this presupposition across his career, most fully in *The Moral Dimension*. Where law-and-economics theorists assume that people endeavor to maximize utility, Etzioni argues that "utility" means not only the pursuit of pleasure but also adherence to moral codes. Where many law-and-economics theorists assume that people attempt to act in strictly rational fashion, Etzioni argues that people select both means and goals within a context of values and norms such that the effectiveness of their actions is en-hanced. And where law-and-economics theorists assume the individual to be the decision-making unit, Etzioni argues that relationships between people frame individuals' decisions.[1]

This chapter examines how law-and-economics theorists characterize fidu-ciary obligation, that is, the legal obligation to act loyally in the interest of

I am grateful to Richard Coughlin, Amitai Etzioni, and David Sciulli for their com-ments on an earlier draft of this chapter, and to Jennifer Hill for suggesting the title.

another. A trustee, for example, owes such an obligation to beneficiaries of a trust, as does an agent to a principal and a corporate director to the corporation and its shareholders. My thesis is that a pervasive assumption of rational calculativeness, if defined to have operative content, leads to inaccurate and unhelpful descriptions of both the content of fiduciary doctrine and judicial behavior in applying it. Moreover, these questions of characterization matter in shaping the continuing evolution of commercial and social norms in the legal community and the broader society. Justifications for commercial behavior and judicial decisions do not develop independently of intellectual constructs. At the least, legal theory ought not witlessly provide the mechanics to undermine the normative core of many existing institutional relationships.

As conventionally understood, outside the realm of law and economics, fiduciary obligation imposes on persons subject to it a distinctive form of obligation. Although the specifics vary among types of relationships, a fiduciary must, within the scope of the pertinent relationship (a matter left considerably to the parties' own agreement to define), abjure the pursuit of self-interest when it conflicts with the beneficiary's interests. In such relationships, unlike those defined solely by contract, the fiduciary is not free to take self-interested actions, even actions not specifically prohibited by the parties' agreement. The law draws what may usefully be called a fiducial line, a fixed point to govern action within the parties' relationship. Like the fiducial line drawn for purposes of navigation or surveying,[2] fiduciary obligation provides a stable plane of reference. It guides the parties' conduct within their relationship, and it permits judges and other observers to assess the propriety of the parties' conduct in the event of disputes.

The scope and consequences of fiduciary obligation can be summarized briefly. The law treats some relationships as inherently fiduciary. These include the relationship between an agent and a principal; a union officer and the union's members; a senior corporate officer and the corporation and its shareholders; a trustee and the beneficiaries of the trust; a lawyer and a client; a guardian and a ward; and a partner and the partnership of which her or she is a member. The precise content of fiduciary obligation in each such relationship varies somewhat, but the basic animating ideas are the same.

Courts also recognize that such a list will never exhaust situations in which fiduciary norms should apply. Courts enforce fiduciary obligation as well in some confidential relationships, namely, "those informal alliances that arise whenever one person trusts in, and relies upon, another . . . any relationship of blood, business friendship or association in which the parties repose special confidence in each other and are in a position to have and exercise, or actually have and exercise influence over each other."[3] By definition, a person believed to lack integrity and a capacity for fidelity cannot be held to a fiduciary duty founded solely in a confidential relationship.[4] No such defense is available in inherently fiduciary relationships. In *Don King Productions, Inc.* v. *Douglas,* a fighter was unsuccessful in establishing that his relationship with a boxing promoter was one of trust and confidence giving rise to fiduciary duties. The fighter testified that he was one of the few people in the world of boxing "that has ever had anything halfway decent to say" about the promoter, a perception the court held to be inconsistent with a high level of trust.[5] On the other hand, had the promoter in fact been a trustee, or an agent, on behalf of the fighter, the fighter's view of the promoter's integrity would not have relieved him from fiduciary duties.

Fiduciary obligation requires the person subject to it to use care in actions within the scope of the relationship and, more distinctively, it prohibits the creation of a conflict between self-interest and the beneficiary's interest. Early in the Anglo-American development of this body of law, *Keech* v. *Sandford* held that a trustee committed a breach of trust by obtaining a renewal of a lease for his own benefit (as the new lessee) when the lessor refused to renew the lease for the benefit of the trust beneficiary.[6] Freed to negotiate to achieve his or her own interests, any trustee might be tempted to prefer them to the beneficiary's interests. The fiduciary prohibition on creating conflicts of interest with the beneficiary encompasses any acts by the fiduciary within the scope of the parties' relationship.

A significant component of the fiduciary's loyalty to the beneficiary is a duty to disclose material information that is broader than the duties of disclosure created by contract law and tort law. In any relationship, a person who has made a factual representation as to a significant matter has a duty to disclose information subsequently acquired if it makes the prior representation untrue or misleading. A fiduciary is under an additional obligation. He or she must disclose material information to the beneficiary whether or not the subsequent information makes a prior representation untrue.[7]

The courts impose distinct remedies in cases of breach of fiduciary obligation: The fiduciary has an obligation to compensate the beneficiary for any loss caused by the breach or, alternatively, the fiduciary has an obligation to account for and disgorge any benefit realized through the breach.[8] Courts impose the obligation to account and disgorge even when the beneficiary cannot show that the breach caused a loss or detriment to his or her position. In *Keech* v. *Sandford,* it is no defense to the trustee that the lessor independently decided not to renew the lease for the benefit of the trust beneficiary. Finally, in some American jurisdictions, breaches of fiduciary duty can expose the fiduciary to liability for punitive or exemplary damages beyond the amounts required to compensate the beneficiary for loss or to disgorge the fiduciary's gain.

One of the major differences between Etzioni's socioeconomics and neoclassical economics is that Etzioni stresses that individuals internalize values and norms from the social context framing economic activity, a fact ignored by neoclassicists.[9] Fiduciary doctrine reveals that in certain economic relationships courts enforce norms and values. They do so regardless of whether the individuals involved have internalized the norms and values and, for that matter, regardless of the individuals' subjective impressions of their own activities.

### Does Judicial Language Matter?

A striking feature of judicial opinions interpreting and applying fiduciary norms is the language used by judges to explain and justify the outcomes they reach. The best-known example appears in Chief Judge Cardozo's 1928 opinion in *Meinhard* v. *Salmon*:

> Joint adventurers, like copartners, owe to one another, while the enterprise continues, the duty of the finest loyalty. Many forms of conduct permissible in a workaday world for those acting at arm's length, are forbidden to those bound by fiduciary ties. A trustee is held to something stricter than the morals of the market place. Not honesty above, but the punctilio of an honor the most sensitive, is then the standard of behavior.[10]

Once bound by fiduciary ties, that is, the rationally calculative pursuit of self-interest is circumscribed by strict rules that favor the interests of the beneficiary over those of the fiduciary. In contrast, prior to forming fiduciary ties, parties deal at arm's length and do not owe each other duties of loyalty. Indicative of the force of Cardozo's formulation, later courts occasionally characterize the conduct expected of a fiduciary as the "punctilio of honor" standard.[11]

Within the law-and-economics genre, many writers characterize fiduciary obligation as a species of contract, in which "the duty of loyalty replaces detailed contractual terms, and courts flesh out the duty of loyalty by prescribing the actions the parties themselves would have preferred if bargaining were cheap and all promises fully enforced."[12] In consequence, as Judge Easterbrook and Professor Fischel wrote recently, fiduciary duties are "not special . . . they have no moral footing, they are the same sorts of obligations, derived and enforced in the same way, as other contractual undertakings."[13] I return later in this chapter to the substantive import of this passage.

More generally one might wonder what to make of the language used in opinions like *Meinhard,* replete as it is with noncontractual-sounding terms and explicit references to morality. Easterbrook and Fischel observe that "we seek knowledge of when fiduciary duties arise and what form they take, not a theory of rhetoric—a theory of what judges *do,* not of explanations they give."[14] This characterization seems to misalign the scholar's project of explanation with the phenomenon to be explained, namely, judging. What judges do, they do with words, words purposively chosen to explain and justify the decision being made. A judge's use of words to explain and justify a decision is not an exercise in mere rhetoric.

Interestingly, other law-and-economics writers acknowledge implicitly that intellectual fashion and the language it attracts matter because people internalize and act upon their justificatory and explanatory devices. Implicitly these writers concede ground to the territorial claims of socioeconomics, even as they continue to prefer to treat individuals as autonomous decision makers. In this light, in his recent writing economist Oliver Williamson frets about what he calls "spillover effects." He appreciates that rational calculativeness can pervade spheres of commercial activity that become dysfunctional when people do not act cooperatively, or can even pervade personal relationships where trustful behavior is essential.[15] One consequence of spillover is that participants become unduly concerned with monitoring each other's inputs and precisely calibrating rewards. The consequences, though, may undermine the purpose of the enterprise. For example, the aesthetic quality of an orchestra's output is not likely to be furthered by precise physiological measurement of each player's effort or by a compensation scheme that rewarded such effort. One visualizes the violinists' elbows swinging farther and the flautists blowing harder, while in the imagination's ear the music deteriorates audibly.

Personal relationships, those created by love, friendship, and family ties, are undermined by participants who engage in ongoing rational calculations of their prospects to "trade up" to a better friend, lover, or family member. Early in Louis Begley's recent novel, *As Max Saw It,* the narrator (Max) reflects on the collapse of his long-lived relationship with Kate: "Ultimately it was the faint indignity of being the abandoned party, and the inconvenience, I minded the most. Kate's skin had begun to coarsen; she was smoking too much; and she had become shrill. In time, I might do better."[16] This passage skillfully leaves the reader with doubts of many sorts about Max. Even if his statement that he might do better is an attempt to rationalize away his loss, he seems, on balance, to be more comfortable with believing himself a cad than a lover left behind. To be sure, the world of personal relationships is more complex than can be addressed within the ambit of this modest chapter. In some relationships, both parties may be attentive to prospects of trading up; or one may be aware of the other's propensity to trade up but love the person unconditionally nonetheless.

Professor Williamson's response to spillover risk is to isolate relationships of personal trust from the proper sphere of calculative behavior. Apart from relationships of personal trust, Williamson argues that calculative excess should be checked by promoting awareness of the spillover effect, discussed above, and of the nonpecuniary satisfactions that follow in relationships in which exchanges are not monitored too closely.[17] We derive satisfactions of many sorts, he argues, from relationships in which we have a generalized expectation of reciprocity but do not feel compelled to maintain precise accounts of exchanges.

Even with these concessions, Professor Williamson's preference is to cloister trust in the isolated sphere of noncommercial personal relationships. Fiduciary doctrine, instead, treats trust as a more general phenomenon, as a set of expectations about another's behavior to be valued and protected in both personal and commercial relationships when those expectations are well founded. In any event, even given Professor Williamson's starting point, choices about language matter. Such choices are likely to figure in the spillover phenomenon, for example, because they reflect and influence acceptable patterns of explanation and justification for behavior. Even internal monologues (like Max's) are attempts to justify our conduct to ourselves.

### Enabling Efficient Breaches

To assess the substantive import of the law-and-economics claim that fiduciary obligation is simply a type of contractual obligation, it is helpful to test the validity of assertions about the nature and operation of contract law as applied to fiduciary obligation. One basic point should be acknowledged at the outset. Enforceable contracts, like most relationships that carry a court-enforced fiduciary obligation, begin with a voluntary association and agreement among the parties. An exception in the fiduciary realm, however, is a constructive trust. Here courts impose a remedy to disgorge property on a person who might not have intended a fiduciary relationship with the trust's beneficiary. The more general point is that the law of contract does not encompass or exhaust the legal consequences of *all* voluntary agreements and associations. Many voluntary relationships have their own distinct set of legal norms, such as those applicable to marriage, divorce, and dispositions of property intended to be effective upon the owner's death. For that matter, norms defined by tort law—like fraud and product liability—also apply to voluntary relationships, agreements, and transactions. If I lie to you about my company's earnings to induce you to invest in it and you lose money as a result, your remedies against me are not confined to contract law, but are enhanced by the tort law remedies for fraud. Thus, my concern is limited to claims that can be made distinctively about contract law, within the range of legal norms applicable to all voluntary relationships.

Contract law, many writers have noted, is morally unconcerned with whether promises are kept; rules specifying remedies for breach of contract at most compensate the nonbreaching party for the value that would have been conferred by the other party's performance, and in many respects such rules operate to undercompensate. Writing in 1897 (well before the emergence of the contemporary law-and-economics movement), Justice Holmes asserted, "the duty to keep a contract at common law means a prediction that you must pay damages if you do not keep it—and nothing else . . . you are liable to pay a sum unless the promised event comes to pass."[18] In any event, you the actor are free, having entered into a contract, to calculate and act upon the course that best furthers your self-interest. Indeed, many contemporary legal theorists maintain that breaches of contract are efficient and should be encouraged to the extent they are efficient. If the breaching party can fully compensate the nonbreaching party and use his or her productive capacity to greater gain elsewhere, the breach is efficient. And contract law is stingy in its computation of damages, a trait that makes some breaches efficient at the margin that would not be were contract law damages more expansive. Contract damages in the United States, for example, do not include attorneys' fees incurred by the nonbreaching party to recover after a breach has occurred, nor do they include punitive damages or damages for pain and suffering.

In striking contrast to contract law, the norms that courts enforce as fiduciary obligations operate to discourage the calculated pursuit of self-interest that could otherwise be justified as producing an efficient breach of contract. For starters, the beneficiary has the remedial option of compelling the fiduciary to account for and disgorge any profit gained through a breach, as a distinct alternative to seeking compensation for loss. A rationally calculative beneficiary who sues his fiduciary should, of course, choose the remedy that yields the larger recovery. In this respect remedies for breach of fiduciary obligation resemble those generated by norms of property law. Courts do not, as a general matter, permit a private party to take another's property even if the taker can demonstrate that he or she will be able to use the property to generate greater gains than can its owner. Such remedies operate ex ante to deter breach. That is, knowing in advance of any breach that no gain may be retained, the rational fiduciary does not breach his or her duty, especially if it is known that the breach is likely to be detected by the beneficiary. This is clearly a "social context" in Etzioni's sense, one that economic actors either internalize and act upon voluntarily or find instead that their breaches lead to extracontractual sanctions in litigation. Put more metaphorically, once the fiducial line is drawn, the well-known legal consequences of breach make it idle for a fiduciary to reckon the gain a breach would produce.

The language in opinions like *Meinhard* v. *Salmon*, moreover, is uncongenial to concepts like efficient breach precisely because it articulates normative footings for fiduciary duty. Emphatic judicial emphasis on punctilios of honor and duties of finest loyalty, if internalized by private parties, discourages the calculated pursuit of self-interest. Justice Holmes, as it happens, observed that his conception of contract "stinks in the nostrils of those who think it advantageous to get as much ethics into the law as they can."[19] The incorporation of ethical norms into a portion of the law is a major feature of judicial opinions analyzing alleged breaches of fiduciary obligation, a feature that distinguishes fiduciary relationships from those in which concepts like efficient breach are useful. Indeed, judges' language encourages persons in positions subject to fiduciary norms to internalize them. Such internalization, in turn, reduces breaches of the norms, which in turn reduces the frequency of successful lawsuits brought by beneficiaries. This effect can be characterized within the typology of compliance developed by Etzioni. Actors who internalize fiduciary norms have a form of moral involvement, a "positive orientation of high intensity" toward the interests of the beneficiary.[20] To some extent, as I explain below, they fulfill their duties for reasons apart from remuneration.

Ironically, concepts of efficiency and anticipated economic benefit are nonetheless useful in understanding some of the reasons why people enter into fiduciary relationships. Given the prospective liability, why would anyone join a partnership? Why would anyone other than an altruistic family member serve as a trustee or a guardian? Why (for that matter) does anyone become a lawyer? One hypothesis is that people who subject themselves to fiduciary norms fail to understand and properly account for their risks of liability, risks that may seem remote when the relationship is initially undertaken. As a general explanation, this hypothesis is not plausible; too many people—many of them demonstrably clever and well informed—have served as fiduciaries. A more plausible hypothesis for the assumption of fiduciary obligation in commercial settings is simply a well-founded calculation of personal benefit through conduct that conforms to fiduciary norms. Prospective partners, for example, anticipate mutual advantage through their association; some fiduciaries, like trustees and lawyers, additionally anticipate future benefit by developing a reputation for faithful and competent service. Indeed, a prospective beneficiary who realizes that breach will not be efficient for his fiduciary can assign a more certain value to their relationship and pay for the fiduciary's services knowing that breach should not be an attractive option for the fiduciary. Moreover, many people are attracted to a profession like the law for reasons that are not evidently self-interested, including the opportunity to be of service to others.

In contrast, the contract law world of efficient breach is less certain; a contracting party lacks accurate foresight into future developments that would make breach attractive to the other party and will always lack full information about the other party's propensity to breach the contract if self-interest so dictates. Of course, if these risks can be identified with precision, they can be insured against. The magnitude of the risk in any particular relationship will be difficult to assess because the likelihood of a self-interested breach is impossible to predict, even if the party has a known track record. Pricing the insurance would thus be difficult. In any event, to the extent any risk is insurable, the insurance is not free. Nor do markets for insurance themselves operate without cost or friction.

In commercial settings especially, it is helpful to distinguish between motives for entering into a relationship, which are likely to be self-interested, and norms that govern conduct within the relationship once it is formed. The relative certainty created by a fiduciary norm, oddly enough, should facilitate more accurate calculation of whether entering into a particular fiduciary relationship will be advantageous. Such certainty—created by the legal norm applicable to the relationship—substitutes for contractually defined insurance against a set of risks surrounding the party's future self-interested conduct. It also obviates or, at least, reduces the loss described by Roger Cotterrell that otherwise results as "the pace of economic, financial life . . . slows as individuals calculate more carefully and more reluctantly whether and when to involve themselves in relationships of reliance which appear to them increasingly insecure."[21] And once in a relationship, fiduciary obligation reduces the costs of ever-vigilant distrust of the other party. In short, fiduciary norms reduce a commercial form of entropy. Along related lines, Robert Cooter and Bradley Freedman argue that the law of fiduciary duty deters misappropriation of the beneficiary's property by presuming that misappropriation has occurred in many situations in which the beneficiary would have difficulty establishing its actual occurrence. As a result, at the outset of any relationship governed by fiduciary norms, the beneficiary's confidence in the other party is enhanced.[22] Within an established fiduciary relationship, to betray the beneficiary's confidence will not be advantageous to the fiduciary.

Most economic actors have relationships with many other actors, among them relationships governed by fiduciary norms and others governed by general contract law. Etzioni's description of "mixed-scanning strategy" is helpful in understanding how the same actor makes decisions appropriate to each relationship.[23] Initially the actor makes a fundamental (or contextualizing) decision to assess whether primacy must be given to an interest other than his or her own. Then, turning to the matter at hand, the actor makes the bit (or item) decision. As Etzioni observes, the fundamental decision (Do fiduciary norms apply?) sets the context for the bit decision. Incremental bit decisions, in the absence of the correct fundamental decision, risk liability for breach of fiduciary duty.

## Carving Out and Contracting In to Duties

To be sure, the precise or technical content of fiduciary norms varies among types of relationships. The duties applicable to corporate directors under the general fiduciary aegis of loyalty are not identical to trustees' duties. Variability also occurs because the parties' own agreement significantly shapes the relationship and the norms applicable to it. This point, of course, is crucial in evaluating the law-and-economics claim that fiduciary norms are in essence contractual. My concrete focus will be examples drawn from the law of trusts, but other areas of the law would, I think, support the general points.

A trust is "a fiduciary relationship with respect to property, subjecting the person by whom the title to the property is held to equitable duties to deal with the property for the benefit of another person, which arises as a result of a manifestation of an intention to create it."[24] The settlor, who creates the trust and transfers title to the property to the trustee, would typically manifest his or her intentions in a written trust agreement. A typical trust agreement designates the beneficiary, specifies the nature and extent of the trustee's powers regarding trust property, and determines the trustee's duties. In particular, trust law recognizes that "the terms of the trust"—the provable manifest intention of the settlor—determine the nature and extent of the trustee's duties and powers.[25] In the absence of terms determining otherwise, the trustee—among other duties—must keep and render accurate accounts and furnish accurate information to the beneficiary, use the skill and care of a prudent person in administering the trust, deal impartially with beneficiaries, segregate trust property from the trustee's own property, and use reasonable care to preserve trust property and make it productive. Most fundamentally, the trustee has a duty of loyalty "to administer the trust solely in the interest of the beneficiary" and, in dealings with the beneficiary, to deal fairly with him and "communicate to him all material facts in connection with the transaction which the trustee knows or should know."[26] All such duties, though, are subject to "the terms of the trust."

On closer inspection, trust law differs significantly from contract law. It limits the efficacy both of carve-outs from otherwise applicable fiduciary duties, as well as transaction-specific waivers or consents to transactions that constitute breaches of trust. Although a trust agreement may include exculpatory provisions that relieve the trustee of liability for breach of trust, exculpatory provisions are ineffective to relieve the trustee from liability to account for any profit derived from breach of trust. Nor may the trustee be exculpated against liability resulting from breaches of trust committed in bad faith or with reckless indifference to the beneficiary's interests.[27] Even when the beneficiary consents to a transaction, if the trustee has an interest in it adverse to the beneficiary's interest, the beneficiary is not bound unless the transaction is fair and reasonable.[28]

One reason for these restrictions is definitional. If a trust agreement could effectively relieve the trustee of his or her duty to account for profit derived from a breach of trust, the trustee would not be a fiduciary in any operative sense. The settlor would have created a relationship other than a trust. The transaction purportedly creating the "trust" would, in effect, be a gift of the property to the trustee. After all, the trustee would be free to use it solely in his or her own interests. A separate reason for the restrictions is prudential. Trustees, it is feared, may take advantage of beneficiaries both in drafting trust instruments and in procuring consent to problematic transactions.

In any event, the concept just explicated is that of carving out from otherwise applicable fiduciary duties through the terms of an instrument or other agreement. In many respects, agreements subject to general contract law proceed in the opposite direction—the parties contract into duties, and contract law imposes on each party only those duties of performance that the party agreed to assume. Contract law, to be sure, has some mandatory content, which I discuss below, but the defining feature of the process of contracting is the specific identification and assumption of duties.

Given this background, how can law-and-economics theorists characterize fiduciary obligation as essentially contractual? They can do so only by using the construct of the hypothetical contract. Easterbrook and Fischel argue that fiduciary obligation is contractual because "the duty of loyalty replaces detailed contractual terms," and courts specify the content of the duty by imposing on the parties the terms they hypothetically would have agreed to "if bargaining were cheap and all promises fully enforced."[29] But if the parties to an actual relationship do not bargain out its terms fully, how do we know what they would have agreed to? Why assume that, in any particular relationship, a bargain reached by the parties would replicate the law of fiduciary obligation as it presently exists?

Indeed, the limits that trust law invariably imposes on general exculpations and transaction-specific consents manifests skepticism of actual bargains and agreements. Actual bargains reflect each party's intensity of need or desire to conclude a deal and each party's skill in bargaining to achieve specific ends (which contract law itself does not require be candidly disclosed to the other party). Nor does the parties' opportunity to bargain foreclose judicial imposition of fiduciary duties when a dispute later arises. For that matter, courts impose relatively exacting forms of the duty of loyalty in relationships in which the parties likely had an actual opportunity to bargain over the terms of their relationship. *Meinhard* v. *Salmon*, the origin of the "punctilio of honor" standard, involved a two-person joint venture in real estate in which the joint venturers had a detailed written agreement. Likewise, many courts impose fiduciary duties on fellow shareholders in small, closely held corporations but not in larger publicly traded corporations.[30] If fiduciary obligation were a judicially crafted substitute for the parties' own bargain, one would expect the obligation to operate more stringently when the parties lacked a realistic opportunity to bargain and less stringently in cases like *Meinhard* and closely held corporations.

## Mandatory Elements of Contract Law

The parties' express agreement does not control all aspects of a relationship governed by the general law of contract. Mandatory rules of law supplement and supersede the private rules created by the parties' agreement. For example, such mandatory rules prohibit fraud, require certain agreements to be in writing to be enforceable, and limit the parties' ability to specify freely the remedies that apply in the event of breach.[31] More generally, contract law includes a mandatory duty to act in good faith in the performance and enforcement of the contract. That contract law imposes such a duty suggests a convergence between contract law and fiduciary obligation, because both require other-regarding behavior.

The extent of the convergence, however, is far from complete. Many contract cases, in fact, hold that self-interested behavior is not a breach of contract, even when the legal framework is expressly understood to include a duty of good faith and the self-interested conduct injures the other party. In a leading example, *Metropolitan Life Insurance Co.* v. *RJR Nabisco, Inc.*, RJR Nabisco incurred enormous amounts of additional indebtedness to fund a leveraged buyout transaction.[32] The impact—clearly foreseeable—of the additional borrowing was to reduce sharply the market value of debt securities previously issued by RJR Nabisco. The court held that the subsequent borrowing did not violate any duty of good faith owed by RJR Nabisco to its prior creditors; had they wished to constrain its ability subsequently to borrow massive amounts of money, the loan instruments could have so provided.

In short, the contractual duty of good faith is not fiduciary obligation labeled in different language; it does not proscribe self-interested conduct that, as in *RJR Nabisco,* could readily be addressed in the parties' agreement.[33] Instead, the contractual duty of good faith prevents parties from evading the consequences of the express commitments they have made and from abusing the other party. For example, if a shoe manufacturer enters into a contract with a leather supplier to buy all its requirements of leather for some period of time, the buyer's duty of good faith limits the quantity of leather it may demand to one determined "in good faith."[34] But the leather supplier is free, unless the contract explicitly provides otherwise, to furnish leather to the manufacturer's chief competitor. On the other hand, a director of an incorporated shoe manufacturer would owe fiduciary duties to the corporation and its shareholders; if the director acquired an undisclosed interest in the competing manufacturer, the director would have breached his or her fiduciary duty of loyalty. Interestingly, even many law-and-economics theorists characterize as "opportunistic" conduct that seems excessively self-regarding, and the term "opportunism" always conveys moral disapproval in this literature.[35]

## Conclusion

My central point is that many aspects of judicial behavior resist explanation if one seeks to explain them by appealing to a robust assumption that all human conduct is driven by the rationally calculative pursuit of self-interest. The operation of fiduciary doctrine is distinctive and, in particular, dissimilar in major respects to general contract law because its function is different. Courts protect expectations of loyal behavior within specific types of relationships. The value of fiduciary obligation in commercial settings is precisely that its imposition is known to proscribe certain types of self-seeking conduct. Paradoxically, drawing the fiducial line by requiring other-regarding conduct from one party can be beneficial to all within a relationship.

A broader point is the role of fiduciary obligation in contributing to what Etzioni calls a "responsive community," one that is "much more integrated than an aggregate of self-maximizing individuals" and that also resists the more constricting structure of repressive or authoritarian communities.[36] In commercial settings, fiduciary obligation facilitates investment, for all the reasons I have explained. It also facilitates the operation of institutions like pension funds and charitable trusts. In many respects, the community generally benefits. True, the initial impact of fiduciary obligation is on particular relationships among individuals, but its larger impact reaches, and indeed underlies, many of the societal units on which Etzioni's analysis focuses.

Finally, fiduciary obligation restricts a private form of corruption, that is, an economic actor's use for self-interested ends of power over others' property. Such corruption is inconsistent with nurturing, as Etzioni advocates, community-sustaining centripetal forces.[37] In a capitalistic market economy, centripetal forces that sustain community cannot flourish if major economic actors make decisions that are visibly tainted by self-interest. Fiduciary obligation, by constraining the self-interested use of power, helps to institutionalize Etzioni's "social context."

## Notes

1. Amitai Etzioni, *The Moral Dimension*, p. 4.
2. See *Oxford English Dictionary*, 2d ed.

3. *United States* v. *Reed*, 601 F. Supp. 685, 712 (S.D.N.Y. 1985).

4. See *Don King Productions, Inc.* v. *Douglas*, 742 F. Supp. 741, 770 (S.D.N.Y. 1990).

5. Ibid.

6. *Keech* v. *Sandford*, 25 Eng. Rep. 223 (1726).

7. *Merrill Lynch, Pierce, Fenner & Smith, Inc.* v. *Boeck*, 377 N.W. 2d 605, 614 (Wis. 1985) (Abrahamson, J., concurring).

8. See *Restatement (Third) of Trusts* §205.

9. Etzioni, *The Moral Dimension*, p. 5.

10. *Meinhard* v. *Salmon*, 259 N.Y. 458, 164 N.E. 545, 546 (1928).

11. See *Wartski* v. *Bedford*, 926 F. 2d 11, 20 (1st Cir. 1991) (standard applicable to partner);' In re Van Swearingen Corp., 155 F.2d 1009, 1011 (6th Cir. 1946) (standard applicable to trustee); Alterman v. State, 615 So. 2e 640, 648 (Ala. App. 1993) (standard applicable to construction contract adviser).

12. Frank H. Easterbrook and Daniel R. Fischel, "Contract and Fiduciary Duty," p. 427.

13. Ibid.

14. Ibid., p. 429.

15. Oliver E. Williamson, "Calculativeness, Trust and Economic Organization," pp. 481–83.

16. Louis Begley, *As Max Saw It*, p. 10. As it happens, the fictional Max is a law professor, a point that need not detain us.

17. Williamson, "Calculativeness, Trust and Economic Organization," pp. 481–84.

18. Oliver Wendell Holmes, "The Path of the Law," p. 462.

19. Ibid.

20. Amitai Etzioni, *A Comparative Analysis of Complex Organizations*, pp. 10–13.

21. Roger Cotterrell, "Trusting in Law," p. 95.

22. See Robert Cooter and Bradley J. Freedman, "The Fiduciary Relationship: Its Economic Character and Legal Consequences," p. 1074.

23. Amitai Etzioni, *The Active Society*, ch. 12.

24. *Restatement (Second) of Trusts* §2. The existence of a trust for legal purposes does not require trust beneficiaries to demonstrate that they actually reposed psychological trust in the trustee. For treatments of the psychological and institutional circumstances of trust, see Diego Gambetta, ed., *Trust: Making and Breaking Cooperative Relations;* and Bernard Barber, *The Logic and Limits of Trust.*

25. Ibid., 164(a).

26. Ibid., 170.

27. Ibid., 222.

28. Ibid., 216 (3).

29. See Easterbrook and Fischel, "Contract and Fiduciary Duty," p. 427.

30. Compare *Noakes* v. *Schoenborn*, 116 Or. app. 464, 841 P. 2d 682 (1992) (holding that controlling shareholder in closely held corporation is a fiduciary toward minority shareholders) with *Kahn* v. *Sprouse*, 842 F. Supp. 423 (D. Ore. 1993) (court declines to apply *Noakes* principle when public market exists for minority's shares).

31. For a theoretical treatment, see Michael J. Trebilcock, *The Limits of Freedom of Contract.*

32. *Metropolitan Life Insurance Co.* v. *RJR Nabisco, Inc.*, 716 F. Supp. 1504, 1516–23 (S.D.N.Y. 1989).

33. Ibid., p. 1519. See also William W. Bratton Jr., "Self-Regulation, Normative Choice, and the Structuring of Corporate Fiduciary Law," pp. 1122–28; Deborah A. DeMott, "Beyond Metaphor: An Analysis of Fiduciary Obligation," pp. 892–902.

34. See Uniform Commercial Code §2–306(1).
35. For a fuller discussion, see Deborah A. DeMott, "Do You Have the Right to Remain Silent: Duties of Disclosure in Business Transactions."
36. Etzioni, *The Moral Dimension*, p. 8.
37. Amitai Etzioni, *Capital Corruption*, p. 185.

## References

American Law Institute. *Restatement (Second) of Trusts*. St. Paul, MN: American Law Institute Publishers, 1959.
———. *Restatement (Third) of Trusts*. St. Paul, MN: American Law Institute Publishers, 1992.
Barber, Bernard. *The Logic and Limits of Trust*. New Brunswick, NJ: Rutgers University Press, 1983.
Begley, Louis. *As Max Saw It*. New York: Alfred A. Knopf, 1994.
Bratton, William W., Jr. "Self-Regulation, Normative Choice, and the Structuring of Corporate Fiduciary Law." *George Washington University Law Review* 61 (April 1993): 1084–1129.
Cooter, Robert, and Freedman, Bradley. "The Fiduciary Relationship: Its Economic Character and Legal Consequences." *New York University Law Review* 66 (October 1991): 1045–75.
Cotterrell, Roger. "Trusting in Law." *Current Legal Problems* 46, part 2 (1993): 75–95.
DeMott, Deborah A. "Beyond Metaphor: An Analysis of Fiduciary Obligation." *Duke Law Journal* (November 1988): 879–924.
———. "Do You Have the Right to Remain Silent: Duties of Disclosure in Business Transactions." *Delaware Journal of Corporate Law* 19, no. 1 (1994): 65–102.
Easterbrook, Frank H., and Fischel, Daniel R. "Contract and Fiduciary Duty." *Journal of Law and Economics* 36 (April 1993): 425–46.
Etzioni, Amitai. *The Active Society: A Theory of Societal and Political Processes*. New York: Free Press, 1968.
———. *A Comparative Analysis of Complex Organizations*. New York: Free Press, 1975.
———. *Capital Corruption: The New Attack on American Democracy*. New York: Harcourt Brace Jovanovich, 1984.
———. *The Moral Dimension: Toward a New Economics*. New York: Free Press, 1988.
Gambetta, Diego, ed. *Trust: Making and Breaking Cooperative Relations*. New York: B. Blackwell, 1988.
Holmes, Oliver Wendell. "The Path of the Law." *Harvard Law Review* 10 (March 1897): 457–78.
Trebilcock, Michael. *The Limits of Freedom of Contract*. Cambridge, MA: Harvard University Press, 1993.
Williamson, Oliver E. "Calculativeness, Trust and Economic Organization." *Journal of Law and Economics* 36 (April 1993): 453–86.

# 6

# Sociology, Economics, and Normative Action: Notes Toward a Theory of Middle Height

*Göran Therborn*

## Sociology and Economics

Amitai Etzioni's *The Moral Dimension* offers an excellent entry into a discussion of both the relationship of sociology to neoclassical economics and the current tasks of sociological theorizing. With regard to the former, it seems to me that a good deal might be gained from finding a nonpolemical baseline, a sort of basic common ground upon which to make and debate mutually intelligible critical assessments. One possible starting point, very natural for a sociologist and also nonbiased against neoclassical economics and rational choice models generally, is a framework of social action. This framework does not exhaust social scientists' concerns, since they are also concerned with the operation and change of systems and systemic processes, whether economic, cultural, political, or social. And it may be argued that a common ground is more easily found in terms of action. It harbors, without discrimination, the approaches of Gary Becker, Jürgen Habermas, Talcott Parsons, and those of most twentieth-century Marxists, from V.I. Lenin to Adam Przeworski or Edward Thompson.

Most, if not all, social scientists would probably accept "explanation" as at least one major task of social theory and the practice of social science. The explanation of social action, then, appears to be a good vantage point from which to grasp the different approaches typical of sociology as well as economics, "rational choice" and its alternatives.

Let us then lay out the analytic skeleton of explanations of action. The basic elements are: a set of actors, a set of situations (or conditions), and a set of actions. In idealist emanationism the situations would disappear, and in extreme structuralism the actors would be reduced to situations; but here we are concerned with mainstream, cross-disciplinary social science. Given the task of explaining social action, we are left with two dimensions along which we can distinguish how social scientific modes of explanations treat the set of actors and the set of situations.

Explanatory factors may be divided into variables and givens or randoms. The latter are by no means synonymous, but they have one important thing in common, namely, we do not have to investigate them. From a perspective of empirical social science, we may find a metalanguage capable of grasping what Etzioni calls the "paradigmatic struggle" within contemporary mainstream social and behavioral science.

Moving from left to right in Table 6.1, game theory is a nonempirical theory of rational strategic action that can take as predeterminedly given both the actor, as rational anybody, and the situation as a payoff matrix (Luce and Raiffa 1957; Harsanyi 1982). The explanatory focus is on questions such as: What is the optimal strategy for each player in the given game situation? and, Does the game have one equilibrium, or more than one? But game theory is also being extended to games in multiple arenas, games nested within others, such as institutional or constitutional games (Tsebelis 1990), in which the basic explanatory logic becomes similar to that of economics.

In the characteristic economic mode of explanation, action is explained by variations of the situation, basically by changes in (relative) prices and incomes (Becker 1976). Actors are given, assumed to be utility maximizers with "stable preferences": "Preferences are assumed not to change substantially over time, nor to be very different between wealthy and poor persons, or even between persons in different societies and cultures. . . . The assumption of stable preferences provides a stable foundation for generating predictions about responses to various changes" (ibid., 5). As Przeworski (1986, 88) puts it, the power of neoclassical economics lies in being able to "separate the analysis of *action at a particular moment* from everything that created the conditions under which this action occurs" (emphasis added). Situational variability consists of the probable cost–benefit consequences of different options at moments of choice. When (probable) incentives change, actors act differently, but in predictable ways.

The assumptions of maximizing behavior and stable preferences do not necessarily require that preferences be exclusively egoistic or pecuniary, nor even that they be universally the same (compare Becker 1991; 1993; Hechter, Opp, and Wippler 1990, 3–4). The "utility function" of a particular set of actors may be specified in different ways, and in ways differing from that of other sets of actors. Nor do the two assumptions necessarily require that actors have unlimited information-processing and calculating capacities. Limitations can be treated as "constraints" of "income, time, imperfect memory, and calculating capacities,

Table 6.1

**Modes of Explaining Human Action**

| Actors | Situations | |
|---|---|---|
| | Given/Random | Variable |
| Given/Random | Game Theory | Neoclassical Economics<br>Rational Choice<br>Behaviorist Psychology |
| Variable | Mainstream Sociology<br>Anthropology<br>Political Science<br>Dynamic Psychology | (Composite models) |

and other limited resources, and also by opportunities available in the economy elsewhere" (Becker 1993, 386; compare North 1990, ch. 3). The crucial point is that the baseline for economic explanations and predictions is actors with given preferences, decision rules, and constraints.

The contrast between mainstream economic and sociological approaches, but also their common ground, is well illustrated by a renowned article by George Stigler and Gary Becker (1977). Couched in a very different language, Stigler and Becker do something familiar to sociologists, and particularly to "anti-positivistic," "humanistic" sociologists. They engage in "interpreting" human behavior in interpretative economics. In particular, they reinterpret what the family does or "maximizes" and then apply this reinterpretation to specific situations, for instance, to the increasing amount of time that people spend listening to music. They interpret this as "the marginal utility of time allocated to music is increased by an increase in the stock of music capital" (ibid., 79). They also apply their reinterpretation to advertising by showing that it does not change tastes, only prices, and that it makes households believe that they get more out of the product advertised (ibid., 84). The attractiveness of this approach, its preserved "generality and power," is a matter of taste—a point I shall not dispute here, even if I do not hide my own sociological and socioeconomic preferences. Taste aside, however, this approach should remind us of the common ground of economics and sociology theorized by the greatest twentieth-century sociologist, Max Weber (compare Therborn 1976, 290).

But the contrast of disciplinary concerns is even more striking. After arguing extensively for *de gustibus non est disputandum* (here meaning roughly, "tastes need not be bothered with," e.g., that the effects of addiction and advertising may be explained by changes in psychologically redefined prices and incomes), Stigler and Becker (1977, 89) add as an aside at the end: "Needless to say, we would welcome explanations of why some people become addicted to alcohol and others to Mozart!" This is the kind of question with which sociologists begin.

Sociologists—and anthropologists and mainstream political scientists—start from the expectation that actors differ across categories and groups of various sorts as well as over historical time. In this sociological-anthropological vision, social action varies because actors vary. They belong to different groups, genders, classes, societies, or, in more recent formulations, they have different amounts of social capital or are embedded in different social networks (Granovetter 1985; Burt 1993).

An important goal of the research agenda is to find out how actors differ. What kind of people listen to or produce what kind of music or use what kind of drugs in what ways? The interpretative sociologist would then ask, What meaning does music have for different kinds of people? The answer would normally not be derived from a very general theory, one equivalent to a theory of consumer choice. Rather, it would come either from a much more ad hoc theory of culture produced in the same way as the typical theory or theoretical derivation in economics, namely, by armchair creativity, or it would come after empirical investigation. While most sociologists tend to defer to their theoretical gurus, sociology is nonetheless much more of an empirical discipline than economics. The proof of the sociological pudding is still in the eating rather than in the looking.

On the other hand, sociologists tend to take as random or given the variation of situations or circumstances of action. They may well take into account, in a way similar to economic explanations, the variability of actors as a constraint. A sociologist of crime would naturally look into patterns of criminality under different regimes of sanctions but would normally not try to assess how different penalties would affect the frequency of a certain kind of deviant action (compare Scull 1988).

In interpretative sociology, the situation is given by actors' definition(s) of it. The options available to the sociological actor typically vary—not with the immediate action situation but, rather, with the actor's values, norms, or interpretation of the situation and with the actor's location in the social structure.[1] Sociologists' tendency not to bother with situational variation is expressed in the old quip that sociology is the discipline that explains why people do not have any choice.

Etzioni's *The Moral Dimension* fits very well into this schema as a sociological counterblast to neoclassical economics. Situational variability is secondary at most because "the majority of choices people make . . . are completely or largely based on normative-affective considerations . . . and . . . the limited zones in which other, logical-empirical . . . considerations are paramount, are themselves defined by N/A (normative-affective) factors that legitimate and otherwise motivate such decision-making" (1988, 93). Etzioni argues further (ibid., 95): "The majority of choices involve little information processing (about the situation) or none at all, but . . . they draw largely or exclusively on affective involvements and normative commitments (of the actors)." In other words, actors care little about how the situations in which they are involved have changed but instead act upon their own actor-specific involvements and commitments. Actors' "habit" and "inertia," not prices and efforts, govern most choices (ibid., 161). Also Etzioni sees the neoclassical assumption of stable or given preferences as a "most important difference" to his own approach, according to which normative-affective factors "account for an important part of the variance among preferences and for changes in them" (ibid., 112).

In brief, our simple scheme above seems to be able to locate both Gary Becker and Amitai Etzioni in the same table. Labeling is not what I am driving at, however. Rather, my aim is to lay out challenges to mainstream economics and mainstream sociology.

These challenges appear to be, on the one hand, the sociological questioning of the given/randomness of actors with their stable preferences and given constraints, and, on the other hand, the economic questioning of the given/randomness of situations (either given as reducible to the structural location, to the interpretations and/or the evaluations of the actors, or randomly variable).

A composite model is not necessarily a solution to these challenges. Parsimony is not just an aesthetic rule of scientific practice. It has a practical aspect as well. The practice of explanation is not made easier by adding to the number of variables. In the end, I think some composite model may offer an advance, but not until it is explicitly formulated and elaborated. To this end, arguments in favor of concentrating on the variability either of actors or of situations are both legitimate. On the other hand, what the sociological position calls for is an explicit, systematic formulation of the variability of situations, or, alternatively, of the latter's negligible randomness.[2]

## For Theories of Middle Height

Etzioni's *The Moral Dimension* is a true specimen of grand theory, dealing with issues of human nature, the foundation of our society, and the foundations of the social sciences. As such it is a major contribution to central controversies of contemporary politics and ethics as well as to the "paradigmatic struggle" in the social sciences. Grand theory has always been an important part of the sociological enterprise, inspiring and enriching the latter.[3] Etzioni's latest variety of it has even provided the impetus for an interdisciplinary scholarly movement, "socio-economics."[4]

However, like everything else in our embattled discipline, grand theory is also an object of criticism. There is also much frustration and irritation with its high-flying generalizations and abstractions. It is almost half a century since Robert Merton, with characteristic wisdom and civility, put forward the case for "theories of the middle range."[5] Having an ecumenical conception of social science, my intention is not to argue for one against the other.[6] Rather, I wish to plead for the raison d'être of a particular kind of theory alongside all others.

The Mertonian divide now needs a distinction itself. Alongside theories of the middle range, which deal with limited ranges of data, we also may distinguish theories that employ a wide range of data but at a medium level of abstraction. I call these "theories of middle height," because they have limited ambitions of abstraction but nonetheless attempt to cover a wide range of empirical cases. In brief, their height of abstraction is modest, but their range of intended coverage is grand.

The current state of the sociological discipline calls out for this partition of the Mertonian middle with regard either to range or to height. The current pluralism of most sociology departments, as well as of the discipline and its major associations, means that grand theories, even Luhmann's total system of theory, simply occupy competing corners in a vast hall where sociologists of all kinds mill around and pick up news and ideas. The risk of any premature closure of sociological theorizing is much smaller than in Parsons's day, when he set out to conquer the commanding heights of American sociology. The hopes of rapid scientific advances—even in the looser Franco-German conception of science— are also less bold today, so the "right" choice of an overall disciplinary strategy is not taken as seriously as it was forty or fifty years ago. However, what suffers in today's pluralist competition is theoretical work on sociological articles of wide-ranging everyday use. The usefulness of such work tends to be inversely correlated with the best way of making a theoretical career. The former had better not express itself either in catchy personal neologisms or in novel theoretical discourses that seek the dazzling effects of stardom. Theories of middle height, by contrast, do not aspire to tower above the bulk of sociological practice: They aim for the widest possible range of application.

A theory of norms, or, better, a theory of normative action, would be a theory of middle height in this sense.[7] While neither a grand theoretical scheme nor necessarily even part of one, it is a wide-ranging theory aimed at encompassing a vast number of social phenomena. While drawn to the moral dimension of human action and society, a theory of norms would be reticent to address fundamental or foundational issues. It would instead concentrate on specifying the range of normative action and systems of action and on finding out what determines variation in the strength of norms and in the content of norms. In general, it would clarify the explanatory power of norms.

As a discipline, sociology would benefit a great deal from hard and concentrated work on theories of middle height. Apart from norms and normative action, there are several other very important topics suitable for and in strong need of such theorization: identity, social cognition (reviving the sociology of knowledge), institutions, the dynamics of value change—and even networks/social capital, where a respectable amount of work is being done.

This chapter, however, is more modest. It limits itself to reflecting upon the tasks of a more elaborate theorization about norms and normative action in the face of the recent challenge from rational choice theory and the lately reinvigorated debate between sociology and economics.

## Normative and Non-Normative Action

Unless otherwise specified, a norm is taken here as a statement—implicit or explicit—about a course of action that is either a proscription or a prescription. A norm in this sense says Do!, or Don't! By normative action, I mean action wholly or mainly driven by the actor's norms. The variation of normative action is, therefore, basically the variability of the actors, not that of the situations they are in. Determinant is the intrinsic message of the norm, not the consequences of following it in different situations. From the perspective of empirical research, the direction and the variation of normative action are better explained by actors' norms and their variation than by the variable cost–benefit outcomes of the situations of action.[8]

On the other hand, while all normative action is basically actor-driven rather than situation-driven, the opposite does not hold. Structuralist, including social network, explanations of action derive from the structural location of the actor, not from his/her norms. Sociological man, contrary to the argument of some people, is not necessarily norm-ruled.

I do not pursue here norms other than prescriptive/proscriptive ones—such as norms that are definitions—other than to point to one similarity between the malfunctioning of definitional and prescriptive norms. Normative expectations remain correct, even if mistaken, and albeit disappointments are interpreted differently in the three cases (of definition, description, and prescription). What does not correspond to a definitional norm is not genuine; it is false. What differs significantly from the state or the curve of normalcy is abnormal, deviant.[9] Action not according to normative prescription is incorrect, unjust. As long as the norm is valid, it is not affected by mistaken expectations, and in principle the validity of the norm, in all three mentioned senses of the word, is unlimited (compare Luhmann 1991, 69). Here is an important aspect of the contribution of norms to social order.

There are many kinds of prescriptive norms, but I am not certain much is gained by a major classificatory effort. Different sorts of norms seem to have different depths, though. To the extent that this holds, an ordering of norms can be useful. One distinction that I have found useful is that between norms of conduct, execution, and distribution.[10] The first refers to people's behavior in certain social worlds, that is, to actions that pertain to their individual and collective identity. The second refers to people's contributions to a social system, as a husband, an employee, or a citizen. Distributive norms, finally, regulate people's allocations of risks and opportunities, rewards and sanctions, the products of their social effort.

Norms are usually not single rules, but rather form parts of hierarchically ordered systems, ranging from supreme principles to rules of situational application (compare Habermas 1992, 25, 309). This provides normative action with an intrinsic flexibility often overlooked both by rationalists and their critics. Placing Merton's (1957, 140) approach in a slightly different context, we may distinguish three modalities of normative action: innovative, conformist, and ritualistic. They are listed in ascending order of loyalty to the most situationally specific norms of behavior in a system. While the precise location of their boundaries may be open to interpretation, the innovator, the conformist, and the ritualist are clearly recognizable types in the operation of religious, political, and occupational systems.

With a focus on normative action, the source of norms becomes secondary, whether the law, a current and proximate social milieu, or an object of identification more distant in time and space. Normative action encompasses any action governed by legal, social, and moral norms. Still, the actor's relationship to the source is important, and I shall return to this issue below.

In this light, James Coleman's (1990, 243) way of defining a norm is not very fruitful, namely, that "a norm exists only when others assume the right to affect the direction an actor's action will take." This definition's relevance to a theory of normative action is undermined by the fact that he never elaborates the self–other distinction underlying it. Yet, Coleman makes at least three major contributions to a theory of norms. First, he offers a catching interpretation of the meaning of social norms.[11] For him, social norms cope with the "externalities of action," with how my actions create problems for others. Second, he makes a very illuminating distinction between different kinds of relations between the targets and the beneficiaries of norms (ibid., 248). Third, he charts some of the conditions for "the realization of effective norms" (ibid., ch. 11).

Coleman's work highlights an irony of contemporary sociology. Since Merton's (1957, ch. 5) work on anomie, the main impetus for theorization and investigation of norms has come from people skeptical about their importance, from proponents of individualist rational choice who are concerned about the latter's limits.[12]

For some purposes it may be useful to distinguish normative action from *normatively oriented* action, although the boundary may often be difficult to establish empirically. There are different ways of taking the normative situation into account when deciding upon a course of action, what the law says, the normative conceptions of other people, and so forth. This taking into account may be, at one pole, only a purely instrumental cost–benefit calculation (e.g., the risks of breaking the law or otherwise offending the norms of others) and, at the other, following a norm (e.g., always abiding by the law, always paying attention to others). Whereas the poles isolate non-normative and normative action, respectively, in between there is a range of possibilities, a range of normatively oriented action.

The nonconsequentialist feature of normative action should not be left unqualified, however.[13] Normative action disregards the consequences for the actor but not necessarily for others. Max Weber ([1919] 1988, 551) once made a famous distinction between *Verantwortungsethik* (ethics of responsibility) and *Gesinnungsethik* (ethics of ultimate ends) that pinpointed the difference between consequentialist and nonconsequentialist normative action. Contemporary legal systems have moved away from the classical maxim of legality, *Fiat iustitia, pereat mundus* (Let justice be done, may the world perish), into consequentialist applications of law (compare Luhmann 1991, 68–69).

## On the Variability of Normative Action

Normative action should be seen as a variable rather than a taxonomic category. Under what conditions do actors act more or less according to norms? It seems that four conditions are crucial, and they place themselves in a two-dimensional property space. One dimension is that of the two basic elements of explanations of action, the actor and the situation; the other is the temporal dimension of the extension of the two, synchronic or diachronic. We then see that the power of norms should vary with:

1. The social context of the actor.
2. The actor's socialization history.
3. The location of the situation in the context of a system of action.
4. The location in history of the situation and of the pertinent system of action.

   In the following subsections I focus on the first two conditions and on the effect of the history of the situation. I focus on condition 3 and the pertinent system of action in the next major section below.

### The Social Context of the Actor

Looking at the first condition, my first point is that the more homogeneous the normative environment and the more insulated it is from other conceptions of action, the more normative action should be expected. This is, of course, the sociological logic of cloisters, communes, and totalitarian states. But there is also another sociological logic involved. Other things being equal, any sociological perspective should lead us to expect that the more economic and social inequality there is, the more heterogeneous the normative environment and the less normative the action. In other words, there is a trade-off between the freedom of the privileged and their security from crime. Inequality may also give rise to normative rebellion against perceived injustice, but that is another issue, to which I shall return below.

   My second point is that other things being equal, too, the frequency of action according to norms should be expected to vary positively with the visibility, or

scrutinizability, of the action. This is not the same thing as arguing that normative action depends on monitoring and the risks of discovery. This would be a
rationalist reduction. Rather, my thesis is that action in accordance with norms
comprises a spectrum of reasons, from instrumental calculation to normative
action, and that normatively oriented action is directly affected by visibility.
Over time, indirect effects on the behavior of actors who had internalized norms
are also likely via the effects of homogeneous environment. If I see a lot of
people breaking the prevailing norm and getting away with it, this is likely to
bring me and others like me to ask whether it is worthwhile to follow the norm.
The answer to this question is not determined, but it is probable that some will
answer it negatively.

My third point holds in similar ways, namely, that direct and indirect, the
amount of normative action should correlate positively with actors' dependence
on a norm-carrying ambience (compare Hechter 1987; Coleman 1990, 379). Actors are more likely to act normatively in relation to workmates and comembers of
organizations and gangs than to absent owners, customers, and members of other
organizations and gangs. But dependence is not sufficient to determine the lateral
extension of normative action. In addition, there is also the identification effect of
"imagined communities" (Anderson 1983). To the extent that human community
is imagined to end at the boundary of the nation, normative action ends there, too.
The other is subhuman, whether Jew, Gypsy, Slav, Ustasha, Chetnik, Turk, or
something else. The breakup of Yugoslavia has reproduced a good deal of the
ugliest sides of World War II. The range of normative action weakens beyond the
range of collective identification. The stronger the identification of the actor with
the norm source, the stronger and more stable the normative action.

One empirical implication of this is that the norm-following conduct of actors
A through N is affected by what happens to S (the source). If the latter is
weakened or discredited, or becomes more distant socially—through whatever
process of differentiation—the less the norms of S will be followed. Actors may,
of course, identify with another norm source. But this is likely to take some time.
So, ceteris paribus, less/more identification with a given norm source should
yield weaker/stronger normative action. A norm source may be anybody: your
mother, your older brother, your local community, the church, a management
guru, a political party, and so forth. But some norm sources are very unlikely
ever to be identified with. Their capacity to instill normative action then tends to
be nil. Jailers and prison wardens are an obvious example, in spite of their
monitoring facilities and the prisoners' dependence on them.

My fifth point is that the stability of normative action also depends on the
depth of internalization. The more deeply internalized a norm, the less susceptible it is to external modification and change. Social prescriptions and proscrip-
tions are not of one piece. Rather, they should be seen as perched on a ladder
down into the self of the actor. Those further down in the well of action are not
likely to be perceived by the actor as norms or obligations but rather as the

natural or human way of doing things (compare Turner 1989, 96–97). When they are not followed by the actor or by his/her milieu, the effect is one of revulsion, disgust, shame. And vice versa, following them has no connotation of constraint.

My hypothesis is that internalization varies with the character of the norm and with the socialization of the actor. The norms most amenable to deep internalization seem to be those having to do with the conception of self, with one's body and person, needs, integrity, and honor.[14] The deepest norms tend to be norms of personal conduct rather than executive or distributive norms of fairness and justice, although the latter also vary widely in their degree of internalization. These deep norms vary across civilizations and between classes and genders of the same civilization. Some of the best examples refer to norms of edible foods and cleanliness and hygiene. An everyday example common to contemporary Western societies is gender differences in internalizing norms of cleanliness. Women seem to have a tendency to internalize the latter more deeply, which creates friction in many couples. Modern women easily face two unattractive alternatives: either do unjustly more household chores than their male companions, or feel disgust at the amount of dirt insouciantly tolerated by the latter.

Finally, my sixth point, without claiming exhaustiveness, is that the prevalent modality of normative action, whether innovative, conformist, or ritualistic, tends to vary with the social status of the actor in the pertinent normative milieu. Under conditions of stable power relations, innovative action is most likely to originate with actors with the most resources, and ritualistic action with those having the least resources; the highest proportion of conformists should be found in the middle. Several reasons may contribute to this pattern, including variations in knowledge of alternatives, margins for experimentation, and risks of being sanctioned by others.

### The Actor's Socialization History

Turning to the second condition, the effects of the actor's history of socialization, the longer and the more devoted the process of socialization of the actor, the more prone he/she should be to normative action. The longer you have been employed or the longer you have been a member of some organization, the more I would expect you to have internalized the norms of the organization. However, devotion and commitment are likely to be more important than time. So, we had better look out for what might determine the former at the societal as well as at the family level. Here, I think the crucial variable is the self-confidence of the agencies of socialization.

Normative action is basically inner-directed, either by the internal processes of the individual actor or by that of the collective of which she or he is a part. Inner-directedness presupposes a certain amount of self-confidence, the capacity of the self to steer its own course regardless of outside pressures. Without it, it does not make any sense to inculcate an inner compass of conduct into one's children, pupils, or members. Self-confidence in this sense is a social and a historical variable. It varies among parents, and it varies across societies. It may be regarded as a product of a basic trust in certain important aspects of the environment instilled by early socialization (compare Moore 1978, 109).

Self-confidence comes either from the experience of success in realizing one's goals or from the embrace of transcendental values. Other things being equal, then, we should expect the children of religiously or otherwise ideologically committed parents and/or of successful parents, and of ideological or successful communities and societies, to be more normatively socialized than those of failed or defeated parents and societies.

For the Mediterranean societies in general and for Sicily in particular, the Swiss ethnologist Christian Giordano (1992) has pointed to the anomic effects among those "betrayed by history" (compare Banfield 1958). The important thing with success here, though, is hardly the amount of it but rather the divide between realization and failure or defeat/decline. In class terms, then, my hypothesis is not that the amount of normative socialization is a linear function of parental socioeconomic success. It is that downwardly mobile, marginalized, or marginal parents should be expected to devote less energy to the socialization of their children than those of other classes.

Apart from the time and the intensity of one's socialization, one's likelihood of acting normatively is significantly affected by the continuity or discontinuity of one's biography, from socialization as a child or an adult to one's current context of action. In other words, the more social upheaval over time, the more mobility—horizontal or vertical—between different social milieus, the more instrumental and the less normative the action. The breakdown of a previous strong normative order should be particularly favorable to egoistic instrumentalism. Contemporary China and Russia illustrate this dramatically. Less drastically, rapidly upwardly mobile parents should be expected, other things being equal, to be less committed to normative action, as well as to the normative socialization of their children, than stable or only incrementally mobile ones.

In short, lack of self-confidence coming from social failure or defeat and a self-confidence bolstered by an eminently lucky biographical rupture are both likely to affect negatively the normative action of the offspring.

### The Effect of the History of the Situation

Looking at the fourth condition, the history of the situation of action also impinges upon the expectability of normative action.

The interaction of norm and interest produces certain threshold effects. If the reward for normatively deviant action suddenly increases, or if previous social controls suddenly lapse, we should expect a sizable increase in instrumental action. Alternatively, if the reward system suddenly departs negatively from previous custom, we should expect a surge in collective action driven by a sense of injustice. Over time a certain moral economy tends to get established, whatever its origin, and attempts to change it are likely to trigger normative rebellion on the part of the disadvantaged (compare Thompson 1991 and Swenson 1989). The point is not, of course, that the disadvantaged are likely to protest against a change, something any rational choice theorist would also tell you, but rather that time tends to leave a moral patina on any state of affairs and that, therefore, the losers of change are likely to react with a sense of moral outrage out of proportion to the absolute amount of change proposed (i.e., much more strongly and united than against the same amount of change from a recent baseline). Whether this means that moral outrage is more strongly correlated with duration than with the size of what is lost is a hypothesis worth probing.

### Role-Plays, Markets, and Power Plays

Although now perhaps out of fashion, there was something fruitful to the society–economy conception of Parsons and Smelser (1956) as one of system and subsystems. It seems pertinent to distinguish systems of action characterized by different normal, that is, usually expected, determinants. In this vein we may distinguish normative and non-normative systems of action, each defined by a typical set of expectations. We are not excluding the possibility or actual occurrence of deviation from expected behavior.

But we should also be aware of another fruitful distinction in this context, namely, that between the constitution or the framework of a system of action and expectations with regard to moves within it. In other words, I postulate without argument the old Durkheimian thesis about the noncontractual elements of the contract. It appears no longer to be a bone of contention with neoclassicists, from James Buchanan to Douglass North. For anyone doubting its truth, the experiences of the former USSR in getting markets to function in the absence of a reliable legal framework of property rights, agency rules, and so forth should serve as a good reminder. What is normatively regulated about markets is, above all, it should be emphasized, their character as systems of choice.[15] To be able to function as systems of voluntary exchange, markets need to have their participants protected against regular lapses and compensated for any occasional lapses.

In spite of the logic of the four cells shown in Table 6.2, there are, in fact, only three social systems of action. The parentheses around Personal Morality is meant to indicate that, although this kind of action fortunately does occur, and although its frequency is at least conceivably amenable to sociological explanation, it is an individual line of action. It refers to the actions of the Prince Myshkins or the Oskar Schindlers.

The systems of action do not necessarily exhaust social action. Systemness is defined in terms of expectations, and many actions occur not only unexpectedly but also in the absence of any clear expectations at all. Depending on how

Table 6.2

**Systems of Action**

|  | Framework of action | |
| Field of action | Normative | Non-normative |
| --- | --- | --- |
| Normative | Role plays | (Personal morality) |
| Non-normative | Markets | Power plays |

strictly and narrowly we define expectations—in terms of specification, range, and stability—the systemness of action will vary. I think a rather narrow conception of systemness is the more promising strategy at this stage of theorizing. This gives us some islands of relatively firm ground from which we may set sail later and with less formidable tasks of navigation. The boundaries between the systems of action are permeable, but (in principle) not fuzzy. An actor usually has an effective option of crossing the boundary, but not without risk. Transgression is trespass. Within a given system of action, however, norms may enter as constraints to market action and, vice versa, considerations of the outcome may facilitate role enactment.

The most important normative framework of modern societies is constituted by law. Power plays, then, are enacted in the interstices or beyond the reach of law. However, if we stick to a narrow sense of systemness, power plays should also have something patterned to them. There may be a definite set of actors and a definite, interdependent set of goals among the actors. The most important power plays are interstate relations, although from the Nuremberg trials, the UN Charter, and the Council of Europe a normative framework is being built. There are also nonstate social relations, that is, systems of action either in the absence of a state legal framework (such as when states break up or down) or in areas where the legal order is suspended or normally evaded. In summary, personal morality is not a social system, and power plays occur primarily outside law. By contrast, in stable modern societies, role-plays and markets make up the most important systems of action.[16] Markets are all systems of action in which sets of suppliers and demanders, observing one another, try to get as much as they can out of situations of action under the constraint of a framework of voluntary exchange. Their competition under these conditions is what gives the market its systematic quality, its marketness. Such markets may well comprise a "marriage market," a dance-place or singles-bar "sex market," as well as product, labor, or financial markets.

While underscoring that well-functioning markets are normatively regulated and that market actors may bring normative considerations to bear upon their strategic behavior, I distinguish markets from another kind of stable, regulated system of action. Role-play seems an appropriate concept (as the normative counterpart to markets). We may define a role as a set of normatively expected courses of action. It ties in with the neoclassical sociological role concept (compare Merton 1957, 368). I would also suggest it to be useful to accept Giddens's (1984, 86) criterion for applying the latter, that is, to "definite settings of interaction in which the normative definition of 'expected' modes of conduct is particularly pronounced." We may define a role as a set of normatively expected courses of action.

The recourse to the theatrical metaphor of "play" is intended to convey that we are concerned here with action rather than with structure, to which the usual notion of role structure would be more apt. Role-plays are social scripts that actors may interpret and enact differently and that may be staged differently by superordinate powers, that is, directors. In role-plays actors act according to their roles, like theater or film actors acting their parts of the script. The systemness is constituted by the role-set, the set of encounters regulated by a particular, at least implicitly coherent, body of norms. Role-plays may be nested, like a play containing a plot and subplots.

Acting in social role-plays is both normative and normatively oriented. At the margin it may even be quite instrumental. What is decisive in the jargon of choice theory is a lexicographical ordering of actions, in other words, courses of action that are not tradable. You may very well try to be the best and the highest rewarded of all actors, but you are not allowed to trade your play and your part in the play for that of another. As an actress portraying Miss Julie, for instance, you have a choice of interpretations that may be governed by ogling at the probability of critical or public success. But in order to portray Miss Julie, there are a number of actions you have to do, and a number of ones you cannot, regardless of their cost or benefit. And you are not allowed to trade a part of your Miss Julie role against a part of your excellent capacity for portraying, say, Mary Stuart.[17]

In role-plays every part has a value, but none has a price. But how valuable are social role-plays? Giddens (1989) apparently considers them insignificant, like many other postfunctionalist theorists. In a more than 700-page-long treatise, "role" is mentioned only once, in passing, and it is listed in neither the glossary of basic concepts nor the important terms. I think this view is mistaken. Every modern society has at least two major social theaters in which important role-plays are performed every day. One is the world of work, with its huge number of job-roles, each with its norms about what to do, what not to do, and how to do it. It should be added that jobs are roles, even if the job is to operate on the market. The salesman, too, has his part.

Even the professor of neoclassical economics at a private university has a script to act, that is, of teaching certain things at certain specified times, of how to relate to the president, to the dean, to colleagues of various rank, to students, to organizations and people outside the university. Let us grant that he is likely to respond to economic incentives, but as long as he is a university professor he is largely bound by academic norms, or else he risks sanctioning if discovered violating them. A professor of neoclassical economics is not expected to trade grades or results of research to the highest bidder, for instance.

The other major social theater is that of organized representation, with its plays of democratic politics, association, and lobbying. What a government minister, a politician, a delegate, or a representative may or may not, must or must not do is largely prescribed by constitutions and statutes, directives, and public opinion. Less specific than working or representing, and therefore less useful in explanation, is speaking or writing a language in which parts are allocated by the grammar, syntax, and pragmatics of the language. Language and communication are, characteristically, the big holes in James Coleman's (1990) 950-page-long foundations of social theory. While cautiously refraining from any unreconnoitered forays into the sociology of language, I would add that even though linguistic norms, and their human variety, are not very easy to squeeze into rational choice interpretations of "the emergence of norms," the former should not be taken as given either. Because languages and linguistic norms have changed and are changing, a theory of norms and normative action should include a theory of language change.

The enacting of normative role-plays constitutes "obligatory action" or "rule-following" behavior in the sense of March and Olsen (1989, ch. 2). But norms are more specific than the "rules" of March and Olsen and many other "institutionalists." For them, rules are "the routines, procedures, conventions, roles, strategies, organizational forms, and technologies around which political activity is constructed. We also mean the beliefs, paradigms, codes, cultures, and knowledge that surround, support, elaborate, and contradict those roles and routines" (1989, ch. 2).

The extent of normative role action depends on the strength of role-plays in a given society rather than on the rewards or sanctions offered in situations of action. Whether you can bribe somebody in an occupational role, private or public, is likely to depend more on the kind of society the role-incumbent is in than on the size of the bribe. In some societies, most people are corrupt; in others, the corrupt are only the exceptions.

Markets and role-plays more often have a symbiotic than a competitive relationship. In many contexts, markets allocate the tickets to the plays going on. The labor market allocates tickets to the occupational role-plays, the electoral market to the plays of representations, and the sex and marriage markets allocate the tickets to the family plays.

The interrelationships among personal morality, power plays, role-plays, and markets vary historically. Indeed, it may be argued that they constitute a central part of the history of modernity. In this context, however, I confine myself to post–World War II history. Both the world of work and that of organized representation have probably become more strongly normative in the past half-century. Professionalization as well as general service jobs, tend to increase the norming of work, including the importance of learning and internalizing norms about how work should be done. The growth of associations and the tendency toward more media scrutiny of politicians increase the significance of norms of representation.

On the other hand, there are also large areas in which role conduct has clearly decreased in recent decades. Roles of gender, age, and family have, on the whole, strongly eroded. Over the long historical run, one may suspect that agrarian, industrial—now postindustrial—urban, and personal modernity have involved a decline in work and family norms/roles, whereas civic and political modernity have spawned more political ones. Without focused empirical investigation it would be foolhardy to assert anything about the net historical development of social roles in the recent period. Then again, such an inquiry may be interpreted as part of the research agenda generated by a theory of norms and normative action.

## Why Norms Change

Norms provide a concrete direction to normative action. As such, the variation of the former is subordinated to that of the latter. People either act normatively or not, and if they do, then the question arises, according to which norms? However, the variability of norms constitutes an important object of investigation itself, and I offer the following hypothesis: The power and the content of a given (body of) norm(s) are likely to change for five reasons, at least.

First, change occurs because of a change in the significance of the actions, and not only to the beneficiaries of the norm. From Coleman (1990, 248) we learn the distinction between beneficiaries and targets of a norm and the extent of their variability. Long before, Merton (1957, chs. 4–5) taught us the differentiating impact of the social structure upon conformity and nonconformity to norms. Between a norm source and its targets or carriers we should expect differentiation, and thereby friction or tension. This provides us with some important sociological entries into the processes of norm formation and change.

One proposition is that norms attenuate over time and, in the long run, become obsolete or unimportant to their beneficiaries. This, in turn, follows from beneficiaries' changed conditions and the changing sources of their rewards. For instance, the strict norms imposed upon the members of combat units—whether military, political, or religious—will lose their significance to unit leaders during times of peace and compromise. Or, the conduct of children becomes less important to parents who work outside the home and whose pay is sufficient to support the family. At the same time (during the nineteenth and early twentieth centuries), the significance of children increased to nation and state builders who were concerned with developing and recruiting conscript armies. Thus, prevailing norms about children change with the significance attributed to children (compare Therborn 1993).

Similarly, the introduction of market elements into role-plays, such as into public health services or public bureaucracies, is a signal that the norms of professionalism and public service have become less significant. The net outcome of such changes cannot be predicted from a theory of norms alone. But the latter should lead us to expect a decline in the observance of norms of, for example, professional integrity, honesty, and objectivity.

Second, when the relations of power between the targets and beneficiaries of a norm change, the norm's stringency and, in cases of major power change, its target are likely to change, too. When women gain access to employment and/or education, the sway of male power and patriarchal norms is likely to decrease. There may then emerge norms of gender equality and antisexism, with men as targets. Likewise, the legitimate power of the boss varies with his relative strength vis-à-vis employees. Furthermore, changes in social relations of power tend to lead to political as well as judicial changes through new legislation as well as new interpretations of existing laws. A discrepancy between the power of the norm source and others' identification with the norm is likely to result in patterned, or "institutionalized" norm evasion, that is, in tacit counternorms (compare Sztompka 1986, 218 on Merton).

Third, to the extent that identification with a given norm source[18] changes, the strength of this norm (complex) in relation to other possible norms will change correspondingly. That is, normative action tends to increase and to stabilize with the success of the norm source in its own terms and, correspondingly, to weaken with the weakening of the norm source. The spread of religions and political ideologies, with their specific calls for normative action, is governed by the competitive force of the religions/ideologies in question. True, identification with a norm source is not reducible to the latter's success or failure. There is always leeway for tragic or heroic identifications. Yet, with this probabilistic qualification, the thesis holds true, I would suppose, at least until I am convinced otherwise by empirical research, the provocation of which I would happily acknowledge.

Fourth, norms are always subject to interpretations, which also tend to change over time. Routine is a leveler, not only a resistant to change. Routine accounts for a certain amount of norm erosion, while certainly stopping far short of leaving the realm of normatively oriented action. The words of the norm source are subject to interpretation by norm carriers, and the ensuing routines may be seen as resulting from an equilibrating process between the values and interests of the source and the carriers. Still, a certain amount of norm (re)interpretation, or norm erosion, may be necessary for an operation to function as expected. This interesting aspect of normative life is highlighted by the occasional recourse by employees to "work to rule," which is not a special treat of servility but a weapon of trade union struggle against the employer.

Fifth, new knowledge of effects of action tends to push new norms. Norms are significantly driven by prevailing conceptions of knowledge. Recent medical knowledge about the relationship between smoking, cancer, and the effects of passive smoking, that is, the externalities of smoking, have given rise to a massive body of new norms against smoking. However, knowledge is not necessarily scientific. New social forces coming, for instance, out of changes in the division of labor generate their own specific knowledge about society and social action, and thereby push new sets of norms. More generally, any body of norms is at risk with each new generation, which has new experiences of the world and is prone to alter the priorities of prescription and proscription.

## Unpacking Institutionalism

Institutionalism has become a catchall for everybody dissatisfied with neoclassical economics and rational choice. Around institutions gather people from economics (Hodgson 1988; Williamson 1985), economic history (North 1990), politics (March and Olsen 1984; 1989), and sociology (Powell and DiMaggio 1991; Granovetter 1991), and from the war camp of rational choice (Hechter, Opp, and Wippler 1990). However, there is little consensus about what it is they gather around. And whatever it is, it usually is perceived only according to vague contours. Valiant efforts at conceptual clarification, such as those by Jepperson (1991) and Ostrom (1986), highlight the complexity of the phenomenon of institutions.

The bundle of institutions needs to be untied. Norms and normative action are one part, and to clarify and specify them is to unpack the big bag of institutionalism.[19] A theory of norms and normative action can also contribute to the two important agendas of socioeconomics and communitarianism that Amitai Etzioni has drawn up.

## Notes

1. The latter may sometimes be referred to as the "situation" of the actor, but that situation is a more or less permanent feature of the actor, not to be conflated with the circumstances of a piece of action to be explained. The alternatives are culturally defined or "structurally patterned" (compare Stinchcombe 1975, 14 ff.) in relation to which action situations are not held to "differ very importantly." In his analysis of arguably the most lucid of sociological explainers, Robert Merton, what Stinchcombe calls "the socially structured alternatives" (ibid., 12) in Merton's theory are, in fact, the actor-situation distinction used here, alternatives "structured" by the actor's cultural belonging and structural location.

2. Compare G. Therborn, "Sociology as a Discipline," 1994.

3. Etzioni has given us at least one more great work of grand theory, *The Active Society*.

4. The Society for the Advancement of Socio-Economics (SASE). See also Etzioni and Lawrence (1991).

5. Merton then reacted to a paper by Talcott Parsons presented at the 1947 meeting of the American Sociological Association. See Merton (1968, ch. 3).

6. As would not, presumably, Etzioni, since he has operated at both levels.

7. Such a theory would, of course, fall into what Merton explicitly called a theory of middle range (Merton 1968, 40), but so would, for example, a "theory of mobility into topmost positions in groups" (ibid., 61). The issue here is not where to draw a line of demarcation between a theory of middle range and one of middle height. My intention, from the height of Merton's shoulders, is only to point to a situation and a problem, which Merton had less reason to bother with in the forties or even in the sixties.

8. From the importance and the legitimacy accorded to interpretative theory in both economics and sociology, it is realistic to expect a considerable area of action for which the "better" explanation will largely be a matter of different theoretical taste.

9. The disciplinary and coercive potentiality of this use of the norm is highlighted by Foucault (1977, 184 ff).

10. This trio corresponds in part to philosophical conceptions of justice as commutative, social or productive, and distributive, but, in particular, norms of conduct match only occasionally with commutative norms of fair exchange.

11. I prefer the more agnostic "meaning" to the more pretentious "origin" or "function," as coping with "the externalities of action," with problems having to do with my actions affecting other people as well.

12. Ullmann-Margalit (1977) is another example, from a narrow game-theoretical perspective. Significant sociological works in between, though, are Moore (1978), Popitz (1980), and Rossi and Berk (1986).

13. As it is, for example, in J. Elster's (1989, ch. 3) otherwise significant contribution.

14. Another formulation of these kinds of deeply internalized norms of conduct is Pierre Bourdieu's (1979, 190) concept of "habitus."

15. And not of force or fraud.

16. It should be noted that I am not talking about the economy and the noneconomy. That is another distinction cutting across the present one of markets and role-plays. After all, there are, or there were, market economies and nonmarket economies.

17. A game is also a role-play in the same sense. When playing soccer, for instance, you are not allowed to trade your preference for, say, boxing.

18. Merton (1957, 357th ff.) dealt with this issue in the context of "reference groups."

19. The big task of unpacking the institutional argument is looked at from a different angle by Richard Scott (1991).

## References

Anderson, B. 1983. *Imagined Communities*. London: Verso.

Banfield, E. 1958. *The Moral Basis of a Backward Society*. New York: Free Press.

Becker, G. 1976. *The Economic Approach to Human Behavior*. Chicago: University of Chicago Press.

———. 1991. *A Treatise on the Family*. Cambridge, MA: Harvard University Press, rev. ed.

———. 1993. "Nobel Lecture: The Economic Way of Looking at Behavior." *Journal of Political Economy* 101: 385–409.

Bourdieu, P. 1979. *La Distinction*. Paris: Ed. de Minuit.

Burt, R. 1993. "The Social Structure of Competition." In *Explorations in Economic Sociology*, ed. R. Swedberg, 65–103. New York: Russell Sage Foundation.

Coleman, J. 1990. *Foundations of Social Theory*. Cambridge, MA: Belknap Press.

Elster, J. 1989. *The Cement of Society*. Cambridge: Cambridge University Press.

Etzioni, A. 1968. *The Active Society.* New York: Free Press.

————. 1988. *The Moral Dimension.* New York: Free Press.

Etzioni, A., and Lawrence, P., eds. 1991. *Socio-Economics.* Armonk, NY: M.E. Sharpe.

Foucault, M. 1977. *Discipline and Punishment.* New York: Pantheon.

Giddens, A. 1984. *The Constitution of Society.* Cambridge, UK: Polity Press.

————. 1989. *Sociology.* Cambridge, UK: Polity Press.

Giordano, C. 1992. *Die Betrogenen der Geschichte.* Frankfurt: Campus.

Granovetter, M. 1985. "Economic Action and Social Structure: The Problem of Embeddedness." *American Journal of Sociology* 91: 481–510.

————. "The Social Construction of Economic Institutions." In Etzioni and Lawrence 1991, 75–81.

Habermas, J. 1992. *Faktizität und Geltung.* Frankfurt: Suhrkamp.

Harsanyi, J. 1982. *Papers in Game Theory.* Doordrecht: D. Reidel.

Hechter, M. 1987. *Principles of Group Solidarity.* Berkeley: University of California Press.

Hechter, M.; Opp, K-D; and Wippler, R., eds. 1990. *Social Institutions.* New York: Aldine de Gruyter.

Hodgson, G. 1988. *Economics and Institutions: A Manifesto for a Modern Institutional Economics.* Philadelphia: University of Pennsylvania Press.

Jepperson, R. 1991. "Institutions, Institutional Effects, and Institutionalism." In Powell and DiMaggio.

Luce, R.D., and Raiffa, H. 1957. *Games and Decisions.* New York: Wiley.

Luhmann, N. 1991. *Soziologie des Risikos.* Berlin: de Gruyter.

March, J., and Olsen, J. 1984. "The New Institutionalism: Organizational Factors in Political Life." *American Political Science Review* 78: 734–49.

————. 1989. *Rediscovering Institutions.* London: Macmillan.

Merton, R. 1957. *Social Theory and Social Structure.* 2d ed. Glencoe, IL: Free Press.

————. 1968. *Social Theory and Social Structure.* 3d ed. New York: Free Press.

Moore, B., Jr. 1978. *Injustice: The Social Bases of Obedience and Revolt.* New York: M.E. Sharpe.

North, D. 1990. *Institutions, Institutional Change and Economic Performance.* Cambridge: Cambridge University Press.

Ostrom, E. 1986. "An Agenda for the Study of Institutions." *Public Choice* 48: 3–25.

Parsons, T., and Smelser, N. 1956. *Economy and Society.* Glencoe, IL: Free Press.

Popitz, H. 1980. *Die normative Konstruktion der Gesellschaft.* Tübingen: J.C.B. Mohr.

Powell, W., and DiMaggio, P., eds. 1991. *The New Institutionalism in Organizational Analysis.* Chicago: University of Chicago Press.

Przeworski, A. 1986. "Le défi de la méthodologie individualiste à l'analyse marxiste." In *Sur l'individualisme,* eds. P. Birnbaum and J. Leca, 77–106. Paris: Presses de la Fondation Nationale des Sciences Politiques.

Rossi, P., and Berk, R. 1986. "A Conceptual Framework for Measuring Norms." In *The Social Fabric,* ed. J. Short, 7–105. Beverly Hills, CA: Sage.

Scott, R. "Unpacking Institutional Arguments." In Powell and DiMaggio 1991, 164–82.

Scull, A. 1988. "Deviance and Social Control." In *Handbook of Sociology,* ed. N. Smelser, 667–93. Newbury Park, CA: Sage.

Stigler, G., and Becker, G. 1977. "De Gustibus Non Est Disputandum." *American Economic Review* 67: 76–90.

Stinchcombe, A. 1975. "Merton's Theory of Social Structure." In *The Idea of Social Structure Papers in Honor of Robert K. Merton,* ed. L. Closer, 11–33. New York: Harcourt Brace Jovanovich.

Swenson, P. 1989. *Fair Shares.* Ithaca, NY: Cornell University Press.

Sztompka, P. 1986. *Robert K. Merton: An Intellectual Profile.* London: Macmillan.
Therborn, G. 1976. *Science, Class and Society.* London: Verso.
————. 1993. "The Politics of Childhood: The Rights of Children in Modern Times." In *Families of Nations,* ed. F. Castles, 241–91. Aldershot, Dartmouth.
————. 1994. "Sociology as a Discipline of Disagreements and as a Paradigm of Competing Explanations: Culture, Structure and the Variability of Actors and Situations." In *Agency and Structure: Re-orienting Social Theory,* ed. P. Sztompka. Philadelphia: Gordon and Breach.
Thompson, E. 1991. *Customs in Common.* London: Merlin Press.
Tsebelis, G. 1990. *Nested Games.* Berkeley: University of California Press.
Turner, R. 1989. "The Paradox of Social Order." In *Theory Building on Sociology,* ed. J. Turner, 82–100. London: Sage.
Ullmann-Margalit, E. 1977. *The Emergence of Norms.* Oxford: Clarendon Press.
Weber, M. (1919) 1988. "Politik als Beruf." In *Gesammelte Politische Schriften.* Tübingen: J.C.B. Mohr.
Williamson, O. 1985. *The Economic Institutions of Capitalism: Firms, Markets, Relational Contracting.* New York: Free Press.

# 7

# Another Look at Etzioni's Concepts

*David Sciulli*

The conceptual decisions that major social theorists make early in their careers typically orient them across their later works. Talcott Parsons, for instance, drew a sharp line early between rational action and nonrational action and then spent his career exploring the analytical components of the nonrational realm as well as their implications for empirical research. To this end, he endeavored in the 1930s to identify within the nonrational realm a distinct arena of action, namely, "voluntaristic action." Throughout his career, Parsons felt that he could ground the cumulative findings of the social sciences by identifying the interrelationship between voluntaristic action and social order. On this ground he could translate into a common language the findings that social scientists discover at different levels of analysis, couched in the terminologies of different theories, disciplines, and methodologies. Everything that Parsons subsequently wrote from the 1950s through the 1970s about law and community, professions and universities, can be read as an ongoing effort on his part to identify how voluntaristic action is institutionalized and, with this, to account for the possibility of social order. Rarely do major social theorists reconsider or rework their earliest conceptual decisions.[1]

Amitai Etzioni made a significant set of conceptual decisions in his influential early work on organizations, and these decisions eventually led him to three other sets later in his career: (1) the decision that there is an irreducible or unalterable human nature, including an identifiable set of substantive human needs (namely, affection and recognition); (2) the decision that liberal democracy is not an automatic outcome of modernity itself or the product of some hidden hand (this decision eventually led Etzioni to call for a shoring up of the substantive norms of community; (3) the decision that rational action is "anti-

135

entropic," as opposed to following Weber and then Parsons in appreciating that rational action analytically defined disrupts institutional arrangements unique to contemporary democracy.

One purpose of this chapter is to explore the interrelationship among these conceptual decisions spanning Etzioni's writings from the 1960s into the 1990s.[2] I show that given his earlier approach to organizations, Etzioni was literally driven to the first two conceptual decisions as he sought a grounding or standard of comparison upon which to base his calls for an "active society" (Etzioni 1968), "responsive society" (Etzioni 1991), and "communitarianism" (Etzioni 1993). Etzioni needs a grounding because he wishes to establish that his criticisms of existing social arrangements involve more than his subjective interpretations of the times or his personal preferences for reform. Etzioni's move to his third conceptual decision—about rational action being anti-entropic—is consistent with his efforts to influence public policy making in the United States. He appreciates that only those criticisms and prescriptions consistent with the optimism of contemporary American pragmatism can gain influence in the policy-making arena. Those consistent with Weber's pathos or critical theorists' radicalism cannot expect to receive a hearing.

Taken together, Etzioni's conceptual decisions pose an important challenge to liberal complacency. They challenge the faith that a "hidden hand" not only brings supply and demand into equilibrium but also somehow yields automatically a benign social order, an institutional arrangement capable of supporting democracy. However, Etzioni's third conceptual decision not only blocks his social theory off from critical theorists' radicalism and Weber's pathos; more ironically, it distances him from appreciating the contemporary conceptual implications of the American founders' republican vigilance. It also brings a significant conceptual inconsistency into his own social theory. Put differently, the American founders' republican vigilance is itself inconsistent today with assumptions about institutional equilibrium that may be traced no earlier than to the late nineteenth century and the rise of American pragmatism and contemporary liberalism. In this light, Etzioni's rejection of liberal complacency moves him toward the founders' position (and toward Weber and critical theory). The problem is that the founders' republican vigilance is inconsistent with Etzioni's immediate turn to a grounding in substantive norms of human nature and in substantive norms of community. Republican vigilance instead rests on the grounding of a procedural normative mediation that, in turn, is unique to secure, fully established democracies.

Another purpose of this chapter is to present this procedural normative mediation and to demonstrate both its institutional significance and its contingency. I do so by drawing a conceptual distinction that Etzioni failed to draw in his work on organizations. I then use this distinction to shed light on some of the problems of interpretation with which he is currently grappling in the public policy arena. These problems begin to reveal why American pragmatism and contemporary liberalism are not likely to be augmented by the shared substantive norms of community that Etzioni has in mind (as do also Robert Bellah, Philip Selznick, Michael Sandel, and Alasdair MacIntyre). Rather, they are more likely to be augmented by extending republican vigilance from (1) the founders' concerns about the arbitrariness of government to (2) contemporary concerns about the arbitrariness of corporations, professions, and other intermediate associations that exercise collective power within American society. This is more likely, however, only to the extent that the American social order remains integrative, at least in part, rather than becoming more exclusively controlling. To be sure, this extending of republican vigilance can then frame communitarianism as envisioned by Etzioni and others. But my point is that Etzioni's three conceptual decisions in themselves neglect the need for this extension.

## From Organizational Compliance to Integration and Control

In *A Comparative Analysis of Complex Organizations* ([1961] 1975) Etzioni developed a middle-range theory suitable for the comparative empirical study of organizations by constructing models or ideal types of the sources of compliance within complex organizations.[3] Etzioni appreciated that Weber's ideal type of bureaucracy is not applicable to many existing organizations, and yet the only alternative model of compliance at the time was the one being offered by the human relations school. This alternative focused on workers' motivations, not on organizational structures (ibid., xiii).

In Etzioni's usage, compliance is a "relationship consisting of the power employed by superiors to control subordinates and the orientation of the subordinates to this power" (ibid., xv).[4] The importance of this definition, as Etzioni well appreciates, is that it combines structural and motivational factors in accounting for orderly organizational behavior. His point in combining these two sets of factors was that this permits him to explore the proposition that differences in the presence of both sets, and in how they are combined, can account for other differences among organizations. The latter include: differences in organizational goals, differences in organizational representatives' behavior, and differences in the extent of consensus and type of communication within organizations. Etzioni's first major conceptual decision in his already promising career, therefore, was his assertion that there are three major sources of intraorganizational compliance, namely, coercion, economic or pecuniary incentives, and normative values. He added that these same three sources also provide the foundations for social order overall (see note 3). Thus, he concludes that three ideal types exhaust the possible types of compliance and types of social order more generally: coercive, utilitarian or remunerative, and normative.

Missing from Etzioni's typology, however, is a conceptual distinction that crosscuts each of his three types of compliance, and the reason it is missing is that Etzioni treated the sociocultural or institutional context of contemporary democratic societies as given (ibid., xx).[5] The distinction I have in mind is that between organizational compliance or social order that rests on individuals' demonstrable social control and organizational compliance or social order that rests in some part on individuals' possible social integration.

Organization constituents' compliance or orderly behavior is possibly based on their social integration when they can at least recognize and understand in common what is being expected of them. Put more precisely, it rests on their at least recognizing and understanding in common the shared social duties that are being sanctioned within the organization.[6] Correlatively, when these shared social duties lack the qualities of recognizability and understandability, organization constituents' orderly behavior is based strictly on their demonstrable social control (see Sciulli 1992, 30). I have shown elsewhere that there is an irreducible threshold that any set of sanctioned duties must cross in order to be recognizable and understandable, and this threshold is comprised exclusively of procedural norms (developed by Lon Fuller 1964/1969, 46–84). Under modern conditions, the qualities of recognizability and understandability are not grounded more immediately upon individuals' sharing of any identifiable set of material interests or, for that matter, any identifiable set of substantive normative beliefs (Sciulli 1992, 111–14). This is the case because organization constituents are typically (1) heterogeneous individuals, not homogeneous individuals, and because they typically occupy (2) competing positions, not fully coordinated or "consensual" positions. Thus, value-neutral social scientists cannot simply posit that organization constituents typically share the same material interests or the same substantive normative beliefs.

What is the threshold of procedural norms that keeps open the possibility that even heterogeneous individuals and competing groups can at least recognize and understand in common what is being expected of them? The rules or social duties being sanctioned within and by any organization can only be recognized and understood in common by everyone affected when they are: enforced generally rather than unevenly; publicly declared; prospective; intelligible, capable of being performed; constant rather than passing; and consistent with actual organizational behavior.[7] Those organizations that institutionalize their administrators' or managers' fidelity to this threshold of procedural norms are organized in a collegial form in particular. They are not organized in a bureaucratic form that institutionalizes a top–down chain of command, nor in a formally democratic or plebiscitary form that institutionalizes majority rule, nor in the patron–client form that institutionalizes relationships of personal trust and dependence (ibid.). Collegial formations are often found at sites of professional practice, including corporate research and development divisions. They are found at sites where organization constituents deliberate over the meaning of qualitative information affecting their clients' lives and livelihoods. They may be found, albeit less frequently, in corporate boards of directors and decision-making structures of top management (see Sciulli, forthcoming).

Again, this distinction between possible social integration and demonstrable social control cuts across each of Etzioni's types of compliance. Normative appeals to secure compliance are possibly integrative only to the extent that administrators or managers enforce these appeals in ways that are consistent with the threshold of procedural norms; whenever they fail to do so, their normative appeals are demonstrably controlling. After all, how can anyone be said to be integrated within an organization when he or she cannot even understand what administrators or managers are expecting? Similarly, material incentives and even exercises of coercion are possibly integrative when they are exercised consistently within the threshold of procedural norms; when, instead, they are exercised in ways that encroach against this threshold, they, too, are demonstrably controlling.

Etzioni approaches this distinction when he says that normative appeals are more likely to be considered legitimate by participants than either material incentives or exercises of coercion ([1961] 1975, 15). But this insight obscures the fact that some normative appeals can be strictly controlling, even if they happen to be acceptable subjectively to organizational participants (and thereby legitimate). Relatedly, it also obscures the fact that when material incentives and even exercises of coercion are kept consistent with the threshold, observing social scientists may note value-neutrally that organizational orderliness is a product of constituents' possible integration. It is not reducible to their demonstrable control (whether through manipulation or what Habermas calls "systematic distortion"). In short, social scientists can apply this threshold value-neutrally in comparative and historical studies, thereby securing a critical distance from all actual organizational practices, whether within authoritarian regimes past or present or within Western democracies today.

Still, even in the absence of the integration/control distinction, Etzioni's thesis regarding how power is neutralized within organizations is extraordinarily suggestive. He insists that "most organizations emphasize only one means of power." This is the case because when two are employed they tend to neutralize each other (ibid., 6–7). Exercises of coercion (for instance, in prisons) typically generate alienation among subordinates so that normative appeals then lose effectiveness (ibid., 27–31). Similarly, when people are being paid to comply (for instance, in nonprofessional industries), it is then generally fruitless to appeal to their ideals. Etzioni adds that neutralization can also occur when organizational elites use methods of compliance that seem inappropriate to the particular organization or activity in question (ibid., 8). For instance, to the extent that people believe it is not appropriate to use economic pressures to attain religious goals, the use of material incentives in religious organizations will not be as effective as their use in corporations.

With this in mind, Etzioni sees individuals' involvement in organizations ranging from alienative (or disorderly) involvement to moral (or orderly) involvement, and then he treats all forms of calculative or pecuniary involvement as falling somewhere in between (ibid., 9–11). What typically happens, he believes, is that an organization's "compliance relationship" interrelates a type of incentive with a type of involvement experience because this "congruence" tends to enhance its effectiveness (ibid., 12–13). Thus, coercion is interrelated with alienative involvement, remuneration with calculative involvement, and normative incentives with moral involvement.[8]

Instead of distinguishing social integration from social control,[9] Etzioni posits that individuals' involvement in an organization is affected by two factors, namely, legitimation and gratification (ibid., 15–16). First, individuals must perceive directives to be legitimate (which, following Weber, he treats as resting on participants' subjective beliefs about the authority of the source of the directives).[10] Second, the directives must not otherwise frustrate subordinates' needs, wishes, and desires. These two factors already reveal why Etzioni would in time make the first two conceptual decisions mentioned at the outset of this chapter. He is already assuming that the legitimacy of directives rests on some group's shared substantive normative beliefs about authority; he is assuming, that is, that the group identifies positively with the organization (e.g., ibid., 68).[11] Moreover, he can only explain and predict directives' effects on individuals' needs, wishes, and desires in comparative perspective if human needs, beyond bare survival, are finite, irreducible, and universal. That is, he can only explain and predict this if human nature literally places non-negotiable limits on organizational effectiveness, specifically, on how authorities anywhere can exercise their organizations' collective power effectively.

Putting the impetus for Etzioni's later conceptual decisions differently, consider what his options were once he overlooked the possibility of grounding the comparative study of organizational compliance on a threshold of institutionalized norms (which was easy to do in 1961, given that Fuller did not publish his "internal morality of law" until 1964).[12] Etzioni was left essentially with only two other places to look for a suitable conceptual grounding for his criticisms and proposed reforms. He could look above the institutional level to an explicitly formulated evolutionary theory. Here his choices would be either to adopt a benign, Lockean view of the rise of modern democracy or else a more jaundiced, Weberian view of systemic tendencies toward authoritarianism. The problem is that in the absence of the threshold of procedural norms and the distinction between social integration and social control, neither choice is satisfactory. The Lockean view ultimately supports the liberal complacency of neoclassical economics and rational choice theory, not Etzioni's criticisms and proposed reforms of American democracy. The Weberian view, in turn, is too dark and pessimistic to appeal to American policy makers who share the optimistic tone of American pragmatism.

The other place where Etzioni could look for a suitable conceptual grounding for his criticisms and proposed reforms was below the institutional level. Here he could explore the internalized substantive norms that individuals somehow share within identifiable groups, as "communities" or belief.[13] Taken by itself, however, this would leave him with pluralism—group relativism—rather than with a grounding for criticisms and reforms. On what basis other than the rational choice criteria of economic efficiency and administrative effectiveness could Etzioni or anyone else then criticize any group that maintained compliance or orderliness in noncoercive ways? Etzioni could only escape relativism—and thereby secure a grounding beyond neoclassical or rational choice calculations of efficiency and effectiveness—by linking his turn to internalized norms to purportedly fundamental human needs that speak to qualities of life that are extraeconomic and nonrational. This linkage is critical to his project: It allows Etzioni to assume that the norms that individuals typically internalize as their own lived beliefs and aspirations are relatively delimited and implacable rather than open-ended and malleable.

## Human Nature and Needs

Since 1968 (1968b) Etzioni has assumed that "we cannot be successfully socialized into structures that are incompatible with our nature" (1991, 19).[14] He assumes this because he assumes that "there is a basic, underlying human nature that cannot be altered." However, problems of interpretation invariably surface whenever this grounding is brought to social scientific research. These problems may be found in Etzioni's own efforts (1) to establish that there really are basic human needs, (2) to specify how they may inform empirical study, and (3) to account for their origin. Rather than demonstrating that basic human needs actually exist in all places at all times, Etzioni simply asserts it. This must be the case, he believes, because full socialization is not possible under authoritarian conditions (ibid., 126). He had to assert this, however, because of the conceptual decisions he made in his earlier work on organizations.[15] He had essentially pushed himself into a corner. I return to this issue below.

Looking at the third issue noted above, the origin of human needs, Etzioni argued in a 1968 article in the *American Sociological Review* (at page 155) that "it is fruitful to assume that there is a universal set of basic human needs which have attributes of their own which are not determined by the social structure, cultural patterns, *or socialization processes*."[16] Yet, in 1991 (at page 126), he held that rather than being God-given or genetically driven, basic human needs are "the product of *one basic form of socialization* [italics added] that we all undergo." Selznick (1992) has similar difficulties identifying the source of basic human needs, as did some critical theorists earlier who tried to identify workers' "objective interests" (see note 22).

Looking at the second issue, informing empirical study, Etzioni identifies affection and recognition as basic human needs.[17] In his words these are "functional prerequisites of human beings" (1968b, 158). Yet, how does Etzioni know that these needs are basic, that "the person can be denied [this] specific kind of experience only at the cost of an intra-personal tension" (ibid., 154)? He says that this is confirmed by an "empirical check": "if both socialization costs and those of social control [in a society or a collectivity] are higher for persons who have been socialized into roles in which their needs for affection and recognition are infrequently satisfied than for roles which offer more frequent satisfaction of these needs" (ibid., 159, emphasis removed). To his credit, Etzioni acknowledges that he simply asserts this empirical check as a general research orientation. He is "not aware of existing studies which directly test these propositions, or the data of which have a direct bearing on them" (ibid., 160). Thus, he can illustrate its utility only "on an informal basis." After presenting hypothetical (that is, informal) illustrations, he concludes:

> [I]f recruitment to one kind of role must be more selective than to the other, i.e., more persons must be screened before "suitable" ones are found, and if the criterion of selection is not special skill but ease-of-socialization or search for abnormal personalities, this is also indicative of the "unnatural" quality of the particular kinds of roles, sub-structure, or sub-culture [being studied]. (ibid., 161)

Can any of these assumptions or propositions be substantiated by social scientific findings? They might be, but their substantiation reveals problems of interpretation, not the self-evident workings of an irreducible human nature.[18] The major problem of interpretation that arises when relying on a theory of human nature to study variations in collectivities and societies is that the theoretical (and clinical) literature itself is marked by a great divide. On one side are Nietzsche, Freud, and others who emphasize the importance of mature or self-disciplined exercises of power and sexuality (or other manifestations of individual aspiration). On the other are Kant, Durkheim, and others who emphasize the importance of affection and recognition (or other manifestations of group solidarity).

What Etzioni, Selznick, Bellah, and other communitarians ignore in placing so much emphasis on the irreducibility of human nature is that contemporary studies also indicate that there is a class bias on each side of the great divide I just noted: Cultural and social elites (along with the working class, ironically) elevate indifference above affection and most types of recognition (Bourdieu 1979; Cookson and Persell 1985). By contrast, the middle class sublimates the lure of power and sexuality in favor of conformity and an ongoing quest for the love of others (Bellah et al. 1985). Following Durkheim, Selznick holds, for instance, that anxiety originates in "unrestrained aspirations" (1992, 144). But followers of Nietzsche and Freud locate the source of anxiety in infantile taboos and restrictions that the middle class in particular internalizes.

Etzioni comes closest to appreciating this class distinction when he concedes that traditional Japanese were "offered fewer opportunities for affection than traditional Mexicans," and yet the latter may have paid a higher personal price for their socialization than the Japanese cost of a higher incidence of ulcers (1968b, 162–63). Nietzsche's way of addressing those who are driven to seek the affection of others was to say that may those who prize a long and pleasant night's sleep never awake (see Kaufmann 1973 for a popularized updating of the Nietzschean position). Freud's way—always more subtle, to be sure—was to point out that the middle class sublimates sexuality and aggression at the cost of its own psychic well-being. The middle class lives in a world marked by infantile taboos and restrictions. As a result, these individuals often fail to attain the mature self-discipline of adults who take responsibility for their own actions and yet live on the surface—Neitzsche calls it "oblivion"—rather than internalizing the middle class's anxieties and fears. When sociologists talk generally about motivation or human nature, they tend to adopt uncritically the middle class's sense of well-being (e.g., Turner 1988). This is illustrated most self-evidently in introductory textbook discussions of deviance: Beyond the offenses to life and property that are sanctioned by basic criminal law in any modern society, the behavior filling these textbook chapters is typically that labeled deviant by the middle class, and the lower middle class at that (e.g., Gans 1988). The same behavior is seen differently by elites and, at least to some extent, by the working class as well.

Selznick seems more attuned to the great divide when he links culture to human nature by way of motivation in his discussion of "cultural destruction" (see Habermas 1973, on "motivation crisis"). Cultural destruction, he contends, is marked by a loss of motivation and by activities robbed of symbolic meaning (1992, 7). Like Etzioni, Selznick also believes that "without an understanding of human nature, we are hard put to criticize existing conditions, personal or social, from the standpoint of critical morality" (ibid., 120). He believes, too, that an "ontology of human nature" contains "a content that transcends cultural differ-ences and provides material for moral ordering" (ibid., 134). Yet, like Etzioni, Selznick then runs into numerous problems of interpretation as soon as he wishes to evaluate the moral worth of specific societies at specific times.

As one example, Selznick links human nature to morality by way of an Aristotelian notion of well-being: a life of virtue. But then he hedges: "[A] telos does not necessarily specify an outcome" but, instead, may refer to an end-state as "the integrity of a process, as when we say law inclines toward the progressive reduction of arbitrariness in official conduct, or when we identify scientific ideals of free, rigorous, and self-corrective inquiry" (ibid., 149–50). With this, however, Selznick has eliminated any need to refer to an irreducible human nature; he may instead focus exclusively on the organizational requirements for mediating arbitrariness and institutionalizing inquiry. With this hedge, moreover, Selznick calls into question everything he said earlier about an ontological or immutable human nature. Quoting George Santayana approvingly, he acknowl-edges that under modern conditions man becomes "more complex" and, as a result, "less stably organized" such that "the telos [the quest for moral well-being] may be experienced as dim and incoherent rather than clear and compel-ling" (ibid., 151, the last quotation is Selznick's, the first two are his uses of

Santayana). If people can become more complex, and thereby less stably organized, how can Etzioni or anyone else assume a priori (see page 141) that "we cannot be successfully socialized into structures that are incompatible with our nature"?

As another example of the problems of interpretation that Selznick acknowledges, consider the following passage: "It is always easier to identify pathologies and establish thresholds than it is to say objectively what is psychic health, maturity, or fulfillment" (ibid., 171). If man becomes "more complex," and if we cannot speak objectively of fulfillment, then what exactly does human nature as a grounding or standard of comparison contribute to the social sciences?

Yet another illustration of problems of interpretation may be found in Selznick's discussion of the moral weakness that can accompany successful socialization into a local community (ibid., 179–80). Overcoming anti-Semitism and ethnocentrism, he points out, requires not only enlarged experience beyond that found in any local community but "may also require at least some sacrifice of social cohesion and personal security" (1992, 180). In other words, Selznick appreciates that this overcoming is more than routine socialization typically achieves. "Routine socialization *inevitably* establishes a cultural hegemony" (ibid., 181, my emphasis).

These problems carry the discussion to another issue of significance that I raised earlier, namely, why has a social theorist as sophisticated as Amitai Etzioni decided to operate on the basis of such grand assumptions about human nature, knowing full well that these assumptions are both controversial and difficult to substantiate? I believe that the answer lies in Etzioni's oversight of the social integration/social control distinction (or some equivalent) early in his career coupled with his continuing interest in nonetheless establishing a ground—a secure standard of comparison—upon which to locate "active societies" or "responsive societies" in comparative perspective. In Etzioni's own words from the 1960s to the 1990s:

> Theories without a conception of human needs (which have specific attributes of their own) are open to a conservative interpretation, of individuals and groups that are expected to adapt to the society as it is. . . . [By contrast] [t]heories which assume autonomous human needs provide an independent basis with which to compare societies to each other . . . and they lead one to expect pressure to change existing societies and cultures toward more responsive ones. (1968b, 168)

> One can determine that one society is more responsive to human nature than another only if one assumes a basic underlying human nature. (1991, 126)[19]

Rather than moving immediately to the grounding of human nature, value-neutral social scientists can instead first identify increases or decreases in the possibility of responsiveness within and across societies by employing the social

integration/social control distinction in monitoring arbitrariness. Put more specifically, they can first establish at least tentatively at this institutional level the
possibility of responsiveness within particular sectors of any given society. They
may well find that certain federal agencies are more capable of responsiveness
than others, and that the same holds true for certain industries, certain universities and hospitals, and certain local governments and police departments. Once
they establish this, social scientists may then turn, if they wish, to fathoming
these organizations' actual responsiveness to individuals' needs.

Failing to draw this distinction or some equivalent at an institutional level,
Etzioni is left with little alternative other than to point to egregious instances of
abuse, such as Nazism, to illustrate the merits of his approach to socialization.
Yet, even here, with extreme cases in view, he fails to make his case by social
scientific standards of verification or falsification. Again, in his words: "If full
socialization were possible, people in a Nazi society should be able to be made
as content as those in a democratic one. This is neither the case nor a normatively sound position" (1991, 126). Etzioni is surely correct in assessing this
position's normative merits. But the literature hardly eliminates it from the realm
of possibility in practice. William Sheridan Allen ([1965] 1984) offers an elaborate case study of the Nazis' takeover of a small German town and the aftermath,
covering a period from 1922 to 1945. It is not self-evident from his account that
either the costs or the effectiveness of socialization of most townspeople were
much different than in comparable towns in democratic societies during the same
period, or even today. Whether these people were more or less "content" than
their counterparts elsewhere is a matter open to interpretation rather than one that
social scientists can decide a priori.[20] Relatedly, is it self-evident in the literature
that socialization was more costly and less effective for whites in the American
South during the 1940s and 1950s than elsewhere in the United States? Additionally, is it self-evident in the literature that socialization was more costly and less
effective for whites in South Africa through the 1980s than elsewhere in Africa
or, for that matter, in Europe or the Middle East?[21]

My point is not to dismiss this line of inquiry. Rather, it is to suggest that
hinging historical or cross-national comparisons immediately on a purportedly
irreducible human nature leaves social scientists with an unnecessarily wide
latitude. They are left free to insert their own subjective interpretations (and
aspirations) into basic descriptions of events, let alone into subsequent explanations. My point is that this latitude is considerably reduced, and the issues involved rendered more manageable, if the social integration/social control
distinction is brought first to the study of basic institutional arrangements. Moreover, the findings that result can then be used to frame subsequent studies of
socialization, including those that do not hinge on grand claims regarding human
nature.

Etzioni's writings illustrate both the interpretive problems created by any
subinstitutional approach, and, ironically, they also illustrate the likelihood that

an alternative, institutional approach will prove more fruitful. He uses his standard of basic human needs to isolate authentic, alienating, and inauthentic social conditions (1968b, 170–74). Social conditions are *authentic* "when the appearance and the underlying structure are both responsive to basic human needs," *alienating* "when both the appearance and the structure are unresponsive," and *inauthentic* "when the underlying structure is unresponsive but an institutional or symbolic front of responsiveness is maintained." Yet, Etzioni concedes that "institutions are easier to study from this viewpoint" than individuals (ibid., 175). In addition, he cannot imagine a fourth possible combination appearing for very long in practice, namely, "an alienating appearance covering a responsive reality" (ibid., 174).

However, the "underlying structure" to which Etzioni refers in this trichotomy can be identified. It is marked by the presence of collegial formations, the only form of organization capable of institutionalizing organization constituents' fidelity to the threshold of procedural norms I discussed earlier. Collegial formations are often found at sites of professional practice. They institutionalize heterogeneous individuals' and competing groups' ongoing deliberations over how best to characterize qualities valued by themselves or by clients, and then how best to maintain or attain these qualities.

With this insight, the fourth possible combination comes readily into view: It occurs, in practice, when collegial formations are present and yet are seen by outsiders as "elitist" and thereby lack popular acceptance or legitimacy. After all, why is it not possible for democratically elected public officials—to say nothing of appointed public and private officials—to be more interested either in maximizing patronage or in promoting a substantive policy agenda than in exhibiting fidelity to existing collegial formations or in otherwise remaining vigilant in mediating arbitrary exercises of collective power? And why is it not possible for these official actions to gain broad popular support? In short, an institutional approach to the underlying structure returns the discussion to identifiable characteristics of organizations supporting modern democracy. It turns the discussion away from the more speculative issues of basic needs and human nature.[22]

## Community and Shared Substantive Norms

In my view the single most important decision that Etzioni made early in his career at a conceptual level was to substitute a critical stance for neoclassical economists' and rational choice theorists' liberal complacency. Even as his view of human nature is the opposite of the American founders (who were hardly optimists), his rejection of liberal complacency nonetheless moves his social theory closer to the founders' republican vigilance.[23] Yet, I show in the next section (on "Entropy, Order, and Institutionalized Norms") that Etzioni's view that rational behavior is intrinsically anti-entropic is then inconsistent with republican vigilance and instead consistent with liberal complacency, and thereby with rational choice theory and American pragmatism.

Liberal complacency revolves around an implicit evolutionary theory, a faith that institutional arrangements tend—somehow—automatically toward a benign equilibrium. This faith is found today, for instance, in economic and legal contractarians' unargued assumption that maximizing corporate shareholders' private wealth invariably carries two institutional benefits for the larger social order: It maximizes social wealth and contributes automatically to a relatively benign social order, one capable of supporting limited government and citizen vigilance (e.g., Easterbrook and Fischel 1991). By contrast, republican vigilance rests more explicitly on an opposite view of institutional evolution. It is more skeptical about the relationship between economic success and institutional equilibrium. It holds that whether any modern social order institutionalizes norms that mediate exercises of collective power short of abuse and arbitrariness is, always and everywhere, only a contingent possibility. This institutional arrangements, a relatively benign social order, is never an automatic outcome of economic success alone, of individuals' strictly rational, maximizing behavior.

Etzioni's own rejection of liberal complacency comes through not only in *The Active Society* (1968a) but also in his works of the 1980s and 1990s.[24] Consider the following warnings and observations that inform his call for communitarianism:

1. If the language of rights is not curbed short of devaluing the "currency of rights," there will be "a universal backlash against rights" (1993, 6).
2. "[T]he best way to curb authoritarianism and right-wing tendencies [in the United States] is to stop the anarchic drift [toward individualism] by introducing carefully calibrated responses to urgent and legitimate public concerns about safety and the control of epidemics" (ibid., 11).
3. Regarding today's "moral confusion and social anarchy" (ibid., 24), "in private matters such as family relations and business transactions and in public spheres from elected office to voluntary organizations, our moral foundations are crumbling, and shoring up is overdue" (ibid., 29).
4. "Ask yourself what the alternatives are to the exercise of moral voices. There are only two: a police state, which tries to maintain civil order by brute force, or a moral vacuum in which anything goes" (ibid., 37).
5. Authoritarian voices have surfaced in the United States in response to crime, drugs, and AIDS, and yet radical individualists play into the hands of authoritarians by condemning communitarian responses (ibid., 163–64).

Rather than being irremediably value-laden, Etzioni's critical stance toward contemporary American society contributes an important advance to functionalism at a conceptual level. Parsons endeavored to identify those institutional, organizational, and interpersonal practices—those institutionalized manifestations of voluntaristic action—that are functional for social order as such. By contrast, Etzioni states explicitly—and correctly—that the very terms "functional" and "dysfunctional" make little sense unless they refer to maintaining and adapting a certain type of social order, namely, a pluralist democracy.[25]

Still, just as Etzioni moves immediately to a substantive normative concept of human nature (tied to affection and recognition), rather than operating through a procedural normative mediation (yielding the social integration/social control distinction), he also moves immediately to a substantive normative concept of community. I showed above that the effort to locate a responsive society is made more manageable by first bringing the social integration/social control distinction to the analysis of existing institutions and organizations. Now I want to illustrate that this distinction permits us to see three patterns in Etzioni's examples of communitarian practices: First, some of his examples are amenable to restatement as procedural norms of behavior that, as such, can inform cross-national and historical comparison. Second, and more curiously, some are reducible to strictly rational sanctions rather than rely on moral appeals of any kind. Third, others that do reflect Americans' purportedly shared substantive norms turn out to be either trivial or unworkable (thereby casting doubt on the very presence of such norms, or on their importance).[26]

Consider the following examples that Etzioni cites or proposes as communitarian practices, all in the context of today's intensifying global economic competition, corporate restructurings, and the middle class's transfer of psychic interest and symbolic gratification from geographic units to corporate bodies of various types (Reich 1991):

1. Requiring airline pilots, school bus drivers, and others "who directly hold others' lives in their hands" to be tested for drug and alcohol use (Etzioni 1993, 2), plus sobriety and drug checkpoints on highways.[27] Putting this proposal more generally, Etzioni advocates "that we agree with one another that we shall make a contribution to public safety and public health by accepting some measures that do encumber us to some extent but allow significant benefits to the community" (ibid., 167).
2. The illustrations of "community prodding" toward conforming to traffic norms at a Stanford University intersection, to norms of lawn upkeep in suburbs, and to norms of garbage sorting in urban cooperatives (ibid., 32–33).
3. Promoting "communitarian families," in which both parents engage actively in children's upbringing, creating "a climate that fosters finding agreed-upon positions that we can favor authoritatively" (ibid., 25).
4. Asserting that parents have "a moral responsibility to the community to invest in proper upbringing of children," Etzioni advocates that parents establish cooperative arrangements to spend time at child centers (since so many are poorly run) (ibid., 58–59). He also calls upon the federal government to ensure two years of unpaid leave from work to raise newborns and to initiate a GI bill that gives parents "points" toward education or retraining if they stay home (1993: 71).

5. In an effort to stem the tide of divorce, Etzioni offers suggestions for counseling and waiting periods before marriage or divorce and new mechanisms that would come into play in the event of divorce: registering parents' social security numbers on childrens' birth certificates in order to ensure child-support payments and enforcing a three-way division of family assets so that children get a share (ibid., 78–83).

6. Seeing that student employment at McDonald's is "uneducational," "a breeding ground for robots," rather than something more benign (like the lemonade stand or newspaper delivery route of old), Etzioni calls for: limits on the hours of employment, school credit only for jobs that meet educational criteria, enhanced job supervision and training, inspection by school representatives ‧ and direction by school counselors, parental steering away from fast-food jobs, and dedication of "a significant share of teen earnings" to the family (ibid., 109–12).

7. The proposal that "communitarian justice" for the disadvantaged rests first on personal self-help, then neighborhood self-help, and finally community self-help (for instance, in local fire companies), with governmental help only for "severely limited communities" (ibid., 144–46).[28]

Etzioni's two most impressive calls for reform, which escape the criticisms that I raised at the top of the list, are directed toward schools and toward ensuring that communitarianism does not slide down the "slippery slope" to majoritarianism and then authoritarianism. Etzioni envisions a "communitarian school" in which discipline and homework are stressed far more than is the case today, plus he couples his discussion of schooling with a call for a year of national service (ibid., 89–115). This is a potentially important response to the "motivation crisis" that Habermas so presciently discussed in *Legitimation Crisis* (1973).

Etzioni's discussion of limits on the community and the safeguards needed to avoid the "slippery slope" are an important supplement to his deontological position, which holds that people may be bound by shared moral duties and commitments (1989, 402). Following Kant and Durkheim, this position assumes "that individuals have acquired a set of shared moral commitments that legitimate the social order and that lead them to treat others the way they seek to be treated themselves" (ibid., 407; also 1990, 149; and Selznick 1992, 32–34). What makes this potentially threatening to civil liberties—prone to sliding toward authoritarianism—is that Etzioni and other communitarians have difficulty identifying which community they have in mind: Is it a local, state, or national community, or is it "nongeographic communities that criss-cross the others, such as professional or work-based communities" (1993, 31–32, 119–22; 1990, 143; Selznick 1992, 371; I address this issue also in chapter 12 of this volume)?

This uncertainty in identifying the community adversely affects Etzioni's communitarianism even at its points of greatest strength and, certainly, magnifies his position's weaknesses. One strength of his position is his critique of the rights-based language of law and politics and his call for an alternative, responsibilities-based language (e.g., 1993, 5–7). As Etzioni sees it, communitarianism revolves around a nexus of four reform measures (ibid., 123–32): (1) emphasizing habits of the heart or internalized values and norms that are already widely shared; (2) balancing the relationship between career and community bonds; (3) making the physical environment more community-friendly and less anomic; and (4) promoting volunteer efforts that are not trivial (his central example is voluntary emergency medical technicians who serve unpaid). Selznick puts well the thrust of such reforms: "[A]t bottom, the communitarian challenge is a demand for more extensive responsibility in every aspect of personal experience and social life" (1992, 385).

However, sociologist Selznick, who is also a legal scholar, appreciates well how uncertainty in identifying the community undercuts these calls for responsibility. He sees that American courts can visualize individual rights much more sharply than they can visualize corporate responsibilities of any kind, including community responsibilities. The issue of whether girls under the age of eighteen should be permitted to secure an abortion without their parents' consent illustrates the limits of judicial vision today. If one answers that girls have this right, then one is essentially saying that the family has no court-enforceable responsibilities here as a corporate entity. Alternatively, if one answers that the family does have such responsibilities, then one is clearly subordinating individual rights. Behind this decision, however, is one's image of the family as a corporate body: Is the family viewed as responsible and facilitative, or as patriarchal and thereby unnecessarily constraining?[29] As Selznick puts the matter in another context, institutions—including corporate entities of any kind—are the chief agencies and most reliable safeguards of community only to the extent that they are respected (ibid., 370).

The social integration/social control distinction that I proposed earlier is designed to identify when certain corporate entities merit respect, namely, when they adopt and maintain the collegial form. However, this standard does not serve well in distinguishing families because, like religious congregations and residential communities, these are corporate entities whose members share substantive norms more immediately, unmediated by the collegial form of organization. Families in particular rarely institutionalize the threshold of procedural norms I discussed earlier, nor is it vital to any existing democracy that they do so. Rather, families are by their very composition more hierarchical. This means, however, that they carry as much potential for caprice and abuse as for affection and support. The same is true of religious congregations and residential communities. They, too, institutionalize more immediately a particular way of life, thereby sanctioning some set of substantive norms of behavior rather than a procedural normative mediation.

Still, the social integration/social control distinction can be used to identify those corporate entities in which individuals are employed that do indeed merit judicial protection on a public law ground. These are the corporate entities that mediate exercises of collective power short of abuse and arbitrariness. Such corporate entities may be found not only in professional associations and at sites of professional practice (such as hospitals and universities) but also, more surprisingly, within for-profit corporations themselves (see Sciulli, forthcoming, for an extended discussion of corporations in this light).

The other great strength of Etzioni's communitarianism is his identification of four specific "notches on the slippery slope" designed to prevent benign community responsibility from sliding inadvertently toward a more malevolent majoritarianism (1993, 177–90). First, communitarian norms and values will not subordinate individual liberties unless there is a clear and present danger. The latter is involved, in Etzioni's view, when airline pilots drink alcohol or take drugs on the job, or when they do so at other times in ways that affect their job performance. Second, communitarian norms and values will not subordinate individual liberties when alternative ways to proceed remain available. Etzioni's first concern here is "to look for ways that do not require any reinterpretation of the Constitution" (ibid., 181). Thus, instead of banning cigarette advertising, and thereby raising First Amendment issues, Etzioni prefers raising taxes on cigarettes. Third, even when these first two requirements are met, a third requirement is that any adjustments in the law and in behavior should be as unintrusive as possible. Fourth, and relatedly, whatever policies are adopted should carry as few externalities or side effects as possible. Even as these notches are an undeniable strength of Etzioni's communitarian position, his uncertainty in identifying the unit of community that he has in mind nonetheless exposes a danger. This danger is revealed when Etzioni says, in discussing the third notch, that "it is best to try other ways first, although the law should not be treated as immutable" (ibid., 181).

Here is where my proposed distinction between social integration and social control again comes into play. Resting on a procedural normative threshold that mediates arbitrary exercises of collective power, it specifies where law is indeed immutable—if one wishes to maintain a relatively benign social order and governing regime. The law is immutable where changes permit or encourage encroachments against the threshold. Correlatively, the same threshold also helps to identify where the law may be subject to negotiation and renegotiation, namely, where changes neither involve nor encourage encroachments. Selznick acknowledges this when he insists that we must distinguish conventional morality (which may tolerate anti-Semitism and ethnocentrism) from critical morality (which does not) on the basis of some "threshold standard of critical morality" (1992, 409).

Finally, the major weakness of Etzioni's communitarianism, which his uncertainty in identifying the unit of community exacerbates, is its prudishness. Etzioni is sensitive to this criticism, and he often offers reassurances that he is not interested in fostering a new Puritanism. Nevertheless, he tends to treat extramonogamous sexuality among adults as a far greater threat to the larger social order than seems self-evidently appropriate or defensible. Nowhere in Etzioni's works does one find Freud's greatest contribution, namely, his clinical observations that adults sublimate aggression and sexuality at some price of psychic imbalance. Moreover, this price escalates considerably—into outright discontent—whenever civilization endeavors to canalize aggression and sexuality entirely into acceptable routes, that is, routes that appeal to the middle class and lower middle class in particular. Consider the sweeping nature of the following statement by Etzioni: "Social attitudes toward sex often speak volumes about how a society approaches moral and social matters in general" (1993, 27). Now Etzioni says this in the context of discussing parents' instructions to their children "about sexual matters," and yet he immediately connects this discussion to other issues, including malingering at work and absenteeism, drug or alcohol use at work, uses of physical force against others, and the declining prestige or status of family life.

The grand sweep of Etzioni's concerns about extramonogamous sexuality is particularly evident when he accepts the strategy of publicly humiliating adults who solicit prostitutes (ibid., 140). It is one thing to be concerned about how unregulated prostitution can disrupt the life of an otherwise vibrant neighborhood, and it is also legitimate to raise, in an age of AIDS, the public health concerns attending the purchasing of sexual favors from strangers, but it is quite another to advocate public humiliation of consenting adults more or less as an end in itself. Etzioni's reassurances notwithstanding, this moves him beyond community-mindedness. He neglects the fact that communities are filled with adults who can be expected to act like adults. He instead treats communities implicitly as designed far more exclusively with children in mind, and the adults be damned. Put differently, it is one thing to advocate that communities see to it that there are "child safe zones"—schools, playgrounds, family restaurants— wherein adults are expected to defer to children's sensibilities, but it is another thing to advocate that communities make it difficult for adults to find places where they may act as they wish, without any concern whatsoever for children's sensibilities.

### Entropy, Order, and Institutionalized Norms

I mentioned earlier that even as Etzioni's critical stance moves his social theory closer to the founders' republican vigilance, his view that rational action is intrinsically anti-entropic moves his social theory in the opposite direction, toward liberal complacency. In exploring why this is the case, consider what people are doing when they act normatively rather than instrumentally. They are subordinating considerations of efficiency in production and effectiveness in administration to an ongoing effort to maintain or enhance some quality in their lives. They are mediating their obvious self-interest in maximizing the production of some quantity of goods or in maximizing the delivery of some quantity of services by an ongoing effort, say, to maintain a clean environment or a friendship, a religious tradition, or "family values." In these four examples, the norms involved are substantive orientations for exercising power, not procedural mediations of such exercises. The larger point, however, is that the value people place on these or any other qualities in their lives eludes ready measurement and quantification. It thereby eludes pricing in the marketplace. Indeed, the very suggestion that these qualities' value may be measured or priced is a clear sign that instrumental considerations of efficiency and effectiveness are already encroaching into—"colonizing"—the particular areas of everyday life in question.[30]

As I just noted, aside from the substantive normative qualities that individuals may value in family and friendships and in religion and environment, normative action may also revolve around institutional arrangements that anchor procedural normative qualities within intermediate associations. Individuals act on such qualities at times when they endeavor to uphold the integrity of a university, a hospital, or any other site of professional practice in the face of economic pressures to the contrary.

Turning to a related issue, individuals' efforts to attain or to maintain either substantive qualities or procedural qualities in their everyday lives may very well be self-interested. After all, when they dedicate themselves to maintaining their friendships or to maintaining the integrity of sites of professional practice, they are not necessarily acting altruistically. However, they are necessarily acting in ways that, by definition, are nonmaximizing. As a result, their actions are also by definition noninstrumental, and thereby nonrational. The term "voluntaristic action" is appropriate in these cases because (1) their activities are secular, directed to ends in the world rather than to purported spiritual or metaphysical ends, and (2) their actions are always only contingently stabilized or institutionalized in the face of economic pressures favoring normatively unmediated maximizing behavior.[31]

That individuals' voluntaristic actions may be self-interested rather than altruistic is evident in cases where they maintain a friendship for strictly personal reasons, whether material or affective. More importantly, individuals may maintain the integrity of a professional practice by acting strictly self-interestedly to protect and advance their own positions within universities, hospitals, or corporate research and development divisions. Yet, their actions are still normative rather than maximizing and rational. They are maintaining certain qualities in their everyday lives that, in turn, normatively mediate how they then define their own personal interests as individuals (whether material or affective), and then, certainly, how they may instrumentally advance them. Put succinctly, in these cases individuals' positional interests can normatively mediate how they literally define, and then act upon, their rational self-interests.

The affective stake that people may or may not develop in their friendships and residential communities is certainly a matter worthy of empirical inquiry and theoretical attention (beginning first and foremost with Books Eight and Nine of Aristotle's *Nicomachean Ethics*). But for the purposes of this chapter a more critical distinction is that between (1) individuals' rational self-interests at relatively fluid sites of economic activity, including stock markets and retail stores, and (2) individuals' normative positional interests within more structured situations, including intermediate associations such as hospitals, universities, and other sites of professional practice.[32] Economists and rational choice theorists may well deny the significance of affect and other norms at more fluid sites. They may emphasize instead the more compelling pressures of instrumental calculations of material (and quantifiable) success and failure. The psychological motivations of relatively detached individuals, after all, are open to interpretation, including interpretations that reduce their behavior to strictly rational calculations of material outcomes. But what economists and rational choice theorists cannot deny is that there are *institutionalized norms* at more structured sites of economic activity *that are unique to relatively benign social orders*. They cannot deny this, because professional associations as well as American courts at times enforce these norms (most particularly when they impose fiduciary duties of care and loyalty on those holding positions of power within corporations and other intermediate associations). In other words, they cannot deny the presence of institutionalized norms within structured situations without simultaneously either (1) neglecting an entire set of professional behavior and judicial behavior or else (2) distorting this behavior's meaning for those directly involved as well as its institutional significance for the larger social order.

The two distinctions that I just drew—between voluntaristic action tied to maintaining qualities in everyday life and rational action tied more immediately to maximizing behavior, and between positional interests and self-interests—not only expose limitations in the capacity of neoclassical economics and rational choice theory to orient empirical research in the social sciences, they also expose problems with Etzioni's conceptual decision at the outset of *The Moral Dimension* (1988a), namely, to characterize rational action as intrinsically anti-entropic (also Etzioni 1986b). The issue of entropy in the physical sciences, the inexorable loss of heat, becomes the issue of arbitrary exercises of collective power in the social sciences—not the issue of a more secular decline in social order as such.[33] Put more specifically, if strictly rational action is left unmediated by institutionalized norms, it results inexorably in institutional outcomes that may be found in all modern social orders, including those that are self-evidently authoritarian. It does not somehow result automatically in those institutional outcomes that uniquely support democratic political and legal regimes.

If the notion of normative behavior being institutionalized means anything, it means that individuals are operating within structured situations, not more fluid sites of contracting. Within structured situations their strictly rational behavior in advancing their own immediate interests is mediated by nonrational qualities of life of one kind or another, some of which the courts ultimately uphold on public law grounds. The question is why would any modern society retain any institutionalized norms from its preindustrial past that mediate—and thereby seemingly complicate rather than self-evidently facilitate—its domestic economic efficiency and international economic competitiveness? One answer is that certain nonrational norms may actually turn out to facilitate, not complicate, efficiency and competitiveness. Rather than mediating individuals' maximizing behavior, these nonrational norms may somehow augment and enhance it. Social theorists who explicitly or implicitly offer this answer to the question hold that individuals behave rationally when they "choose means most suitable to their ends" and also remain open to evidence and to reason (Etzioni 1988a: 91, 136, 144). But this definition of rational action then lands them in a contradiction. On the one hand, they say that "instrumental rationality is not judged by the consequences but by the process of decision-formation." Thus, rational behavior "actually means behavior 'in line with rational decision-making'" (ibid., 148; also 1986b, 69–72). On the other hand, they assume, often without argument but at times explicitly, that instrumentally rational behavior is integrative in and of itself; it is anti-entropic or benignly ordering (1988a, 151).

There is, however, a quite different answer to the question above. Institutionalized norms remain in place within some modern societies precisely because they mediate efficiency and competitiveness in serving a decidedly qualitative, that is, voluntaristic, outcome. They contribute to a qualitative relationship between economic and noneconomic institutions that is capable of supporting a democratic political and legal regime in particular. Being qualitative, this outcome, this institutional relationship, is nonrational and thereby mediates individuals' strictly rational behavior. Put more precisely, it mediates their rational behavior short of abuse and arbitrariness even if such exercises of collective power would otherwise prove to increase efficiency and competitiveness. Social theorists who offer this answer define rational behavior more analytically. They define it as the selection of instrumental means to maximize the attaining of quantities of goods, goods whose value is readily reducible to their price in the marketplace. With this, these social theorists escape the contradiction noted above. They also simultaneously establish that normatively unmediated rational action is entropic. It drifts inadvertently from maximizing behavior to arbitrary exercises of collective power.

Etzioni contends that rational action is anti-entropic or potentially integrative in itself precisely because he does not keep his definition of rational action analytical. Instead, he brings nonrational elements of mediation into his very definition of rational action.[34] These elements may be found when Etzioni refers to an individual's internal reflection over goals and means before acting rationally, and then also to individuals' deliberations with others when arriving at collective or corporate decisions (e.g., 1986b, 69–72; 1988b, 95–103). Neither reflection nor deliberation, however, is the most efficient or effective instrumental means to maximize the attaining of quantities of goods or services. Being noninstrumental, these elements of action are instead nonrational. Neoclassicists have always sensed the importance of keeping the definition of rational action analytically precise. But they went too far by initially assuming without argument that individuals and groups have perfect information when they act rationally (see Etzioni's discussion of March and Simon at 1986b, 69). All that they needed to assume was that individuals and groups act immediately, without reflecting or deliberating, and that—somehow—maximizing behavior results.[35] In turn, the most that Etzioni or anyone else can say when the definition of rational action is kept analytically precise is that only normatively mediated rational action can *possibly* be anti-entropic or benignly ordering.[36]

Consider what happens if a theorist does not explicitly interrelate the presence of institutionalized norms with mediations of abuse and arbitrariness, and thereby with the possibility of maintaining limited government and citizen vigilance over it. The theorist then cannot establish, with reasons, why institutionalized norms remain present at all. Their presence becomes a matter of individuals' strictly personal, subjective decisions—as reflections of their internalized norms, their purported altruism. These decisions become more and more difficult to justify with reasons as inefficiencies become more and more evident. Their presence then becomes reducible to sheer habit. This is essentially the position of the New Institutionalism in organization theory, and it may be found as well in the "traditionalist" or "communitarian" approach to corporate law (see Millon 1993 for a recent literature review).

### Notes

1. Although this does happen. Anthony Giddens began his career with a zero-sum conception of power, one that he drew explicitly in reaction to Parsons's view that power may expand and, as a result, not always be exercised at others' expense. By the 1970s, Giddens explicitly adopted Parsons's view, at times mentioning the connection to Parsons, at times not.

2. Etzioni acknowledges in the opening to his collected essays, *A Responsive Society,* that his work rests on "a limited number of concepts, linked by an overarching theory." He adds that his 1967 article in the *American Journal of Sociology,* "A Theory of Societal Guidance," "best summarizes my overall approach" (1991, xiii).

3. Etzioni returns to "grand theory" whenever he explores whether and how these sources of compliance affect the larger social order ([1961] 1975, xi–xv, 26; also see Etzioni 1958).

4. Elsewhere ([1961] 1975, 3) Etzioni says "compliance refers both to a relation in which an actor behaves in accordance with a directive supported by another's power, and to the orientation of the subordinated actor to the power applied."

5. The same conceptual distinction is also missing from Etzioni's later (1988a, b) impressive effort to identify the normative-affective factors that orient individuals' selection of goals and choice of means.

6. Whether they otherwise believe these duties are legitimate, or otherwise accept them, is a separate issue.

7. Selznick repeats this procedural threshold but characterizes differently what it accomplishes (1992, 438). In his view it marks a threshold of law's effectiveness and justness. In my view it is more basic, marking a threshold of law's very intelligibility.

8. However, Etzioni notes in his 1975 revised edition that Heiskanen found his compliance theory to be untestable because there is no evidence of pressure toward "congruence," as organizations endeavor to increase their effectiveness ([1961] 1975, 98).

9. This aside, there are all sorts of gems in this first major work by Etzioni. For instance, economists and sociologists today fight ceaselessly over how to define or locate the corporation's boundaries. Is the corporation a fluid site of contracting, such that its boundaries are permeable? Or is the corporation an entity with firmer boundaries? Etzioni's answer is straightforward and compelling: He reminds social scientists that any organization, including any corporation, is an intermediate association that, as such, exercises collective power. Then he adds that an organization's boundaries span all actors who are marked by at least one of three dimensions of participation: involvement, subordination, and performance. Thus, even the lowest-level employee is an organization constituent, but the typical customer or client is an outsider ([1961] 1975, 20–21). Etzioni does not say so, but major customers or clients are likely constituents by his criteria.

Also, three very important contributions may be found in Etzioni's later works: first, his discussion (in *Challenge,* 1985a) of the relationship between economic incentives and governmental commands; second, his argument (in *Economics and Philosophy,* 1986a) for the empirical significance of a "moral utility" above and beyond the economists' reduction of utility to the pursuit of pleasure, interdependent satisfactions, or a formal rank ordering of preferences; third, his effort (in the *Journal of Economic Psychology,* 1988b) to define normative-affective action positively, rather than leaving it as a residual category, as a deviation from the rational model informing neoclassical economics.

10. Etzioni treats normative compliance, whether in religious organizations, political organizations, or hospitals and universities, as resting primarily on individuals' internalizing directives, and thereby accepting them as legitimate ([1961] 1975, 40). He acknowledges that professional organizations add material incentives to their normative controls (ibid., 51–53). But he is careful throughout his discussion to remind the reader that he is assuming all of the organizations he discusses are located in modern democratic societies (ibid., 41, note 2).

11. And he is assuming that normative controls exercised within the institutional context of a modern democratic society—unlike material incentives or coercive sanctions—are somehow inherently integrative rather than controlling (e.g., [1961] 1975, 74–75). This assumption runs through the literature on social control generally, and it bespeaks an unfounded faith—as opposed to a more value-neutral suspension of any such assumption—that existing liberal and social democracies somehow automatically rest today, and for perpetuity, on relatively benign social orders. There is no existing social theory, nor any body of empirical research, that supports this faith. It is simply a prejudice that pervaded American social science in particular after World War II and still persists today, even if more implicitly and in weakened forms.

12. In the early 1960s Parsons was only beginning to abandon his earlier Weberian approach to law and social control and to adopt independently an approach closer to Lon Fuller's. Within a decade, Parsons and Fuller would be team-teaching at Harvard.

13. Bellah's phrase, "community of memory," is telling in this light.

14. Etzioni's position is akin to that of American pragmatists, yet grander: "Fundamental to the pragmatist argument is the view that social experience everywhere, if allowed to follow its natural course, will provide at least minimal opportunities for such positive goods as cooperation, reconciliation, personal autonomy, and enlargement of self" (Selznick 1992, 80).

15. Selznick points out that "Marxist doctrine needs a theory of human nature because without it there can be no secure basis for social criticism, especially radical criticism" (1992, 136). I would add that Marxist theory needs such a theory precisely because it lacks any credible theory of organization, any theory of institutionalized collective power (Sciulli 1992). Etzioni launched his own criticisms of contemporary democracies from the more promising point of departure of an organization theory. But I just showed in the previous section that he failed to consolidate his point of departure as a grounding or critical standard of comparison.

16. Etzioni's emphasis in this sentence begins after the term "basic human needs," but I reduce it for present purposes to the last three words.

17. Consider how these are related to the two factors Etzioni had earlier said affected organizational constituents: legitimacy and gratification (see page 140 above). Both revolve around constituents' subjective acceptance of their situation, and subjective beliefs can be the products of successful control—manipulation or systematic distortion—rather than of integration.

18. This is precisely the reason why Habermas initiated a "procedural turn," steering critical theory away from any and all substantive groundings, whether a theory of capitalist breakdown or a theory of objective interests (see note 22).

19. Selznick is similar, yet slightly more defensible, because he links both cultural development and cultural destruction to human nature via the issue of motivation (e.g., 1992, 7–8; also 149–55). By his account, not only can a loss of motivation lead to cultural destruction, the loss of a strong cultural context can lead to "a loss of spiritual well-being."

20. This is not to say that there are no significant differences at all in comparative perspective. My point simply is that socialization practices, taken in themselves, are not likely to reveal them. This is the factor, however, upon which Etzioni relies heavily to confirm his assumptions about human nature and basic needs.

21. Selznick, for instance, adds the following three sentences to his account of "the pragmatist argument" quoted in note 14: "It would be fatuous to suppose that individuals always do or can achieve these benefits [of cooperation, reconciliation, personal autonomy, and enlargement of self]. Mostly they are frustrated or the outcome is distorted. That is why a moral theory is needed, one that builds upon and yet transcends the promise of ordinary experience" (1992, 80).

22. Critical theorists, both those who predated Habermas's procedural turn away from seeking a grounding on any substantive normative standard (e.g., Lukacs, Marcuse) and those who later resisted taking this turn (at least for a time, e.g., Agnes Heller), all foundered in their efforts to identify basic human needs beyond those of bare physical survival. See Heller (1972) for one of the best statements.

23. Consider the following passage: "[F]ree individuals require a community, *which backs them up against encroachments by the state* and sustains morality by drawing on the gentle prodding of kin, friends, neighbors, and other community members, rather than building on government controls or fear of authorities" (Etzioni 1993, 15, my emphasis).

24. He notes that his work "has become ever more explicitly concerned with moral consideration," and he adds that "my work was never value-free, nor is that of any other social scientist I know" (1991, xvi). Still, this last is an overstatement. Etzioni's earlier works, including *The Active Society,* were more analytical and value free than his later works on communitarianism. Also, *The Moral Dimension* can claim value neutrality as an analysis of the limitations of assumptions underlying neoclassical economics.

25. I show in a separate volume that this is one of six reformulations that are needed to convert Parsons's functionalism into a non-Marxist critical theory, one that I call "societal constitutionalism." Because Parsons referred always to social order as such

rather than to the type of social order that he arguably had in mind implicitly, his works have suffered from an unfortunate but nonetheless accurate criticism. Brazil, for instance, has been a remarkably orderly society through civilian and military rule alike, and yet Parsons's social theory, as it stands, can tell us very little about the Brazilian social order. Yet, if Parsons's social theory is reformulated as addressing a benign or nonauthoritarian social order in particular, then it may well tell us more about Brazil than specialists in the area currently tell us. In fact, I would generalize this point: If an elaborate social theory fails to orient empirical research in fruitful directions beyond what specialists in an area are already studying, then there is no good reason to take the social theory seriously at all (other than as a catalogue device in competition with many others).

26. I should point out that I am examining critically the concepts of community and communitarianism at a scholarly level. Nothing I say in this section, however, should be read as an indictment or rejection of communitarianism as a social movement in the policy-making arena. Liberalism, after all, has long fostered scholarly disputes at a conceptual level, and yet who today would indict or reject classical liberalism (which American Republicans and Democrats share) as a social movement in the policy-making arena? Quite to the contrary, I see communitarianism as an extraordinarily important countertrend to the American drift toward individualism that Bellah and his colleagues (1985) so eloquently described in case studies and examined in theory and that Etzioni (1993) so forcefully confronts in practice. However, my point in saying this rests, again, on my presupposing that the social integration/social control distinction is already being brought to the study of the policy-making arena itself. That is, as long as advocates of communitarianism do not threaten or jeopardize the islands of possible social integration in today's sea of demonstrable social control, then advocates of individualism (such as the ACLU) cannot legitimately claim greater moral authority for their own position. The same holds true, of course, for advocates of individualism: To the extent that they do not threaten or jeopardize these islands, then the dispute between individualists and communitarians is strictly a policy dispute. Neither side can credibly claim greater moral authority than the other. However, if the social integration/social control distinction is not brought to this and other policy disputes, then everything is muddied. Each side postures by staking out some moral stance or another and then labeling the other less moral or principled. The distinction at least permits observing, value-neutral social scientists to adjudicate between such claims, isolating those that have merit and dismissing those that are simply power plays presented ideologically in the rhetoric of morality. See Ringer (1969/1990) for an excellent discussion of how German academicians once employed a rhetoric of morality even as they themselves routinely encroached against the threshold of procedural norms that mediates arbitrariness, at times actually encouraging the Ministry of Education to engage in such encroachments. Readers should not assume that responsible contemporary American voices are immune from ideological posturing. The lead Sunday editorial in the *New York Times* on November 13, 1994 carried the title, "Newt Gingrich, Authoritarian." *Times* editors have every right to engage stridently if they wish in a substantive policy dispute with the new Speaker of the House of Representatives. But on what reasoned basis do they label him "authoritarian" nearly two months before he assumed office and exercised collective power at all, let alone arbitrarily?

27. Etzioni's analogy to the installation of metal detectors at airports is powerfully drawn, and particularly his point that the ACLU opposed this move, too, as an infringement on civil liberties—all evidence to the contrary notwithstanding.

28. Similarly, across his impressive book, *The Moral Commonwealth* (1992), Selznick emphasizes the importance of moral content—that is, of "warranted" substantive norms of behavior. Yet, his own specific references to the moral content of behavior are both rare and thin. As one example, in the context of discussing existentialism, he says: "Without

an appreciation of content—the values and demands of parenthood or citizenship, for example—we lose purchase on the moral order. We may know what it means to be oneself, but not what it means to be a self worth knowing" (ibid., 73). Relatedly, he insists that a collective belief in the value of family life "is more firmly based on funded experience than, say, a belief in the intrinsic worth of higher education for everyone" (ibid., 22). As in political discourse, these references to family values are vague, and family court judges, for instance, need far greater guidance than Selznick is providing. Even when Selznick is most courageous, his position remains vague. He argues, for instance, that the *Roe* decision on abortion is acceptable and yet it fails to recognize the full range of values at stake. "The alternative is to treat the sanctity of human life, and related values bearing on procreation, as values belonging to the community as a whole" (ibid., 417). The issue, of course, is what specifically are the community's values that trump the decisions of individual women?

29. See the Popenoe contribution to this volume (chapter 8), and in particular his citation for a 1993 debate in the *Journal of Marriage and the Family*.

30. The term is taken from Habermas's notion of the "colonization of the lifeworld" by systemic forces of rationalization.

31. These activities are voluntaristic in the sense that I have reconstructed from Parsons's writings (Sciulli 1986).

32. See Sciulli (forthcoming) for an extended discussion of positional interests. I show that English and American courts have extended judicial protection to certain positional interests since the fourteenth century as part of the uniquely Anglo-American fiduciary law tradition (see also DeMott's contribution to this volume, chapter 5). Without using this terminology, this legal tradition has nonetheless always emphasized the importance of the courts' maintaining islands of possible social integration within the sea of demonstrable social control that characterizes a fledgling and then firmly institutionalized market society.

33. This is the case because when social order is disrupted at one level, it is simply transferred to some higher or lower level. It does not give way suddenly to a Hobbesian war of all against all. Thus, when Beirut became most dis-ordered, during the 1970s and 1980s, solidarities intensified below this level, within religious factions, and they may also have intensified above this level, within Pan-Arab or regional organizations. Rather than seeking examples of entropy in social life, therefore, one is better advised to monitor rises and falls of arbitrariness at each level of social organization and also within each sector of a modern society.

34. And Etzioni cannot sustain his own wording. He reverts at times to the second approach to rational action, particularly when he refers to the normative-affective "capsule" within which rational action typically occurs (e.g., 1991, 452–68; 1988b, 95–103; 1985b, 249–61).

35. Etzioni sees that neoclassicism rests on Locke's social contract theory (1967, 24). Yet, he does not himself abandon the premises of this theory because, in his view, the alternatives are less appealing, namely, some variation of romanticism or else the view that society and history are driven by forces that cannot be subjected to human guidance or control. I have alluded to a third alternative, however, one closer to the founders' republican vigilance than to Locke's liberal complacency: Accept that Hobbes's social contract theory is more internally consistent than Locke's (even if a war of all against all is a limiting case), and then appreciate that only if procedural normative mediations of arbitrariness are firmly institutionalized can a modern social order support a democratic political and legal regime. Weber failed to distinguish this threshold from the imposition of some set of substantive norms by force or caprice, and this accounts for his pathos.

36. Or, Etzioni can say that rational action is anti-entropic for the self rather than for

the larger social order. Since Etzioni often refers to the psychological discipline that rational action requires, this may be a legitimate way to read all of his references to anti-entropy.

## References

Allen, William Sheridan. (1965) 1984. *The Nazi Seizure of Power: The Experience of a Single German Town 1922–1945*. Rev. ed. New York: Franklin Watts.
Bellah, Robert N.; Madsen, Richard; Sullivan, William M.; Swidler, Ann; and Tipton, Steven M. (1985) 1986. *Habits of the Heart: Individualism and Commitment in American Life*. New York: Harper and Row.
Bourdieu, Pierre. (1979) 1985. *Distinction: A Social Critique of the Judgment of Taste*. Cambridge, MA: Harvard University Press.
Cookson, Peter W., Jr., and Persell, Caroline Hodges. 1985. *Preparing for Power: America's Elite Boarding Schools*. New York: Basic Books.
Easterbrook, Frank H., and Fischel, Daniel R. 1991. *The Economic Structure of Corporate Law*. Cambridge, MA: Harvard University Press.
Etzioni, Amitai. 1958. "Democratic and Non-Democratic Supervision in Industry." *Journal of Human Relations* 6: 47–51.
———. (1961) 1975. *A Comparative Analysis of Complex Organizations: On Power, Involvement, and Their Correlates*. Rev. ed. New York: Free Press.
———. 1967. "A Theory of Societal Guidance." In *A Responsive Society*, 23–42.
———. 1968a. *The Active Society: A Theory of Societal and Political Processes*. New York: Free Press.
———. (1968b). "Basic Human Needs, Alienation, and Inauthenticity." In *A Responsive Society*, 153–85.
———. 1984. *Capital Corruption: The New Attack on American Democracy*. New York: Harcourt Brace Jovanovich.
———. 1985a. "On Solving Social Problems: Inducements or Coercion?" In *A Responsive Society*, 265–77.
———. 1985b. "Encapsulated Competition." In *A Responsive Society*, 247–64.
———. 1986a. "The Case for a Multiple-Utility Conception." In *A Responsive Society*, 418–51.
———. 1986b. "Rationality Is Anti-Entropic." In *A Responsive Society*, 67–90.
———. 1988a. *The Moral Dimension: Toward a New Economics*. New York: Free Press.
———. 1988b. "Normative-Affective Factors: Toward a New Decision-Making Model." In *A Responsive Society*, 91–123.
———. 1989. "Toward Deontological Social Science." In *A Responsive Society*, 401–17.
———. 1990. "Liberals and Communitarians." In *A Responsive Society*, 127–52.
———. 1991. *A Responsive Society: Collected Essays on Guiding Deliberate Social Change*. San Francisco: Jossey-Bass.
———. 1993. *The Spirit of Community: The Reinvention of American Society*. New York: Simon and Schuster.
Fuller, Lon L. (1964/1969) 1975. *The Morality of Law*. Rev. ed. New Haven, CT: Yale University Press.
Gans, Herbert J. 1988. *Middle American Individualism: The Future of Liberal Democracy*. New York: Free Press.
Habermas, Jürgen. 1973. *Legitimation Crisis*. Boston: Beacon Press.
Heller, Agnes. 1972. "Towards a Marxist Theory of Value." *Kinesis* (graduate journal in philosophy: Southern Illinois University at Carbondale) 5: 7–76.
Kaufmann, Walter. 1973. *Without Guilt and Justice: From Decidophobia to Autonomy*.

New York: Peter H. Wyden.

Millon, David. 1993. "Communitarians, Contractarians, and the Crisis in Corporate Law." *Washington and Lee Law Review* 50: 1373–93.

Reich, Robert B. (1991) 1992. *The Work of Nations.* New York: Vintage.

Ringer, Fritz K. (1969) 1990. *The Decline of the German Mandarins.* Hanover, NY: University Press of New England, Wesleyan University Press.

Sciulli, David. 1986. "Voluntaristic Action as a Distinct Concept: Theoretical Foundations of Societal Constitutionalism." *American Sociological Review* 51: 743–66.

———. 1992. *Theory of Societal Constitutionalism.* Cambridge: Cambridge University Press.

———, forthcoming. *The End of Corporate Governance: A Study in Societal Constitutionalism.*

Selznick, Philip. 1992. *The Moral Commonwealth: Social Theory and the Promise of Community.* Berkeley: University of California Press.

Turner, Jonathan. 1988. *The Structure of Social Interaction.* Stanford, CA: Stanford University Press.

# Part III

## Socioeconomics and Communitarianism: Research

# 8

# Family Values: A Communitarian Position

## *David Popenoe*

Most Americans now agree that the past three decades have not been kind to the American family. During this period—one in which many observers were proclaiming with great insistence that "the family is just changing, not declining"—the social institutions of marriage and the family, in fact, have weakened more, as measured by a variety of indicators, than during any other period of similar length in the history of our nation (Popenoe 1993a). In view of today's sky-high divorce rates, burgeoning nonmarital pregnancy rates, and nearly a quarter of all American children still living below the poverty line, even archprotagonists of "family diversity" are now muting their efforts to retire the concept dear to the hearts of each generation's conservatives: family decline.

Despite growing agreement that the family is declining and not just changing, however, many Americans have great difficulty coming to grips with the moral dimensions of this contemporary family trend. Perhaps we should merely acquiesce to it, as for the most part we have been doing. Times do change, after all, and maybe we need the family less than we used to. And anyway, has not one's family become a strictly private matter, something that should not be the business of the rest of us?

Unfortunately, the "family values debate" in this nation has become heavily politicized and polarized between conservatives and liberals. On the right, the self-avowed "profamily" forces have taken moral positions—such as the prohibition of homosexuality, premarital sex, pornography, and abortion—that are thoroughly unacceptable to those who stress individual rights. To save the family, they argue, we must try to stamp out many undesirable patterns of individual behavior. The forces of the left, in their turn, have tended to denigrate or dismiss the family, often perceiving it to be an institution that is inherently patriarchal, inegalitarian, detrimental to women, and a bulwark of derided "bourgeois values." Even the simple phrase "the family" is a negative to many liberals, as they sense in its use a moral absolutism and threatened social straitjacket. The much preferred term is "families," which implies that everyone should have freedom of choice in family matters.

What is the reasonable person to believe? Which of the many family-value issues in the national debate today should command our greatest attention and concern? A communitarian perspective can help to provide the answer. In a national sociocultural movement led by Amitai Etzioni, communitarians call for a reawakening of our allegiance to the shared values and institutions—most of all the family—that sustain us in a way that balances individual rights with social responsibilities. Communitarians argue that if we keep our eye on the central issues—the strengthening of the social order and the welfare of children—neither the position of the right nor the left is very helpful in coming to grips with what ails the American family. And, surprisingly, the most important family concern has barely been mentioned in the public debate.

As I shall document in this chapter, there is much social science evidence to support the middle-of-the-road communitarian position. A close look at recent social trends and at the accumulating social science evidence on matters concerning the family finds that the case for the various right-wing "prohibitions" is not very compelling; these prohibitions are at best peripheral to the goal of shoring up family life in America. Yet, in sharp contrast to the left-wing emphasis on family diversity, the evidence also suggests that a very high value should be placed on what communitarians advocate: the two-parent, child-centered nuclear family.

Communitarian advocacy for the intact nuclear family, however, should not imply support for continuing the traditional form of the nuclear family—male-dominated and with women restricted to the mother/housewife role. This is a critical distinction, one typically lost in the current debate. Maintaining the traditional nuclear family, as some conservatives demand, is socially impossible, if not also morally unwise. But disowning the nuclear family so as to cleanse ourselves of its traditional form, the disturbing message of much leftist thought, is surely a classic case of throwing out the baby with the bathwater.

## Family Change and Communitarian Values

What does it actually mean to say that the family is an institution in decline? Let us consider first what a social institution is: a way of organizing human behavior in such a way that society's needs are best served. A social institution consists essentially of normative, accepted codes that indicate how people should act in a certain area of life. As a socially sanctioned unit of child rearing, the family was probably the first social institution in evolutionary terms, and it is one of the few social institutions that is universal—found in some form in every known society.

One reason that the institution of the family is universal is that every society has a paramount need to raise children. Children come into this world totally dependent, and they must, for a longer portion of their lives than for any other species, be taken care of and taught by adults. Almost all societies have assigned this task to the biological parents (assuming they exist), or at least to the biological mother. In all societies the biological father is identified where possible, and in most societies he plays an important role in his children's upbringing. Beyond this, family form varies considerably, ranging from the nuclear form, with the two parents living apart from their relatives, to families where the grandmother or other relatives play a major role.

Until recent centuries, however, adult family members did not necessarily consider child rearing to be their primary task. As a unit of rural economic production, the family's main focus was economic survival. Rather than the family existing for the sake of the children, it could be said that the children, as needed workers, existed for the sake of the family. One of the monumental family transitions in history, therefore, was the rise in industrial societies of what we now refer to as the traditional nuclear family—husband away at work, wife taking care of the home and children, and the family unit living apart from relatives. The primary focus of this historically new family form was indeed the care and nurturing of children, and parents dedicated themselves to this task. It was within this family form that western egalitarian democracy, with its emphasis on the relatively autonomous yet socially responsible individual, came to full fruition. And it was this family form that generated the individuals who were responsible for the tremendous intellectual and economic achievements of the industrial era (Berger and Berger 1983; Sagan 1987).

In the past thirty years modern societies have been witness to another major family transformation—the beginning of the end of the traditional nuclear family. Three important changes have occurred. First, many parents voluntarily have broken their nuclear family ties (at a rate currently estimated to be over 50 percent), and many mothers have decided voluntarily to forgo marriage, with the consequence that, for the first time in history, a surprisingly large number of children are being raised in single-parent households, apart from other relatives (Organization for Economic Cooperation and Development 1990). Second, women in large numbers have left the role of full-time mother and housewife to go into the labor market. And, third, the main focus of the family has shifted away from both economic production and child rearing to a paramount concern for the psychological well-being and self-development of its adult members. As one indication of the strength of this new focus, parents increasingly tend to break up—even when they still have children at home to raise—if their needs for psychological stability and self-fulfillment are not met in the marriage relationship.

Through all of these recent shifts, the family has lost tremendous social power in society. Once the only social institution in existence, it is now small, fragile, and overshadowed by both the state and the market. People today spend a smaller portion of their lives actually living in families than at probably any other time in history (Watkins, Menken, and Bongaarts 1987). This trend of family decline, of course, is strongly associated with such concurrent cultural trends as increasing individual autonomy, choice of lifestyles, material affluence, social power for women, and tolerance of individual and cultural diversity. It reasonably can be said that, in many respects, the family's decline is the adult individual's gain.

One thing that has not changed through all the years and all the family transformations, however, is the need for children to be raised by adults, the raison d'être of the family in the first place. Especially in modern, complex societies, in which children need an enormous amount of education and psychological security in order to succeed, active and nurturing relationships of adults to children are critical. Yet today's children probably spend less time with adults, including their parents, than in any other period of history. Absent fathers, working mothers, distant grandparents, anonymous schools, and transient communities are all indicators of a dramatic decrease in child-centeredness, not only within the family but within society as a whole. (Even the speed of modern life is antichild; children thrive at a much more patient, casual pace of living.)

Underlying this decrease in child-centeredness is the radical individualism of modern societies—the preoccupation with personal expression, occupational success, and material gain (Bellah et al., 1985, 1991). Except insofar as they represent means of personal expression for adults, and thus the enhancement of adult self-development, children increasingly are seen as a hindrance to leading "the good life" (Hewlett 1991). This is a fundamental reason why the birth rate is now below that necessary even for the replacement, much less the growth, of the population.

In summary, the trends of modern living—most of all within the family—are leaving children stranded and isolated in their wake. The condition of the family is probably the single most important factor accounting for today's record-high, and in many cases increasing, rates among juveniles and adolescents of delinquency and violence, suicide, depression, obesity/anorexia, drug abuse, and nonmarital pregnancies (National Commission on Children 1991; Select Committee on Children, Youth and Families 1989). High rates of these personal and social problems are found at all class levels and among all sectors of our population.

How should we as a society respond to this socially destructive situation, one that augurs so poorly for the future? Government programs of various sorts may help. But the only long-run solution is a shift in the cultural values by which we live, a shift from family-demeaning to family-supportive communitarian values.

With respect to the universal moral choice between individual autonomy and social obligation, between promoting individual development and fostering social order, societies historically have tended to suppress the individual in favor of strengthening the social. But today, the United States is at the opposite end of the continuum. Individuals have more autonomy than ever before in history, and it is the social that has become problematic. What is problematic is not only that normally interpreted as social breakdown, for example, the extraordinarily high rates of crime, but also the fact that the social order has become less able to nourish individual development. If the social sciences have taught us anything, it is that, for maximum personal growth, individuals must live in a reasonably cohesive and stable social order. Yet increasingly, and despite the high value we place on self-development, people are seemingly more fearful, anxious, and stressed (Myers 1992; Oldenquist 1986). Their self-development is being inhibited.

A cohesive, stable, and nourishing social order, communitarians believe, is based on each member's fulfilling his or her social obligations and commitments. But what is a social obligation? What commitments do individuals have to society as a whole? Beyond pursuing one's self-interest, how should one's social duties be fulfilled? There is the obvious, albeit minimal, answer to these questions involving a "live and let live" principle. In pursuing one's own self-interest, one should not unduly impair the ability of others to pursue their self-interest. To this minimal answer can be added another obvious yet fundamental principle: One should be a "good citizen" and vote, take an interest in public issues, and participate in community activities.

Yet by far the most important social obligation that each individual can fulfill is to responsibly and successfully raise a child to adulthood. It is clearly in everyone's best interest that adults raise their offspring to be healthy, happy, and productive members of society. On such an obligation, the next generation's character, and thereby the future of society, depends.

### The Key Moral Issues

This brings us to the central question of taking a communitarian position in regard to current family trends. Communitarians believe that the highest social value should be placed on parent-child relationships and the fostering of a child-centered society. It is essential to proclaim that children are a society's most important asset, and that once born, they should be loved and valued at the highest level of priority. A "secure base," in the words of John Bowlby (1988), should be a part of every child's birthright.

This moral priority evinces the unequivocal affirmation of monogamous, procreative marriages and of strong, enduring families whose members have time for each other, do many things together, communicate well with one another, and mutually foster the social values on which the good society depends: sharing, cooperation, commitment, and social responsibility. Each of the specific moral positions outlined below stems from this overriding focus on the social importance of strong families and child-centeredness.

## Marital Dissolution

The first issue to be considered is the most important of all to the promotion of strong families and child-centeredness. Yet surprisingly, of the moral issues taken up in this chapter, it is the least widely discussed. There are no national antidivorce movements like those for antiabortion, no national commissions examining the problem of divorce like those for pornography, and few indignant outcries from the pulpit about marital dissolution of the kind heard frequently about premarital sexuality.

The results of ongoing research in the social sciences strongly confirm the negative effects of a high divorce rate, especially on children (Dawson 1991; Emery 1988; McLanahan and Sandefur 1994; Wallerstein and Blakeslee, 1989). Indeed, few bodies of social research have had such consistent findings. But with the well-founded statistical expectation that at least one marriage in two contracted today will end in divorce or separation, moral (and legal) restraints on divorce have obviously weakened enormously (Martin and Bumpass 1989). To be divorced was once a highly stigmatized status; today it has almost become the norm (Glendon 1987; Jacob 1988; Phillips 1988). We have had a divorced president, most religious congregations now contain a large number of divorced members, and even many religious leaders are in second marriages.

A reinstated moral (to say nothing of legal) prohibition against divorce would be an unreasonable intrusion on person liberty. Especially when children are not involved, the case in many marriages today, there is little social benefit in trying to keep two people together who are miserable in each other's company. Companionship has become the main reason for marriage, and when this is no longer obtainable, people should have the right to move on (Cancian 1987). A society that values companionate marriages with strong emotional ties must at the same time expect a relatively high divorce rate.

Yet from the perspective of children and the stability of family life, divorce has become too easy, too accepted. There is a new mind-set that divorce is now an acceptable possibility in each person's life. People enter marriages realizing that if things do not work out, there is a quick remedy. Indeed, some lawyers now tell people when they marry that they should spend as much time planning for their divorce as they spend planning for their marriage. Worst of all, having children is no longer a compelling reason not to divorce; couples with children divorce at a rate only slightly lower than couples without children (Waite and Lillard 1991). In a momentous change of opinion over the last twenty-five years, the great majority of Americans today believe that "a married couple should not necessarily stay together for the sake of the children" (Thornton 1989; Thornton and Freedman 1983).

The new attitude toward divorce strikes at the very heart of the family institution. If all families consisted of nothing but an intimate relationship between two adults, society could probably survive a relatively high breakup rate. But when children are the involuntary victims of the breakup, we are all losers. Greater moral concern about the dissolution of families when children are involved, therefore, is absolutely essential. Making divorce involving children somewhat more difficult in legal terms provides one answer. But constant moral reaffirmation of the importance of lasting marriages and some cultural re-stigmatization of divorce when children are involved are more important in the long run. This moral position draws support from the fact that two family-related conditions in life are still deeply desired by almost all young people: a divorce-free home in which to grow up and a stable marriage of their own as adults.

With such a moral position about family dissolution comes a correlate—one in favor of the intact, nuclear family. Not all intact, two-parent families are successful at raising children. And single-parent families and stepparent families, which today are typically the product of divorce, can often be very successful at this task. Many social scientists have worked diligently to document these facts. Yet the statistical evidence is overwhelming that an intact family is the better vehicle for child rearing (Angel and Angel 1993; Garfinkel and McLanahan 1986; Hetherington and Arasteh 1988). Moreover, it is what children want. For people living in alternative family forms, real sensitivity and often material assistance from others are indispensable. But to waver on the fundamental importance of the intact family in the interest of, for example, promoting "diversity" or "tolerance" is to weaken a moral message on which the very future of society depends.

### Gender Roles

At the heart of the breakdown of the modern family are changing gender roles. More than anything else, strengthening the modern family involves finding ways to improve intimate, long-term relationships between men and women and ways of assisting them in their joint task of child rearing. Unfortunately, partly because the moral issues involved are so complex and difficult to unravel, the gender-role debate is not often cast in moral terms.

Let us begin with the gender-role issue of married women in the labor force, for it is one of the most widely discussed but easiest to resolve. Most men of late middle age and older look back with nostalgia to the era of the traditional nuclear family. But social conditions unquestionably have changed. In what represents a tremendous historical shift, only about one-third of the adult life of the average married woman today will be spent as the mother of at-home children. Even if one were to assume that a woman's main purpose in life was to be a mother and housewife, it is clearly unreasonable for most married women to devote their entire adult lives to these two roles because of later ages at first marriage, average family sizes of less than two children, and much longer life spans (Bergmann 1986; Bianchi and Spain 1986; Davis and van den Oever 1982; Filene 1986; McLaughlin et al. 1988).

If for no other reason, then (other reasons are discussed below), the family era of economically dependent, full-time housewives should be regarded as a thing of the past. Women today are socialized and educated, as are men, to enhance their personal development, make an economic contribution, and contribute fully to public life. For women, as well as for men, the central problem in the organization of adult life is not work versus children but how best to encompass both paid work and raising children.

Dramatic though the demographic and economic changes have been, however, the issue of married women in the workforce and the demise of the separate-sphere family is only the tip of the iceberg in the gender-role debate. The heart of the matter is the way in which men's and women's "inherent nature" is perceived and the expectations we have about their "proper" roles and behavior within the family and within society at large. Again, the debate about male-female similarities and differences has become so polarized between right and left and has taken on so many ideological-political overtones that reasoned discussion is difficult. Also, the position at which one comes into the debate depends on the cultural context. In many contexts, one might emphasize male-female similarities. But in America today, communitarians can reasonably say, it is important to consider more carefully some differences.

The view of the extreme right is that men and women are biologically and irrevocably different in so many fundamental respects that they necessarily should inhabit separate spheres of life, with women taking domestic roles and meeting the emotional-expressive needs of society and men taking work and public roles and thus meeting society's instrumental needs. Man at work and woman at the hearth, it is argued, is not only in the best interest of society but is how the world has always been and ever shall be.

One problem with this viewpoint, as noted above, is that the conditions of life have changed markedly, making such traditional gender roles now largely obsolete whether one supports them or not. Another problem is that differences between men and women have been so exaggerated and distorted throughout history that much of social life has been unfavorable to women. Men have frequently used their public power to the detriment of women. Also, because a wide range of emotions and behaviors is found within both females and males, with much overlap between the two groups, the locking of each sex into separate spheres retards personal development and violates personal liberty.

Some evidence suggests that, at least in modern societies, those members of each sex who have the highest levels of self-esteem and self-confidence tend to exhibit a balance of "male" and "female" characteristics and virtues, so-called psychological androgyny (Cook 1985; Spence and Helmreich 1978; Kaplan and Sedney 1980). For this and other reasons, the notion that men and women ought to be socialized to be more alike is worthy of support. It is in society's best interest to promote more sensitive and caring men who take a greater interest in domestic roles, especially child rearing, and more self-confident and assertive women who are active in work and public life. Indeed, the successful experiences of the Scandinavian nations, where this has been a goal of public policy, indicates that such socialization is clearly possible (Moen 1989).

In contrast to the extreme right, the extreme left takes the view that there are no socially important biological differences between men and women other than childbearing. It is asserted that virtually all male-female differences in psychology and behavior are culturally determined and therefore subject to the human will to change. The implicit (and sometimes explicit) goal of such change is social androgyny—the social identity of men and women. In the utopian society of the extreme left, one would never be able to predict by sex alone what social roles a person will play in life (Okin 1989). Such androgyny-oriented intellectuals see the perfect society as one in which men would do 50 percent of the domestic work, including child rearing, and women would do 50 percent of the public work.

While the right-wing view of male-female differences is detrimental to women, the left-wing view is detrimental to the family. The well-functioning family has always been based on a division of labor that reflects the different abilities and motivations of each sex in child rearing; motherhood and fatherhood have never been thought of as the same. Universally, women have cared for very young children, and men have typically played the child-care roles of provider, protector, and backup assistant. No research has demonstrated that men and women, who obviously reflect the sexual dimorphism found throughout the higher animal kingdom that is related to the biology of reproduction, are not also fundamentally different in other ways, such as in the ability to nurture infants. Without substantial evidence to the contrary, we cannot assume that men and women, given their radically different reproductive roles, could ever be psychologically and behaviorally the same. Many communitarians believe (myself of course included), therefore, that we should think about gender roles and male-female equality more in terms of complementarity, symmetry, and equivalency than in terms of identity (Popenoe 1993b; Rossi 1985).

Although it has brought many benefits to men as well as to women, the gender-role revolution of recent decades has not been kind to families (Friedan 1981; Mintz and Kellogg 1988). The negative effects on the family probably stem mostly from the rapid pace at which the revolution has taken place. But the extraordinary emphasis on gender similarities and workplace equality between men and women, although necessary to counteract the kinds of social distortions still reflected in the views· of conservatives, has downplayed women's reproductive role and thus tended to denigrate motherhood (Gallagher 1989; Hewlett 1986; Mason 1988). And the desirable efforts to change the role expectations for "husband" and "wife," so as to reduce male dominance and female subordination in the home, have tended to undermine the more socially important roles of "father" and "mother" (Johnson 1988).

The gender-role revolution is implicated in today's historically high marital dissolution rates (Blumstein and Schwartz 1983; Cherlin 1992). Gender roles within marriage have become increasingly ambiguous and are thus a frequent cause of marital discord (Hochschild and Machung 1989). This may be particularly true of economic roles: There is some evidence that the closer a wife's income gets to that of her husband's, the higher the probability of divorce (Cherlin 1979; Ross and Sawhill 1975).

The consequences of the gender-role revolution on women have received the bulk of scholarly attention, but equally important have been the consequences, mostly unintended, on men. Men, for example, seem increasingly reluctant to commit to a relationship. And when they do commit, they are less likely to stay committed. In addition to the fear of failure in a high-divorce era, one broad reason for the decline in marital commitment among men is that men's traditional reasons for getting married have been weakened. Through the removal of the double standard of sexual behavior, for instance, women have gained most of the sexual freedoms that men have long held. But this change has also diminished one of the main reasons why men marry—to obtain regular, legitimate sex. Men can now get as much legitimate sex as they want outside of marriage.

Another reason men traditionally have married is to become an economic provider. One important factor in the positive correlation between a wife's income and the chances of divorce, noted above, has been labeled "the independence effect." Because women are more able to maintain themselves economically, they are less likely to stay in an unhappy marriage. But the other side of the coin is that because women are more able economically to maintain themselves, men have less reason for marrying and less compunction about breaking up a marriage once they are in it.

A fundamental problem these few examples point out is the failure to recognize that men and women are in many ways different. They have different sexual drives, different propensities toward children, different perspectives on relationships, different conceptions of morality, and perhaps even speak a different language (Gilligan 1984; Moir and Jessel 1991; Pool 1994; Tannen 1990). They also have different reasons for marrying. A major social task that lies ahead, therefore, is how better to organize the modern family in recognition of these differences without retracting the positive benefits of the gender-role revolution. This is no easy task. But one starting point is to view marriage not as a tie between persons with identical roles but as a complementary relationship between persons who will each bring different outlooks and abilities to the union.

It is both significant and hopeful that in modern societies today the emergence of a new realism about family matters has appeared, one that bodes well for the future of the family and the needs of children. The gender-role debate is turning more in the direction of frankly discussing gender differences. A growing number of women has begun to rethink their lives and their careers along lines different from those of men, with a new interest in "sequencing" work and family pursuits, for example, in a way that enables them to spend more time with very young children (Cardozo 1986). In view of the new work roles of women, many men are becoming more actively involved in child rearing. And the structure of the workplace is becoming more supportive of families and children, with the emergence of parental leave, flexible hours, and other measures that enable both parents to better combine paid work with child care. All of these trends, most communitarians believe, should vigorously be encouraged.

### The Subsidiary Moral Issues of the Right

Strong positions on four other moral issues—the prohibition of homosexuality, pornography, premarital sex, and abortion—have been forcefully put forth by the right in America as part of a "profamily" agenda. Although these issues have an obvious family-relatedness, they are much less important to the promotion of strong families and child-centeredness, as we shall see, than the issues considered above. They are also highly controversial. Few communitarians, including Amitai Etzioni, have taken a public position on all of them. But I shall nevertheless sketch out a possible communitarian position, while recognizing that not all who claim the mantle of communitarianism will agree with me entirely.

### *Homosexuality*

Homosexuality is probably second only to abortion in being the most controversial social issue in America today. Yet the controversy over homosexuality greatly overemphasizes its moral significance as a threat to families. On this issue, and several of those discussed below, the distinction between prohibition, tolerance, and affirmation is important. The debate over homosexuality has tended to be between those who favor outright prohibition and those who favor unequivocal affirmation. The position advocated here is that society should, in support of personal liberty, tolerate a wide range of sexual practices, including homosexuality. In support of the family, however, society should not necessarily affirm every aspect of homosexuality and the homosexual lifestyle as the moral or social equivalent of heterosexuality. As the basis of family life, and thus the key to both social order and societal continuation, heterosexuality should continue to command a high status as a social value.

Moral positions on homosexuality often rest on whether homosexuality is seen as biologically or culturally determined. Many homosexuals have striven in recent years to document that homosexuality is entirely biological, or "essentialist," in character. Like left-handedness or color blindness, it is argued, a person is born either homosexual or heterosexual, and little cultural conditioning, to say nothing of personal or social choice, is involved. In keeping with this assumption, a common (and almost certainly erroneous) assertion is that homosexuals make up "about 10 percent" of every population.

As I read the available evidence, it does not support the essentialist position. A biological proclivity may be a necessary, but it is not a sufficient, cause of most homosexuality. Homosexuality is most likely the result, as John Money (1988) has concluded, of (still undetermined) biological factors in combination, at certain critical stages of individual development, with a social learning or conditioning component. The same holds true for almost all human behavior.

That societies differ greatly in both the prevalence of homosexuality and in their acceptance of homosexual practices supports the proposition that homosexuality is a partly learned (culturally induced) phenomenon. Some societies appear to be almost entirely free of overt homosexual practices. Others, such as some American Indian tribes, have sequential bisexuality built into their cultures. (Typically, immediately after puberty boys go through a culturally approved stage involving homosexual practices but as adults become exclusively heterosexual.) Another societal variation is the concurrent bisexuality of adult Greek males, who have sex both with boys and with their wives. Further support for the proposition that homosexuality is a cultural phenomenon comes from the fact that societies, such as our own, have changed greatly over time in the prevalence of, and attitudes toward, homosexual practices (Greenberg 1988).

It is also important to stress that the term homosexuality refers to a wide spectrum of phenomena, ranging from casual and one-time sexual encounters between persons of the same sex, through bisexuality, to persons who believe that they were born homosexual and have never been erotically attracted to the opposite sex. This suggests that the mix of biology and culture in the creation of homosexuality can be quite variable.

Humans are a remarkably sex-oriented species, and we engage in far more sexual activity than is necessary for procreation. Not only does much of our sexual activity have pure pleasure as its goal, but many people seem fully capable of having other than heterosexual interests. The sex drive can manifestly be focused on a wide variety of objects: people of the same sex, inanimate objects, animals, and one's own manipulations. Indeed, a sizable number of males in our society are presumed to have engaged in some nonheterosexual practices at some time during their life.

In the Judeo-Christian tradition, a strong moral stand has been taken against all nonheterosexual sex practices: masturbation, bestiality, and homosexuality (as well as "kinky" heterosexual practices). Yet on scientific grounds it is difficult to make the case that any of these practices, on their own, have a sufficiently negative social or personal impact to warrant moral, much less legal, prohibition. We should be tolerant of these practices when they are engaged in voluntarily, in private, and do no harm to others.

Such tolerance, however, needs to be distinguished from full affirmation. Societies that place a high value on individual rights and freedoms should tolerate a wide array of homosexual practices, but societies dedicated to the promotion of strong families and child-centeredness should not at the same time advocate or affirm all of the values associated with homosexuality as it is expressed today.

Much of the homosexuality we see about us today goes well beyond occasional or even regular homosexual practice. In recent decades, and apparently for the first time in world history on anything like the present scale, many homosexuals are pursuing a separate and exclusive homosexual lifestyle. Indeed, the label "homosexual" to refer to a particular social status was not even invented until modern times. Throughout history many people have engaged in homosexual practices, but there seem to have been very few exclusive homosexuals of the type that see themselves (and are often seen by others) as a special status apart from heterosexuals. Today's exclusive homosexuals increasingly live apart from heterosexuals and espouse a subculture in which families and children have little place and homosexuality is put forth as the social and moral equivalent of heterosexuality. In the male homosexual world, this subculture is also relatively promiscuous and disparaging of monogamy.

If the exclusive homosexuality and homosexual subcultures becoming so prevalent in the modern world are largely constructed socially, and the evidence strongly suggests that they are, moral questions may properly be raised. Society can reasonably examine the nature of the social construction, for example, and, if necessary, seek changes. If certain political goals of the organized homosexual community are not in society's best interest, it is reasonable that they be challenged. Society can also proscribe certain homosexual practices if they are socially destructive, just as it proscribes some heterosexual practices.

Nuclear familism and homosexualism as lifestyles incorporate contradictory values and views of the world. It would be a moral contradiction for society to affirm and promote the nuclear family, with its basis in heterosexuality and its generation and nurturance of children, while at the same time affirming and promoting all of the values of the homosexual subculture. Fully aware of this contradiction, the homosexual community has assumed a leading role in attempts to redefine the family under the banner of "family diversity" and to cast doubt on the validity and importance of heterosexuality. If they are really concerned about the well-being of the family, the moral agents of society should oppose these attempts.

As a case in point, one of the interesting moral questions that has arisen in recent years concerns the granting of legal and church marriages to homosexual couples. Through legal and religious marriage, many homosexual couples wish both to fall under the jurisdiction of family law (with its legally enforceable rights and duties) and to be provided with the spiritual blessing of the church. In considering this issue one should keep in mind that the main social purpose for the institution of marriage is the insurance of family stability for children (Davis 1985; Houlgate 1988). This institutional purpose, and therefore the importance of the social institution in general, would surely be compromised by incorporating the marriage of same-sex couples.

It is important to add, however, that society has a stake in the promotion of monogamous relationships among homosexuals and in protecting weaker partners in homosexual relationships from exploitation. For this reason, it seems reasonable to establish for homosexual couples marriagelike "domestic partnership" laws, along with their religious equivalents, that could extend to such couples some of the rights and responsibilities of the institution of marriage.

## Pornography

Commercial pornography, mainly consumed by men, is pervasive in modern societies. Recently, the prohibition of pornography has become a burning issue that allies strange bedfellows—radical conservatives and radical feminists. Conservatives believe that it is helping to destroy marriage, while radical feminists hold that it promotes rape and sexual violence and is inherently degrading to women. Evidence to support these positions is limited (Zillman and Bryant 1989). Some experimental evidence suggests that the repeated viewing of sexual violence on the screen desensitizes and disinhibits men and fosters attitudes that at least trivialize rape. There is much less evidence that a moderate use of nonviolent "erotica" pornography weakens marriages. Relevant to this issue is the fact that Japan, a very low-rape and strong family country, has a thriving market for pornography, much of which is extremely violent, and that the pornography industry has flourished in Sweden and Denmark, where women have a higher status than probably anywhere else in the world.

It is important to distinguish between the different kinds of pornography. Much current pornography, for example, that available in the friendly local video store, merely portrays sex acts in which people morally and legally may engage in private. Such a portrayal of common reality (albeit in a distorted, exaggerated, and sleazy way) is certainly not everyone's cup of tea, but in this liberal age the case for its strict prohibition due to some overriding social reason is not an easy one to make (Hawkins and Zimring 1988; Randall 1989). At the other extreme is pornography that portrays, purely for the purpose of perverse titillation, patently offensive and illegal acts, for example, sex with children and physical violence against women. The case for banning such obscene pornography is compelling.

The social problem of pornography is in some ways similar to that of alcohol. Like alcohol, pornography is something many people (men) desire, and, when used strictly in moderation, it appears to be relatively innocuous from both a personal and social standpoint. As in the case of the public management of alcohol, the moral or legal prohibition of all forms of pornography is not the answer. In addition to the virtually insuperable difficulties of enforcing such a prohibition, it would probably do little to promote strong families. Yet all pornography should be kept out of the hands of children, and the availability of even legalized pornography to adults should be controlled.

## Premarital Sex

One of the most prominent norms of the Victorian era was the stricture concerning sex before marriage. It applied mainly to women, however, and was part of the now-infamous double standard. In this regard we have truly been through a social revolution in the past thirty years: Few people today, women or men, marry as virgins or even desire their spouse to be a virgin (D'Emilio and Freedman 1988). Yet the "profamily" right still seeks to morally enforce this norm of sexual behavior.

If there were evidence to show that waiting until marriage to have sex would significantly strengthen marriages, a case could perhaps be made for continuing the moral prohibition of premarital sex—although for egalitarian reasons it should apply to both men and women. But I know of no such evidence. To the contrary, members of fundamentalist and conservative Protestant denominations, for example, who almost surely practice premarital sexual continence more than the rest of the population, have a relatively high divorce rate (Kitson, Babti, and Roach 1985). Indeed, it is a plausible proposition that some premarital sexual experience actually enhances the institution of marriage.

In any event, two features of modern life suggest that it is highly unrealistic to continue to expect premarital sexual abstinence. First, the time period between puberty and marriage has lengthened dramatically (Modell 1989). Average first-marriage ages today are about twenty-four for women and twenty-six for men. This is some ten to fifteen years after puberty, which in turn comes at an earlier stage of life than ever before in history. Second, our culture and mass media have become highly charged with sexually oriented material.

We might be able to make some modifications in our culture, but we cannot do much about the long period of time between sexual awakening and the marital state. Marriages at younger ages might be a solution, but such marriages are ill-advised on other grounds. Victorian norms prohibiting premarital sex, therefore, seem clearly outmoded.

Moral concern should be focused not on the prohibition of premarital sex but on sexual promiscuity, teenage sex, and unprotected sex. Society does have an important stake in seeking to limit all three of these phenomena. Sexual promiscuity, the frequent and indiscriminate changing of sex partners, may well endanger marriages by establishing behavior patterns that are antithetical to stable, long-term relationships. Teenage sex, in the sense of sexuality engaged in by immature individuals, is an important moral issue because it involves individuals who are not yet mature enough to successfully envelop sexuality within a loving relationship. And the vast social problems of abortion, unwanted children, and teenage parents, to say nothing of contagious disease, dictate that all premarital sexuality that is unprotected by the use of safe and effective contraceptives should be considered morally out of bounds.

### Abortion

Finally, a very brief word about what is undoubtedly the most divisive domestic issue in America today (and one of the most divisive in our nation's history)

(Luker 1984; Rosenblatt 1991). This is obviously not the place to engage the terribly thorny moral questions that have dominated the abortion debate, such as at what point a fetus becomes a human life and whether or not abortion should be included under a woman's right to privacy (Tribe 1990). Many reasonable moral grounds exist for limiting, if not prohibiting, the practice of abortion, and almost no society morally condones abortion under any and all circumstances (Glendon 1987). Yet as a threat to the institution of the family, the practice of abortion as it exists in America does not appear to be a serious concern.

From a moral perspective focusing strictly on strong, child-centered families, abortion is best viewed in connection with birth control. With current technological knowledge, there is no way to have a satisfactory birth-control system without the possibility of using abortion as a backup when other methods of birth control fail, a not-infrequent occurrence given the current level of contraceptive technology. To oppose abortion is to oppose having a satisfactory birth-control system.

Of course, one can argue that any form of birth control is antichild, and in the sense that it prevents children from being conceived, that is true. Yet the world hardly needs more unplanned children. What it needs is more wanted children, whose parents are able to rear them to become healthy, happy, and self-reliant adults.

At least in a comparison of nations, there is no evidence that tolerance of abortion is associated with antichild attitudes. In fact, quite the opposite appears to be the case. Japan, for example, which typically receives very high marks for child-centeredness, has since World War II been highly tolerant of abortion. And many European nations in which abortion has not generated the controversy found in the United States have stronger commitments to children than does our nation. It is important to add, however, that in most of these nations restrictions on abortion—and general moral concern about abortion—are considerably greater than what is advocated by radical American prochoicers (Glendon 1987).

## Conclusion

In trying to decide what positions to take in today's family-values debate, the reasonable person faces an agonizing quandary. Not only are firm cultural guidelines weakening, but the moral stands advocated by the right and the left are highly contradictory. The extreme right advocates a policy of return to the family form of an earlier era, while the extreme left advocates what often seems a virtual abandonment of the nuclear family in favor of alternatives.

The communitarian position lies between the two extremes. Our principal concern, according to communitarians, should be for strong and successful nuclear, child-rearing families. Evidence from the social sciences convincingly supports the view that such families are a fundamental social necessity with no adequate substitutes. Once this moral focal point is established, positions on such family-related issues as divorce, homosexuality, and abortion tend to fall into place.

There is no going back to the traditional male-dominated, separate-sphere nuclear family of an earlier era. Changes in values and in the structure of society have made that family form obsolete. What we should be fostering instead are nuclear families in which women and men are equal partners—equal in power and decision making and providing complementary and equivalent contributions. Two key characteristics of the traditional nuclear family, however, should be preserved at all costs: an enduring sense of family obligation and the desire to put children first.

## References

Angel, Ronald J., and Angel, Jacqueline L. 1993. *Painful Inheritance: Health and the New Generation of Fatherless Families.* Madison: University of Wisconsin Press.

Bellah, Robert N.; Madsen, Richard; Sullivan, William M.; Swidler, Ann; and Tipton, Steven M. 1985. *Habits of the Heart.* Berkeley: University of California Press.

———. 1991. *The Good Society.* New York: Alfred A. Knopf.

Berger, Brigitte, and Berger, Peter L. 1983. *The War Over the Family: Capturing the Middle Ground.* Garden City, NY: Anchor.

Bergmann, Barbara R. 1986. *The Economic Emergence of Women.* New York: Basic Books.

Bianchi, Suzanne M., and Spain, Daphne. 1986. *American Women in Transition.* New York: Russell Sage Foundation.

Blumstein, Philip, and Schwartz, Pepper. 1983. *American Couples.* New York: Pocket Books.

Bowlby, John. 1988. *A Secure Base: Parent-Child Attachment and Healthy Human Development.* New York: Basic Books.

Cancian, Francesca M. 1987. *Love in America.* Cambridge: Cambridge University Press.

Cardozo, Arlene Rossen. 1986. *Sequencing.* New York: Collier Books.

Cherlin, Andrew. 1979. "Work Life and Marital Dissolution." In *Divorce and Separation*, eds. G. Levinger and O.C. Moles, 151–66. New York: Basic Books.

———. 1992. *Marriage, Divorce, Remarriage.* Cambridge, MA: Harvard University Press.

Cook, Ellen Piel. 1985. *Psychological Androgyny.* New York: Pergamon.

Davis, Kingsley, ed. 1985. *Contemporary Marriage: Comparative Perspectives on a Changing Institution.* New York: Russell Sage Foundation.

Davis, Kingsley, and van den Oever, Pietronella. 1982. "Demographic Foundations of New Sex Roles." *Population and Development Review* 8, no. 3: 495–511.

Dawson, Deborah A. 1991. "Family Structure and Children's Health and Well-Being: Data from the 1988 National Health Interview Survey on Child Health." *Journal of Marriage and the Family* 53, no. 3: 573–84.

D'Emilio, John, and Freedman, E. 1988. *Intimate Matters: A History of Sexuality in America.* New York: Harper and Row.

Emery, Robert E. 1988. *Marriage, Divorce, and Children's Adjustment.* Newbury Park, CA: Sage.

Filene, Peter G. 1986. *Him/Her Self: Sex Roles in Modern America.* Baltimore: Johns Hopkins University Press.

Friedan, Betty. 1981. *The Second State.* New York: Summit.

Gallagher, Maggie. 1989. *Enemies of Eros.* Chicago: Bonus Books.

Garfinkel, Irwin, and McLanahan, S.S. 1986. *Single Mothers and Their Children: A New American Dilemma*. Washington, DC: The Urban Institute.

Gilligan, Carol. 1984. *In a Different Voice*. Cambridge, MA: Harvard University Press.

Glendon, Mary Ann. 1987. *Abortion and Divorce in Western Law*. Cambridge, MA: Harvard University Press.

Greenberg, David F. 1988. *The Construction of Homosexuality*. Chicago: University of Chicago Press.

Hawkins, Gordon, and Zimring, Franklin E. 1988. *Pornography in a Free Society*. Cambridge: Cambridge University Press.

Hetherington, E. Mavis, and Arasteh, Josephine D., eds., 1988. *Impact of Divorce, Single Parenting, and Stepparenting on Children*. Hillsdale, NJ: Lawrence Erlbaum.

Hewlett, Sylvia Ann. 1986. *A Lesser Life*. New York: William Morrow.

———. 1991. *When the Bough Breaks*. New York: Basic Books.

Hochschild, Arlie, with A. Machung. 1989. *Second Shift: Working Parents and the Revolution at Home*. New York: Viking.

Houlgate, Laurence D. 1988. *Family and State: The Philosophy of Family Law*. Totowa, NJ: Rowman and Littlefield.

Jacob, Herbert. 1988. *Silent Revolution: The Transformation of Divorce Law in the United States*. Chicago: University of Chicago Press.

Johnson, Miriam M. 1988. *Strong Mothers, Weak Wives: The Search for Gender Equality*. Berkeley: University of California Press.

Kaplan, A.G., and Sedney, M.A. 1980. *Psychology and Sex Roles: An Androgynous Perspective*. Boston: Little, Brown.

Kitson, Gay C.; Babri, K.B.; and Roach, M.J. 1985. "Who Divorces and Why?" *Journal of Family Issues* 6, no. 3: 255–93.

Luker, Kristin. 1984. *Abortion and the Politics of Motherhood*. Berkeley: University of California Press.

McLanahan, Sara S., and Sandefur, Gary. 1994. *Growing Up with a Single Parent*. Cambridge, MA: Harvard University Press.

McLaughlin, Steven D. et al. 1988. *The Changing Lives of American Women*. Chapel Hill, NC: University of North Carolina Press.

Martin, Teresa Castro, and Bumpass, L.L. 1989. "Recent Trends in Marital Disruption." *Demography* 26, no. 1: 37–51.

Mason, Mary Ann. 1988. *The Equality Trap*. New York: Simon and Schuster.

Mintz, Steven, and Kellogg, Susan. 1988. *Domestic Revolutions: A Social History of Family Life*. New York: Free Press.

Modell, John. 1989. *Into One's Own: From Youth to Adulthood in the United States 1920–1975*. Berkeley: University of California Press.

Moen, Phyllis. 1989. *Working Parents: Transformations in Gender Roles and Public Policies in Sweden*. Madison: University of Wisconsin Press.

Moir, Anne, and Jessel, David. 1991. *Brain Sex*. New York: Lyle Stuart.

Money, John. 1988. *Gay, Straight, and In-Between: The Sexology of Erotic Orientation*. New York: Oxford University Press.

Myers, David G. 1992. *The Pursuit of Happiness*. New York: William Morrow.

National Commission on Children. 1991. *Beyond Rhetoric: A New American Agenda for Children and Families*. Washington, DC: U.S. Government Printing Office.

Okin, Susan Moller. 1989. *Justice, Gender, and the Family*. New York: Basic Books.

Oldenquist, Andrew. 1986. *The Non-Suicidal Society*. Bloomington: University of Indiana Press.

Organization for Economic Cooperation and Development. 1990. *Lone-Parent Families*. Paris: Organization for Economic Cooperation and Development.

Phillips, Roderick. 1988. *Putting Asunder: A History of Divorce in Western Society.* Cambridge: Cambridge University Press.

Pool, Robert. 1994. *Eve's Rib: Searching for the Biological Roots of Sex Differences.* New York: Crown.

Popenoe, David. 1988. *Disturbing the Nest: Family Change and Decline in Modern Societies.* New York: Aldine de Gruyter.

———. 1993a. "American Family Decline: 1960–1990: A Review and Appraisal." *Journal of Marriage and the Family* 55, no. 3: 525–42.

———. 1993b. "Parental Androgyny." *Society* 30, no. 6: 5–11.

Randall, Richard S. 1989. *Freedom and Taboo: Pornography and the Politics of a Self Divided.* Berkeley: University of California Press.

Rosenblatt, Roger. 1991. *Life Itself: Abortion in the American Mind.* New York: Random House.

Ross, Heather L., and Sawhill, I.V. 1975. *Time of Transition: The Growth of Families Headed by Women.* Washington, DC: The Urban Institute.

Rossi, Alice S. 1985. "Gender and Parenthood." In *Gender and the Life Course,* ed. A.S. Rossi, 161–92. New York: Aldine de Gruyter.

Sagan, Leonard A. 1987. *The Health of Nations.* New York: Basic Books.

Select Committee on Children, Youth and Families. 1989. *U.S. Children and Their Families: Current Conditions and Recent Trends, 1989.* Washington, DC: U.S. Government Printing Office.

Spence, J.T., and Helmreich, R.L. 1978. *Masculinity and Femininity: Their Psychological Dimensions, Correlates and Antecedents.* Austin: University of Texas Press.

Tannen, Deborah. 1990. *You Just Don't Understand: Women and Men in Conversation.* New York: William Morrow.

Thornton, Arland. 1989. "Changing Attitudes Toward Family Issues in the United States." *Journal of Marriage and the Family* 51, no. 4: 873–93.

Thornton, Arland, and Freedman, D. 1983. "The Changing American Family." *Population Bulletin* 38, no. 4. Washington, DC: Population Reference Bureau.

Tribe, Laurence H. 1990. *Abortion: The Clash of Absolutes.* New York: W.W. Norton.

Waite, Linda, and Lillard, Lee A. 1991. "Children and Marital Disruption." *American Journal of Sociology* 96, no. 4: 930–53.

Wallerstein, Judith S., and Blakeslee, S. 1989. *Second Changes: Men, Women and Children a Decade after Divorce.* New York: Ticknor and Fields.

Watkins, Susan Cotts; Menken, Jane A.; and Bongaarts, John. 1987. "Demographic Foundations of Family Change." *American Sociological Review* 52, no. 3: 346–58.

Zillmann, Dolf, and Bryant, Jennings, eds. 1989. *Pornography: Research Advances and Policy Considerations.* Hillsdale, NJ: Lawrence Erlbaum.

# 9

# Community Building in Industrial Relations: Creating Conditions for Workplace Participation

*Wolfgang Streeck*

Ever since encountering their Japanese competitors in the increasingly integrated world markets of the 1970s and 1980s, managers, policy makers, and unionists in Western countries have been looking for ways to make labor–management relations in the workplace more "cooperative." In the new world of post-Fordist production and competition, cooperation no longer simply means the absence of conflict. It requires rather a high degree of positive social integration, with workers accepting responsibility for high performance and willing managers delegating that responsibility to frontline workforces. Indeed, the kind of work reform seen by many today as the only possible defense against being outcompeted by the Japanese social system of production would appear to amount to nothing less than an exercise in community building: mutual acceptance of responsibilities and obligations in addition to rights and entitlements; development of a common sense of purpose and a shared long-term view; willingness to contribute and perform even where contributions and performance cannot easily be monitored; and generally the building of "trust" in the other side's "goodwill."

The main part of this chapter was presented at a conference on "International Evidence: Worker–Management Institutions and Economic Performance" in Washington, DC, March 1994. The conference was organized by the Work and Technology Institute as a contribution to the work of the Commission on the Future of Worker–Management Relations, which was created by President Clinton and chaired by former Secretary of Labor John Dunlop.

The new thinking is reflected in the leading concepts in contemporary Western discussions on work reform, "involvement," and, less nebulous, participation. Today everybody agrees on the desirability, if only for economic-competitive reasons, of a participatory organization of work that emphasizes decentralization of competence, decision making, and responsibility; less bureaucratic supervision and more self-monitoring of workers; high skills and high "professional" consciousness; flexible and broad task assignments; and intensive horizontal cooperation in work teams. The issue is no longer whether a reorganization of work along these lines is desirable, but how one can get there out of the still largely Taylorist organizational culture inherited from the past.

As far as I can see, at the core of most of the debate on the latter point is the question of the effect of formal institutions regulating the employment relationship on community building and trust formation. To managers in particular, the great attraction of the Japanese model, as they read it, includes the apparent absence in it of formal rules; the weakness of unions, as manifested by their company patriotism; the unitary rather than pluralist character of workplace governance; the way internalization of company goals by an involved workforce seems to bring with it unquestioned acceptance of authority and hierarchy; and broad managerial powers and prerogatives supported by high social integration of the organization and a shared enterprise culture. If the purpose of work reform in the West is to increase flexibility and eliminate the rigidities bred by adversarialism, the lesson from Japan seems to be that this can best be achieved by abolishing formal rules and institutions, in particular collective representation, government legislation, and trade unions with commitments extending beyond the limits of the envisaged enterprise community and that interfere with direct communication between management and individually empowered workers. "Involvement" and "trust," the Japanese case seems to confirm, cannot be prescribed; they must come about voluntarily and spontaneously among individuals working together for common objectives, requiring above all the removal of formal institutions that only cultivate artificial differences.

Contrary to this is the view that, even if managerialist interpretations of the Japanese experience are correct, in Western countries the formation of trust at the workplace requires some form of constitutionalization of industrial relations, so as to balance the stark asymmetries in power and mutual dependence between individual workers and their employers and thereby prepare the ground for individual involvement and participation. Low trust and absence of community in the workplace, rather than being caused by formal rules and institutions, negotiated or legislated, are seen in this perspective as a structural condition in any marketlike system of employment; indeed, not only are rules and institutions not the source of low trust, rather it is only through a well-designed set of such rules and institutions that low trust can be managed and mitigated so that something like a workplace community can emerge as a result. In practical discussions on industrial relations reform, this controversy boils down essentially to three issues that I will subsequently develop: (1) the role of collective participation, or workforce representation, in bringing about individual participation, or worker involvement, in an advanced, decentralized organization of production; (2) the potential contribution of legal rights of workforces and workers to participation, as opposed to voluntary arrangements agreed to locally between employers and workers; and (3) the relationship between a post-Fordist organization of work, on the one hand, and unions and collective bargaining, on the other.

### Is collective participation of workforces necessary or helpful for expanding individual, direct participation of workers in new forms of work organization?

Direct participation, or "involvement," of workers in production may be distinguished from collective participation of workforces through rights and procedures of information, consultation, and codetermination (in short, through "ear," "voice," and "muscle"),[1] raising the question of how the two may be related to each other. As indicated, at one extreme is the view that transition toward a post-Taylorist organization of work makes collective participation dispensable, or may even be obstructed by it. Alternatively, it has been argued that new forms of work organization are most likely to emerge and persist where they are supplemented by, and indeed negotiated through, mechanisms of collective participation. At its core, this controversy is over whether a participatory organization of work is likely to be broadly and successfully instituted as part of the intelligent manager's bag of tricks, or whether it is more likely to come into existence as a result of joint regulation involving management and some representation of the workforce as a whole.

This issue has many facets, and a wide variety of empirical evidence may be brought to bear on it. There is, for example, the German discussion in the late 1960s and early 1970s on the relationship between *Mitbestimmung am Arbeitsplatz* (codetermination on the job) and *Mitbestimmung auf Betriebs- und Unternehmenebene* (codetermination at the plant and enterprise level). At the time the prevailing view among union officials was that decentralization of participation to individual workers and work teams would undermine collective participation by work councils and centralized representation through unions. The legacy of this debate persisted well into the early 1980s, when pressures for participatory work reorganization began to come from management rather than from within the unions, raising concerns among the latter about a possible preemption of work council and union rights by managerial "empowerment" of workers and work groups. As Lowell Turner and others have shown, however, union attitudes soon shifted, and the powers of work councils were increasingly used to demand and negotiate work reforms involving direct participation (for example, through group work). In an important sense, this amounted to a fundamental rehabilitation of the *Mitbestimmung am Arbeitsplatz* movement, confirming its claim that direct participation by workers in the organization of production is compatible with collective participation and representation.

Two slightly different but related aspects of the matter dominate the American debate of the 1990s. The first, as I see it, concerns the viability of management-initiated direct participation schemes that are not embedded in some system of collective ear, voice, or muscle. There seems to be growing evidence that worker–management cooperation in a reorganized, more decentralized labor process is more effective and longer-lasting in firms where there is also some form of collective participation—in the United States typically through unions, in other countries often through work councils. Quality circles, total quality management, shop-floor programming, teamwork, and so forth, seem to be more universal, and less likely to disappear when the manager who introduced them changes jobs, where they are not just unilaterally instituted by management but negotiated, regulated, and jointly implemented by management and a collective representative of the workforce (Kelley, Mishel, and Voos). The situation seems to be similar in Britain, where work reform and worker–management cooperation appear more likely to occur in unionized than in non-unionized firms (Marginson).[2] It may also be interesting to compare the success of the Swedish work reform movement in the 1980s, which took place in a context of strong unionism and legal rights to codetermination, to the much less impressive outcome of the attempts of French employers in the 1970s, before the Auroux reforms, to move beyond Taylorism without the support of, and indeed often with the intention to undercut, unions or legal bodies of collective participation.

Second, there is in the American discussion the view that any collective participation of workforces, at least in the United States, would primarily be used by unions and workers to defend traditional rights to job control and seniority, and the rigid Taylorist work organization on which these are conditional. Change toward a post-Taylorist work organization is therefore believed to be ultimately possible only in a "union-free environment."[3] In part, this may have to do with American labor law, which is often claimed to force unions into an adversarial mode vis-à-vis management—an image that was reinforced by several recent court cases in which unions used the Wagner Act to have arrangements for labor–management cooperation in nonunionized firms declared management-dominated and, therefore, illegal "labor organizations." While, as has been said, there are indications that the situation may be very different in unionized firms,[4] the generic problem remains that in a participatory organization of work, it is often hard to distinguish the functional organization of the labor process from the representative organization of workers, which is bound to raise problems regarding either the independence of unions and, where they exist, work councils or the ability of management to adjust work organizations to changing economic and technological needs.

**Does workplace participation require legislation, or
should public policy wait for employers to introduce
participation arrangements voluntarily and at their discretion?**

Legislative intervention would seem to be particularly suitable for instituting collective participation, but it may also be used to set up or facilitate direct, individual, shop-floor or on-the-job participation. Note that legislation may support collective participation by creating nonunion institutions like work councils, by reinforcing union rights in the workplace, or by any combination of the two. It may also support individual participation by creating bodies of collective participation capable of or even charged with negotiating its terms.

The case against legislative intervention is, interestingly enough, often based on the presumed economic benefits of workplace participation, not just for workers but also for employers and their firms. If participation is indeed as productive as is claimed, so the argument runs, managements can be trusted to introduce it on their own; if they don't, this only proves that participation is less economically beneficial than its proponents maintain. Against this one may cite the observation that in many countries and firms changes toward a participatory organization of work that is also more competitive were first demanded by unions and work councils in opposition to initial resistance to change of employers, who often consider any form of workplace participation an intrusion on their managerial prerogative. Collective participation in particular tends to be resisted by employers, even where there is evidence that it may make direct participation, with its economic benefits, easier to introduce and sustain. If a case can be made that employer voluntarism is not sufficient for desirable changes in the workplace to occur at the right pace or on a broad enough scale, and that employers left to their own devices tend to be more reluctant in introducing workplace participation than they should for their own good or that of the economy, this would speak strongly for legislative intervention.

Looking at the international evidence, most advanced industrial countries today do have legislation on collective participation in the workplace, conferring on workforce ear, voice, and, more rarely, muscle the status of enforceable legal rights. It is important to note that there is legislation of this kind even in Sweden and Italy, where industrial relations are traditionally voluntaristic and workplace participation is effected through unions rather than work councils. In the 1970s both countries, which up till then had left the regulation of labor–management relations in the workplace exclusively to unions and management, felt a need to use, legislation to ensure that workforces as a whole were given an opportunity, at the minimum, to form and express collective views on the way their firms were managed.[5] Countries with a longer tradition of legal intervention and a history of workplace participation through work councils, like Germany, the Netherlands, France, and Spain, also legislated in the 1970s and early 1980s to strengthen workplace participation rights. While most of this legislation was concerned with collective participation, the French laws of 1982 (the so-called Auroux legislation) also gave explicit rights—of "expression"—to work groups and individuals. The two major countries that remained unaffected by this international wave of legislation—which coincided with the beginning of the continuing massive technological and organizational restructuring of advanced capitalist economies—were the United States and Great Britain.

In general, it seems that governments that legislate on workplace participation pursue two major objectives. The first is to ensure that participation is more universal than it would be were its institutionalization left to the goodwill and prudence of managements and the policies and market power of unions. Universality may be deemed desirable either because participation at the workplace is regarded as a right of industrial citizenship that government is obliged to extend to all workers, or because of a belief that the economic benefits of participation should not be kept from workers or industries whose employers have not yet understood them or do not care about them. Second, by enshrining the ground rules of workplace participation in formal law, governments remove certain parameters of workplace labor relations from the discretion of the two sides, and thereby from their local haggling and struggling. Legislation may thus relieve local industrial relations from potentially divisive subjects.

Also, by taking the basic rights and procedures of workplace participation out of local contention, legislation discourages attempts, especially by employers, to do away with them unilaterally under economic distress or to threaten to do so unless workers make substantive concessions. Legislation may thus make both sides devote their efforts and inventiveness to cooperative pursuits and positive-sum games, protecting employers from the temptation to seek advantage in creating a "union-free environment," and workforces from the need to hedge against employers defecting from participation regimes and reasserting their managerial prerogatives if they see fit. Constitutionalization of workplace relations may in this way directly contribute to trust formation and community building.

An important question regarding legislative intervention is how detailed, prescriptive, and rigid it should be. Broad legislation that leaves much discretion to the local parties may in effect hand over the existence of effective workplace participation to the whims and vagaries of local power relations or managerial idiosyncrasies and may fail to give reality to the idea of a universal right of industrial citizenship. Still, conditions do differ among different plants and firms, so legislation must allow for its implementation to be adjustable to local circumstances and unforeseen variation. Frequently, therefore, legislation limits itself to mandating unions and employers to work out the details of participation arrangements between them. This is true especially in Sweden, where the codetermination legislation of the 1970s requires unions and employers' associations at the national level to elaborate the terms of workplace participation by national agreement; that agreement, in turn, provides for plant-level agreements to be negotiated between individual employers and union workplace organizations. In other countries, such as Italy, governments historically refrained from legislating on participation altogether, leaving the subject to regulation by national collective bargaining, or helping to bring about agreement by threatening to legislate in cases where employers and unions failed to provide for workplace participation on their own.[6]

The most common approach, it appears, is for governments to lay down in formal law the most basic substantive rules for workplace participation—what broad rights workforces are to have with respect to information, consultation, and codetermination—and otherwise create a set of procedures by which they may be elaborated and adjusted to local conditions. This is in practice the case even in a superficially highly legalistic system like the German one, where formal agreements and informal understandings between work councils and management at the local level specify and modify the relatively detailed prescriptions of the Works Constitution Act (*Betriebsverfassungsgesetz*).[7] Such local flexibility would seem particularly desirable where legislation, as is usual, deals primarily with collective participation, and where the latter is used to negotiate and implement direct participation on the shop floor and in the organization of work. The country where the formal law leaves more room than anywhere else for flexible local elaboration of participation arrangements is probably Italy. While that room seems to have been used very well in the past two decades, when a wide variety of work council–like information, consultation, and codetermination arrangements emerged under the auspices and in the legal form of union workplace organizations, it is interesting to note that there is now a growing consensus in Italy that the time may have come for some form of consolidation of workplace participation through legislation.[8]

**What is the proper relationship between workplace participation, on the one hand, and unions and collective bargaining, on the other?**

Conventionally, comparative industrial relations distinguishes between two models of workplace participation: one in which workforces exercise information, consultation, and codetermination rights through unions and collective bargaining, and another in which such rights are vested in union-independent works councils. Upon closer inspection, however, this distinction appears less than categoric:[9]

1. Even where workplace participation is operated through unions in the absence of legally based work councils, distributive wage bargaining is typically kept separate from information, consultation, and codetermination procedures; where it is not, the latter are not likely to function well.[10] Such separation is easier to achieve where wage bargaining is centralized and conducted by "external unions" above the individual firm, with "internal unions" limited in their activities to workplace-specific subjects other than wages. To protect the

differentiation between collective bargaining and workplace participation, workplace unions in systems without union-independent work councils often create special bodies, such as joint-consultation committees, to serve as channels for (collective) workplace participation unrelated in particular to wage bargaining. This applies widely in Japan, and increasingly in unionized American firms trying to build labor–management cooperation.

2. Even where workplace participation is vested in legislated work councils, these are in countries in which such councils exist in close relation to union workplace organizations, so much so that they often are "union-independent" only in formal status. In fact, the European legislation of the 1970s and 1980s that revived and strengthened workplace participation in response to technological and economic change also strengthened the links between unions and work councils, allowing, and indeed often prescribing, closer cooperation and coordination between the two. Work councils as bodies of collective participation were in this way moved closer to unions as agents of collective interest representation and were in the process infused with a range of representative functions in addition to the purely consultative ones they had served before. The reason seems to have been that, as long as councils were merely mechanisms of consultation between employers and workforces on production matters, they neither attracted much interest from the workforce nor were of much use to employers, especially as these employers found themselves increasingly in need of active consensus, as distinguished from passive acquiescence, of their workforces on a growing number of complicated issues arising from industrial restructuring.

European reforms of workplace participation in the 1970s and 1980s, through legislation or other means, responded to a generally perceived need for institutions that, while not directly involved in distributive conflict, enabled employers and workforces regularly to exchange information, discuss projects and proposals, and work out agreements on increasingly complex and open questions of, for example, work reorganization, training, and technology use. In countries with traditionally union-based workplace industrial relations, where this required supplementing representation with participation, unions in a growing number of workplaces supported the creation of joint union–management committees, sometimes also including nonunionized workers, that superseded the exclusively consultative council system of the postwar period, often after the unions' own status at the workplace had been strengthened by legislation. In countries with legally based work councils, on the other hand, governments recognized a need for supplementing participation with representation and thus legalized closer connections between councils and unions. In effect this resulted in considerable convergence between systems with union-based and with legally based workplace relations.[11]

This is not to say that the formal distinction between workplace unions and work councils became altogether irrelevant. Where unions and councils coexist, the former's legal rights provide workforces with a resource additional to union power in inserting themselves in workplace decision making. Also, work council independence from unions seems to help the latter isolate workplace participation from collective wage bargaining, and thus maintain their monopoly over the bargaining process. Still, unions are typically deeply involved in the operation of workplace participation through work councils, even where these are legally based. Often unions take the initiative in the creation of councils, and indeed they usually have legal privileges in doing so. Where council seats are not altogether reserved to unions, their candidates usually win most of them.[12] Unions also provide training and advice to elected council members and often have legal rights of access to council meetings. Frequently, full-time union officials join work council negotiating teams or sit on joint labor–management committees. As a result, unions tend to be highly successful in recruiting into their membership work councillors originally elected to their positions as nonunion candidates.

Work councils seem to work best with strong unions involved in their operation and while preserving the distinction between participation and collective bargaining, especially over wages. A central issue for the institutional design of workplace representation through a work council system, therefore, is how to encourage cooperation and mutual support between councils and unions, linking interest representation with workplace participation without undermining the necessary differentiation between the two and yet still allowing for both cooperation in production and conflict over distribution to proceed on their own terms.[13] For this to be possible, unions may themselves have to change their modus operandi and organizational structures. Legislation may help them in this, for example, by giving them access to resources, from state or employers, for building a training and support system for elected work council members.

A related question concerns the effect of work councils, or statutory participation arrangements in general, on the organizational fortunes of unions. A frequently held view, especially in the United States, with its history of company unionism, is that councils may weaken unions or make them altogether dispensable by offering workers a less costly alternative form of representation. If American employers advocate councils, they usually do so for this reason, which is why American unions often view councils with suspicion. In European countries, the problem is mainly discussed in terms of the effect of councils on the willingness of workers to join unions and pay union dues; there are some indications, although not conclusive, that such "crowding out" may have occurred in Spain, and to a lesser extent in the Netherlands and Germany. It has been argued, however, and the fear has been expressed, not least among American employers, that councils may to the contrary provide unions with access, for example, in the course of council elections, to a large number of workplaces they would otherwise be unable to penetrate. In this vein, the remarkable stability of German unionism in the 1970s and 1980s was often explained by hidden "union security" effects of the German work council system.

However this may be, union membership may certainly decline for reasons that have nothing to do with work councils, as in France, where councils are weak, or in the United States, where they are nonexistent. In such countries, work councils may in fact be the only chance for the vast majority of workers to achieve some form of participation including, however limited, representation in the workplace. And perhaps unions may also recover a degree of organizational strength and influence, not least over work reform, if only after considerable internal rebuilding that enables them to offer support and guidance to workforces in workplace participation arrangements.

In summary, in countries where trust between management and labor does not come about "naturally," or cannot be mandated by management as a condition of "lifelong" employment, unilateral introduction by individual firms of trust-requiring, post-Fordist work organizations may be less than optimally effective. Successful community building may in such conditions, then, depend on successful institution building backing the desired "involvement" of individual workers in a functional organization of decentralized competence with reliable, noncontestable opportunities for collective workforce participation and interest representation, not least with respect to the terms of involvement, and allowing for simultaneous articulation of conflicting as well as common interests. Low trust, that is, is most likely to be neutralized where it is institutionally recognized, offering it legitimate opportunities for expression that do not interfere with cooperation and creating safeguards that remove attacks on the other side's status as a legitimate party from each side's strategic arsenal or render such attacks counterproductive. It would seem that, precisely where the objective is cooperation and trust between management and labor in private firms operating in competitive markets, there is ample room and indeed high demand for good public policy and intelligent institutional design overcoming endemic failures of both corporate hierarchies and markets in fostering socially integrated work communities between employers and employees.

### Notes

1. Collective participation may be vested in work councils, workplace unions, or any combination of these. I will return to this aspect below.

2. Just as in the United States, there are no work councils in Britain that could speak on behalf of the entire workforce.

3. Or, more generally, in the absence of any form of collective expression of workers that is not unilaterally instituted and controlled by management. A weaker version of this is the belief that where management has accepted direct participation through work groups and similar structures, collective participation is no longer needed since individual workers can speak for themselves and, indeed, have enough freedom built into the perfor-

mance of their work tasks to ensure that their interests are adequately taken into account.

4. Although we have no knowledge of the number of cases in which unionized workforces have successfully opposed post-Taylorist work reform.

5. While both countries relied on workplace unions as their chosen instrument of participation, what they were de facto instituting were rights of participation for a plant's entire workforce. In Sweden, the level of unionization is so high that for all practical purposes the unions represent all workers. In Italy, unions made it their policy after the *autunno caldo* of 1968 to include nonmembers among the workers' councils, even though these were formally, under the *statuto dei lavoratori* of 1970, workplace union representations (*rappresentazione sindacale aziendale*). In a similar way, although in collective bargaining instead of participation, U.S. labor law ensures the identity of union and workforce representation in the workplace through the principles of sole bargaining agent and universal union membership once a union has been duly certified.

6. Note, however, that in practice this remained largely without consequence, apparently because the relation between individual participation and collective representation (in France specifically, through both unions and work councils) remained unresolved and confusing.

7. There is also the possibility in Germany for national collective agreements expanding on legal participation rights. Interestingly, this is not favored by employers, who, in Germany at least, prefer legal rules. Italian employers, by comparison, seem to prefer regulating workplace participation by collective agreement so as to avoid legislation. The difference is not necessarily in different preferences for rigidity or flexibility; it may be that where participation is already instituted by law, collective bargaining on top of legislation may seem to give too many advantages to the unions.

8. This was written before the 1993 election of the Berlusconi government.

9. Remember also that union-based workplace participation may be enabled by formal law, not just by voluntary industrial agreement, and that participation through non-union work councils may be based on collective industrial agreement rather than legislation.

10. For example, the labor–management consultation arrangements in British firms in the 1950s and 1960s withered away under management suspicions that they were abused by the unions for collective bargaining purposes and under union suspicions that management used them to limit the scope of bargaining.

11. See my summary chapter, "Work Councils in Western Europe: Cooperation Through Representation." In *Work Councils: Consultation, Representation, Cooperation.*, eds. J. Rogers and W. Streeck. Chicago: University of Chicago Press, 1995.

12. In all countries, unions have certain privileges in nominating candidates, and generally election procedures are written so as to give a degree of preference to union tickets.

13. Arguably, the country where this has been the least well accomplished is Spain, where work councils are de facto union workplace organizations with full rights to collective wage bargaining; as a result, there seems to be relatively little information, consultation, and codetermination on production matters in Spanish firms.

# 10

# Decoding the Language of Etzioni's Moral Dimension in Complex Organizations

*Calvin Morrill*

In *The Moral Dimension,* Amitai Etzioni presents a perspective of social action that seeks to bridge the gap between the idealized images of the undersocialized rational actor and the oversocialized romantic communitarian. He argues that people attempt to balance these "codeterminants" of action—what he refers to as the "I & We"—into a "judicious mix" during day-to-day affairs (1988, 67). A crucial question left unanswered by Etzioni is how people make sense of the mixture of self-interest and moral commitment in their decision making and routine actions. This is not simply an information-processing problem (i.e., How do I effectively manage information about self-interest and moral commitment in my decisions?) or a maximization problem (i.e., Do I prefer to maximize self-interest or moral commitment?). It is a question that fundamentally links sense making about the codeterminants of action to social context.

Portions of the data herein were presented at the annual meetings of the National Academy of Management, Anaheim, CA, 1988. Support for this work was provided by a Junior Fellowship at Harvard Law School and the Program in Law and Social Sciences of the National Science Foundation (#SES–8508349). I especially thank Albert Bergesen for theoretical leads in this chapter and David Sciulli for carefully commenting on a penultimate draft. William Bailey, Donald Black, Judee Burgoon, Elisabeth Clemens, Sharon Conley, Herbert Gans, Scott Jacobs, Sally Jackson, Deborah Kolb, Peter Manning, Dirk Scheerhorn, Ellen Snyderman, Harrison White, and members of the Social Organizational Seminar at the University of Arizona led by Walter Powell made several helpful comments on earlier drafts of the manuscript.

In this chapter, I compare the narratives told by corporate executives in two *Fortune* 500 organizations about their handling of day-to-day conflict with colleagues. The mix of self-interest and moral commitment is readily apparent in routine conflict management because it fundamentally involves the pursuit of grievances (either formally or informally) and often reveals the underlying normative contours of social contexts (Black 1990; Clark 1988; Morrill 1995; Ross 1993a; 1993b). Moreover, the focus on corporate elites fills in an oft-cited gap in "studying up" normative life in contemporary society (e.g., Nader 1969). Although individuals undoubtedly have personal idiosyncrasies in the way they tell stories, my argument is that conflict management narratives can be viewed as symbolic collective representations of organizational contexts. Such narratives typically contain accounts for action and references to salient social identities that link them to institutionalized vocabularies of motive (Mills 1940). Taking this perspective, the repertoire of vocabularies of motive available in particular organizational contexts becomes crucial for understanding how executives come to make sense of their own actions and interpret future actions.

In the pages that follow, I present a theoretical framework for understanding conflict management narratives as symbolic collective representations. This framework is followed by discussions of the methods and research sites used in the current investigation and a quantitative analysis of executive narratives for conflict management. I conclude with implications for understanding the moral dimension in executive action, managerial decision making, and organizational control at the executive levels.

## Language and Social Context

Sociolinguists across a number of disciplines have argued that the type of social context in which people routinely communicate exerts certain constraints and opportunities on their speech. In turn, the type of speech used can shape and reinforce the selective perception of the speaker, as well as the pragmatics for navigation through social structures (e.g., Applegate and Delia 1980; Atkinson 1985; Giglioli 1972, 14). Basil Bernstein's classic theory of speech codes and social context offers a useful predictive theory regarding the relationship between speech and social context.

### *Speech as Collective Representation*

Bernstein (1964; 1975) classifies speech into two speech codes—the restricted and the elaborated—each of which exhibits certain foundational elements. Restricted codes are

> comparatively simple in structure. We can go a little further and say that in the case of a restricted code the vocabulary will be drawn from a narrow range. . . .

> [It] will not facilitate the speaker in his attempt to put into the words his purposes, his intent, his unique experience in a verbally explicit form. (Bernstein 1964, 57)

In elaborated codes, by contrast:

> [T]he speaker will select from a side range of syntactic options or alternatives. . . . [T]he code through its planning procedures will facilitate the speaker in his attempt to put into words his purposes, his discrete intent, his unique experience in a verbally explicit form. (ibid., 57)

Restricted codes thus carry with them more general meaning about their local contexts without explicitly communicating it through content. Elaborated codes contain much wider ranges of linguistic vocabulary and syntax, exhibit greater flexibility, and are more likely to contain explicit information about the social contexts in which they occur. Although Bernstein appears to have had something of an absolute difference in mind in his original formulations, it is clear that the differences between restricted and elaborated speech codes can be treated on a relative basis as well. Indeed, the concepts may be most useful when comparing the differences between speech codes found in different contexts.

Restricted and elaborated codes develop in social contexts best described by Durkheim's (1933) classic distinction between mechanical (in which social order is based on structural continuity and cultural similarity) and organic solidarity (in which social order is based on structural and cultural differentiation):

> [Restricted codes] will arise where the form of the social relation is based on closely shared identifications, upon an extensive range of shared expectations, upon a range of common assumptions. Thus a restricted code emerges where the culture or subculture raises the "we" above the "I." . . . The use of a restricted code creates social solidarity at the cost of verbal elaboration of individual experience. The type of social solidarity realized through a restricted code points toward mechanical solidarity, whereas the type of solidarity realized through elaborated codes points toward organic solidarity. The form of communication reinforces the form of the social relation. (Bernstein 1975, 147)

In this way, language forms can differentially embed Etzioni's "I & We" codeterminants of action in social contexts.

Applied to the study of managerial discourse, this framework would suggest that restricted conflict management narratives will (1) carry more implicit meaning; (2) assume more tacit knowledge by the listener about the events being discussed; (3) emphasize group rather than individual actions or consequences; and (4) be relatively uniform across executives in terms of linguistic style and conflict management forms mentioned. Elaborated conflict management narratives should (1) carry more explicit meaning (i.e., events should be more "spelled out"); (2) focus on individuals and their personal relationships; (3) contain a wider range of conflict management; and (4) be more personalistic.

One would also expect restricted conflict management narratives to be associated with (1) managerial contexts with pervasively shared assumptions and relatively stable, overarching valued systems; (2) clearly defined boundaries between subdivisions; (3) a great deal of face-to-face interaction between managers; and (4) continuity in managerial-rank membership. Elaborated conflict management narratives should predominate under the opposite conditions associated with restricted narratives: in managerial contexts with multiple or ambiguous value systems, fluid divisional and departmental boundaries, personnel flux, and a lack of social interaction among its members.

### Conflict Management Accounts as Vocabularies of Motive

Scott and Lyman's (1968) arguments concerning accounts provides a link across speech codes, social context, and vocabularies of motive. Scott and Lyman classify accounts into two basic types: justifications or excuses. Justifications focus on the acceptance of responsibility by the actor for an action (or actions) and the reasons why such actions were taken. Excuses are attempts to evade responsibility for actions by denying the link of acts or events to a speaker. In conflict management narratives, such accounts focus attention on why actors managed conflict as they did.

Scott and Lyman (1968), drawing on Mills (1940), argue that affinities exist between accounts and the social contexts in which they are produced. If so, it may also hold that there are affinities between speech codes and accounts. One might expect that actors speaking predominantly in elaborated conflict management narratives would use more justifications spelled out in great detail, emphasizing individual responsibility and the tie of actors to conflict management actions. Restricted narratives, in contrast, would contain excuses that would deny individual responsibility and agency while at the same time attributing conflict management actions to contextual norms and organizational health concerns.[1]

### Identity

The way people define themselves in social situations is an important component of any vocabulary of motives because such identities often carry with them expectations for why particular actions are taken (Tajfel 1978; 1981). In cohesive social contexts, individuals often define themselves in terms of particular social categories: those categories based on the attributes of the group to which they belong. Individuals in cohesive social contexts—where restricted narratives are found—may even define themselves wholly in terms of their group membership to the exclusion of individual attributes (Turner 1982). Therefore, one would expect the identification of principals in restricted narratives to contain references to collective agents and for elaborated narratives to contain references to individual agents.

To summarize the hypothesized relationships between conflict management narratives, accounts, and identities: Under conditions of high group solidarity among corporate managers, one would expect a predominance of restricted conflict management narratives containing accounts that excuse conflict management actions and refer to the relevant principals in terms of collective identities. Under conditions of low group solidarity among corporate managers, one would expect a predominance of elaborate conflict management narratives that contain accounts that justify conflict management and refer to the relevant principals in terms of individualistic identities.

## Method

### Research Sites, Access, and Informants

I selected two research sites for the present investigation based on a combination of opportunity, feasibility, and comparability. The opportunity arose for access to the two sites during the course of a larger multisite field study of organizational conflict. Executives in firms I was already studying referred me to informants in the two organizations under study in the present research. Both of the firms operated primarily in the geographical locale of my larger study. Finally, executives who referred me to these firms suggested that they might offer an intriguing comparison because of the similar sizes of their executive ranks and their prominence as "utility" providers, while at the same time exhibiting divergent recent histories, internal organizational structures, and relationships with government regulators.

General Utility (GU; a pseudonym) sells and provides the infrastructure for natural gas in a large metropolitan area. It has 30,000 employees and twenty-one executives (with the title of vice president or higher) and generated five billion dollars in revenues during 1986. Commco (also a pseudonym) provides communications services and infrastructure in several states. It has 60,000 employees, twenty-one executives, and generated eight billion dollars in revenues during 1986. I gained access to each site through a management consultant who worked with both firms for several years. In each firm, a vice president granted a preliminary interview. Once I established rapport with these informants, I used a "snowball" technique to generate contacts with other informants in the firms (a more detailed account of access appears in the methodological appendix in Morrill 1995). The average age of executive informants at GU and Commco was 55 years, with a range of 35 to 66 years. Most executives had postgraduate degrees. All but two top managers were male northern European Americans.

## Fieldwork

I engaged in fieldwork at each firm's headquarters during a ten-month period in 1985. During this time, at least one site visit was made per week, per firm. Site visits consisted of several data collection activities: (1) semistructured interviews with fifteen of twenty-one executives at GU and sixteen of twenty-one executives at Commco; (2) conversational interviews (e.g., Dalton 1959) with twelve managers and clerical staff members at GU and ten managers and clerical staff members at Commco; (3) observations of staff meetings, executive meetings, and daily work routines; and (4) the collection of company newsletters, brochures, and internal memos. In all, I spent 113 hours at GU and 108 hours at Commco distributed over the ten-month period of fieldwork.

Semistructured interviews consisted of several sets of moderately scheduled questions. An initial set of questions focused informants on the internal and external contexts of their firms and their personal careers. A second set of questions focused informants on their routine interactions with subordinates, superiors, and peers. A third set of questions focused informants on narratives and accounts of conflict they had experienced firsthand as principals. The techniques in this last set of questions derive from fieldwork strategies used by anthropologists to collect memory cases of conflict from disputants and informants in cross-cultural research on disputing (e.g., Llewelyn and Hoebel 1941, 20–40; Nader and Todd 1978, 5–8). Cases are bounded by the substance (issues) of a conflict and can contain several forms of conflict management. I asked informants to specifically relate stories of conflict management, which, as much as possible, I attempted to allow to unfold naturalistically as the informants told them.[2]

## Analysis

I used a constant comparative method (Glaser and Strauss 1967) to code the data. I first open-coded the data into two broad domains: context and conflict management narrative data. Two categories emerged within each context domain, each with its own subcategories: (1) internal context (formal structure, informal relations and culture, and physical layouts) and (2) external context (market type and position, resources available for organizational growth, and regulatory relations with the state). Five categories emerged in the conflict management narratives: (1) conflict issues; (2) conflict management actions; (3) narrative "elaboration"; (4) the social identities of the principals as framed by the speakers; and (5) accounts for conflict management. Several subcategories were taken from relevant literatures and also emerged from the data analysis itself. I discuss each of these subcategories in subsequent sections.

One important limitation of the present study concerns the nature of the communication data. The data were collected at my prompting rather than naturalistically among the informants themselves. Such data could therefore suffer from social desirability effects, performance effects as a result of the interview situation, or a systematic difference in the rapport established between the informants and me. I gained access through identical methods and believe that my rapport with informants in each setting was approximately the same as evidenced to my access to meetings and daily routines in each setting. The analyses that follow demonstrate systematic narrative consistencies *within* organizations and systematic differences *between* organizations. It is difficult to believe that interviewer effects would have such consistent effects on every informant. Moreover, studies of informant accuracy indicate that informants deeply embedded in a particular context tend to be biased in their self-reports of that context toward its normative parameters. That is, reports about particular events in a setting well known to an informant, to the extent they are distorted or remembered inaccurately, are biased toward what usually happens in that setting. One could reasonably argue that communication data collected in the present study—while not collected from naturally occurring conversations among informants—approximates the narratives and accounts that conventionally occur among informants in the two research sites.

## Organizational Contexts

### *Internal Contexts*

GU has experienced few changes in its formal structure or executive personnel during the past ten years. The firm still contains only three ranks at its executive level: vice president, senior vice president, and the chief executive officer of the firm. Seventeen of the twenty-one executives who fill these ranks have worked with the company for over twenty years. One senior vice president commented: "Most of us [GU executives] have spent our whole lives in this company. We've grown up with it." In general, there is relatively dense social interaction among GU managers. Telling evidence for this assertion derives from several quantitative and qualitative sources. I asked the GU executives to estimate the content of their face-to-face communications with their colleagues in terms of three categories: task only, social only (personal matters such as those related to family or off-site recreational activities), and work and social combined. I also requested that informants make their lists add up to 100 percent. On average, executive informants reported that they engaged in conversations with their colleagues that focused on work-only issues 35 percent of the time, social-only issues 23 percent of the time, and work and social issues combined, 42 percent of the time. I then asked the GU executives I interviewed what percentage of their colleagues they would label as acquaintances, friends, or close friends. I again requested that each executive make his percentages total 100 percent. The average percentages across the GU informants (n = 15) were: close friends ($\bar{x}$ = 31 percent), friends ($\bar{x}$

= 45 percent), and acquaintances ($\bar{x}$ = 24 percent). Moreover, executive informants reported on average nearly nine face-to-face contacts per week with their colleagues. Illustrations of face-to-face contacts include group meetings, dyadic meetings, lunches, telephone conversations, or after-hours activities. Although most executives were not connected via E-mail on a regular basis, a few executives reported using an electronic memo system on occasion, which I did not count as a face-to-face contact.[3]

Qualitative evidence for the shared community among GU executives can be found in the way executives refer to themselves and the company. Executives typically refer to the firm as the "utility," and to themselves as "utility men." Many executives, when I asked what their responsibilities were at GU, began their responses with, "Well, I'm a utility man." These labels derived from the greetings GU service people are taught to give upon arriving at a customer's home (e.g., "I'm the utility man" or "I'm from the utility company"). They would then give a cursory (but friendly) description of their duties, typically punctuated with some technical labels about their work. Pictures and plaques on executive office walls further underscore the connections between GU executives and their identification with the firm. Many of them portray social events attended by executives or awards related to GU's sports teams in local corporate sports leagues. Dense interaction of this sort also strengthens the boundaries between GU executives and lower-tier managers.

Despite the overall cohesion among GU top managers, subvariation in the culture and structure at the executive level also exists. Such variation is most apparent in the public affairs office, which was created in the late 1970s to handle marketing, public relations, and communications with regulatory agencies. Three of the company's four newest vice presidents, with responsibility for marketing, regulatory lobbying, and legal affairs, could be found in this department. Public affairs underwent three reorganizations during my fieldwork, replaced its head once, and hired several staff personnel who had little direct experience with the firm (particularly lawyers). As the CEO noted in an interview: "Public affairs is the one department in our firm that we don't know much about. We've tried a lot of things in there that aren't part of our mainstream; hired a lot of people who aren't utility men because we have situations that need to be handled that people who grew up in the firm can't handle. I'm still not sure that any of it is working." Indeed, these changes have created the conditions for partially undermining the overall normative control (e.g., Etzioni 1961) that forms the underlying basis for control among GU executives. I discuss organizational control at a more general level later in the chapter.

Turning to Commco, it contained six office ranks, extending from the chief executive officer/president to assistant vice presidents. It also contained several more departments and divisions than GU. More importantly, Commco underwent several reorganizations in the 1980s, replaced more than half of its executive personnel, reclassified nearly all of its managerial personnel, and embarked on an unprecedented (in its history) expansion of its products and services. All of this created a world of internal uncertainty and differentiation among Commco top managers, the likes of which GU managers only read about in the newspapers. These conditions also coupled with an atomized social world among Commco executives relative to executives at GU. Commco executives reported less than three face-to-face contacts per week with their colleagues. They were also more likely to classify their colleagues as acquaintances ($\bar{x}$ = 68 percent) than friends ($\bar{x}$ = 22 percent) or close friends ($\bar{x}$ = 10 percent). In contrast to GU informants, Commco executives reported that they engaged in conversations with their colleagues that focused on work-only issues 59 percent of the time, social-only issues 18 percent of the time, and work and social issues combined, 23 percent of the time.

The physical layout of Commco's headquarters reinforces executive social fragmentation. The firm's headquarters occupies several different buildings spread out in a large metropolitan area. Several executives reported that they found it difficult to fight through the congestion of the city to meet with their peers face-to-face. Mandatory retreats, begun in the early 1980s, appear to have done little to increase the cohesion among Commco's top managers. As one executive put it, "Executives at [Commco] are like different planets orbiting around different suns."

Unlike GU executives, Commco executives responded to my questions about their responsibilities with detailed descriptions of their individual activities and how those activities related to those of their peers and outside competitors. One vice president even remarked: "I really don't see myself first as a [Commco] executive [making quotation marks in the air with his hands]. I run a very independent operation; with my own style." A senior vice president underscored this point with a lengthy discussion of the company's philosophy of profit centers. Each profit center is largely responsible for its own revenues and operating costs and has relative autonomy over its personnel and budgetary issues. Commco executives also hoped their communication patterns with colleagues would change. As one senior executive noted: "We run a very complex operation that requires a level of communication among our units that we don't presently enjoy. We have gone off on our own, with the profit center idea as our motto."

*External Contexts*

The external contexts of GU and Commco also differ. GU has operated in the same economic domains for the past several decades. The company recently expanded its overseas operations and some of its agreements with local municipalities to supply infrastructure. Yet, its growth still remains moderate. Indeed, the decline of the nuclear energy industry has even reduced some of the expected competition from other energy sources. GU's marked stability contrasts sharply with Commco's dramatically turbulent external context. Commco split from its parent in 1982 to enter into a highly volatile, previously noncompetitive market for communications products. It has also experienced constant conflict over rate increases with regulatory agencies in recent years.

## Conflict Management Narratives

### Conflict Issues

Table 10.1 contains a distribution of conflict issues mentioned in executive narratives collected at GU and Commco. In some instances, executives used these categories themselves to talk about conflict issues.[4] In other instances, category labels are composites of similar issues.

• *Business strategy* issues refer primarily to instances in which executives called into question the appropriateness of pursuing particular domestic marketing and sales strategies, joint ventures with other firms, and overseas ventures.
• *Ethical* issues involved unauthorized uses of company resources (e.g., planes, expense accounts), lying to colleagues, and divulging company strategy to competitors.
• *Managerial style* issues largely refer to personal comportment, treatment of subordinates, and the way executives make decisions (i.e., how they search for information, whether or not they are willing to take a stand at a decision point, etc.).
• *Organizational structure* issues involved grievances about chains of command and reorganizations.
• *Personal performance* issues were nearly always centered on what aggrieved parties termed "unjust" budget processes.
• *State relations* issues focused on strategies used to "manage" state regulatory agencies, including the appointment of former executives to the commissions and lobbying efforts with various commissions.

GU executives reported conflict over breaches in managerial style and ethics most often, while Commco executives reported trouble over organizational structure and business strategy most often. This is predictable. One expects a pervasively shared set of expectations among GU executives to produce more grievances and conflicts defined as normative breaches of personal behavior than at Commco. One also expects conflict over strategy and structure to be modal at Commco because of different normative orders and accompanying expectations associated with numerous reorganizations since the early 1980s.

### Conflict Management Actions

A seemingly paradoxical mix of discipline and negotiation emerged when GU managers referred to their own actions and those of their adversaries. Discipline

Table 10.1

**Conflict Management Issues in General Utility and Commco Narratives**

| Issue | General Utility | | Commco | |
|---|---|---|---|---|
| Business strategy | 7.7% | (3) | 22.9% | (11) |
| Ethics | 28.2% | (11) | 6.3% | (3) |
| Managerial style | 35.9% | (14) | 10.4% | (5) |
| Organizational structure | 12.8% | (5) | 25.0% | (12) |
| Personal performance | 5.1% | (2) | 12.5% | (6) |
| Resource allocation | 10.3% | (4) | 14.6% | (7) |
| State relations | 0.0% | (0) | 8.3% | (4) |
| Totals | 100.0% | (39) | 100.0% | (48) |

*Note:* $X^2 = 19.55$; df = 6; $p < .01$.

refers to negative sanctions directed at subordinates, and negotiation refers to discussions ostensibly aimed at constructing a mutually agreeable solution. Typically, discipline in a conflict management action is associated, across a wide variety of cultures, with institutionalized hierarchies (Baumgartner 1984; Morrill 1989). Negotiation is less typical (Black 1990). However, the presence of both kinds of conflict management may be explained by examining who negotiates with whom. In all but five of the fifty-one times in which negotiation was mentioned in the narratives, it occurred between colleagues of equal rank within the GU managerial hierarchy. Other than the dyadic conflict management actions of discipline and negotiation, GU executives most frequently report third-party interventions, whether appeals for partisan support or appeals for neutral settlement—again consistent with general theories of third-party dispute intervention (Black and Baumgartner 1983).

A different profile emerges from Commco executive narratives. Commco top managers mentioned avoidance as the modal conflict management action, that is, the curtailing of social interaction with offending parties. Toleration (inaction), noncooperation (intentionally not fulfilling obligations to a colleague), and verbal confrontation were then mentioned most frequently as conflict management actions. Interestingly, Commco executives saw their adversaries using far more discipline against them than they saw themselves using against others. The categories in Table 10.2 derive from the cross-cultural and organizational literatures on conflict management (e.g., Baumgartner 1988; Black 1990; Black and Baumgartner 1983; Kolb and Bartunek 1992; Morrill and Thomas 1992), as well from informants themselves. Table 10.2 addresses my hypothesis that more restricted conflict narratives would contain a narrower range of conflict management actions, and, indeed, GU executives did mention a narrower range of conflict management forms in their narratives than Commco executives mentioned in their narratives.[5]

Table 10.2

**Self and Adversary Conflict Management Actions in General Utility and Commco Narratives**

| Action | General Utility | | Commco | |
|---|---|---|---|---|
| Self | | | | |
| Avoidance | 3.2% | (2) | 26.2% | (21) |
| Discipline | 23.8% | (15) | 5.0% | (4) |
| Negotiation | 36.5% | (23) | 10.0% | (8) |
| Noncooperation | 0.0% | (0) | 15.0% | (12) |
| Settlement appeals | 9.5% | (6) | 3.8% | (3) |
| Support appeals | 12.7% | (8) | 7.5% | (6) |
| Toleration | 4.8% | (3) | 17.5% | (14) |
| Verbal confrontation | 9.5% | (6) | 15.0% | (12) |
| Subtotals* | 100.0% | (63) | 100.0% | (80) |
| Adversary | | | | |
| Avoidance | 2.9% | (2) | 26.3% | (25) |
| Discipline | 21.4% | (15) | 12.6% | (12) |
| Negotiation | 37.1% | (26) | 6.3% | (6) |
| Noncooperation | 1.4% | (1) | 18.9% | (18) |
| Settlement appeals | 7.1% | (5) | 5.3% | (5) |
| Support appeals | 17.1% | (12) | 4.2% | (4) |
| Toleration | 0.0% | (0) | 15.8% | (15) |
| Verbal confrontation | 12.9% | (9) | 11.6% | (11) |
| Subtotals** | 100.0% | (70) | 100.0% | (95) |
| Totals | | (133) | | (175) |

*Notes:* $^*X^2 = 24.33$; df = 7; $p < .001$. Percentages are rounded off to 100.
$^{**}X^2 = 41.08$; df = 7; $p < .001$. Percentages are rounded off to 100.

### Narrative Elaboration

Narrative elaboration captures the degree to which speakers explicitly spelled out the meanings and contexts for action within their narratives. I had difficulty operationalizing elaboration into meaningful categories, but I drew from both Bernstein (1964; 1974) and developed others as I coded my findings. Most of the categories for elaboration are self-explanatory, but excerpts from the narratives may help to clarify them:

1. *Attributions of adversary intent.* Commco speaker: "This was no accidental outburst. Phil intended to confront me on his problems with the divisional allocations."

2. *Background events.* Commco speaker: "The problems occurred during the second quarter and came right on the heels of a shake-up in marketing."

3. *Conflict management actions.* GU speaker: "We had a number of one-on-ones [negotiations] to figure out the situation and get it resolved."
4. *Consequences of events.* Commco speaker: "The entire negotiation had a lasting effect on me, Joe, and Carol."
5. *Personalities of principals.* Commco speaker: "He is the type of guy that always seems to be in a battle with someone. . . . It's some sort of vanity psyche, I think."
6. *Reference to contextual norms.* GU speaker: "When you get this far, everyone has the same thing in mind—what's going to work for the utility."
7. *Relations between principals prior to the conflict.* Commco speaker: "I didn't know him at all because he came from an electronics firm, but I could tell right away he was very cocky and wanted to make a name for himself."
8. *Time sequencing.* GU speaker: "First, we got together people from public relations for some preliminary talks. Then we got everyone together without our CEO. Finally, we pulled in the CEO for the final meeting."

In both corporate settings, speakers focused their narratives on how they and their adversaries managed their conflicts and on the background events leading up to their grievances, although Commco executives expended more words on background events than their counterparts at GU. Commco executives spent more time than GU executives on intent, personalities, relationships, and time sequencing, although these categories are still dwarfed by the time spent on background events and conflict management actions. GU executives expended six times as many words in their narratives on contextual norms as did Commco executives. GU executives also spent little time on attributions of adversary intent, consequences of events, personalities, relationships between principals, or the time sequencing of the events in the narrative. These patterns are consistent, respectively, with the expectations regarding restricted and elaborated narratives presented earlier.

### Collective and Individual Identity

Table 10.4 contains the distributions of references to individual and collective identities in managers' narratives. GU speakers consistently elevated the "we," to use Etzioni's terms, over the "I" in their narratives. They consistently referred to themselves and their adversaries collectively, typically using "we" as in "we had a problem. . . ." Such collective labeling occurred even when the principals in a narrative were individuals rather than departments or divisions. At Commco, informants were nearly uniform in referring to themselves and their adversaries as individuals, using proper names, nicknames, and personal pronouns. In many narratives involving interdepartmental conflict management, speakers focused on the "individuals" or "personalities" involved.

Table 10.3

**Percentage of Words Devoted to Elaboration Dimensions of General Utility and Commco Narratives**

| Dimension | General Utility | | Commco | |
|---|---|---|---|---|
| Attributions of adversary intent | 3.0% | (545) | 6.0% | (5,284) |
| Background events | 16.9% | (3,086) | 26.9% | (23,776) |
| Conflict management actions | 42.8% | (7,805) | 36.9% | (32,582) |
| Consequences of events | 2.0% | (363) | 3.0% | (2,641) |
| Personalities of principals | 2.1% | (379) | 7.0% | (6,164) |
| Reference to contextual norms | 21.9% | (3,993) | 3.1% | (2,701) |
| Relations between principals prior to the conflict | 8.0% | (1,452) | 10.0% | (8,806) |
| Time sequencing | 3.3% | (600) | 7.1% | (6,266) |
| Totals | 100.0% | (18,223) | 100.0% | (88,220) |

Table 10.4

**Identities of Selves and Adversaries in General Utility and Commco Narratives**

| Identities | General Utility | | Commco | |
|---|---|---|---|---|
| Selves* | 100.0% | (42) | 100.0% | (50) |
| Individual identity | 42.9% | (18) | 86.0% | (43) |
| Collective identity | 57.1% | (24) | 14.0% | (7) |
| Adversary(ies)** | 100.0% | (34) | 100.0% | (41) |
| Individual identity | 32.4% | (11) | 87.8% | (36) |
| Collective identity | 67.6% | (23) | 12.2% | (5) |

$^*X^2 = 19.03$; df $= 1$; $p < .001$.
$^{**}X^2 = 5.98$; df $= 1$; $p < .05$.

## Accounts

A quick inspection of Table 10.5 reveals that GU speakers were more likely to offer excuses rather than justifications for their conflict management. GU executives excused their conflict management most often by citing a lack of knowledge (as in, "If we had known the city would pay for the utility lines, we would never have sent it up the line to corporate to get it straightened up"). The next most mentioned excuse among GU executives focused on scapegoating (as in, "They pulled us into a tense confrontation with their pompous pronouncements"). Excuses involving the local context frequently occurred as well in GU narratives (as in, "It just goes with the territory of being a manager: Sometimes you have to come down hard on subordinates"). Excuses based on personalities

Table 10.5

**Justifications and Excuses for Conflict Management in Executive Accounts at General Utility and Commco**

| Account type | General Utility | | Commco | |
|---|---|---|---|---|
| Justifications* | | | | |
| Denial of injury | 9.7% | (3) | 25.8% | (25) |
| Denial of victim | 12.9% | (4) | 19.6% | (19) |
| Normative | 35.5% | (11) | 8.2% | (8) |
| Organizational health | 29.0% | (9) | 15.5% | (15) |
| Self-interest | 12.9% | (4) | 30.9% | (30) |
| Subtotals | 100.0% | (31) | 100.0% | (97) |
| | | | | |
| Excuses** | | | | |
| Context | 24.0% | (12) | 16.7% | (6) |
| Lack of knowledge | 40.0% | (20) | 8.3% | (3) |
| Personalities | 10.0% | (5) | 44.4% | (16) |
| Scapegoating | 26.0% | (13) | 30.6% | (11) |
| Subtotals | 100.0% | (50) | 100.0% | (36) |
| | | | | |
| Totals | | (81) | | (133) |

*Notes:* $^*X^2 = 20.29$' df $= 4; p < .001.$
$^{**}X^2 = 18.42;$ df $= 4; p < .001.$

occurred least frequently and rarely focused on individuals. Instead, GU informants concentrated on what one might call a "group personality," as in this response to my question to an executive about why a public affairs executive aggressively dressed down a colleague in an interdepartmental meeting: "We have type A departmental personality in public affairs."

GU executives tended to justify their conflict management on normative or organizational health grounds. For example, one GU vice president justified his verbal confrontation of a colleague during an argument by saying: "We all have the right to be honest with each other at the utility. We were just acting like utility men." An organizational health justification sounded like this: "We pulled together to stop Operations from making a lousy decision about our newest subsidiary." Much less prevalent were justifications based on denials of injuries, denials of victims, or self-interest.

Commco speakers were more likely to justify rather than excuse their conflict management actions. Their most prevalent justifications focused on self-interest: "I knew that if I didn't negotiate with her, it would stunt my career." Or: "I knew in the end that it could cost the firm some money, but it could be my ass if I confronted him. So I let the issue slide and tried to look out after my own ass." This last account demonstrates the degree to which self-interest manifested itself in Commco narratives—even at the expense of organizational health. Self-interest also crept subtly into other forms of justifications, as in this denial of injury to an adversary justification: "There was no harm in saving a little skin off my butt and not talking to him for a few weeks about the problem." Denying that their adversary was a "victim" (e.g., had a legitimate grievance) also occurred frequently in Commco narratives, such as this statement regarding the disciplining of an executive for not making required field visits: "She hadn't been out to see those switching stations for several months. She deserved, no, she was begging to be left off the switching planning committee." Organizational health justifications (in this instance, for noncooperation) sounded like this: "Look, if she doesn't have the numbers from me for the marketing agenda, she can't lose the company a bundle by screwing up the forecast, now, can she?" Normative justifications were least prevalent in the Commco narratives. Nearly all of the normative justifications (six out of eight) related by Commco executives drew on the "way things were" prior to the numerous reorganizations Commco experienced in the 1980s rather than the current normative order.

Accounting for conflict management by reference to personality and scapegoating represented the largest percentage of excuses found in Commco narratives. These types of accounts tended to be quite personalistic and in some cases even took on a psychoanalytic bent. For example, one Commco executive accounted for her toleration of a male colleague in the following manner: "I have some sort of anal retentive complex. I always want things just right and not messy so I hold everything in." Another Commco executive illustrates scapegoating to explain a series interdepartmental negotiations over authority disputes: "Because of Bill, I had to hash out a really complex set of agreements between sales and marketing over several weeks' time. He's really the fly in the ointment." Less prevalent in the Commco narratives were environmental and lack-of-knowledge excuses. Almost all of the environmental excuses were collected just prior to leaving the field as Commco faced increasingly stiff challenges from competitors entering markets the firm had historically dominated. For instance, one executive explained his toleration by simultaneously alluding to the firm's external environment, his personal lack of knowledge, and his self-interest: "The way this business is changing, I couldn't jump down Carol's throat because of the marketing screwup. Besides, I might be out of a job at some point and need her help. Anyway, I'm not sure I have enough information to really know how big the problem is anyway."

## Decision Making and Control in Executive Contexts

As the foregoing analyses suggest, vocabularies of motive are systematically associated with conflict management narratives embedded in particular types of social contexts. Restricted narratives are associated with the dense social relations, shared values, and cultural continuity found among GU executives, whereas more elaborated narratives are associated with the fragmented social ties and cultural discontinuity found at Commco. Executives' accounts of their conflict management actions systematically varied as well. Elaborated narratives tend to contain self-interested justifications, whereas restricted narratives tend to contain excuses that disconnect individual agents from responsibility for their actions.

A central implication of my findings is that the balance between the "I & We" is in many ways not set by the individual but by the contexts in which individuals find themselves. Individuals learn vocabularies of meaning as well as local social pragmatics and repertoires of balancing self-interest and moral commitment. This does not mean that executives are oversocialized dupes. They make choices and at times consciously balance self-interest and moral commitments in their work and personal lives. But they do so within social contexts that contain normative contours for their choices. As such, executives do not sit above their organizations like Napoleonic men and women on white horses looking over their troops. Like their subordinates, they are embedded in social contexts, albeit ones typically not seen by outsiders.

A second implication of my findings is that the tendency toward elaborated or restricted narratives may also be emblematic of particular decision-making practices among managers. March (1988) argues that decision making in organizations is less rational choice (based either on organizational health or self-interest) than that of a fit between rule-conditioned procedures and outcomes accepted as appropriate. If so, managers who experience strongly held values associated with restricted narratives may be especially prone to organizational inertia. Decision makers under these conditions may even fall prey to what Argyris (1982) terms "defensive routines" that freeze managers into particular ways of thinking and acting. By contrast, elaborated narratives may cut two ways. On the one hand, they may be an indicator of greater decision-making flexibility among managers. On the other hand, the verbosity exhibited in elaborated communication may also lengthen decision-making processes and increase decisional uncertainty because of the speech code's greater variety (e.g., Weick 1979).

A third implication of my findings relates to how speech codes linguistically enact organizational controls. Scholars have argued that structural systems of control operating at the lower levels of an organization are based on self-interested incentives that feed into the organization's collective goals (Etzioni 1961; 1965; Tannenbaum 1968). Executives largely escape close monitoring in such systems of control. At the tops of corporations, then, control is enacted through the selection of particular types of managers, typically those who are socially similar in gender, class background, experiences, and education to executives already in place (Kanter 1977; Moore 1962; Morrill 1995). Social similarity of this kind provides a general perspective on managerial pragmatics, but it does not ensure that executives will act in accordance with local organizational goals and definitions of firm success (e.g., Fligstein 1990). The question is, How are local organizational controls enacted and reinforced among top managers? A starting point for answering this question may be found in White and Eccles (1986; see also White, 1986), who argue that control "must work out of the energy asserted by people keeping their own footings in their immediate social milieus. Control exists when the efforts of actors to achieve their own goals yield a self-reproducing social structure" (White and Eccles 1986, 132). Control in this sense does not require direct monitoring or intervention (the constant supervision and sanctions, for example, of a shop-floor steward). It requires minimally that actors have vocabularies or motives for their continued and consistent participation in the local social structure. Speech codes and types of accounts within them are two basic elements in such control systems.

In this light, consider Ouchi's (1980) three ideal types of organizational control. "Clan control" exists when organizational members believe that "individual interests are best served by a complete immersion of each individual in the interests of the whole" (ibid., 136).[6] "Market control" relies on specific contracts of relatively independent actors. "Bureaucratic control" captures the incentive systems prevalent at the lower and middle levels of most formal organizations. Restricted speech codes and clan control have obvious, natural affinities. Restricted codes reflect and reinforce behavior as collective experience via their form and content (e.g., via accounting practices, as at General Utility). The individualistic and self-interested nature of elaborated codes has affinities with contractually oriented market control, as illustrated by the narratives at Commco. Restricted and elaborated codes can both be associated with different types of bureaucracies or even substructures within the same organization (e.g., the public relations department versus other departments and divisions at GU). A punishment-oriented bureaucracy (Gouldner 1954) that emphasizes rigid subordination of individuals to rules might be associated with restricted codes. A representative bureaucracy (ibid.) that emphasizes democratic decision making might be associated with elaborated speech codes.

This analysis only begins to explore the self-interested and moral dimensions of linguistic forms in organizational contexts. We need to collect decision-making narratives from a greater variety of domains. We also need to explore a number of questions concerning codes, accounts, and agency. As examples, under what conditions is agency deleted from executive narratives and accounts by the use of the passive voice and nominalized verbs (e.g., "downsizing," "retrenchment," "relocating")? What are the communicative impacts of these linguistic moves on relevant audiences (both within and outside organizations)? How do linguistic codes cue or constrain the salience of organizational identities (e.g., Albert and Whetten 1985)? We need to explore the relationship between cognitive complexity and decision-making effectiveness (Bartunek, Gordon, and Weathersby 1983). Research on communication and cognition indicates that cognitive complexity enables speakers to use more elaborated speech, but the issue is whether speech codes are an observable manifestation of cognitive complexity (e.g., Applegate and Delia 1980) and how they relate to decision-making effectiveness.

Finally, we need more ethnographic studies of the moral dimensions of organizational elites. If we are to understand the efficacy of Amitai Etzioni's perspective for creating a "new socioeconomics" with greater interpretive and predictive power at both the micro- and macrosociological levels, we need ethnographies at the top social hierarchies. With the exception of a handful of ethnographies over the past forty years (e.g., Dalton 1959; Jackall 1988; Kanter 1977; Kotter 1983; Mintzberg 1973; Morrill 1995), much of what we know about the moral life of corporate elites derives from macrosociological studies of power elites (e.g., Domhoff 1967; Mills 1951; 1956; Mintz and Schwartz 1981; Useem 1984). As we learn more about elites, we are finding that the same conceptual tools and field methods used to study normative life in lower social positions prove useful for studying elites. The perspective offered here resonates with this general argument and advances only a few of the insights that studies of speech codes and managerial decision making may yield for the study of the moral dimension in social life.

## Notes

1. Organizational health concerns could focus on a variety of issues relevant to the survival of an organization, including increasing or maintaining shareholder dividends, increasing or maintaining market shares, and creating organizational structure conducive to individual and collective productivity. Specific issues within these broad contours emerged from informants themselves.

2. At GU, I tape-recorded thirteen out of fifteen executive interviews, and at Commco, eleven out of sixteen executive interviews. Taping hinged on informants' approvals. Only narratives taped in each firm were used in the present analysis. These methods yielded thirty-five GU narratives (averaging 3:56 minutes in length, with a range of 1 to 16 minutes, and a mean number of words of 552) and thirty-three Commco narratives (averaging 15:31 minutes in length, with a range of 11 to 33 minutes, and a mean number of words of 2,520). I also reconstructed and analyzed untaped narratives from field jottings. They appear to have similar characteristics to the taped narratives, except that untaped narratives may be a bit shorter than taped narratives and sometimes contain more delicate issues related to unethical behavior by colleagues. It is interesting to note that GU executives provided many more conflict management actions per minute of narrative than Commco executives. This pattern fits with the compact nature of the restricted narratives at GU and the more elaborated nature of the Commco narratives, in which informants attempted to spell out a variety of details of the events and personalities surrounding each conflict management action.

3. For an extended discussion of these measures at both GU and Commco, see Morrill (1995).

4. The comparative nature of the study necessitated creating a set of categories that could be used consistently across the two sites. However, such a strategy is a balancing act uncomfortably placed between the neatness of analytically general categories and local meanings that may not be transferable across different social contexts. As much as possible, I attempted to create a parsimonious typology that allows for analytic comparison but also approximates local meanings within each research site.

5. The standard deviations for the four distributions provide rough estimates of the number of actions across the categories in each distribution: GU references to self (SD =

7.13), GU references to adversary (SD = 8.24), Commco references to self (SD = 5.59), and Commco references to adversary (SD = 6.74). Lower standard deviations mean that the number of actions in each category lie closer to the mean for that distribution and are thus more evenly distributed across the categories in that distribution. The higher the standard deviations, therefore, the more likely that a few categories within each distribution contain large amounts of the conflict management actions.

6. Note the similarities between "clan control" and Etzioni's (1965) conception of normative compliance, in which organizational members are folded into collective goals via a shared sense of moral purpose.

## References

Albert, Stuart, and Whetten, David A. 1985. "Organizational Identity." In *Research in Organizational Behavior*, vol. 7, eds. L.L. Cummings and Barry M. Staw, 263–95. Greenwich, CT: JAI Press.

Applegate, James L., and Delia, Jessie G. 1980. "Person-Centered Speech, Psychological Development, and Contexts of Language Usage." In *The Social and Psychological Contexts of Language*, eds. Robert St. Claire and Howard Giles, 245–82. Hillsdale, NJ: Lawrence Erlbaum.

Argyris, Chris. 1982. *Strategy, Change, and Defensive Routines*. Boston: Pitman.

Atkinson, Paul. 1985. *Language, Structure, and Reproduction: An Introduction to the Sociology of Basil Bernstein*. London: Methuen.

Bartunek, Jean M.; Gordon, Judith R.; and Preszler, Rita Weathersby. 1983. "Developing 'Complicated' Understanding in Administrators." *Academy of Management Review* 8: 273–84.

Baumgartner, M.P. 1984. "Social Control from Below." In *Toward a General Theory of Social Control*, vol. 1, *Fundamentals*, ed. Donald Black, 303–45. Orlando, FL: Academic Press.

————. 1988. *The Moral Order of a Suburb*. New York: Oxford University Press.

Bernstein, Basil. 1964. "Elaborated and Restricted Codes: Their Social Origins and Some Consequences." In *American Anthropologist: The Ethnography of Communication* [special issue], vol. 66, eds. John J. Gumperz and Dell Hymes, 55–69. Washington, DC: American Anthropological Association.

————. 1975. *Class, Codes, and Control*. New York: Schocken Books, 1975.

Black, Donald. "The Elementary Forms of Conflict Management." In *New Directions in the Study of Justice, Law, and Social Control*, ed. School of Justice Studies, Arizona State University, 43–69. New York: Plenum Press.

Black, Donald, and Baumgartner, M.P. 1983. "Toward a Theory of the Third Party." In *Empirical Theories About Courts*, eds. Keith O. Boyum and Lynn Mather, 84–114. New York: Longman.

Clark, James. 1988. "Presidential Address on the Importance of Our Understanding of Organizational Conflict." *Sociological Quarterly* 29: 149–61.

Dalton, Melville. 1959. *Men Who Manage: Fusions of Feeling and Theory in Administration*. New York: Wiley.

Domhoff, William G. 1967. *Who Rules America?* Englewood Cliffs, NJ: Prentice-Hall.

Durkheim, Émile. (1893) 1933. *The Division of Labor in Society*. New York: Macmillan.

Etzioni, Amitai. 1961. *A Comparative Analysis of Complex Organizations*. New York: Free Press.

————. 1965. "Organizational Control Structure." In *Handbook of Organizations*, ed. James G. March, 650–77. Chicago: Rand McNally.

————. 1988. *The Moral Dimension: Toward a New Economics*. New York: Free Press.

Fligstein, Neal. 1990. *The Transformation of Corporate Control.* Cambridge, MA: Harvard University Press.

Giglioli, Pier Paolo. 1972. "Introduction." In *Language and Social Context,* ed. Pier Paolo Giglioli, 7–17. New York: Penguin Books.

Glaser, Barney G., and Strauss, Anselem L. 1967. *The Discovery of Grounded Theory.* Chicago: Aldine.

Gouldner, Alvin W. 1954. *Patterns of Industrial Bureaucracy: A Case Study of Modern Factory Administration.* New York: Free Press.

Jackall, Robert. 1988. *Moral Mazes: The World of Corporate Managers.* New York: Oxford University Press.

Kanter, Rosabeth M. 1977. *Men and Women of the Corporation.* New York: Basic Books.

Kolb, Deborah M., and Bartunek, Jean M., eds. 1992. *Hidden Conflict in Organizations: Uncovering Behind-the-Scenes Disputes.* Newbury Park, CA: Sage.

Kotter, John P. 1983. *The General Managers.* New York: Free Press.

Llewellyn, Karl N., and Hoebel, E. Adamson. 1941. *The Cheyenne Way: Conflict and Case Law in Primitive Jurisprudence.* Norman: University of Oklahoma Press.

March, James G. 1988. "Introduction: A Chronicle of Speculations about Organizational Decision Making." In *Decisions and Organizations,* ed. James G. March, 1–21. Oxford: Basil Blackwell.

Mills, C. Wright. 1940. "Situated Actions and Vocabularies of Motives." *American Sociological Review* 5: 904–13.

———. 1951. *White Collar: The American Middle Classes.* New York: Oxford University Press.

———. 1956. *The Power Elite.* New York: Oxford University Press.

Mintz, Beth, and Schwartz, Michael. 1981. "Interlocking Directorates and Interest Group Formation." *American Sociological Review* 46: 851–69.

Mintzberg, Henry. 1973. *The Nature of Managerial Work.* New York: Harper and Row.

Moore, Wilbert. 1962. *The Conduct of the Corporation.* New York: Random House.

Morrill, Calvin. 1995. *The Executive Way: Conflict Management in Corporations.* Chicago: University of Chicago Press.

———. 1989. "The Management of Managers: Disputing in an Executive Hierarchy." *Sociological Forum* 4, 387–407.

Morrill, Calvin, and Thomas, Cheryl King. 1992. "Organizational Conflict Management as Disputing Process: The Problem of Social Escalation." *Human Communication Research* 19: 400–28.

Nader, Laura. 1969. "Up the Anthropologist: Perspectives Gained from Studying Up." In *Reinventing Anthropology,* ed. Dell Hynes, 284–311. New York: Random House.

Nader, Laura, and Todd, Harry F. 1978. *The Disputing Process: Law in Ten Societies.* New York: Columbia University Press.

Ouchi, William G. 1980. "Markets, Bureaucracies, and Clans." *Administrative Science Quarterly* 25: 129–41.

Ross, Mark Howard. 1993a. *The Culture of Conflict: Interpretations and Interests in Comparative Perspective.* New Haven, CT: Yale University Press.

———. 1993b. *The Management of Conflict: Interpretations and Interests in Comparative Perspective.* New Haven, CT: Yale University Press.

Scott, Marshall B., and Lyman, Stanford. 1968. "Accounts." *American Sociology Review* 33: 46–62.

Tajfel, Henri, ed. 1978. *Differentiation between Social Groups: Studies in the Social Psychology of Intergroup Relations.* London: Academic Press.

———. 1981. *Human Groups and Social Categories: Studies in Social Psychology.* Cambridge: Cambridge University Press.

Tannenbaum, Arthur S. 1968. *Control in Organizations*. New York: McGraw-Hill.

Turner, John C. 1982. "Towards a Cognitive Redefinition of the Social Group." In *Social Identity and Intergroup Relations*, ed. Henri Tajfel, 15–40. Cambridge: Cambridge University Press.

Useem, Michael. 1984. *The Inner Circle: Large Corporations and the Rise of Business Political Activity in the U.S. and the U.K.* New York: Oxford University Press.

Weick, Karl. 1979. *The Social Psychology of Organizing*. Reading, MA: Addison-Wesley.

White, Harrison C. 1986. "Agency as Control." In *Principals and Agents: The Structure of Business*, eds. John W. Pratt and Richard J. Zeckhauser, 187–212. Boston: Harvard Business School Press.

White, Harrison C., and Eccles, Robert G. 1986. "Control Via Concentration? Political and Business Evidence." *Sociological Forum* 1: 131–51.

# Part IV
## Obstacles to Community

# 11

# The Moral Dimension of Feminist Theories: Implications for Pay Equity

*Paula England and Linda Markowitz*

Comparable worth is an increasingly salient public policy issue in the United States. Yet, there is still misunderstanding about what comparable worth is and disagreement within the feminist community about why it should exist. The purpose of this chapter is twofold: First, to explain what comparable worth is, we define the most common implementation of comparable worth, the point factor system. Explaining the point factor system shows under what conditions and to what extent comparable worth will reduce the sex gap in pay. Our description reveals that point factor systems can be implemented in more or less radical ways, either to challenge the very definition of skill, or more modestly to enhance women's position within the already existing definition. Second, we analyze how more or less radical approaches to implementing comparable worth relate to the distinctions between three broad feminist paradigms: liberal feminism, Socialist/Marxist feminism, and radical/cultural feminism. We conclude that the three paradigms do not differ so much in whether or not to endorse the idea of comparable worth; rather, they differ in their normative recommendations of how to implement a pay equity scheme. Thus, we see that the most philosophical and normative questions about this debate are closely linked with particulars of implementation.

At first glance, comparable worth sounds very much like the more familiar issue of "equal pay for equal work," which refers to men and women in the *same* job, with the same seniority, performing the same work equally well, but being paid differently. But comparable worth is a different issue. It is distinct because it refers to comparisons between the pay in *different* jobs, jobs that differ in that they entail at least some distinct tasks. The comparisons are between one job that is largely male and one that is largely female. The allegation of discrimination is the claim that the difference between the pay of the two jobs results from gender bias in wage setting rather than from other factors. For example, women workers for the city of San Jose discovered in the mid-1970s that secretaries were generally earning less than workers in male jobs that required no more than an eighth-grade education, including, for example, men who washed cars for the city (Blum 1991, 60). Eventually, women in San Jose succeeded in getting the city to do a job evaluation study that showed, for example, that nurses earned $9,120 per year less than fire truck mechanics, and legal secretaries made $7,288 less than equipment mechanics (ibid. 82–83).

The unabated increase in women's employment makes the issue of comparable worth more prominent; as employment becomes the norm for most women most of the time, the consequences of facing discriminatory wages increase. Women's wages are also more crucial than ever to women and children because of increases in single adulthood, single parenthood, and divorce. Between 1960 and 1980, the percentage of women from 25 to 29 who had never married went from 13 percent to 23 percent, and the percent of women aged 30 to 34 who had never married went from 7 percent to 12 percent (England and Farkas 1986). About half of the cohort born in the early 1950s (Cherlin 1981) and two-thirds of those marrying today are projected to experience divorce. Out-of-wedlock births rose from 5 percent of all births in 1960 to 18 percent in 1980. Between 1960 and 1988, the proportion of children living in a household containing a married couple went from 91 percent to 79 percent for whites and from 69 percent to 39 percent for African Americans (Ellwood and Crane 1990).

Less obvious to many is the importance of wages to women who are married to men who earn an adequate "family wage." A long line of research on marital power (reviewed in England and Kilbourne 1990) has shown that women's employment and the relative earnings of husbands and wives affect the balance of power in marriages. When women's earnings are lower, even when they are making valuable contributions in the form of home management and child rearing, their bargaining power vis-à-vis their husbands is substantially lower than is that of women with higher earnings. Thus, comparable worth is valuable to women inside marriages; if the reform raises married women's wages relative to married men's, we can expect it to raise women's relative power within marriage closer to parity with men's.

Largely as a result of feminist efforts from within unions and political groups, forty-two states have passed legislation mandating some data collection on the equity of their pay structures for state employees, twenty-one have done a formal pay equity study, and twenty have made some pay equity adjustments (National Committee on Pay Equity 1989). Recently, however, advocates have faced organized resistance to the concept by the Reagan/Bush administrations (e.g., U.S. Commission on Civil Rights 1985), the Chamber of Commerce and other organizations representing employers, neoclassical economists who see it as a violation of "market wages" (Killingsworth 1990), and the religious right (Schlafly 1984). This resistance has seriously slowed and weakened comparable worth initiatives.

## Implementing Comparable Worth Through Job Evaluation

Job evaluation is seen by comparable worth advocates as a tool to achieve equitable pay for women's jobs. Indeed, Remick (1984, 99) defines comparable worth as the "application of a single, bias-free . . . job evaluation system within a given establishment across job families, both to rank jobs and set salary." Despite this link between job evaluation and comparable worth, the use of job evaluation predates the comparable worth debate by decades. In the 1940s a number of firms began to use job evaluation because they found that it reduced disputes with unions (Northrup 1980; Patten 1987). Job evaluation provided a technical means to rank jobs so that the relative pay of jobs was not subject to negotiation unless the content of a job changed. Thus, while employers still had to bargain about overall pay levels, job evaluation saved them from negotiating about each job individually. Job evaluation has been in common use by many large employers since World War II. Among large firms responding to one survey, 56 percent used job evaluation for managerial jobs, and 67 percent used it for nonsupervisory office jobs (Akalin 1970). Small firms are less apt to use job evaluation (Schwab 1984). The federal government and most state governments use job evaluation, while local governments vary as to whether they use it. Overall, experts estimate that half (Schwab 1984) to two-thirds (Belcher 1984) of U.S. workers are in jobs where wages are affected by job evaluation.

In all methods of job evaluation, it is the requirements of the job that are evaluated, not the performance of a given individual within the job. It is taken for granted that within any one job, different individuals are paid different amounts because of differences in merit or seniority. However, each job generally has a pay range to which such individual variation is confined. For example, the pay in one job may range from $800 to $11,000 per month, while in another it ranges from $950 to $12,500 per month. The second job has a higher pay level, whether defined by the bottom, midpoint, or top of the pay interval. Job evaluation is a way of deciding which jobs will have a higher pay level than others according to a standardized way of evaluating the demands of the job.

Most applications of job evaluation do not have pay equity between male and female jobs as a goal. This use of job evaluation is a phenomenon of the last fifteen years and is limited almost exclusively to job evaluations mandated by states or localities for their public sector employees. A few corporations have undertaken job evaluation with pay equity between male and female jobs in mind, but they are the exception (Bernstein 1986). Yet, job evaluation has an importance for comparable worth far beyond the pervasiveness of its current use. This is because proponents of pay equity want to see job evaluation practiced much more universally as a strategy to correct sex bias in the relative pay of jobs.

The basic idea of comparable worth is simple: Some female-dominated jobs unfairly are assigned lower wages than some male-dominated jobs, solely because those jobs are filled largely by women rather than men. The practice of comparable worth, however, is not as simple as the idea. How does one conclude that gender is the main cause of pay differences between two jobs—one filled largely by men and one by women? How do we know that the jobs' differential pay does not result from differences in their demands for skill or adverse working conditions? This question poses a certain dilemma for the comparable worth advocate because what counts as a skill or an adverse working condition is constructed socially. How one defines these social constructs depends as much on one's interests and assumptions as on empirical truths. For this reason, the job evaluation process is critical. The group that controls the job evaluation process will be able to shape the outcome of comparable worth to some degree. The process of job evaluation is generally controlled by managers, who are often guided by consulting firms. However, nonmanagerial employees, union representatives, and/or citizens (in the case of the public sector) sometimes participate in the process. Since the outcome may be affected by who participates in the process, this is one source of political contestation when job evaluation is to be used to achieve pay equity for women and/or people of color (Steinberg and Haignere 1987; Acker 1987). The issue raises questions about who the relevant stakeholders in the outcome are and how their possible rights to participation in deciding wages are weighed against those of owners or managers in a firm or governmental body. In the remainder of this section we describe the most common job evaluation technique used in pay equity studies in the public sector, the point factor system,[1] and briefly outline how each step in the point factor system is subject to social construction, and hence, gender bias.

The point factor system, like other job evaluation systems discussed above, was not created with the sole purpose of redressing issues of gender pay inequity. The goal of the point factor system is to "objectively" evaluate the skills and other demands on workers for each job. This is done using several steps: describing a job, choosing compensable factors and rating jobs on these compensable factors, assigning weights to the factors to get total points for each job, and using points to set pay. These steps are discussed below.

The first step of the point factor system is to assemble written descriptions of each job (Beatty and Beatty 1984). There are several ways to gather information for the descriptions. One survey of job evaluators found that 90 percent talked to supervisors to obtain information, 60 percent talked to incumbents, and 44 percent observed the job being performed (Schwab and Heneman 1986). Steinberg and Haignere (1987) suggest the use of surveys of incumbents. Such surveys were used in the New York State pay equity study (Steinberg et al. 1986).

Whatever method is used to assemble the information, the general purpose of a job description is to describe the actual tasks performed in each job, as well as the skills, effort, responsibilities, and working conditions associated with the job. This could include what education and prior experience is required to work in the job. It may include how much of one's time is spent on various tasks. It may also include the number of employees, clients, or dollars of budget for which job incumbents are responsible. Overall, the intent is to provide an accurate description of what is demanded of one holding the job.

In this step, differences in outcomes occur depending upon which group gets to provide job descriptions. Managers, incumbents, and feminist groups tend to focus on different aspects of a job as being important. For instance, Acker (1989) shows that in Oregon's managerial-controlled comparable worth reform, skills most commonly found in female-dominated jobs, such as responsibility for the care of persons, were not included in job descriptions, whereas responsibility for physical objects was. Moreover, when managers evaluated positions defined as nonsupervisory, they did not include supervisory tasks within the job description, even when job incumbents engaged in such tasks. Thus, the group controlling this first step of assembling job descriptions has substantial power over which out of many tasks are included in the job description. This then affects results, since a prerequisite to a job characteristic being compensated via a job evaluation is that it is measured.

In the Oregon case, for instance, male employees did not agree with how the female employees evaluated female-dominated jobs, although the female employees agreed with how the male employees evaluated male-dominated jobs. Male employees steadfastly claimed that female-dominated jobs were less tricky and intricate and more routine than male-dominated jobs, and thus deserved less compensation than male-dominated jobs. They held this view despite the fact that they had never held the female jobs and despite evidence provided to them by female employees that their work positions were far from repetitive and routine (Acker 1989).

The second step in a point factor job evaluation is to choose the "compensable factors," the factors that will determine monetary compensation, and to rate each job on each factor. While plans differ in how many factors they use, the most common compensable factors used tap skill, effort, responsibility, and working conditions. "Working conditions" refers to unpleasant, stressful, or dangerous aspects of performing the job.

Steinberg and Haignere (1987, 168–69) argue that the following adverse working conditions are common to women's jobs but are often not included as (or as a part of) compensable factors, and thus are given no weight in job evaluation: sitting for long periods of time without a break; communication stress from dealing with upset people; stress from distractions; stress from visual concentration (e.g., on video display terminals); stress from exposure to sick and disabled persons; stress from receiving work from numerous people; and stress from working in an office where people come and go. The most common job evaluations in use in industry and government have only one (if any) factor for working conditions. In many job evaluation systems, this factor taps only those onerous working conditions typical to men's jobs, such as lifting heavy objects, exposure to dirt, or potential for physical danger. This has an adverse impact on the points women's jobs receive, and thus on women's wages.

In the third step, evaluators must decide whether or not each factor is equally important. For example, should adverse working conditions be given a weight equal to skills requiring education? The relative weight given to a factor will determine the relative dollar return to increments of that factor compared to other factors if the job evaluation is used to set pay. There are two ways to determine the weights of factors, the a priori and policy-capturing methods.

In a priori systems (such as the commercial Hay or Willis plans) the weights of factors are determined in advance by management or consultants. The weights are often hidden, implied in the scoring systems. For example, if there are four factors, and one factor ranges from 0 to 10 while the other three range from 0 to 5, and total points are calculated by adding up points on each factor, roughly speaking, this leads to giving a weight to the first factor that is twice as large as the other three. Firms and governments that use a priori systems often use commercial systems from major consulting companies. Most consulting companies use the same implicit weights for all their clients, weights that they have found to "fit" general market realities. Such weights tend to conserve the existing job hierarchy (Acker 1989). For example, responsibility for managing workers is usually weighted much more heavily than responsibility for the well-being of students, patients, or clients of the organization. This is a political choice that could well be different if managers or consultants dependent on management for business did not control the job evaluation process. Because comparable worth argues that factors associated with female-dominated jobs are undervalued, it is an important consideration in favor of the a priori method that it has the potential to change the lack of value female-dominated jobs face by changing weights so that factors associated with female-dominated jobs (such as responsibility for nurturing clients or stress from working for numerous people) are given more value. However, this is unlikely to occur with standard job evaluations in use by management and management-oriented consulting firms.

Policy-capturing systems determine the weights of factors using current pay practices of the employer as the criterion. This is generally done with a multiple regression analysis that predicts jobs' pay from their points on all the factors.[2] The regression analysis estimates a coefficient for each factor. The coefficient for each factor reveals the weight it is being given in the employer's current pay practices. This is the sense in which this type of job evaluation "captures policy" with its analysis of how existing pay corresponds to the various compensable factors.

Policy-capturing regression analyses may use all jobs in the establishment as observations in the analysis. Alternatively, the analysis may use only "key" or "benchmark" jobs as observations. Key or benchmark jobs include those in which hiring is done from outside the organization, as well as those that are most comparable to jobs in other organizations (Schwab 1980; Schwab and Wichern 1983). These are the jobs most directly affected by external labor market conditions. Because of this, by using key jobs, policy-capturing systems of determining weights are affected by the relative weights given to various compensable factors in the external labor market.

Because the policy-capturing method takes the present wage system as the database from which to calculate weights, if female-dominated jobs are undervalued because factors on which they score high receive low weight, their pay is likely to remain low after the policy-capturing job evaluation has been implemented. Thus, if workers in female-dominated jobs were well informed and had a large say in the process of job evaluation, a policy-capturing system might not be the method they would prefer to see used, although, as discussed above, an a priori analysis guided by a management-oriented consulting firm may be no better.

In the fourth step, points from the different jobs must be totaled so that wages can be determined. This is calculated by putting the score for each factor for a given job into the equation (containing a constant and a slope or weight for each factor) obtained from either the a priori weight selection or the policy-capturing regression analysis. This allows one to calculate the pay that we would expect this job to have based on its scores on each of the compensable factors, given their weights.

Often a scattergram is drawn of total job points against pay. Pay is generally measured with the bottom, top, or midpoint of the pay interval set by policy for each job. Each point in the scattergram represents one job. The location of the point from left to right is determined by the number of total points the job was given in the job evaluation. The vertical location of the point is determined by the job's current pay. The best-fitting line through the scatter of points is called the "policy line" or "pay line." There will always be some scatter of points about the line, but in general the points cluster around a line, indicating that there is a substantial correlation between points and pay. Jobs above the line are those that are paid more than average for their number of points. Jobs below the line are paid less than average for their number of points. Pay equity studies generally find a pattern similar to that shown in Figure 11.1. Most male jobs are above the line. Most female jobs are below the line. In fact, sometimes we draw two lines, one through the male jobs and one through the female jobs, referred to as the male and female lines.

At this point the employer decides what pay changes to make as a result of the job evaluation. Pay equity advocates generally advocate raising female jobs to the male pay line. This increases the overall wage bill. Another alternative is to move female jobs to the overall pay line. (See Figure 11.1 for a hypothetical example of a male job line, female job line, and overall pay line.) Then what is to

Figure 11.1 **Scattergram Plotting Job Pay Against Total Points, Where Female Jobs Pay Less than Male Jobs with the Same Number of Points**

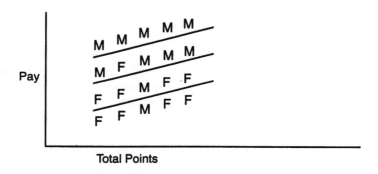

*Note:* "F" denotes predominantly female job; "M" denotes predominantly male job. Units of analysis are jobs. If a policy-capturing or a priori job evaluation found a relationship between points and pay like that in this figure, the conclusion would be that predominantly female jobs are paid less than predominantly male jobs of comparable value to the employer, that is, that the sort of discrimination at issue in comparable worth has been documented. The top line is the best-fitting line through the male jobs, referred to as the "male line," the bottom line is the best-fitting line through female jobs, the "female line," and the middle line is the best-fitting line through all jobs, sometimes called the "policy line" or "pay line."

be done about the many male jobs already paid more than this overall pay line? It is not conventional to lower existing workers' wages, although not doing so guarantees that pay equity will increase the overall wage bill. However, sometimes jobs above the line are "red-circled" for slower raises and/or for two-tier wage systems in which new hires in the job are paid according to the policy line while incumbents are paid the old, higher wage. The two systems then gradually converge through differential raises and/or attrition. This option is less expensive to employers than raising the pay of female jobs to the current male job line, but it is generally more expensive than moving all jobs' pay to the overall line even if it entails reducing pay in male jobs. Choices between these alternatives are irreducibly political; they differentially affect the economic interests of owners, workers in "female" jobs, workers in "male" jobs, and unions.

It is interesting to note that despite the lack of control feminists and groups representing employees commonly have over the process of job evaluation, most results from job evaluations find female-dominated jobs to be paid less than male-dominated jobs receiving the same points. This means that regardless of the built-in advantages male employees and managers face with the point factor system, female-dominated jobs are still found to be discriminated against. Hence the appeal of comparable worth to feminists.

## Comparable Worth and Three Feminist Theoretical Perspectives

We have chosen to look at three general theoretical perspectives in the feminist literature: liberal feminism, Socialist/Marxist feminism, and radical/cultural feminism. To be sure, collapsing feminist thought into only three categories oversimplifies existing theory. Many theorists resist any one of these labels. We do not deny variation within feminist theories nor the existence of feminist theories not discussed here. However, we believe understanding the ideas and policies associated with comparable worth is enhanced by looking at a small number of general perspectives, rather than analyzing a myriad of perspectives with minor variations.

### *Liberal Feminism*

Liberal feminism derives from classical liberalism, which underlies most of the political spectrum in the contemporary United States. Liberalism is concerned with questions about the relations of individuals to each other and to the state. Liberalism is individualist in that it advocates rights accruing to individuals rather than collectivities (Gray 1986). All versions of liberalism see limits on what governments can rightfully require of individuals. This stems from the belief that rationality is what is distinctive and especially valuable about humans, and that rationality allows humans to govern themselves (Jaggar 1983). Classical liberals generally excluded women from the natural rights accorded to men because they saw women as less rational than men. Thus, the job of early liberal feminists, like Mary Wollstonecraft ([1792] 1975), was to argue that men and women are fundamentally equal in their potential for rationality. Just as Locke ([1698] 1967) had argued that men do not need a monarch because men are rational, Wollstonecraft argued that women do not need the authority of men because women, too, are rational.

A key tenet of liberal thought has always been the notion of a public/private dichotomy paired with the belief that, due to individual rights, the state should not intervene in what is "private," and that "justice" does not apply to this private sphere. What has been continually under dispute is the location of the boundary between public and private (Jaggar 1983). Gender relations in the family were excluded from the public sphere by early liberals such as Locke (Benhabib 1987). For the most part, liberal feminists (unlike Socialist/Marxist feminists and radical/cultural feminists) have not disputed this. Thus they have focused on women's equal rights in nondomestic matters, such as education, politics, and careers. In general, the notion of equal treatment of men and women in non-household affairs has become *the* liberal notion of feminism. There are, however, some exceptions to this, as when liberal feminists support enforcement of assault laws to prosecute men who rape or beat their wives at home, or when they argue for public support of child care or for laws mandating that employers give parents the job flexibility they need to combine being parents with employment (Okin 1989).

Over time, liberalism has split into two major camps. One camp emphasizes individual rights against the state, and thus opposes state action. These liberals see rights as being negative—freedom *from* interference—rather than positive rights to specific opportunities. In this camp are laissez-faire economists, who oppose state regulation of the economy, and libertarians, who oppose most all state action, whether pertaining to the economy or not. The second camp emphasizes rights to equality of opportunity or treatment. It is this second camp that is now called "liberal" in popular discourse, but both are descendants of classical liberalism.

Libertarianism extends the notion that the state should not interfere with private affairs beyond the economy by moving into areas of civil liberties such as the family, sexual behavior, and speech. Libertarians believe that the state should do virtually nothing except uphold property rights, enforce contracts, and protect individuals' rights to be free from physical assault. Since libertarians want a very limited state, liberal feminists upholding this view obviously oppose laws prohibiting discrimination in employment or any other regulation of employment contracts. This would include opposition to the Equal Pay Act and Title VII, whether interpreted to include comparable worth or not, and to any new legislation mandating wages based on the principle of comparable worth. (For examples of libertarian and laissez-faire feminism, see McElroy 1991.)

The laissez-faire tradition of liberalism is the one most followed in neoclassical economics. Economists take as given some initial distribution of property, goods, and services. By assuming that individuals seek to maximize utility, economists conclude that any two persons who can each make themselves better off by an exchange will do so. Economists define an exchange as leading to a Pareto-superior distribution if both parties view themselves as better off after rather than before the exchange. It follows that if governments do nothing to prohibit exchange or to redistribute resources, a succession of sequentially Pareto-superior moves will occur, leading to a Pareto-optimal distribution. Efficiency is defined in terms of such Pareto-optimality. Using this criterion, redistribution by the state can never improve efficiency, since it is not mutually voluntary exchange; hence the commitment to laissez-faire.

How does this apply to comparable worth? Feminists with the laissez-faire view would argue that the state should not interfere with an employer's right to pay persons in predominantly female occupations an amount they are willing to accept. Nor should it interfere with a potential employee's right to prefer a badly paying job to no job at all. This trade-off might exist if comparable worth regulations required employers to pay more than they currently pay in female jobs and this led them to hire fewer workers in the jobs. Comparable worth is seen to prohibit some exchanges that would move the system toward Pareto-optimality.

Despite these laissez-faire implications of neoclassical theory, there is a diversity of opinion among neoclassical economists about how much governmental intervention into the economy is warranted. Today most labor economists advocate laws against hiring discrimination (hiring an employee based on sex rather than ability to fulfill the requirements of a job), yet they oppose governmental action to require that wages meet comparable worth standards (see, for example, Killingsworth 1984; O'Neill 1984; Polachek 1984). An exception is Bergmann (1985; 1986; 1989), who sees comparable worth as an antidote to the low wages in female occupations that she sees resulting from hiring discrimination in male occupations that leads to crowding and, hence, low wages in female occupations. The opposition of economists to comparable worth is more consistent with the normative leanings of neoclassical theory than is the advocacy by these same people of laws against hiring discrimination. When neoclassical economists advocate laws against hiring discrimination, they are stepping outside the neoclassical paradigm and inserting a notion of equity that cannot be found within the efficiency criterion of Pareto-optimality. Thus, to be consistent, when they oppose comparable worth, it cannot be just a result of the paradigm's hostility to governmental intervention, or they would oppose laws against hiring discrimination as well. The reasons for opposing comparable worth have more to do with their positive belief that if there is discrimination at all it must take the form of barriers to entry into a position (i.e., hiring discrimination), and that requiring comparable worth wages would create disemployment that laws against hiring discrimination do not. In sum, the general belief by feminists in the libertarian and the laissez-faire schools is that comparable worth is interference by the government and, thus, not a desirable solution to the sex gap in pay.

The second strand of liberalism has stressed equality, in contrast to the emphasis upon individuals' freedom from governmental regulation discussed above. The emphasis in egalitarian liberalism has generally been on equality under the law—equality of opportunity or equality of treatment—not on equality of outcomes. That is, inequalities of income, power, or wealth are accepted by most egalitarian liberals as long as opportunities to ascend these hierarchies are reasonably equal and as long as the state and other institutions treat all individuals by the same standards (Brenner 1987).

It is the application of the egalitarian strand of liberalism on the nonhousehold sphere on which liberal feminists have placed most emphasis. Egalitarian liberalism endorses state action in the service of equality of treatment or opportunity outside the family. Feminists have pushed legislative agendas based on this reasoning, supporting the passage and administrative enforcement of laws against discrimination in employment, credit, and educational opportunities.

For many liberal feminists, comparable worth is seen in this same vein. Most liberal feminist organizations, such as the National Organization for Women and the National Women's Political Caucus, have endorsed comparable worth. They view comparable worth as a tool to achieve nondiscrimination in wage setting. They see the issue as a straightforward "equal treatment" issue. Thus, liberal feminists may accept policy-capturing or management-run a priori methods of job evaluation as an approach to comparable worth, even when they embed bias against traditionally female skills into wage systems, as long as male and female jobs are evaluated by the same standard and, thus, the evaluation meets "equal treatment" criteria. Liberals are also likely to accept processes for arriving at pay equity that are controlled by management and lack participation by workers, since many versions of liberalism do not entail a criticism of capitalism or a commitment to democracy in economic institutions. However, given the importance placed on equal treatment by egalitarian liberals, multiple pay plans within an organization would not be acceptable to most liberal feminists.

However, if one follows the egalitarian thrust of liberalism far enough, the call for equality of opportunity leads to a call for greater substantive equality by class, race, and gender. This follows from the fact that inequality in outcomes often creates inequality of opportunity. With respect to class or strata, as long as there is inequality among parents, and children receive financial, cognitive, cultural, or social resources from their parents, groups of children will not have equality of opportunity (England 1988). In the case of gender, without equality between men and women in occupations and earnings, young women cannot have equal opportunity for mentors with similar experiences, role models, and so forth. The argument for race is analogous. When these facts are realized, the liberal criterion of equality of opportunity, rather than being juxtaposed to a criterion of equality of condition, is seen to require greater equality of condition for its realization. Thus, a call for a socialism of sorts can be derived from egalitarian liberalism (Eisenstein 1981). However, most American liberals do not take equality of opportunity this far, either out of fear of the concentration of power in the state required, or because they believe that the possibility of unequal outcomes has incentive-producing effects. It is to a fuller discussion of socialist views, including those derived from Marxism, that we now turn.

### Socialist/Marxist Feminism

In a Marxist view, the concept "species being" is fundamental. The idea is that what is unique and valuable about humans is their exercise of control over nature through their productive labor. Thus, Marx advocated workers' being as autonomous as is possible by the innately interdependent nature of humans, and he believed that capitalism robbed workers of this control. "Labor," as used by Marxists, need not always involve the production of material objects, and physical and mental labor are equally entailed in species being. This contrasts with liberals, such as Locke ([1698] 1967), who view rationality as the essential characteristic of humanity and thus valorize mental over physical labor (Jaggar 1983, ch. 3). Harmonizing with Marx's valuation of productive labor is his assertion that the means and relationships of production are primary to understanding inequality. This is because one's relationship to production ultimately affects the ability to control one's labor power. Under capitalism, Marx argues, capitalists control the labor power of the working class because the working class must sell its labor power to the capitalist class in order to subsist. The hierarchical division of labor and a manager's rights to make decisions about the work process prevent workers from attaining the extent of control that Marx argued to be necessary to fulfill one's species being. Thus to Marxists, the socialism that flows from egalitarian liberalism is inadequate if it does not abolish capitalism.

Orthodox Marxists see employed women as exploited by capitalists, just as male workers are exploited. In addition, many Marxists see sex discrimination in labor markets, which leads women to have even lower wages than men, as a side effect of capitalism. The idea is that discrimination on the basis of workers' sex or race operates to "divide and conquer" workers by deflecting their attention away from the fact that they have a common enemy, capitalism (Edwards, Reich, and Gordon 1975; Reich 1981; Shelton and Agger 1993). None of the proponents of this theory specify, however, that the mechanism that serves to divide and conquer is the form of sex discrimination at issue in comparable worth, that is, the devaluation of women's jobs. However, the theory seems open to the possibility that this could be one such mechanism. The theory is equally consistent with exclusion of women from high-paying jobs or payment of unequal wages by sex within jobs as the mechanism of discrimination that serves to divide and conquer.

But what of homemakers? The most orthodox Marxist position, that of Engels ([1884] 1972), does not see woman as exploited but rather as oppressed by the exclusion from public production that occurred for many women with the development of capitalism (Smith 1978). Engels thought socialism would liberate women to participate in this public production by socializing household work (Jaggar 1983, ch. 4). Marxist feminists (James and Dalla Costa 1973; Seccombe 1974; Smith 1978; Vogel 1983) believe that homemakers are exploited by capitalists. They argue that women's domestic labor maintains and nurtures workers and hence produces a commodity, "labor power." Thus, homemakers engage in production and are exploited in the formal sense of contributing surplus value to capitalists; they are even more exploited than paid workers because they are paid nothing for their reproductive labor (Shelton and Agger 1993). Despite their differences on whether homemakers are exploited, orthodox Marxists and Marxist feminists both agree that women's subordination is derivative of the class relations between capitalists and workers.

Socialist feminists agree with Marxist feminists' contention that women's household labor creates surplus value for capitalism. However, socialist feminists dispute the Marxist feminists' claim that gender inequality is entirely derivative of class relations between capitalists and workers (Hartmann 1981; Jaggar 1983, ch. 6, 10). They argue that women are oppressed by both capitalism and patriarchy, and they see both as systems of material social relations. Patriarchy is a system that includes material social relations of male dominance in how reproduction (sexuality, procreation, the nurturance of people, and household labor) is organized. Some socialist feminists follow Hartmann (1976; 1981) in defining patriarchy as a system involving men's control over women's labor at home and in the paid workplace. Many socialist feminists see the realms of household work and paid production as mutually determining, with neither causally prior, and advocate an abolition of a division of labor based on sex in both paid and domestic labor. (For reviews, see Walby 1986, ch. 2; Shelton and Agger 1993.)

The Socialist/Marxist feminist positions are distinct from the liberal feminist position in several ways. First, those who follow Marxist theory see labor rather than rationality as the criterion of normative claims (Jaggar 1983). Second, some socialist feminists favor collective struggle to achieve the abolition of the sexual division of labor in the home, while most liberal feminists eschew interference by any collective in domestic affairs. In this sense of assuming the necessity of collective approaches to problems, Socialist/Marxist feminists are communitarian, although most communitarians are neither socialists nor feminists. (The links between feminism and communitarianism are discussed in more detail below, when we discuss cultural feminism.) Third, and most important for comparable worth, Marxists and socialist feminists challenge many of the hierarchical aspects of the organization of work under capitalism. The unequal distribution of wealth, the hierarchical division of labor, the valorization of mental skills and managerial tasks, and the extent of inequality in wage distribution are all challenged. In contrast, most liberals accept these inequalities and focus their reforms on ensuring that individuals have equality of opportunity to ascend hierarchies or that individuals of equal merit are treated equally within such hierarchies.

What is the Socialist/Marxist feminist position on comparable worth? Socialists, whether they are Marxists or not, are likely to endorse comparable worth as a worthy reform, although one that is not without dangers, but also to see comparable worth as inadequately radical. Comparable worth does not challenge the distribution of wealth, the hierarchical division of labor, or inequality in the distribution of wages (Brenner 1987). In practice, it tends to narrow the gender gap in wages and compress the overall wage structure, but it leaves many other inequalities intact (Acker 1989). Job evaluation, with its complicated statistical formulas, may reinforce the rule of technical experts and obscure the irreducibly political nature of setting wages. The superior value of mental over manual skills and the greater importance of supervisory over other kinds of responsibility are assumed by job evaluators, and uncontested by liberal feminism, but not acceptable to socialist values (Brenner 1987; Acker 1989; Feldberg 1984). Thus, because of all the aspects of inequality not challenged by comparable worth, and the possibility that job evaluation may legitimate some of these, some socialist feminists criticize comparable worth as inadequately egalitarian (Brenner 1987; Blum 1987; 1991).

Despite reservations, many Socialist/Marxist feminists advocate comparable worth as a reform that could potentially improve the situation of women (Feldberg 1984; Steinberg 1987; Blum 1987; 1991; Acker 1989). Many of the jobs whose wages comparable worth would raise involve nurturant labor, similar to the reproductive labor women do in the home. Thus, there is a normative harmony between the Marxist feminist and socialist feminist claims that those who do reproductive labor in the home are doubly exploited and that the aim of comparable worth is to raise the wages of those who do such reproductive labor in paid employment. Also, comparable worth questions the assumption that wages are determined by the neutral factors of "supply and demand" rather than by gender. This is a challenge to laissez-faire economics and to the idea that wages are not political products (Blum 1991).

On the question of how comparable worth should be implemented, socialists argue for worker participation in the job evaluation process. This follows from the belief that decisions about what job characteristics to include and their relative weights are irreducibly political.

Socialists also oppose lowering any workers' wages to provide funds to raise others' wages; thus, they advocate the use of the "male line" to set wages, bringing the pay of female jobs up to the line that summarizes the relationship between job points and wages among male jobs (see Figure 11.1). One reason that socialists believe in using the male line is to maintain solidarity among all workers as the reform is instituted; solidarity between men and women would be impeded if women's raises were funded by a lowering of men's wages.

Marxists prefer an implementation that raises the overall wage bill, because Marxists' underlying normative theory, following from the labor theory of value, says that all workers, even those in high-wage positions, are exploited by the extraction of surplus value. Thus, any reform that reduced men's wages would heighten their exploitation. If comparable worth raises the wage bill, Marxists see this as a plus, with the hope that wage increases will come out of profits rather than being passed on to consumers. (How this argument applies when the employer is the government is less clear.)

### Radical/Cultural Feminism

Cultural feminists value traditionally female characteristics, disputing the usual deprecation of qualities viewed as feminine (Donovan 1985, ch. 2). Thus, whereas patriarchal and liberal views have elevated the spiritual or rational over the physical, emotional, or intuitive, cultural feminists argue for at least an equal valuation of the latter qualities. Whereas patriarchal views revere the bravery of risking one's life in hunting, sport, or war, the cultural feminist reveres nurturing for its preservation of life. And whereas patriarchal thinkers, classical liberals, and some Marxists have revered humans for their domination over nature, cultural feminism reveres harmony with nature; this aspect of cultural feminism is sometimes called ecofeminism.

The traditionally female characteristics that cultural feminists believe our culture has undervalued include nurturing; nonviolence; sensitivity to the feelings of others; emotional expressiveness; unselfishness; a collective orientation; kinship with, rather than domination of, nature; acceptance of our physical bodies; humility; flexibility rather than rigid adherence to abstract principles; and intuition of wholes. Cultural feminists argue that people have always benefited from women's practice of these skills and values, but this benefit is seldom acknowledged in patriarchal societies. Rather, these virtues have been seen as signs of weakness, lack of proper individuation, or lack of rationality. Traditionally male characteristics are more highly valued in our culture; these include individual ambition, independence, aggressiveness, abstract and analytical rationality, and repression of emotion. Liberal feminists protest the limitations on women's access to public roles, while failing to question whether traditionally male characteristics are appropriate behavior in these roles. In contrast, cultural feminists argue that traditionally male values are inappropriate for human behavior by either men or women in either domestic or public roles, at least without greater balance from traditionally feminine values than currently obtains. (Examples of cultural feminist works are Held 1993; Noddings 1984; C. Keller 1976; E.F. Keller 1985; Starhawk 1987; Tuana 1993.)

In this discussion, we are choosing to combine cultural feminism and radical feminism, though the match is by no means perfect. (For critiques of cultural feminism by radical feminists, see Echols 1983; Hoagland 1989.) Radical feminists see women's subordination to be the fundamental inequality, not a side effect of class inequalities, as orthodox Marxists and Marxist feminists believe. Radical feminists believe that women's subordination is the result of how sexuality, childbearing, and child rearing have been socially organized (Jaggar 1983). Since activities in these spheres have been linked to women and have been deprecated, there is a clear link to cultural feminism.

Radical/cultural feminists argue that the exclusive focus among liberal feminists on allowing women to enter occupational and political positions formerly monopolized by men is misdirected because the values underlying the practice of and disproportionate reward for such positions are wrong for both men and women. For example, while a liberal feminist might fight to get more women into management, a radical/cultural feminist might be equally or even more interested in seeing production organized in a less hierarchal manner so that "manager" and "worker" are no longer job categories, or in increasing the pay and respect given to nonsupervisory workers relative to managers. On these points, socialist feminists would agree with radical/cultural feminists. While a liberal feminist might focus on increasing the number of women scientists, a radical/cultural feminist might place equal importance on changing the extent to which separation between scientists and their subject matter is valued in science.

One theme in cultural feminism is an argument that we should valorize emotional connection, community, and prosocial values more than the liberal tradition has. In this respect, radical/cultural feminists are communitarians. Prominent writers associated with the communitarian critique of liberalism include philosophers Alasdair MacIntyre (1981) and Michael Sandel (1982) and sociologist Amitai Etzioni (1993). Communitarians believe that the bonds of community, and the values that support them, are to be revered. The values that flow from this differ from those in the liberal tradition in that the liberal tradition sees the key moral issue as respecting others' rights to noninterference, whereas communitarians believe that attending to the needs of those in one's community is also a moral necessity. Communitarian ethics are more like what psychologist Carol Gilligan (1982) called the "ethics of care" than what she called the "ethics of rights," with the latter more consistent with the liberal tradition. (For a feminist discussion of this issue, see Kittay and Meyers 1987.) This part of the communitarian critique of liberalism is normative; it is about how we *ought* to act.

A second part of the communitarian critique of liberalism is about how things work, rather than about what ought to be. (We will call this the "positive" analysis.) While this critique does not put forward a moral argument, it is about the force of what Etzioni (1988) has called the "moral dimension" in all human affairs. We might also call this the "social dimension," since values arise from our ties to other people. The existence of this dimension in market institutions poses a challenge to neoclassical economics, or, more generally, narrow versions of rational choice theory. In *The Moral Dimension*, Etzioni (1988) criticizes the neoclassical assumption that the economy is most productive when there is free competition unhindered by government intervention in a population of atomized beings who make choices primarily in terms of profit. An economy constituted of people who behave as portrayed in the economic model could not achieve enough trust and cooperation to be productive in this view. Like feminists, Etzioni and other communitarians realize that socially constructed norms affect the economic realm as well as all other realms.

However, while the radical/cultural feminist position is communitarian (as is the socialist feminist position), not all communitarians are feminist. Indeed, to the dismay of feminists, communitarians such as Sandel (1982) and MacIntyre (1981) write approvingly of families as sites where the values of the community are reproduced, while offering no normative criticism of male domination in the family or community (Friedman 1991; 1992). For centuries, most communities and nations have promoted antifeminist values. Thus, a respect for the moral dimension is no guarantee that the outcome will be feminist—in the sense of reducing male privilege.

For feminists, a problem with the positive analysis of some communitarians is that they implicitly see communities' morality as monolithic. But this is inaccurate; groups who are harmed by dominant values always develop moral discourses of resistance. Thus, the question is not only whether there are aspects of the moral dimension affecting every institution, as Etzioni (1988) tries to show, but whose morality prevails. Etzioni's *The Spirit of Community* (1993) acknowledges the diversity of values in American society and the fact that consensus on all issues is impossible in the foreseeable future. Thus, he suggests building a movement for communitarianism on the basis of the limited values that the vast majority *does* agree upon, such as nonviolence, nondiscrimination, truth, and democracy. This approach guarantees, on the one hand, that most overtly patriarchal values would not be promoted in any communitarian program consistent with his designs; however, it also ensures that a full panoply of policies attempting to root out male privilege would not be a part of such a program.

What position does radical/cultural feminism imply for comparable worth? Radical/cultural feminism is consistent with a version of comparable worth that sees the root of the problem to be a cultural devaluation of some jobs and job characteristics because of their association with women and traditionally female activities. Although the aims of comparable worth reforms are in harmony with radical/cultural feminism, feminists of this persuasion have written and organized little around comparable worth. In part, this is because radical/cultural feminist writers have focused on broad theoretical critiques of androcentrism rather than policy debates. It is also because radical/cultural feminist activists have focused upon starting alternative institutions (such as women's cooperative businesses, spiritual groups, and communes) that embody the values they embrace. Few have engaged in political action aimed at persuading the government to mandate comparable worth or unions to bargain for comparable worth. Working through the male-dominated bureaucratic state or unions has been avoided by many radical/cultural feminists, some of whom advocate separatism from male institutions. Nonetheless, there is a striking harmony between the traditionally female and androgynous activities and skills valued by radical/cultural feminists and the traditionally female jobs that would have their pay elevated by comparable worth.

Yet, some proposed methods of implementing comparable worth entail insufficient cultural change from a radical/cultural feminist's perspective. Many standard applications of point factor job evaluation systems, described above, retain some of the devaluation of women's work that a radical/cultural feminist would want to eliminate. Given their commitment to nonhierarchical practices, radical/cultural feminists would oppose management control of the job evaluation process in principle, as well as because it may lead to correcting only a small part of the cultural devaluation of "female" work that is embedded in current wage systems. For instance, job descriptions tend to be written by supervisors rather than by incumbents, and skills needed mostly in female-dominated jobs are often not included in the job description, giving them no chance to receive a weight of above 0 in wage-setting formulas.

Radical/cultural feminists would object to using policy-capturing approaches to job evaluation because they utilize uncontested, employer-given weights for various job characteristics, and they lead to wage changes only when employers' criteria are being used inconsistently. In the radical/cultural feminist view, many traits are now undervalued when they appear in either men's or women's jobs because of their historic association with women's spheres. Thus an a priori approach to job evaluation that explicitly sets out to give more value to traditionally feminine job characteristics, such as nurturing skills, would be most consistent with the radical/cultural feminist view. However, a priori systems of job evaluation as currently practiced by management consulting firms such as Hay or Willis would not be seen to produce sufficient revaluating of typically female job characteristics.

## Conclusion

We conclude that, although comparable worth may not be at the top of the agenda for any of the three feminist frameworks analyzed, all three paradigms are consistent with the claims of comparable worth, that is, that wage systems contain gender bias and that such bias should be eradicated. In this sense the three versions of feminism agree on comparable worth. However, we also conclude that the three feminisms differ on what are acceptable or desirable ways of implementing comparable worth: Socialist/Marxist and radical/cultural feminism seek more basic changes than does liberal feminism.

Much of the outcome of any comparable worth reform hinges on how it is implemented and who controls the process. The egalitarian school of liberal feminism holds that the government is responsible for enforcing equal opportunity and equal treatment for sex and racial groups in labor markets. Policy-capturing versions of point factor job evaluations are ideal for detecting whether employers are using inconsistent criteria to set wages in "male" and "female" jobs without contesting an employer's right to set the criteria used to determine which jobs will be seen as more payworthy. This version of implementing comparable worth appeals to the "equal treatment" standards of liberals and can be used to argue for comparable worth under the principles of Title VII of the Civil Rights Act (England 1992, ch. 5). However, liberal feminists would not regard as an adequate reform any use of job evaluation that keeps separate evaluation and pay systems for different families of jobs, although many management consulting firms recommend the latter as a compromise between equity and market realities. Today, the more politically influential descendant of classical liberalism is the laissez-faire school, which opposes comparable worth as one more unwarranted intervention by government in the economy. As long as this school of thought dominates, even relatively conservative implementations of comparable worth will be difficult to achieve.

Socialist/Marxist feminism is consistent with comparable worth reforms for two reasons. First, comparable worth challenges the pure laissez-faire notion of markets. Second, the claim that wage systems contain sex bias that should be eradicated is consistent with the socialist feminist notion that patriarchy is present in paid employment. Marxists and other socialists see capitalism, managerial control, and a hierarchical wage system as fundamentally problematic. Since many versions of implementing comparable worth do not contest these issues, the reform is inadequately radical for these feminists. However, Socialist/Marxist feminists may see it as something valuable around which to organize. Socialist/Marxist feminists favor processes of implementation that give control over the process of job evaluation and wage adjustments to workers rather than managers or technocrats in consulting firms. They also advocate systems of wage adjustments that bring female jobs up to the level of comparable male jobs and avoid lowering wages in any job. This flows from their belief that profit is exploitative, so raising the wage bill is not something to avoid, and their desire to maintain solidarity among male and female workers as the reform is conducted.

Radical/cultural feminism focuses on the devaluation of activities and traits associated with women. As communitarians, radical/cultural feminists see social bonds and values based on them as inherently valuable; however, feminists are critical of the values of communities that preserve male privilege. Radical/cultural feminism harmonizes well with the claim of comparable worth that women's jobs and the characteristics associated with them are devalorized in present wage systems. Radical/cultural feminism is consistent with implementing comparable worth through a process of job evaluation that allows for participation by women workers and uses a priori setting of weights to explicitly increase the positive weight given to characteristics commonly found in female jobs, such as nurturant social skills. From a radical/cultural feminist point of view, the usual implementations of comparable worth are insufficiently radical, but the general reform is worthy of support.

## Notes

1. The systems used by the well-known Hay and Willis consulting firms are examples of point factor systems, as is the Position Analysis Questionnaire (called PAQ) (McCormick et al. 1972). Recently the federal government has been moving to a point factor system for its white-collar jobs called the Factor Evaluation Systems (Katz 1984). Point factor systems are the most common choice in the private sector (Schwab and Wichem 1983; Akalin 1970) and have been used in most of the pay equity studies done by states and localities.

2. Minimum, midpoint, or highest pay in each job can be used as the dependent variable for the policy-capturing regression analysis, although this choice may affect the weights (Treiman 1979).

## References

Acker, Joan. 1987. "Sex Bias in Job Evaluation: A Comparable Worth Issue." In *Ingredients for Women's Employment Policy,* ed. C. Bose and G. Spitze, 183–96. Albany: State University of New York Press.

———. 1989. *Doing Comparable Worth: Gender, Class and Pay Equity.* Philadelphia: Temple University Press.

Akalin, Mustafa T. 1970. *Office Job Evaluation.* Des Plaines, IL: Industrial Management Society.

Beatty, Richard W., and Beatty, James R. 1984. "Some Problems with Contemporary Job Evaluation Systems." In *Comparable Worth and Wage Discrimination,* ed. H. Remick, 59–78. Philadelphia: Temple University Press.

Belcher, C.W. 1974. *Compensation Administration.* Englewood Cliffs, NJ: Prentice-Hall.

Benhabib, Seyla. 1987. "The Generalized and the Concrete Other: The Kohlberg-Gilligan Controversy and Feminist Theory." In *Feminism as Critique: On the Politics of Gender,* ed. Seyla Benhabib and Drucilla Cornell. Minneapolis: University of Minnesota Press.

Bergmann, Barbara R. 1985. "The Economic Case for Comparable Worth." In *Comparable Worth: New Directions for Research,* ed. Heidi Hartmann, 70–85. Washington, DC: National Academy Press.

———. 1986. *The Economic Emergence of Women.* New York: Basic Books.

———. 1989. "Does the Market for Women's Labor Need Fixing?" *Journal of Economic Perspectives,* 3, no. 1: 43–60.

Bernstein, Aaron. 1986. "Comparable Worth: It's Already Happening." *Business Week* (April 28): 52, 56.

Blum, Linda M. 1987. "Possibilities and Limits of the Comparable Worth Movement." *Gender and Society* 1: 380–89.

———. 1991. *Beyond Feminism and Labor: The Significance of the Comparable Worth Movement.* Berkeley: University of California Press.

Brenner, Johanna. 1987. "Feminist Political Discourses: Radical Versus Liberal Approaches to the Feminization of Poverty and Comparable Worth." *Gender and Society* 1: 447–65.

Cherlin, Andrew J. 1981. *Marriage, Divorce, Remarriage: Social Trends in the United States.* Cambridge, MA: Harvard University Press.

Donovan, Josephine. 1985. *Feminist Theory: The Intellectual Traditions of American Feminism.* New York: Frederick Ungar.

Echols, Alice. 1983. "The New Feminism of Yin and Yang." In *Powers of Desire: The Politics of Sexuality,* ed. Ann Snitow, Christine Stansell, and Sharon Thompson, 439–59. New York: Monthly Review Press.

Edwards, Richard; Reich, Michael; and Gordon, David, eds. 1975. *Labor Market Segmentation.* Lexington, MA: D.C. Heath.

Eisenstein, Zillah R. 1981. *The Radical Future of Liberal Feminism.* New York: Longman.

Ellwood, David T., and Crane, Jonathan. 1990. "Family Change among Black Americans: What Do We Know?" *Journal of Economic Perspectives* 4: 65–84.

Engels, Friedrich. (1884) 1972. *The Origin of the Family.* New York: International Publishers.

England, Paula. 1988. "Equality of Opportunity, Inequality of Reward, and the Hierarchical Division of Labor." *Free Inquiry in Creative Sociology* 16: 137–42.

———. 1992. *Comparable Worth: Theories and Evidence.* New York: Aldine de Gruyter.

England, Paula, and Farkas, George. 1986. *Households, Employment, and Gender: A Social, Economic and Demographic View.* New York: Aldine de Gruyter.

England, Paula, and Kilbourne, Barbara Stanek. 1990. "Markets, Marriages, and Other Mates: The Problem of Power." In *Beyond the Marketplace: Rethinking Economy and Society,* ed. Roger Friedland and A.F. Robertson, 163–89. New York: Aldine de Gruyter.

Etzioni, Amitai. 1988. *The Moral Dimension*. New York: Free Press.

—. 1993. *The Spirit of Community: The Reinvention of American Society*. New York: Simon and Schuster.

Feldberg, Roslyn L. 1984. "Comparable Worth: Toward Theory and Practice in the United States." *Signs: Journal of Women in Culture and Society* 10: 311–28.

Friedman, Marilyn. 1991. "The Social Self and the Partiality Debates." In *Feminist Ethics*, ed. Claudia Card, 161–76. Lawrence: University of Kansas Press.

—. 1992. "Feminism and Modern Friendship: Dislocating the Community." In *Explorations in Feminist Ethics*, ed. Eve Browning Cole and Susan Coultrap-McQuin, 89–97. Bloomington: Indiana University Press.

Gilligan, Carol. 1982. *In a Different Voice: Psychological Theory and Women's Development*. Cambridge, MA: Harvard University Press.

Gray, John. 1986. *Liberalism*. Milton Keynes: Open University Press.

Hartmann, Heidi. 1976. "Capitaliism, Patriarchy and Job Segregation by Sex." In *Women and the Workplace: The Implications of Occupational Segregation*, eds. Martha Blaxall and Barbara Reagan, 137–70. Chicago: University of Chicago Press.

—. 1981. "The Unhappy Marriage of Marxism and Feminism: Toward a More Progressive Union." In *Women and Revolution*, ed. Lydia Sargent. Boston: South End Press.

Held, Virginia. 1993. *Feminist Morality*. Chicago: University of Chicago Press.

Hoagland, Sarah Lucia. 1989. *Lesbian Ethics: Toward New Value*. Palo Alto, CA: Institute of Lesbian Studies.

Jaggar, Alison M. 1983. *Feminist Politics and Human Nature*. Totowa, NJ: Rowman and Allanheld.

James, Selma, and Dalla Costa, Mariarosa. 1973. *The Power of Women and the Subversion of the Community*. Bristol, UK: Falling Wall Press.

Katz, Paul A. 1984. "The Federal Civil Service." In *Handbook of Wage and Salary Administration*, ed. Milton Rock, 14/1–14/10. New York: McGraw-Hill.

Keller, Catherine. 1986. *From a Broken Web: Separation, Sexism, and Self.* Boston: Beacon Press.

Keller, Evelyn Fox. 1985. *Reflections on Gender and Science*. New Haven, CT: Yale University Press.

Killingsworth, Mark R. 1984. "Statement on Comparable Worth." Testimony before the Joint Economic Committee, U.S. Congress.

—. 1990. *The Economics of Comparable Worth*. Kalamazoo, MI: Upjohn Institute.

Kittay, Eva Feder, and Meyers, Diane T. 1987. *Women and Moral Theory*. Totowa, NJ: Rowan and Littlefield.

Locke, John. (1698) 1967. *Two Treatises of Government*. New York: Cambridge University Press.

MacIntyre, Alasdair. 1981. *After Virtue*. Notre Dame, IN: University of Notre Dame Press.

Martin, Teresa Castro, and Bumpass, Larry L. 1989. "Recent Trends in Marital Disruption." *Demography* 26 (1): 37–50.

McCormick, E.J.; Jeanneret, P.R.; and Mecham, R.C. 1972. "A Study of Job Characteristics and Job Dimensions as Based on the Position Description Questionnaire." *Journal of Applied Psychology* 56: 547–62.

McElroy, Wendy, ed. 1991. *Freedom, Feminism, and the State: An Overview of Individualist Feminism*, 2d ed. New York: Holmes and Meier.

National Committee on Pay Equity. 1989. *Pay Equity in the Public Sector, 1979–1989*. Washington, DC: National Committee on Pay Equity.

Noddings, Nel. 1984. *Caring: A Feminine Approach to Ethics and Moral Education*.

Berkeley: University of California Press.

Northrup, Herbert R. 1980. "Wage Setting and Collective Bargaining." In *Comparable Worth: Issues and Alternatives*, ed. E.R. Livernash, 107–36. Washington, DC: Equal Employment Advisory Council.

O'Neill, June. 1984. "An Argument Against Comparable Worth." In *U.S. Commission on Civil Rights. Comparable Worth: Issues for the 80's: A Consultation of the U.S. Commission on Civil Rights*, 177–86. Washington, DC: U.S. Government Printing Office.

Okin, Susan Moller. 1989. *Justice, Gender, and the Family*. New York: Basic Books.

Patten, T. 1987. "How Do You Know if Your Job Evaluation System Is Working?" In *New Perspectives on Compensation*, ed. D.B. Balkin and L.R. Gomez-Mejia, 10–19. Englewood Cliffs, NJ: Prentice-Hall.

Polachek, Solomon William. 1984. "Women in the Economy: Perspectives on Gender Inequality." In *Comparable Worth: Issue for the 80's*. Vol. 1. U.S. Commission on Civil Rights, ed. Washington, DC: U.S. Government Printing Office.

Preston, Samuel. 1984. "Children and the Elderly: Divergent Paths for America's Dependents." *Demography* 21: 435–58.

Preston, Samuel H., and McDonald, John. 1979. "The Incidence of Divorce within Cohorts of American Marriages Contracted Since the War." *Demography* 16: 1–25.

Reich, Michael. 1981. *Racial Inequality: A Political-Economic Analysis*. Princeton, NJ: Princeton University Press.

Remick, Helen. 1984. "Major Issues in A Priori Application." In *Comparable Worth and Wage Discrimination*, ed. Helen Remick, 99–117. Philadelphia: Temple University Press.

Sandel, Michael. 1982. *Liberalism and the Limits of Justice*. Cambridge: Cambridge University Press.

Schlafly, Phyllis, ed. 1984. "Equal Pay for Unequal Work." In *Equal Pay for Unequal Work*. Washington, DC: Eagle Forum Education and Legal Defense.

Schwab, D.P., and Heneman, H.G., III. 1986. "Assessment of a Consensus-Based Multiple Information Source Job Evaluation System." *Journal of Applied Psychology* 71: 354–56.

Schwab, D.P., and Wichern, D.W. 1983. "Systematic Bias in Job Evaluation and Market Wages: Implications for the Comparable Worth Debate." *Journal of Applied Psychology* 31: 353–64.

Schwab, Donald P. 1984. "Using Job Evaluation to Obtain Pay Equity." In *Comparable Worth: Issues for the 80's: A Consultation of the U.S. Commission on Civil Rights*, 83–92. Washington, DC: U.S. Government Printing Office.

Seccombe, Walter. 1974. "The Housewife and Her Labor Under Capitalism." *New Left Review* 83: 3–24.

Shelton, Beth Anne, and Agger, Ben. 1993. "Shotgun Wedding, Unhappy Marriage, No-Fault Divorce? Rethinking the Feminism-Marxism Relationship." In Paula England, ed., *Theory on Gender/Feminism on Theory*. New York: Aldine de Gruyter.

Smith, Paul. 1978. "Domestic Labour and Marx's Theory of Value." In *Feminism and Materialism*, ed. Annette Kuhn and Annmarie Wolpe, 198–219. London: Routledge and Kegan Paul.

Starhawk. 1987. *Truth or Dare: Encounters with Power, Authority, and Mystery*. San Francisco: Harper and Row.

Steinberg, Ronnie J. 1987. "Radical Challenges in a Liberal World: The Mixed Success of Comparable Worth." *Gender & Society* 1: 466–75.

Steinberg, Ronnie J., and Haignere, Lois. 1987. "Equitable Compensation: Methodological Criteria for Comparable Worth." In *Ingredients for Women's Employment Policy*, ed. Christine Bose and Glenna Spitze, 157–82. Albany: State University of New York Press.

Steinberg, Ronnie J.; Haignere, Lois; Possin, C.; Chertoa, C.H.; and Treiman, D.J. 1986. *The New York State Pay Equity Study: A Research Report.* Albany: Center for Women in Government, State University of New York Press.

Treiman, Donald J. 1979. *Job Evaluation: An Analytic Review.* Interim Report to the Equal Employment Opportunity Commission. Washington, DC: National Academy of Sciences.

Tuana, Nancy. 1993. *The Less Noble Sex: Scientific, Religious, and Philosophical Conceptions of Woman's Nature.* Bloomington: University of Indiana Press.

U.S. Commission on Civil Rights. 1985. *Comparable Worth: An Analysis and Recommendations.* Washington, DC: U.S. Government Printing Office.

Vogel, Lise. 1983. *Marxism and the Oppression of Women: Toward a Unitary Theory.* New Jersey: Rutgers University Press.

Walby, Sylvia. 1986. *Patriarchy at Work: Patriarchal and Capitalist Relations in Employment.* Minneapolis, MN: University of Minnesota Press.

Wollstonecraft, Mary. (1792). 1975. *A Vindication of Rights of Woman.* Baltimore: Penguin.

# 12

# Middle-Class Avoidance, Indifference, and Discrete Nihilism

## David Sciulli

Whatever its other qualities may be, a community is a site-specific collectivity. This is clearly conveyed when sociologists refer to residential communities, whether neighborhoods or small towns, but it comes through, too, even when they refer to occupational or work-based communities.[1] Here they often point to sites of professional practice, to hospitals, universities, and corporate research divisions (e.g., Etzioni 1993, 31–32, 119–222). Whether residential or occupational, the term "community" also conveys, at the very least, that participants share some "common vocabulary of discourse and a background of implicit practices and understandings" (Sandel 1982, 172–73; also Selznick 1992, 358).

One problem that any sociologist faces in emphasizing the importance of community is that references to either residential or occupational communities seem stultifying. These references favor corporate entities that seem unnecessarily to obstruct other institutions and organizations from adapting the larger American society to intensifying global economic competition, ongoing corporate restructurings, and, however regrettable this might be, declining local and familial loyalties. These same corporate entities also seem prone to taxing the will of nonconforming individuals and groups.

Seeing this, Amitai Etzioni attempts to update and sharpen how sociologists approach contemporary communities by presenting the ideal of "responsive

I presented an earlier version of this chapter at the Thirty-first Congress of the International Institute of Sociology on June 21, 1993, at the Sorbonne in Paris. Thanks to Juchuan Wang, a Texas A&M graduate student, for a methodical reading and criticism of this version, and to Amitai Etzioni for written comments on the version that appears here.

community" (1991, 146–49). This ideal draws attention to how a community "expresses, affirms—versus imposes—its common values, ends, and interests" (ibid., 146–47). A responsive community does not operate through the state's coercive mechanisms. Nor does it oppress individuals and groups that fail to conform to a particular way of life or a particular set of substantive norms of behavior. Rather, it tolerates different ways of life even as it operates through "appeals to the 'nobler' part of the self" (ibid., 147; also Selznick 1992, xi). The responsive community "appeals to values that members already possess ('only you can prevent forest fires!') and encourages them to internalize values they currently do not command (before an appeal [about] litter will be effective, individuals are called upon to concern themselves with the environment)" (Etzioni, 1991, 148–49).

Still, Etzioni recognizes that he and other communitarians nonetheless face a problem: "The difficulty here is that communitarians do not draw on one clear substantive account of community" (ibid., 145). Indeed, when it comes to matters of substance, communitarians typically refer vaguely to the values purportedly shared within local communities. They seldom attempt to identify the values shared within occupational communities. A case in point is Philip Selznick's emphasis on the importance for the self of "core participation" in an ongoing community as opposed to "segmental participation" at other sites (1992, 184). Selznick can visualize core participation in geographic communities, and particularly family settings, but he has difficulty describing it at work sites other than those that are particularly regimented (e.g., Selznick ibid., 193).[2] For Selznick: "A group is a community to the extent that it encompasses a broad range of activities and interests, and to the extent that participation implicates whole persons rather than segmental interests or activities" (ibid., 358).

All references to the "integrity" of neighborhoods, small towns, and other localities seem anachronistic, however, in the context of today's global economy and corporate restructurings.[3] As Labor Secretary Robert Reich puts the matter: "The liberal task at hand is not to add legitimacy to the spurious notions of geographic community" (quoted by Etzioni at 1991, 145). Similarly, Selznick acknowledges that critics of communitarianism will point to the seeming anachronism of his own view, namely, that communities properly have the capacity to integrate civility with piety and a compelling respect for ongoing practices (1992, 35).

If Etzioni's communitarianism and Selznick's civility and piety are to be realized in benign ways today, then social scientists should find evidence that the norms and values to which they refer already inform the everyday lives of the middle class—from the upper middle class to the lower middle class. Yet, in the last two decades American and French sociologists in particular have documented that these norms and values are not in evidence across this stratum. They instead report the presence of quite different norms and values, and their findings were anticipated by classical social theorists at the turn of the century who drew attention to the general disruptiveness of modern social change. First, Durkheim established that modern social change uproots individuals from local communities and from earlier personal attachments and normative bonds. This leaves them anomic, adrift from settled moral guidance. Second, Weber added that the institutions of formal democracy—regularly held elections, competing political parties, even basic First Amendment freedoms—can "level" the governed. They can prepare the way for a "mass society" as opposed to sustaining automatically the motivated, vigilant citizenry that the American founders had in mind as the "constituent force" that ultimately ensures limited government and otherwise upholds the Constitution. Finally, Weber also pointed out that to the extent that social order is maintained at all, it may well rest on bureaucratically enforced, strictly formal social controls; it need not rest on individuals' widely shared sense of being integrated with others in local or national communities. Putting the matter more generally, the relationship between modern social change and a democratic political and legal regime has always been more tenuous than certain—to say nothing of the relationship between modern social change and substantive communities of shared values and norms capable of supporting such a regime.

Looking briefly at the United States today, the American middle class is shrinking in size, and its standard of living is deteriorating. Most growth in white-collar jobs has been in low-paying clerical jobs. Between 1975 and 1990, America's 500 largest companies failed to add any jobs to the economy, and their share of the civilian labor force has actually dropped, from 17 percent to 10 percent (Reich 1991, 6). Only working wives have made possible a modest standard of living for many middle-class households, and the result (for better or worse) has been an ongoing disruption of family rituals and practices (Lasch 1991, 479; Reich 1991). If a large and secure middle class is central to any geographic community under modern conditions, whether local or national, then the condition of the American middle class today is more portentous than reassuring.

One purpose of this chapter is to explore the gap between Etzioni's and other communitarians' references to community and the findings of the literature on middle-class beliefs and practices. These beliefs and practices are critical to any renascence of community in the United States in particular because neither a genuinely upper-class culture nor a genuinely working-class culture challenges this country's prevailing middle-class "culture" (Bellah et al. 1985, viii). Bellah and his colleagues describe the beliefs and practices of the established middle class in the United States, and Herbert Gans and Christopher Lasch do the same for the stratum below it, the lower middle class. In France, Pierre Bourdieu and Michel Maffesoli describe more generally the contemporary cultures within which the upper and lower middle class operate.[4] Communitarians may say that they have launched their social movement precisely because a creeping individualism has undermined the middle class's sense of responsibility. But my point in exploring the literature on the middle class is that this stratum is not likely to provide a base for communitarianism, because the latter's appeal for greater unity runs counter to powerful systemic changes currently pressuring the middle class as a whole. One such change is functional differentiation, which results in a breakdown of meaning—of substantive beliefs—by occupation or task. Another is intensifying international economic competition, which disrupts the everyday lives of the middle class in different ways rather than in similar ways, and thereby fragments meaning even further.

Another purpose of this chapter is to go further than establishing today's ongoing breakdown of meaning. It is to establish that the seemingly most responsible stratum, the upper middle class and cultivated elite—the bourgeoisie—engage in what I call "discrete nihilism." This occurs when the bourgeoisie treats basic procedural norms institutionalized within some corporations, professions, and other intermediary associations as if they are as amenable to compromise or pragmatic negotiation—as well as outright encroachment—as the pluralistic substantive norms that animate residential and occupation-based communities. My point in labeling this behavior nihilistic is that these basic procedural norms are unique to contemporary democracies, whereas the substantive norms animating communities are not, even if each community's constituents believe their particular practices maintain valued qualities of life. My point in saying that this encroaching behavior is discrete is that neither the bourgeoisie nor the sociologists mentioned in the previous paragraph appreciate the institutional significance of the first set of norms. These sociologists fail to draw the analytical distinctions that bring their institutional significance into view. Bourdieu in particular sees clearly that the bourgeoisie's general demeanor of indifference—as opposed to that of seeking affection or general recognition—is easily transferred from the arts to the professions. But he, as well as the bourgeoisie whose behavior he studies, fails to appreciate that this transfer can inadvertently challenge basic procedural norms and, with this, inadvertently undermine a quality of social life that is unique to contemporary democracy.

## Americans' Isolation and Disaffection

### The Established Middle Class: From Meaning to Drift

Tocqueville appreciated during the Jacksonian era that Americans were prone to isolation and, as a result, strangely available for despotism. The key element that he saw stemming and reversing this tendency, and thereby stabilizing American democracy, was the presence of active civic organizations across American civil society. Today, Robert Bellah is troubled precisely because he finds that the established American middle class treats its interpersonal and institutional commitments (in marriage, in work, in religious congregations, and in civic organizations) as enhancements of personal well-being. It no longer treats them as institutionalized moral imperatives that, in turn, give their personal lives greater meaning (Bellah et al. 1985, 47; also Lamont 1992, 98 on Americans' emphasis on self-actualization). As a result, the moral commitment that once marked the yeoman citizens whom Tocqueville observed participating in civic organizations, and that later in the century was still broadly shared across the growing American middle class, is giving way today to narrower concerns. On the one hand, there is respect for technical competence (see Reich 1991, 177–95 on symbolic analysts; and Lamont 1992, 40, 92, 240 note 23). On the other, there is tolerance for the aesthetic tastes unique to various self-help groups, what Bellah calls "lifestyle enclaves" (Bellah et al. 1985, 59).[5]

Aside from its changing outlook toward civic associations, the established middle class's view of work has also changed more recently since Bellah's study. Bellah appreciated that corporate managers, professionals, and community organizers rarely see their work as a calling (some exceptions being physicians and ballet dancers) (ibid., 66). They more often see their work either as a job that provides the income they need to enter a consumer economy or else as a career that offers more or less routine advancement through the ranks. What has changed of late is that the trajectory of the typical middle-class career is flatter today than it was before 1984, when a great wave of hostile, bust-up takeovers swept across corporate America. More importantly, continued employment within most corporations is itself contingent today, to say nothing of routine advancement. Not only middle managers but even top managers have lost career security. As a result, other than being a source of income, work has lost even more meaning for most middle-class Americans; it no longer generates a sense of commitment. Using Bellah's terminology, this loss reflects middle-class Americans' drift toward "utilitarian individualism."

In response to this drift, many middle-class Americans seek meaning in family life or, alternatively, in the avocations that Bellah labels lifestyle enclaves.[6] Again using Bellah's terminology, this search for meaning outside of work reflects middle-class Americans' drift toward "expressive individualism." "In a period when work is seldom a calling and few of us find a sense of who we are in public participation as citizens, the lifestyle enclave, fragile and shallow though it often is, fulfills that function for us all" (ibid., 75). The drift toward both types of individualism troubles Bellah. He worries that citizens' earlier, institutionalized sense of commitment offered American democracy more stable normative support and a more resilient infrastructure of personal belief and interpersonal behavior (ibid., 68, 71).

A century and a half after Tocqueville, therefore, Bellah worries that middle-class Americans' strictly instrumental and expressive pursuits are strangely compatible with a stultifying conformism, one that leaves them more available for tolerating abuse and arbitrariness than social scientists today typically acknowledge (ibid., 147–48). This is the case because when individuals no longer turn to long-standing practices or legitimate authority for meaning, they look instead to peers' acceptance to confirm their actions and judgments. The result, in Bellah's view, is a greater division running through American society than anything attributable to the country's cultural diversity. The division is that between (1) a "monoculture" of technical-bureaucratic rationality and (2) the minicultures of individuals' interpersonal beliefs within relationships and enclaves (ibid., 152). The only way to escape or overcome this division while simultaneously lending greater support to American democracy, in Bellah's view, is to shore up a specific set of intermediary associations, namely, "communities of memory" (ibid., 152–53). With this in mind, Bellah contrasts what he calls the empty self of individualism to the constitutive self, which he believes the middle class once developed and maintained within communities of memory.[7] For the moment I note simply in passing that all of Bellah's examples of genuine communities are marked by a particular way of life and by individuals sharing an identifiable set of substantive norms of behavior—whether as ethnic and racial groups or as religious, national, regional, local, neighborhood, or familial groups (ibid., 154). My point is that Bellah does not explore the procedural norms that frame and mediate such communities so that their behavior as corporate entities—their exercises of collective power—remain consistent with American democracy.

Closely connected to the established middle class's turn toward expressive individualism within lifestyle enclaves is their increasing reliance on therapy to ameliorate their remaining interpersonal conflicts. This, too, carries institutional implications: "[T]herapy's stress on personal autonomy presupposes institutional conformity" (ibid., 124). The larger American society may remain buttressed by the formal rule of law, but Bellah finds that most rules actually enforced within occupations simply compel participants' conformity. They seldom capture their spirit as individuals or foster a sense of self-integration (ibid., 126). With this, Bellah reveals two levels of analysis at which sociologists may inquire into the nature of social order in cross-national perspective, even as he focuses on the first, namely, the interpersonal level of individuals' self-integration within communities. The other is the institutional level of corporate entities' social integration within the larger social order.

In Bellah's view, self-integration occurs only within genuine communities of memory, not within lifestyle enclaves.[8] His central point in emphasizing this is that the "prevalence of contractual intimacy [for example, in therapy] and procedural cooperation, carried over from boardroom to bedroom and back again, is what threatens to obscure the ideals of both personal virtue and public good" (ibid., 127). When he refers to the "public good," however, Bellah turns from self-integration to social integration, from the interpersonal level to the institutional level. Yet, much like Selznick's references to the relationship between personal well-being and moral community, Bellah also has difficulty identifying the relationship between his ideals of personal virtue and public good in ways that can escape controversy or competing interpretations in a dynamic, pluralistic society.

### *The Lower Middle Class: Loneliness and Avoidance*

Herbert Gans is also concerned about the institutional implications of the American middle class's individualism, but, unlike Bellah, he explores popular individualism, that of the lower middle class. The stratum that interests Gans spans 40 percent of all American households, those families whose income in the mid-1980s ranged from $15,000 to $37,500. The breadwinners in these families hold factory and service jobs (including semiprofessional positions in fields such as nursing) as well as routine clerical, sales, and technical or bureaucratic office positions. Putting this stratum in context, Gans points out that the vast majority of Americans still hold only a high school diploma; one-fourth of all young Americans fail to graduate from high school every spring. Moreover, the vast majority of Americans today are employed in workplaces with twenty or fewer employees (Gans 1988, 52).

Gans's statistical category of people is in many respects more significant, both economically and culturally, than Bellah's established middle class. Gans's people are not only a numerical majority of all Americans, but they also occupy the very center of American popular culture. Compact discs do not climb the charts and movies do not become blockbusters until they attract a sizable middle-American audience. Relatedly, when the writers of sociology textbooks discuss deviance, they do so explicitly or implicitly against the backdrop of what Gans's people believe is unacceptable or abnormal conduct.

Still, middle Americans' popular individualism is a relatively recent development. It emerged in the late nineteenth century as the family farm disappeared and sales, clerical, and other office positions multiplied (ibid., 14). Rather than mimicking the individualism—either utilitarian or expressive—of the established middle class, popular individualism hinges on "motherhood" values such as generosity, fairness, honesty, personal responsibility, and hard work (ibid., 34). Where Bellah's established middle class lacks a sense of community and yet actively seeks peer support in lifestyle enclaves, Gans's lower middle class avoids all formal organizations, whether public or private. It instead invests its time and energy in family and friends. In a curious way, Gans's people also seek meaning in lifestyle enclaves, but theirs rarely include strangers. Rather, Gans's people essentially recapitulate in contemporary America the "amoral familism" that Edward Banfield (1958) found decades earlier among southern Italians.[9] Banfield saw this both reflecting and accounting for the absence of a commons, of any notable public life. Gans's people, actually, often end up leading lonelier lives than Banfield's people—given the normal course of life stages (that is, children leaving the nest, friends seeking job openings elsewhere) plus the more recent disruptions of American family life in particular (that is, the high incidence of divorce, to say nothing of unhappy marriages) (Gans, 44).

The familism and personalism animating the lower middle class also explains why Gans's people endeavor to avoid any and all contact with state agencies or major corporations. Large organizations make them uncomfortable because they are not skilled at "the antagonistic cooperation . . . which characterizes professional work" (ibid., 51, here Gans quotes David Riesman). Instead, they approach even the largest corporations and governmental agencies with familial models of behavior in mind. They then find rather readily that the behavior of large organizations fails to match these models. This, in turn, confirms their worst fears about strangers.[10] Yet, Gans's people are attached emotionally to the nation and its symbols, such as the flag and Arlington National Cemetery (ibid., 61).[11] Their children not only fight the nation's wars but often volunteer for service rather than wait to be drafted.

Gans's central concern is that the American lower middle class's broadly shared strategy of organizational avoidance results in an ever-widening gap between the workings of America's democratic institutions and the popular individualism of the majority of citizens. Thus, like Bellah, this gap causes Gans to worry about the future of American democracy. Ross Perot likely fills this gap at least somewhat in the United States today, but others, more aggressive in their policy positions, may well fill it in the future. The American left rightly fears popular individualism (Lasch 1991, 37). In France at this writing, it may be that Edouard Balladur (prime minister) and Charles Pasqua (interior minister) fill this gap to some extent.

Even more than Bellah's established middle class, however, Gans's lower middle class is buffeted by systemic economic and social changes beyond their understanding and control. On the one hand, they value home ownership as a means of obtaining personal control over their immediate situation (Gans 1988, 2); their homes offer them havens from the anxieties they experience in approaching formal organizations in particular and from the unwelcome intrusions of strangers more generally. Yet, these are precisely the Americans who find it increasingly difficult in today's domestic economy to buy a home, or to keep it.[12]

Gans's people quite purposefully avoid risk taking, much preferring to play it safe, to adopt a hunkering-down strategy. They are more interested in landing jobs that pay acceptable wages than in entering careers that hold out the promise of steady advancement (ibid., 3). In their eyes work is a necessary evil, even if personally rewarding at times; work is not a voluntaristic expression of their person or being (ibid., 6–9). And yet these are precisely the Americans who most readily lose their jobs in any economic downturn. Thus, their purposeful strategy of risk avoidance ends up exposing them inadvertently to the disruptions of systemic economic changes (in a global economy) and systemic social changes (affecting family life). Their strategy of holding a job, owning a house, and avoiding formal organizations ends up exposing them to unemployment, to bankruptcy, and then to dependence on relatives or, worse, governmental agencies.

In short, the individualism that Bellah sees in the established middle class's utilitarianism and expressivism, Gans portrays, more benignly, as the lower middle class's largely fated efforts at self-improvement (ibid., 105).[13] Christopher Lasch's more recent study (1991) can be read as putting both sociologists' findings into grander theoretical and historical perspective. He notes that American right-wing politicians defer ritually to the "traditional values" of Gans's lower middle class, and yet they remain committed to progress and the goals of unlimited economic growth and acquisitive individualism that attract Bellah's established middle class (ibid., 21). Like Bellah and Gans, Lasch also does not see the danger to American democracy today coming from collectivist movements, either right or left. Rather, he, too, sees the danger coming from a cumulative erosion of the psychological, cultural, and spiritual foundations of American democracy (ibid., 24).

Put more specifically, Lasch is concerned that America today is more a nation of passive consumers than a nation of vigilant citizens (ibid., 68). He interprets both the New Deal and the Progressive Movement as democratizing consumption, not as broadening citizenship (ibid., 70). John Maynard Keynes, who provided Western lawmakers with a theoretical rationale for developing mass consumer societies, appreciated that consumerism steadily erodes the work ethic. Actually, he was convinced as early as the 1920s that the notions of duty and calling were already anachronistic (ibid., 74–75). Today Lasch not only is convinced, with Bellah, that the middle class generally has lost a sense of calling but also that there has been a "collapse" of legitimate or subjectively acceptable authority across American society. In his view this explains why so many American political and social leaders turn to bribery, intimidation, and surveillance in order to maintain their traditional bases of support (ibid., 27–28).

**Taking Stock and Looking Forward**

Lasch's indictment of American leadership brings the discussion to the point I raised earlier about the discrete nihilism of the bourgeoisie. I show in this section that Bellah, Gans, and Lasch are mistaken in seeing the coming crisis of American democracy in psychological and social psychological terms. What is more central than any psychological malaise, or any absence of individuals' internalized subjective sense of integration within communities of memory, is a much more palpable erosion of the institutionalized procedural norms unique to modern democracy. When these norms are firmly institutionalized, the rules or social duties being sanctioned within and by any organization can at least be recognized and understood in common by everyone affected. This is the case because these rules or social duties are: enforced generally rather than unevenly; publicly declared; prospective; intelligible; capable of being performed; constant rather than passing; and consistent with actual organizational behavior (Fuller 1964/1969, 46–84). Those organizations that institutionalize their constituents' fidelity to this threshold of procedural norms are organized in the collegial form in particular, not the bureaucratic form, nor the formally democratic or plebiscitary form, nor the patron–client form of interpersonal trust and dependence (Sciulli 1992). Collegial formations or deliberative bodies are often found at sites of professional practice (as peer review committees, for instance), including universities, hospitals, corporate research and development divisions, and other intermediary associations. At these sites professionals may institutionalize their own ongoing deliberations over the meaning of qualitative information affecting their clients' lives and livelihoods.

My point is that the individualism and pragmatism of the established middle class and upper middle class in particular can contribute to the erosion of these procedural norms. By contrast, the lower middle class's efforts simply to avoid organizations cannot. At first glance, it seems that Pierre Bourdieu (1979) and Michele Lamont (1992) distance the French experience from the American when they observe that the French upper middle class's respect for intellectual honesty poses an alternative to their American counterparts' pragmatism, which is marked by a greater willingness to compromise in order to get along (esp. Lamont 1992, 30). Putting this observation into my discussion above, compromises at sites of professional practice that legitimate encroachments against basic procedural norms contribute to nihilism, even if inadvertently or discretely. Thus, a respect for intellectual honesty seems at first to make this less likely. Yet, Bourdieu (1979, 315) and Lamont (1992, 50–53) both note, too, that the French middle classes are themselves undergoing changes in belief as a result of systemic pressures in the domestic economy and global economy. Self-employed French semiprofessionals and professionals, for instance, act more like American corporate managers. They, too, stress sociability with clients and teamwork with colleagues as opposed to intellectual honesty.

The problem, again, is that camaraderie at work sites can be more forced than voluntaristic, more controlling than integrating. It can become a mechanism of peer conformity and interpersonal social control. As such, it can just as easily support arbitrary exercises of collective power within and by intermediary associations as contribute to a social order capable of supporting democracy. "Indeed, some [Americans] might end up adopting a pragmatic approach to morality as they adapt their beliefs to the situation at hand" (Lamont 1992, 40). American sociologists and political scientists have noted for thirty years that a strictly pragmatic approach to decision making marks the drift of legislative pluralism and judicial balancing, and American legal historian William Hurst points out that the result is "bastard pragmatism," not anything loftier.

Gans captures well the implications of this discussion when he observes that the very concept of citizenship seems anachronistic today because there seem to be no equivalents in society, in everyday life, to the status of citizenship (Gans 1988, 69, 114). I have already proposed a societal equivalent to citizenship, however, namely, professionals' behavioral fidelity to the threshold of procedural norms that is uniquely institutionalized by collegial formations. Once this societal equivalent to citizen vigilance over limited government is brought into view, it exposes to social scientific observation the discrete nihilism of the American and French bourgeoisie.

## Complacency and Vigilance

Lasch traces the disruptiveness and sense of malaise that mark contemporary American society to the modern idea of progress, to producers' and consumers' collective commitment to increase private wealth for perpetuity, as literally an end-in-itself, the "one and only heaven" (Lasch 1991, 43). The ancient Greeks, by contrast, were animated by a quite different collective commitment, namely, that of citizens living in the present with faith and hope.[14] One of Lasch's central points in drawing this stark contrast is that the ancient view of citizenship is actually closer to the American founders' and framers' republican vigilance than to contemporary Americans' more facile complacency and pragmatism (ibid., 46, 50–51).

Republicans associated civic virtue with self-assertion and self-realization, the opposite of Christianity's virtue of self-abnegation (ibid., 173–74). They also condemned a life devoted to maximizing private wealth, but not because they disapproved of selfishness as such. Rather, republicans condemned such a life because they believed that self-interested behavior in the marketplace is insufficiently competitive; it fails to provide talented individuals with sufficient scope to live according to the ancient Greek ethic of excelling in a public realm. Republicans particularly condemned wealthy individuals who bent the rules governing any given practice—public or private—in order to advance their own material advantage. In their view this undermined the game of competition and everyone's opportunities to excel (ibid., 174).

Republicans also shared with the ancients the proposition that the first responsibility of citizens—as opposed to producers and consumers—is to keep government's power limited. This responsibility takes precedence over all others (except those to family and to God) precisely because abusive exercises of collective power destroy the public realm, the only site at which the competitive pursuit of excellence remains a possibility. Thus, American republicans' most important goal after the Revolution was to establish institutions that supported citizen vigilance over limited government. In this endeavor they faced a very practical issue: What kinds of institutional arrangements can help citizens to recognize in common when government's exercises of power become abusive or arbitrary or when government is succumbing to its "encroaching nature"? American republicans' answer was to decentralize governmental power wherever practicable. After all, if citizens are to recognize in common what abusive government is, then they must also be able to recognize in common what limited government is.

With the practical problem in mind of maintaining citizens' shared recognition, and thus their collective vigilance, the framers retained the thirteen colonial legislatures and adopted Montesquieu's idea of dividing governmental powers. These two institutional devices supported citizen vigilance in three ways. First, both devices decentralized and limited government's exercises of collective power. Second, federalism and the division of powers provided citizens with "trip wires" by which they might recognize in common when government succumbs to its "encroaching nature." After all, an encroaching government will at the very least collapse the division of powers and replace federalism with a more centralized administration. Third, both devices also slowed down all governmental actions, thereby giving citizens time to organize popular resistance when necessary, and particularly before an encroaching government becomes too powerful to resist (see Sciulli 1992, 68–69, 202–39 on the allegory of the constituent force).

Thus, "republican virtue" had everything to do with maintaining an "ordered liberty," a "constitutional liberty" (McDowell 1988, 65–66). It had little to do with laissez-faire. Indeed, "the doctrine of laissez-faire was hardly known to the framers of the Constitution" (Bourgin [1945] 1989, 37, 47).[15] To be sure, "republican virtue" included a strong defense of private property, but this was ironically because the framers believed that citizen vigilance as well as limited government rested on a social infrastructure quite inconsistent with laissez-faire. They believed that a republic rested on a social infrastructure marked by three characteristics: first, a proliferation of yeoman farmers, small shopkeepers, and craft laborers; second, a proliferation of intermediary associations across civil society that, by definition, stand between the individual and the state; third, an absence of rich and poor, of wealthy merchants and impoverished laborers.

This reveals why the American founders and framers were so reluctant to grant broad legal support to private commercial activity in the early republic. They did not want to encourage imbalances of private wealth. They feared that a widening gap between rich and poor disrupted social order, eroded citizen vigilance, and thereby posed a threat to the republic itself.[16] In their view, this gap marked England's decadence as a society. England's "mercantile monopolists" used the power of government to secure private economic privileges at others' expense. The framers were convinced that when businessmen were permitted to use government's power in this way, only private disorder and public abuse could result (Sellers 1991, ch. 2; Mark 1987; McDowell 1982, ch. 1–3; McCoy 1980).[17]

The radicalism of Americans' early view of what can be called the institutional externalities of private commercial activity may be appreciated today by putting it into the terminology of contemporary corporate law (see Sciulli, under review): Whenever private contracts that are otherwise legal—and otherwise profitable—make it more difficult for citizens to recognize in common when concentrated wealth or collective power is being used in abusive or arbitrary ways, the courts may legitimately nullify these contracts on this public law ground. The point of American republicanism was precisely that an overriding public law interest, an interest in reducing the institutional externalities of exercises of collective power, legitimately assumes a higher legal status than otherwise lawful and profitable private law contracts. Thus, like other political economists of their day, including Mandeville and Smith, American republicans were concerned first and foremost about the institutional externalities of private commercial activity, not the immediate externalities that more directly affect discrete individuals (such as failed investments or temporary loss of employment).[18] By contrast, a century later neoclassical economists would be concerned far more narrowly with whether corporations maximize their owners' private wealth and with how corporations perform their "production function."[19]

Adam Smith contributed greatly to the modern idea of progress—and to liberal complacency—even as he did not fully embrace the idea himself. He advanced it by rebutting republicans' general concern that unbridled acquisitiveness results invariably in personal unhappiness and civic decline (Lasch 1991, 52). Smith's counterargument was that man's insatiable appetites can drive the economic machine just as surely as man's insatiable curiosity drives the machine of scientific discovery. Still, Smith first referred to the "hidden hand" in *The Theory of Moral Sentiments,* not in *The Wealth of Nations.* He did indeed argue that accumulated private wealth simultaneously advances the public good, even if inadvertently, but he also revealed why he was reluctant to embrace liberal complacency outright (ibid., 54). He observed that even as the division of labor enhances productivity, it also dulls the mind and saps the martial spirit. With this, he still accepted in some part republicans' point that civic virtue, citizen vigilance over limited government, does not spring automatically from the normatively unmediated play of individuals' self-interested behavior in the marketplace (ibid., 56).[20]

After Smith's tempered support for a market society, liberals became ever more complacent with each generation, eventually losing any memory of the founders' concerns about declining citizen vigilance (see Lasch on "Macaulay's complacency," 1991, 58). Complacent liberals' article of faith, inconsistent with Smith's reservations, is that when individuals maximize their own private wealth, they simultaneously (1) maximize social wealth and (2) contribute automatically to a benign or nonauthoritarian institutional arrangement, as if guided by a hidden hand.

At the turn of the twentieth century, however, a full generation before the New Deal and Keynes's *General Theory,* Weber and other major social theorists (with the notable exceptions of Comte and Spencer) would have none of this faith. The best single illustration of their pathos, as contrasted to American liberals' complacency, is found in Weber's discussion of the "ethic of responsibility" in "Science as a Vocation." Weber insisted that even when individuals endeavor to act responsibly within a market society, their actions can still be expected to contribute, even if inadvertently, to modernity's systematic drift toward formal social control and collective abuse. This institutional outcome can be called social authoritarianism. If Weber had not addressed at a conceptual level these institutional externalities of individuals' interpersonal behavior, he would have simply reported whether and how people act responsibly in their everyday lives. Weber would have been a symbolic analyst, not an organizational and institutional theorist, and he would have substituted liberal complacency at a conceptual level for his own pathos, his own version of republican vigilance. What prevented Weber from moving to this lower level of analysis is that, unlike symbolic analysts, he felt compelled to account at a conceptual level for the possibility of there being a nonauthoritarian institutional outcome under modern conditions. The concepts that he developed to this end—rationalization, fragmentation of meaning, bureaucratization, leveling of the governed—highlighted how contingent this possibility is in practice. These same concepts, in turn, framed all of Weber's observations of individual and group behavior.

Lasch correctly criticizes American historians for losing this sense of pathos, for failing to take account "of the possibility of tragedy—missed opportunities, fatal choices, conclusive and irrevocable defeats" (Lasch 1991, 221; also see Selznick on American pragmatists' neglect of "evil," 1992, 31, 172–73). The problem, as Lasch correctly puts it, is that no modern country, including the United States, has yet learned how to reconcile freedom and equality with the wage system, modern finance, and the corporate organization of economic life. Appreciating this, Lasch thinks that the critique of a consumer society implicit in the behavior of Gans's lower middle class merits attention. This behavior by the majority of Americans poses a challenge to social scientists' prevailing faith of liberal complacency (Lasch 1991, 225).[21] Still, Lasch also appreciates that Gans's people are hardly republicans. He concedes that their lower-middle-class culture is provincial. Yet his central point stands, namely, that lower-middle-class culture is also realistic in the context of today's intensifying international economic competition, uncertain domestic economy, and declining material expectations. This stratum's general skepticism about the workings of large public and private organizations provides Lasch with the opening he needs to explore the contemporary merits of republican vigilance.

Still, Lasch goes too far in defending directly the substantive norms of behavior unique to the lower middle class. I proposed earlier that an alternative is to look first at how some intermediary associations today maintain their own integrity by adopting the collegial form of organization, and how the latter helps to institutionalize procedural normative restraints unique to modern democracy. By their very presence in society, these intermediary associations help to mediate short of abuse and arbitrariness: the state's power, their own exercises of collective power, and their middle class membership's strictly self-interested, pragmatic behavior.

Bellah also neglects this alternative because he approaches the professions in a reductionist way. He sees the rise of what he calls a "therapeutic culture" coinciding with the rise of the modern middle class, and he calls the latter's "calculating and ambitious culture" the "culture of professionalism" (Bellah et al. 1985, 119). He uses this label because, for him, a profession is less a calling (marked by devotion to impersonal standards of excellence) than a drive for success (an indefinite goal) (ibid., 119–20). But this way of approaching the professions also hinges too directly on some implicit substantive normative standard of individuals' sincerity or commitment at work. Bellah overlooks the fact that professions, and sites of professional practice, are intermediary associations. Can he really assume that how they are organized—the form in which they are organized—has nothing to do with how individuals actually behave, and then with whether the larger social order is benign or possibly integrative?[22]

Similarly, however insightful Gans might be in saying that the concept of citizenship is anachronistic, he says this against a background belief that even local citizen activism is "professionalized" today. Because Gans, too, is operating implicitly with a substantive normative standard of professional behavior as "sincere" or "genuine," he insists that those individuals who engage in "professionalized" politics are often "unusual people" driven by "unusual motives" (1988, 75). But what does this charge really amount to? Gans is simply saying that political activists, like professional practitioners, are different from the organizational avoiders whom Gans is studying—and this is clearly the case. But how can Gans be so certain that none of their points of difference stem from their ongoing responsibility to exhibit fidelity to procedural norms, and that the latter uniquely mediates arbitrariness at an institutional level? If this is the case, in practice, then, these "unusual people" are maintaining the sense of fair play that Gans's lower middle class also values, even as Gans's people correctly view these same people as strangers who fail to act in familistic or personalistic ways.

### "Orgy" and Indifference in France

#### *Challenges to Morality in Everyday Life*

By contrast to Lasch's effort to escape liberal complacency by drawing on the beliefs and practices of the lower middle class, Maffesoli's "sociology of the orgy" (1985) establishes an important defense of many norms antagonistic to those of Gans's lower middle class, the work ethic in particular. He defines orgy in its etymological sense as a shared emotion, a collective sentiment, a holistic perspective that integrates life, passion, and communal feeling. This occurs today, in Maffesoli's view, when people in cities lose their active selves as they enter a crowd or, better put, as they "flutter" from site of interaction to site of interaction. Maffesoli makes an important contribution by drawing social scientists' attention to the "instant condensations" that people experience at these sites. As he says, these are fragile, fleeting, serial moments, and yet they often elicit strong emotional investments from aggregates of individuals who otherwise are perfect strangers. Thus, orgiasm is the "*jouissance* [playfulness] of the present," coupled with the tragic attitude of ignoring tomorrow (ibid., 10). It is all-encompassing, and thereby enriches the substance of a community's life at the moment. Praising the "impulse to wander," Maffesoli cites Braudillard positively on the "collective compulsion" of some Americans to keep moving along the highway (ibid., 6).

Yet, even as Maffesoli discusses the loss of an active self in many urban settings, he nonetheless also refers constantly to a "living equilibrium" when describing both the local community and the larger social order that frames these passing interactions. These references reveal, ironically, that Maffesoli shares the grand postwar faith of liberal complacency. This is evident when he says off-handedly that "because there is plurality, there is an equilibrium, even if this equilibrium is contradictory or tensional," and elsewhere that "complexity . . . necessitates the art of equilibrium" (ibid., 52, 83).[23] His citing of Pareto before using the concept of equilibrium in these ways is not sufficiently powerful, however, to support such grand statements (ibid., 11). Standing back, these statements also do not follow logically from Maffesoli's own descriptions of orgiastic behavior. An alternative way of casting his findings is to say that because there is plurality there is social control, at least to the extent that social order is being maintained at all. And exercises of social control can either be possibly integrative or demonstrably manipulative or coercive.

One key to understanding Maffesoli's position, and also to appreciating why his references to equilibrium are marks of a complacent liberal, is his distinction between morality and ethics. Morality, by his account, elevates a certain number of behaviors above all others. As a result, it is provincial and ultimately stultifying. Ethics, on the other hand, refers to a different basis for social equilibrium, one based on a "reciprocal relativization" of the different values that may be found not only across local communities but also across the passing settings noted above. Thus, Maffesoli believes that local communities as well as larger social orders rest on what he calls an "ethical immoralism": People accept that their own behavior as well as others' is often tied to the moment. For this reason, they are suitably reluctant to rank certain types of behavior as being more "moral" than others in some grander sense. Still, Maffesoli also correctly notes that even his more modest ethical "ensemble" is formalized only with difficulty (ibid., 8). Moreover, Maffesoli praises plurality and difference even as he concedes that their limiting case is death, not a living equilibrium (ibid., 73).

This brings us to the issue: Are there any limits to plurality and difference, short of death, that are consistent with the ethical in Maffesoli's sense? That is, are there limits that do not simply renew the provincial moralities that the very lived quality of urban settings has already irreversibly challenged? By failing to address at a conceptual level the different forms in which the ethical can be stabilized or institutionalized today (ibid., 7), Maffesoli implicitly shares the postwar faith of liberal complacency. This can be seen when he says, on the one hand, that orgiasm overrides morality by encouraging individuals to engage in spending and loss at the moment, and yet, on the other, he nonetheless believes that such excess always reinforces the ethical.[24] It does so, he says, by reminding everyone of why their "being together" at any site really matters (ibid., 9–10).

The problem with Maffesoli's distinction between morality and ethics is that he defines both concepts in terms of lived experiences and substantive norms of behavior. Then he assumes that, somehow, a cacophony of such experiences and norms contributes automatically to a benign or nonauthoritarian social order. He assumes this by not defining the ethical in particular in terms of the non-negotiable procedural norms that uniquely serve such a social order in two ways. They simultaneously (1) permit plurality and difference, including the excesses of orgiasm in Maffesoli's sense, and (2) mediate exercises of collective power by both residential and occupational communities short of abuse and arbitrariness (Sciulli 1992). There is clearly room for bringing procedural norms into Maffesoli's work because he notes that even in extreme cases of orgiasm, for instance, in Sade's endless game, there are still rules or regulations of one kind or another (Maffesoli 1985, 22, 26). The issue, again, is to identify the sites at which fidelity to procedural norms is non-negotiable, at least if a relatively benign or possibly integrative social order is to be maintained. Once these sites are identified, we can then concede that when orgiasm elsewhere moves beyond these limits, it does not carry institutional externalities; it does not then challenge a benign social order by relativizing it.

Maffesoli is certainly correct, therefore, that the fecundation of the world can occur below the surface, in subterranean dens where even Sade might be welcome. But is it not also the case, both in principle and in practice, that such experiences at an interpersonal level have the greatest potential to reach their fullest and most robust expression in private, when arbitrary exercises of collective power are being restrained at an institutional level? Maffesoli notes that popular *savoir vivre* does not allow itself to be seen except in certain paroxysmic situations such as carnivals (ibid., 31). But what if it does begin to flaunt itself, and thereby seeks protection for its new public exposure, all in the name of plurality or diversity? Again, are the only limits to orgiastic plurality and difference those of traditional morality or Christian prudery? Maffesoli is assuming without argument, without offering the concepts that he needs to support it, that a public world of some legitimacy has already institutionalized some resilient restraints on orgiastic excess. He assumes this complacently, as a state of affairs that is an automatic outcome of the substance of plurality itself. Absent from his work are concepts of republican vigilance that draw attention to the fact that the procedural norms that protect all of us from the worst, from evil, are never automatically institutionalized, whether in France or in the United States.

### Bourgeois Indifference and Contemporary Risk

I turn briefly to Bourdieu's work in order to bring into the discussion the beliefs and practices of yet another stratum within the middle class, namely, the upper middle class and cultural elite, the cultivated bourgeoisie. Bourdieu documents that this group's general demeanor is marked by two central, interrelated characteristics: First, the bourgeois exhibit indifference to the objectifying gaze of others and an "aesthetic disposition," what Bourdieu calls the "pure gaze" of detachment. Second, the bourgeois refuse to invest psychic or emotional energy in the substantive concerns of everyday life and, thus, refuse to take too seriously most matters that concern Bellah's people, to say nothing of Gans's (1979: 5, 35, 53, 207–8). Where Gans's people shrink from the public arena, and even Bellah's people and Maffesoli's orgiasts prefer private enclaves to the public stage, Bourdieu's cultivated bourgeois thrive in the most formal, public settings. Their utter indifference to the opinions and feelings of others actually results in these individuals' appearing to others to be not only nonchalant but relaxed, eminently sociable to any and all who enter their circle. Their general demeanor in public is so unique to the bourgeoisie that it sets them apart from Gans's avoiders and Bellah's individualists as an identifiable tribe. (I show below that Maffesoli's orgiasts span these three tribes.) The members of this third tribe literally use the same words to describe wine that they use to describe architecture (ibid., 53).

Still, the wild card running through Gans's account of the lower middle class ironically runs through Bourdieu's account of the cultivated bourgeoisie, one that he acknowledges in passing (ibid., 297–304): the systemic escalation of financial risk that affects all modern societies and all social classes. Where Gans's avoiders need a steady wage to remain part of a consumer society, and also to stay clear of governmental assistance, the bourgeoisie's way of life hinges on these individuals' having permanently at their disposal great reserves of discretionary wealth. These reserves, like the avoiders' very jobs, have been disrupted by corporate structurings that began in 1984 and continue today. Systemic pressures of market competition have reduced considerably the security of return on all long-term or fixed investments, whether those of material capital or of human capital. Even the most established bourgeoisie in the United States are being encouraged or induced by systemic pressures to take risks with family fortunes, and at times to gamble. At a minimum, these individuals are being induced by systemic pressures to place family fortunes in trust, with fiduciaries taking the risks for them (see Sciulli, forthcoming).

In addition, like Maffesoli, Bourdieu also indirectly affirms liberal complacency. This is evident when he says that the primary experience that all people have of the social world is that of *doxa,* an adherence to relations of order which, for them, are self-evident (Bourdieu 1979, 471). The problem here is that orderly behavior as such may well be automatic or relatively immutable. The limiting case of disorder, after all, a Hobbesian war of all against all, is never realized in practice. Rather, when people reduce their allegiances to the nation or larger social order, they typically transfer them to some clan, family, or local passing grouping. But they never simply fragment, all of a sudden becoming unattached, roving individuals. My point, again, is that a benign or possibly integrative social order is hardly an automatic institutional outcome at any level of analysis, unlike a social order that rests more exclusively on mechanisms of social control that permit or even encourage arbitrary exercises of collective power.

### Discrete Nihilism: From Interpersonal Experience to Institutional Significance

Below I will move the discussion from descriptions of middle-class behavior at an interpersonal level of analysis to explanations of how this behavior affects existing institutional arrangements within modern democracies. First, however, I want to explore how Maffesoli's examples of orgiasm move back and forth from the upper middle class to the lower middle class, from Bourdieu's tribe of the cultivated bourgeoisie and Bellah's tribe of lifestyle individualists to Gans's tribe of organizational avoiders. To this end, it is worthwhile to consider Freud's view of the mature life. In *Civilization and Its Discontents* ([1930] 1961), Freud argued that individuals face life maturely when they no longer rely on religion to escape life's decisions or, certainly, when they do not turn to alcohol or drugs to blunt life's disappointments and hardships. Mature people seek pleasure or happiness open-eyed and clearheaded, and yet the game of life works against them. Moments of pleasure are fleeting, whereas states of pain or unhappiness are an everyday experience. The natural deterioration of the human body is one source of pain. But another is when individuals invest their emotional or psychic energy in others—including spouses and children—who fail to reciprocate. Precisely because the odds against sustained pleasurable experiences are so long, mature individuals tend to moderate their aspirations accordingly. They rein in their emotional investments in others either by isolating themselves or, alternatively, by throwing themselves into their work or professional activity (ibid., ch. 2).

Bellah has already shown us, however, that the established middle class no longer sees work as a calling worthy of such dedication. And Gans has shown us that the lower middle class opts for isolation, even at the price of loneliness. Putting the point at issue more generally and analytically, the experiences of orgiasm lived by the three different tribes of the middle class, and the material and psychic costs that these individuals bear during these experiences, are hardly equivalent. Yet, social scientists tend too often to stand back and chronicle types of behaviors by detaching their descriptions from references to the class or status position of the individuals involved. With this, they collapse the very different meanings that seemingly similar behaviors have for the individuals involved. What social scientists need in approaching these behaviors, then, is some class-neutral standard of behavior that allows them to draw distinctions independently of actors' own subjective interpretations of their meaning. In the absence of such a standard, everyday experience becomes ever more balkanized, too particular to draw meaningful comparisons across.

With this in mind, consider Maffesoli's argument (1985, 1–2) that the individual and the social are being supplanted today by the "confusional." This concept is an important contribution to social theory. Maffesoli is careful to point out that it does not refer to the anomic. Rather, it refers to those very real, substantive norms—concrete ways of life—that both structure and regenerate a community as an ethical immoralism. The confusional, like the orgiastic, is the primordial "being together," where everyone loses his and her active self by entering a state of being where "transgression loses its interest" (ibid., 3–4). In losing their active selves, individuals are free to blossom—both in tenderness and in cruelty (ibid., 5). I would insist that this, too, is an important, indeed a courageous, contribution to social theory.

My point, however, is that social scientists need to look to the institutional level, and to turn away for a moment from the interpersonal level, in developing any standard by which to compare people's lived experience. Consider how this works in comparing Maffesoli's and Bourdieu's work. On the one hand, Maffesoli's orgiasts are engaged so directly in substantive or lived endeavors that their experiences are fundamentally incommensurable, irreducibly pluralistic. On the other hand, Bourdieu's tribe of the cultivated bourgeoisie experiences a far more singular "aesthetic disposition." Clearly, when Bourdieu's tribe experiences distinction and when Maffesoli's tribe experiences pleasure, their individual members need not concern themselves with how their experiences affect existing institutional arrangements. But my point is that it is precisely here where observing, value-neutral social scientists can make their contribution, as Weber did over seventy years ago when he approached the ethic of responsibility not only at an interpersonal level but also at an institutional level.

Bourdieu errs when he insists that the principles by which any given practice is structured can never be informed by any system of universal forms and categories but can only be informed by some particular, site-specific scheme. Bourdieu calls this scheme a "habitus," as opposed to using the more amorphous term "values." His term better captures individuals' practical mastery of everyday conduct (Bourdieu 1979, 466).[25] Yet, American legal theorist Lon Fuller argued persuasively nearly three decades ago that it is mistaken to believe that general norms cannot frame and orient everyday conduct, and particularly within social orders that are relatively benign and that actually do mediate arbitrary exercises of collective power. Habermas has since updated the argument independently and on a loftier theoretical plane: Only procedural norms can keep open the possibility of heterogeneous individuals and competing groups gaining some shared recognition and understanding of the value of the same qualities of life. Bourdieu has not established that even the cultivated bourgeoisie is so homogeneous today (unlike in the past), so lacking in competing factions and incommensurable experiences, that it can establish and maintain a shared recognition and understanding of the value of the same qualities of life independently of any and all procedural normative framing.

Similarly, Maffesoli also cannot neglect the point of Habermas's communicative ethics and Fuller's legal theory. He cannot simply describe orgiasts' substantive norms of behavior and then assume without argument that a benign "ethical equilibrium" somehow results automatically. Yet, like Bourdieu, Maffesoli also provides an important, powerful corrective to Habermas's too easy reduction of the richness of social life to the procedural framework of a benign social order.[26] My point in trying to negotiate between these important contributions is that Maffesoli and Bourdieu need to say more about Habermas's procedural turn, even as Habermas can concede the significance of their efforts to capture the substantive richness of everyday life.

In this light, consider again Maffesoli's distinction between ethics and morality. It is ethics that "must integrate the plurality of values and make them interact for the greatest good of the societal bond" (Maffesoli 1985, 11). He also insists that "if there is a necessity for evil, for disorder, what the orgy demonstrates is that in the end it attains a superior order which brings it closer to the harmony or the coincidence of contraries" (ibid., 79). In both passages, Maffesoli is appealing to an ethics at an institutional level, and yet he persists in defining the latter exclusively in terms of substantive norms.

The problem with this is that neither Maffesoli nor anyone else has any way of knowing when a substantive way of life actually advances the greatest good of a societal bond or when a particular social order is superior to others in substance. If Maffesoli does know this, then surely he must share the standard of comparison that he is using. It is certain that if he does identify it, it will turn out not to rest exclusively on substantive norms; after all, if it does, it exposes Maffesoli to charges of provincialism, including ethnocentrism. Moreover, when orgiasm turns politically nasty, as Maffesoli acknowledges it is clearly capable of doing, where precisely will he or anyone else who appeals directly to the merit of substantive norms draw the line? Why exactly will they draw it to prohibit one type of experience rather than another?

Relatedly, Bourdieu points out that aristocracies are "essentialist" (1979, 24). With this, his study of the cultivated bourgeoisie brings to mind Nietzsche's view of nobility: Being aristocratic or noble in essence, the cultivated bourgeoisie properly escapes the petty rules and regulations governing Gans's lower middle class. The problem, however, is how does Bourdieu or the cultivated bourgeoisie know which rules in particular are petty? How does he or they know when, if ever, rules unique to contemporary democracy are being violated? Or are all restrictions placed on the cultivated bourgeoisie petty by definition? Nietzsche certainly failed to offer the social sciences any political theory with which to draw such distinctions. Indeed, he has no theory of associations or collectivities, whether those worthy of nobles or unworthy. Moreover, he acknowledges that individual nobles can err in estimating the worth or essence of others when they travel to unfamiliar localities ([1887] 1969, Essay One, sections 2–4).

The issue is not whether those in public or private positions of authority are essentialist or whether they actually believe in what they are saying or in what they are doing (Maffesoli 1985, 19). Sincerity in politics, as in corporate management, is unimportant. What is important is how those who occupy positions of power actually behave. What, then, does Maffesoli mean when he refers in passing to the modern world's "soft totalitarianism" (ibid., 94)? What does he mean when he says that the worst totalitarianisms involve a liaison of police and doctors? For his part, Bourdieu talks about the "objective orchestration" of fields of cultural production and fields of cultural consumption (1979, 230). Yet, he also concedes that taste or distinction is endlessly negotiated and renegotiated precisely because "there is no sovereign taste" (ibid., 231). What sorts of concrete behavior is he prepared to acknowledge as cultivated, and what sorts of concrete behavior is Maffesoli prepared to acknowledge as orgiastic, irrespective of who in particular engages in it?

Whatever their answers might be, what is particularly damaging to any modern social order is breakdowns in basic fairness. This is the central message of American republicanism. Such breakdowns certainly occur when doctors and other professionals no longer exhibit fidelity to the procedural norms of their own professions' collegial formations or peer review committees—or, worse, when other members of these formations and committees do not exhibit fidelity to these norms in the first place. It is unimportant whether their behavioral fidelity to these norms is sincere or not. It is also unimportant whether their behavioral encroachments against these norms are prompted by commands from state officials or by more mundane material calculations of self-interest in the marketplace. It is unimportant, too, whether they are prompted toward encroachments by a concern for "hygiene," a concern to enforce some official morality. If professionals exhibit fidelity to the procedural norms institutionalized by collegial formations, it does not really matter at an institutional level whether and how they compromise on substantive issues. Correlatively, if they encroach against the integrity of collegial formations, it does not then matter if they become "principled" in other respects, refusing to compromise on substantive issues.

Some of the excesses of Maffesoli's substantive normative approach to everyday life come to light in his discussion of Mafia clans (1985, 61–64). He may be correct that the Mafia's three principles are distance from authority, self-sufficient aid or self-help, and aid to the needy. But he errs in saying that the Mafia exhibits "powerful systems of social integration" (ibid., 79). He is defining "integration" directly in terms of substantive norms. When it is defined in this way, it is impossible to distinguish between when an orderly situation is the product of successful social control and when it is the product of more voluntaristic affiliation. Similarly, he is too casual in discussing how the rule of law may be replaced by familial social order regulated in invisible and spontaneous ways (ibid., 63). And he is too casual in moving from a discussion of networking in the

Mafia to one of networking in the professions. The same thing happens when he discusses how those who occupy powerful positions secure sexual favors from subordinates (ibid., 152).[27]

Indeed, Maffesoli becomes particularly irresponsible when he says that the "quality of an association is in direct relation to its capacity to know how to channel disorder and violence" and that "the management of death and contradiction is one of the essential qualities of life in expansion" (ibid., 80). Again, it matters a great deal whether the associations managing these matters are organized in the collegial form or whether they are organized in the bureaucratic form. Maffesoli is insightful when noting that excess affirms existence. Yet, he fails to draw important distinctions when he says that playing with institutions and established rules is perhaps dangerous in terms of a career plan, but that this gives daily life "a knock that explodes the overrigidity of the normative imposition" (ibid., 80).

Relatedly, Maffesoli defends the proposition that orgiasm inscribes itself on a background of violence, and he may be right (ibid., 97–98). But social scientists can draw the following distinction: They can distinguish forms of popular cruelty carried on by formally equal adults and then concede that in fluid situations of everyday life people do indeed negotiate these activities among themselves. They can also distinguish, however, the cruelty that professionals and others who occupy positions of power within structured situations can carry on against those who find themselves often unawares within dependent positions.[28] A physician having a drink at a bar who decides to be cruel to other patrons is one thing. A physician in the examining room who decides to be cruel to a patient is another. Both types of behavior may well be manifestations of the orgiastic. But they carry very different institutional implications. The pervasiveness of the first type of cruelty has little to do with whether a social order is benign or malevolent. But the pervasiveness of the second type has a great deal to do with it. American feminists (such as Catherine MacKinnon) collapse both types of cruelty as they condemn everything; Maffesoli collapses both types as he praises everything. The problem is the collapse of this analytical distinction, not the condemnation or the praise (which are both premature).

Bourdieu points out that the working class expects every image to perform a function. Thus, its judgments about art refer to norms of morality or agreeableness.[29] By contrast, the bourgeoisie's "pure gaze" is detached, reflecting the extent to which its life escapes necessity (1979, 5, 30–32).[30] The irony of Bourdieu's description of the cultivated bourgeoisie, however, is that these individuals prefer form to substance until they get to the workings of institutions. Here they prefer substantive outcomes that suit their own interests. They do not exhibit fidelity to institutional forms as non-negotiable normative restraints on arbitrary exercises of collective power. Because Bourdieu approaches the cultivated bourgeoisie by adopting their substantive normative perspective as his own, he fails to address that in these structured situations these individuals are hardly employing a pure gaze.[31] They are rather engaging nakedly in self-interested behavior. This is the best illustration of the bourgeoisie's discrete nihilism, and it also illustrates when Bourdieu exceeds the scope of application of his own conceptual apparatus.

The central theoretical issue in all of this is whether the integrity of the professions and other intermediary associations is irreducibly central to the social infrastructure underlying modern democracy itself.[32] If it is, then the cultivated bourgeoisie's subordination of these units' integrity to their own self-interest is nihilistic. If it is not, then the integrity of the professions is as negotiable across social classes as is the meaning of art and the taste of cuisine. Bourdieu is already assuming the latter when he says:

> [The working class's unwillingness to negotiate everything] is clearly seen when, by an accident of social genetics, into the well-policed world of intellectual games there comes one of those people (one thinks of Rousseau or Chernyshevsky) who bring inappropriate stakes and interests into the game of culture, who get so involved in the game that they abandon the margin of neutralizing distance that the illusion (belief in the game) demands; who treat intellectual struggles . . . as a simple question of right and wrong, life and death. (ibid., 54)

This judgment is as legitimate as any other as a strictly subjective opinion on Bourdieu's part. But one searches Bourdieu's work in vain either for an argument or for citations to an argument that can support his affiliation with the players' point of view. Is it not a more value-neutral stance for a social scientist to refuse to affiliate himself or herself with any class's substantive vision of what is negotiable and what is not negotiable? Also, Bourdieu says that people of refinement know bad taste instinctively, whereas for those who do not, rules are needed. Again, this, too, is fine when discussing cuisine, or art, or home furnishings. But it is another matter when one is endeavoring value-neutrally to monitor how professions and other intermediary associations are organized. Indeed, when Bourdieu discusses the expansion of consultancy and public relations positions that revolve around the marketing of good manners or physical charm, he fails to distinguish professions analytically from semiprofessions. The semiprofessions are indeed more open to manipulation by sons and daughters of the bourgeoisie. But this is precisely because these occupations do not really involve fiduciary relationships with clients; rather, their relationships with clients may legitimately be subordinated to negotiations of meaning and power plays of all kinds (ibid., 153).

The values that the bourgeoisie (or other social classes) bring to the arts, to the theater, and to cuisine are matters of indifference to the social sciences. They are simply to be chronicled value-neutrally, along with how social classes differ in their interpretations of plays and movies and how they variously toss insults at each other, defer to each other, or exhibit indifference to each other. What matters, however, is when social scientists attribute any set of substantive norms to the professions and other intermediary associations. This matters because whether intermediary associations can possibly support a relatively benign social order rests on whether they institutionalize everyone's behavioral fidelity to certain procedural norms. Here is where neither the bourgeoisie nor the lower middle class or working class may simply bring their substantive norms unmediated. Here also is where social scientists may monitor encroachments from any quarter value-neutrally. Compare this proposal to Bourdieu's statement that the precondition for the success of all petit bourgeois associations and social movements is strictly "disinterested," "clean" activity, free of all political compromises (ibid., 457). This may well be a legitimate criticism of the petit bourgeois, but Bourdieu does not have the concepts at his disposal to move it beyond prejudice.

Bourdieu exceeds the scope of application of his own concepts when he uses not only occupations and semiprofessions but also professions proper to illustrate his point that all social positions "are also strategic emplacements, fortresses to be defended and captured in a field of struggles" (ibid., 244–45). Put differently, Bourdieu turns too quickly to the substance of professions, approaching it from the cultivated bourgeoisie's point of view.[33] When the cultivated bourgeoisie is free to experiment on its own, it in essence labels everyone else. It labels others not simply as unrefined but also as—somehow—challenging the "morality" of the larger social order by their very presence. This labeling is not high culture. It is rather low-level social control. It is institutionalized rancor or ressentiment.[34]

The bourgeoisie's institutionalized ressentiment accomplishes two things simultaneously: First, it permits individual bourgeois to believe subjectively that they are personally above ressentiment and mean-spiritedness. Second, it arbitrarily narrows the arena of cultural competition in which the bourgeoisie endeavors to define taste or cultivation. This can be seen both at an interpersonal level and at an institutional level.

At an interpersonal level, Bourdieu's work indirectly exposes a practicable alternative to leftist calls for greater egalitarianism, one quite consistent with Nietzsche's will to power, Freud's will to happiness, and then Maffesoli's will to life: Individual members of the lower middle class or working class may mimic the bourgeoisie's demeanor of indifference. These individuals' overcoming of what Bourdieu calls "petit bourgeois timidity," and their development of an indifference to the objectifying gaze of others, can yield major interpersonal strengths. Part of the overcoming of timidity, of course, is to refuse to accept the bourgeoisie's labeling of new competitors as interlopers. There are hundreds of examples of this occurring in practice today, not only across the music industry and film industry but also across Wall Street and major financial houses.[35]

At an institutional level, the bourgeoisie's highly censored language, its restraint and false simplicity (ibid., 178), is inappropriate within those structured situations in which professionals operate.[36] In these structured situations, where positional power can be abused, the bourgeoisie's highly censored language is both self-aggrandizing and discretely nihilistic. It calls to mind not so much aristocratic privileges as the "mercantile monopolies" against which the American founders and framers rebelled in the late eighteenth century. Thus, irrespective of Bourdieu's collapse of analytical distinctions, his study of the cultivated bourgeoisie nonetheless reveals the latter's discrete nihilism. He notes, for instance, that "one forgets that the dominant class is defined precisely by the fact that it has a particular interest in affairs 'of general interest' because the particular interests of its members are particularly bound up with those affairs" (ibid., 443). I would put this point differently: For the very reason that Bourdieu articulates, the bourgeoisie's indifference to the integrity of certain forms and procedural norms, its unmediated pursuit of its own substantive interests, might very well pose a greater obstacle to "community" than others' more direct encroachments.

## Notes

1. Talcott Parsons (1957), for instance, defined community as "that aspect of the structure of social systems which is referable to the territorial location of persons . . . and their activities."

2. Selznick acknowledges that "locality is a congenial condition and probable correlate" of community, but then he insists that this is not an essential feature. Yet, it is difficult to visualize what the alternatives to locality look like, and his own examples are more troubling than helpful. Selznick says that special-purpose institutions may become communities "when purpose is not very rigidly or narrowly conceived, when leeway is allowed for controversy over ends and means, and when participation is an important part of the individual's life within the organization" (1992, 359). His examples, however, are military and police organizations, as opposed to "marginal business firms" in which ongoing employment is uncertain.

3. These references also seem anachronistic in light of Freudian approaches to the self. For a Freudian, Selznick's core participation is better labeled "infantile engagement," whereas Selznick's segmental participation is the "mature engagement" one finds among adults. Freud emphasized that mature individuals are understandably reluctant to invest their psychic energy in any one activity, and thereby to expose themselves to disappointments and to losses of love by others.

4. Michele Lamont's qualitative empirical study spans Bourdieu's cultivated bourgeoisie, Bellah's established middle class, and Gans's lower middle class (1992, 14).

5. A lifestyle enclave, according to Bellah, is a sectoral organization that individuals freely choose more or less independently of their ethnic and religious affiliations (Bellah et al. 1985, 72–73). Thus, a continuing marriage in America today may itself be a lifestyle enclave (ibid., 74).

6. And the American family, of course, is an institution experiencing considerable flux today. See Popenoe's contribution to this volume (chapter 8).

7. Compare Bellah's distinction to Selznick's distinction between core participation within communities and segmental participation within less significant bodies (Selznick 1992, 184).

8. I show below that Bourdieu and Maffesoli explore essentially this same level, that of self-integration, and they also largely ignore the first level, that of social integration.

The exception in Bellah's case is when he refers to the relationship between community and democracy, and the exception in Bourdieu's and Maffesoli's cases is when each refers, respectively, to the concepts habitus and neotribalism. Much like the way Bellah defines community, they define habitus and neotribalism directly in terms of substantive norms.

9. Compare this to Maffesoli's more positive comments on "Mafia style" affiliations, which are discussed below.

10. Recall Freud's discussion of the stranger ([1930] 1961, 67): "Not merely is this stranger in general unworthy of my love; I must honestly confess that he has more claim to my hostility and even my hatred. He seems not to have the least trace of love for me and shows me not the slightest consideration. If it will do him any good he has no hesitation in injuring me, nor does he ask himself whether the amount of advantage he gains bears any proportion to the extent of the harm he does me. Indeed, he need not even obtain an advantage; if he can satisfy any sort of desire by it, he thinks nothing of jeering me, insulting me, slandering me and showing his superior power; and the more secure he feels and the more helpless I am, the more certainly I can expect him to behave like this to me."

11. When British sociologist Raymond Williams calls this mobile privatization (as cited by Gans), he comes close to Maffesoli's praise for fluttering or serial relationships.

12. Teresa Sullivan, Elizabeth Warren, and Jay Lawrence Westbrook (1989) show that it is Gans's people who most typically file for personal bankruptcy.

13. Similarly, Maffesoli does not see individuals' fluttering from group to group as narcissistic but rather as the "fluidity of neotribalism." Still, Gans sees the major problem facing the American lower middle class as loneliness, not tribal attachments (Gans 1988, 108).

14. By contrast, Judaism and Christianity initiated the notion of future progress (albeit in an afterlife) coupled with an overriding dedication to God (Lasch 1991, 45–46, 50–51). It was this notion that became secularized in the commitment to steady material improvement for perpetuity.

15. Whether or not the American founders and framers were familiar with Adam Smith's writings is a matter of controversy among historians. On the one hand, Bourgin points out ([1945] 1989, 24) that although *The Wealth of Nations* first appeared in 1776, it was not published in America until 1789. He is convinced that Smith's ideas were neither well known nor influential. On the other hand, Gary McDowell finds (1982, 52) that "the exact influence of the Scottish moralists on American thought is impossible to measure, but we do know that, during the American Founding, such Scottish authors as Adam Smith and Adam Ferguson were widely read and discussed and frequently invoked by the proponents of the 'new science of politics.' In particular, James Wilson was responsible for introducing many Scottish Enlightenment theories into American political thinking." Wilson, a signer of the Declaration of Independence, was from Pennsylvania and, McDowell notes, second only to James Madison in his theoretical contributions to the Constitution. He later served as a justice on the U.S. Supreme Court (ibid., 52–53; also McCoy 1980, 13–47). Herbert Hovenkamp (1991, 21–23) argues that Jeffersonians were influenced by Smith's writings, but he is not as clear about Jefferson himself.

16. Even early American liberals, who were otherwise critical of republicans' zeal in condemning private commerce, accepted republicans' view of the social infrastructure supporting citizen vigilance and limited government (Lasch 1991, 195–202). Legal scholars and historians continue to debate the relationship between liberalism and republicanism, for example, Bourgin ([1945] 1989), *Yale Law Journal* (1988), and Sunstein (1990, ch. 1). The same is true about the relationship between democracy and republicanism (e.g., McDowell 1988, 34). Historian Charles Sellers notes, for instance, that early Americans

preferred the term "republican" to the term "democrat" (1991, 31–32).

17. Etzioni's *Capital Corruption* (1984) can claim a direct lineage to this concern of the framers.

18. "Of course I do not believe in literal 'laissez-faire'; I know of no reputable economist who ever did. Certainly neither Smith and Ricardo nor Cobden and Bright would have restricted the state entirely to the negative functions of policing individual liberty and defense against outside attack. No one denies that 'man is a social animal'; and in fact society makes men far more than men make society, meaning by deliberate thinking and action" (Knight [1921] 1948, lii).

19. The corporation's production function is "the physical relationship between [its] output and various inputs, [and it] tells us how much output we can hope to get if we have so much labor, so much capital, so much land, etc." (Samuelson 1948, 521).

20. Lasch notes that Albion Small saw Smith, not Spencer, as the founder of modern sociology (1991, 68–69).

21. Lasch says that in order to renew political life, we must abandon the concept of community and strike out in a new direction (1991, 164). We must question the fatalism that informs both the idea of progress and the lingering fear of disaster (ibid., 170). Lasch is instructed by the works of MacIntyre, Sandel, and Bellah, but he is concerned that they fail to say much about republican virtue (ibid., 172). Selznick (1992) agrees on this point.

22. See my other contribution to this volume (chapter 7) for a discussion of the integration/control distinction.

23. If Maffesoli restricted these references to the tensional equilibrium of the self, without referring in any way to the local order or the larger social order (which he clearly does, e.g., 1985, 11), then matters would be different. Of course, he would also end up with a psychological theory, not a sociological theory.

24. Actually, seen in its most benign light, this is close to the virtue of magnanimity in Aristotle's *Ethics*.

25. Maffesoli traces the term "habitus" to Aquinas (1985, xiii).

26. Maffesoli says in passing that "one has never spoken so much of 'communication' as in this organization of solitude," whose central actor is the individual (1985, 82).

27. Maffesoli is startled by the fact that from 1837 to 1846 32 percent of all births in France were illegitimate. The rate today among African Americans is much higher, exceeding 50 percent, and that for all Americans is approaching 30 percent. Does Maffesoli see substantive normative limits to orgiasm?

28. The English tradition of fiduciary law originated in the fourteenth century precisely in an effort to protect individuals who could not escape positions of dependence. See DeMott's contribution to this volume (chapter 5).

29. Unlike Maffesoli, Bourdieu uses the terms "morality" and "ethics" interchangeably.

30. Lamont (1992) exposes several points at which the outlook of the American upper middle class is closer to that of the French working class than to the French upper middle class.

31. Similarly, Bourdieu sees indifference as central to the everyday life of the bourgeoisie, and yet he later says that indifference in polling questions is a reflection of political impotence (1979, 406). The propensity to speak politically (even in a poll), he argues, is proportionate to the sense of having the right to speak (1979, 411).

32. I present the theoretical rationale for this in *Theory of Societal Constitutionalism* (1992). Now, however, I present the position as a conditional question rather than as a declarative statement that readers would properly expect to be defended at length.

33. What does not need to be brought into Bourdieu's study, to be sure, is the upwardly mobile petit bourgeois's across-the-board asceticism, rigor, and legalism (Bourdieu 1979, 331).

34. The bourgeoisie's capacity to live on the surface is effective in interpersonal relations, for reasons that Nietzsche offered so compellingly in the 1880s and Freud in the 1920s. And yet this capacity, in itself, is hardly equivalent to what Nietzsche called nobility or what Freud thought of as maturity. Nietzsche's strongest criticisms, of course, were directed at those who harbor rancor and ressentiment, this being part of what he called the slave revolt in morality ([1887] 1961, Essay One, section 10).

35. Maffesoli provides a more appealing picture of the working class and its everyday possibilities even in the context of the necessities that constrain it. He does not see them "encountering legitimate culture as a principle of order" (Bourdieu 1979, 387) that they cannot either overcome or ignore. He does not see their only principle as that of conformity (ibid., 380–81). He sees them as the other, always potentially challenging. This approach is important and refreshing, particularly in the post–Cold War era.

36. Bellah points out that Americans today treat their concerns about moral questions as matters of private anxiety. They lack a shared language with which to discuss their central aspirations and fears. Bellah is interested in how Americans today might preserve or create a morally coherent life, as opposed to continuing the instrumental and expressive individualism that isolates Americans from each other. Lasch has problems of language of his own: He adopts the viewpoint of parents raising children as he criticizes contemporary American society (1991, 33). He fails to address the problem that a modern society in which children are safe to walk the streets at night alone may well be a society that is unsafe for adults.

## References

Banfield, Edward C. 1958. *The Moral Basis of a Backward Society*. New York: Free Press.

Bellah, Robert N.; Madsen, Richard; Sullivan, William M.; Swidler, Ann; and Tipton, Steven M. (1985) 1986. *Habits of the Heart: Individualism and Commitment in American Life*. New York: Harper and Row.

Bourdieu, Pierre. (1979) 1984. *Distinction: A Social Critique of the Judgment of Taste*. Cambridge, MA: Harvard University Press.

Bourgin, Frank. 1945/1989. *The Great Challenge: The Myth of Laissez-Faire in the Early Republic*. New York: George Brazilier.

Etzioni, Amitai. 1984. *Capital Corruption: The New Attack on American Democracy*. New York: Harcourt Brace Jovanovich.

———. 1991. *A Responsive Society: Collected Essays on Guiding Deliberate Social Change*. San Francisco: Jossey-Bass.

———. 1993. *The Spirit of Community: The Reinvention of American Society*. New York: Touchstone.

Freud, Sigmund. (1930) 1961. *Civilization and Its Discontents*. New York: W.W. Norton.

Fuller, Lon L. (1964/1969) 1975. *The Morality of Law*. Rev. ed. New Haven, CT: Yale University Press.

Gans, Herbert J. 1988. *Middle American Individualism: The Future of Liberal Democracy*. New York: Free Press.

Hovenkamp, Herbert. 1991. *Enterprise and American Law, 1836–1837*. Cambridge, MA: Harvard University Press.

Knight, Frank. (1921) 1948. *Risk, Uncertainty and Profit*. Boston: Houghton Mifflin.

Lamont, Michele. 1992. *Money, Morals, and Manners: The Culture of the French and American Upper Middle Class*. Chicago: University of Chicago Press.

Lasch, Christopher. 1991. *The True and Only Heaven: Progress and Its Critics*. New York: W.W. Norton.

Maffesoli, Michel. (1985) 1993. *The Shadow of Dionysius: A Contribution to the Sociology of the Orgy*. Albany: State University of New York Press.

Mark, Gregory A. 1987. "The Personification of the Business Corporation in American Law." *University of Chicago Law Review* 54: 1441–83.

McCoy, Drew R. 1980. *The Elusive Republic: Political Economy in Jeffersonian America*. Chapel Hill: University of North Carolina Press.

McDowell, Gary L. 1982. *Equity and the Constitution: The Supreme Court, Equitable Relief, and Public Policy*. Chicago: University of Chicago Press.

———. 1988. *Curbing the Courts: The Constitution and the Limits of Judicial Power*. Baton Rouge: Louisiana State University Press.

Nietzsche, Friedrich. (1887) 1969. *On the Genealogy of Morals*. New York: Vintage.

Parsons, Talcott. 1957. "The Principal Structures of Community." In *Structure and Process in Modern Societies*, 250–79. New York: Free Press, 1960.

Reich, Robert B. (1991) 1992. *The Work of Nations: Preparing Ourselves for 21st Century Capitalism*. New York: Vintage.

Samuelson, Paul A. 1948. *Economics: An Introductory Analysis*. New York: McGraw-Hill.

Sandel, Michael. 1982. *Liberalism and the Limits of Justice*. Cambridge: Cambridge University Press.

Sciulli, David. 1992. *Theory of Societal Constitutionalism: Foundations of a Non-Marxist Critical Theory*. Cambridge: Cambridge University Press.

———. Under review. *The End of Corporate Governance: A Study in Societal Constitutionalism*.

Sellers, Charles. 1991. *The Market Revolution: Jacksonian America, 1815–1846*. New York: Oxford University Press.

Selznick, Philip. 1992. *The Moral Commonwealth: Social Theory and the Promise of Community*. Berkeley: University of California Press.

Sullivan, Teresa A.; Warren, Elizabeth; and Westbrook, Jay Lawrence. 1989. *As We Forgive Our Debtors: Bankruptcy and Consumer Credit in America*. New York: Oxford University Press.

Sunstein, Cass R. 1990. *After the Rights Revolution: Reconceiving the Regulatory State*. Cambridge, MA: Harvard University Press.

Symposium. 1988. "The Republican Civic Tradition." *Yale Law Journal* 97.

# 13

# The Human Rights Challenge to Communitarianism: Formal Organizations and Race and Ethnicity

*Gideon Sjoberg*

The objectives of this chapter are twofold. First, I will outline the central tenets of communitarian thought in sociology (and related disciplines), and I will look at whom the communitarians are debating and why. In articulating the communitarian agenda I consider some of their contributions to social and moral theory and to our empirical understanding of contemporary American society. Second, I will evaluate critically the communitarian effort from two interrelated vantage points—one, the failure of communitarians to address the issues of human rights and, the other, the neglect of major empirical issues confronting members of U.S. society and humankind at large. This second objective requires that we introduce the human rights (in contrast to the ethicist) perspective and that we outline some of the major trends in the global setting that moral theory must come to address.

### The Communitarian Agenda

Without doubt, Amitai Etzioni has been a major figure in shaping the communitarian agenda in the United States. He took the lead in establishing the journal

This is a much revised version of a plenary address at the annual meeting of the Southwestern Sociological Association, San Antonio, TX, March 28–April 2, 1994. I have profited from the comments of Boyd Littrell, Andrée F. Sjoberg, Elizabeth Gill, Kelly Himmel, Kirsten Dellinger, Tim Dunn, Sandy Lemens, and Roger Nett. I am especially indebted to Leonard Cain for his helpfulness. David Sciulli's constructive editorial criticisms also are deeply appreciated.

*The Responsive Community*; he initiated work on "The Responsive Communitarian Platform"; and he has written a widely discussed book, *The Spirit of Community* (Etzioni 1993; compare Etzioni 1991, esp. 127–52).

I discuss Etzioni's salient contributions, along with those of such other sociologists as Robert Bellah, Philip Selznick, and Alan Wolfe, and take into account, at least implicitly, social and moral theorists such as Mary Ann Glendon, William Galston, Alasdair MacIntyre, Jean Bethke Elshtain, Charles Taylor, Michael Sandel, and Michael Walzer. Although these scholars have been associated in one way or another with communitarianism, they differ among themselves, even as one perceives commonalities that set them apart from members of other contemporary schools of thought.

Several features of communitarian theorizing in sociology are worthy of attention. These scholars reassert the importance of the moral dimension in sociological analysis. In so doing, they confront the dominant worldviews of our time—liberalism and utilitarianism. They call for greater responsibility by members of society, as well as adherence to a "common good."

By examining the moral foundations of human activities, sociologists in the communitarian mold stand apart from the logical empiricists, or proponents of the natural science model, who would eliminate all moral issues from sociological investigation. So, too, they stand apart from Weber, Parsons, and others, who call on sociologists to sustain "value neutrality." The communitarians are not averse to speaking of a "moral sociology" or of sociology as a "moral science."

The communitarians call to mind a long-standing cleavage in sociology. In recent decades the dominant perspective of American sociologists—as represented by proponents of value neutrality—has obscured the countertradition that goes back as far as Durkheim. For all of Durkheim's insistence on the rigorous use of the scientific method, he had an abiding interest in the moral dimension of social life (Jones 1994). More recently, however, sociologists such as Pitirim A. Sorokin (Sorokin and Lunden 1959) and C. Wright Mills (1959) advanced, in rather unabashed ways, their own particular moral visions.

The countertradition seems to be reasserting itself in sociology. There are sociologists who have been influenced by Jürgen Habermas (1990) and his moral language. Moreover, recent analyses of rational choice theory (e.g., Smelser 1992; Favell 1993) suggest that the moral foundations of sociology are becoming more open to public scrutiny. Smelser (1992) goes so far as to speak of the "theological foundations" of rational choice theory.

Sociologists can and do contribute to empirical knowledge; they also can and do contribute to moral knowledge. One of the strengths of the discipline lies, as the work of Bellah et al. (1985) attests, in the incorporation of moral analysis into the investigation of empirical issues. The communitarians have reminded us that this is a legitimate sociological endeavor.

In coming to terms with the communitarians, we must recognize that they

have targeted both liberals and utilitarians.[1] The communitarians take exception
to some of the central tenets of contemporary liberalism, particularly as expressed in Rawls's *Theory of Justice* (1971). That Rawls should be singled out is
understandable. After all, he reintroduced morals into contemporary American
philosophy and social theory, and he, according to some scholars, provided a
moral underpinning for the modern welfare state.

Sociologists such as Bellah and his associates zero in on utilitarians, not
Rawlsian liberals. *Habits of the Heart* (Bellah et al. 1985), whatever its failings,
provided a useful counterweight to exchange or rational choice theory at the time
when the latter had attained such a dominant position in sociology. In a somewhat similar vein, Selznick (1993) conceives of his work, *The Moral Commonwealth*, as a corrective to the neoconservative trend in the social sciences.

These critiques of liberalism and utilitarianism, and the resultant counterat-
tacks by natural choice theorists and others, are, at their base, a debate about the
foundations of contemporary democracy. The champions of each perspective
have their own moral vision of a democratic order.

Specifically, the communitarians are opposed to contemporary individualism,
whether of a utilitarian or a liberal variety. By inference, they stand in sharp
opposition to postmodernism. For communitarians duty and responsibility loom
especially important. Etzioni (1993), using Glendon (1991) as a point of departure, is highly critical of "rights talk," which is typically associated with contemporary liberalism. There is, he insists, far too much concern with rights and not
enough with responsibility for one's fellow human beings, especially members
of the family and the larger community.

The family, not the individual, serves for Etzioni and Bellah, for instance, as
the basic building block for the development and maintenance of a good society.
It is noteworthy that the study of the family has been influenced by communitarian thought. The symposium anchored by Popenoe's (1993) essay in the *Journal
of Marriage and the Family* is indicative of this trend. Popenoe expresses an
abiding concern with the decline of parental responsibilities for children. Popenoe, in point of fact, is one of the signatories of "The Responsive Communitarian Platform" (1991/92), and a considerable part of his analysis is predicated on
the presuppositions of communitarian thought regarding the nature of family life.
That his position has evoked sharp criticism from one wing of feminism is
documented by Judith Stacey's (1993) objections to Popenoe's essay.

The communitarians do not stop with a call for familial responsibility. They
also call for individual responsibility to the larger collectivity—the "common
good" or the "good society." Etzioni (1993), in analyzing the common good,
relies on concepts reminiscent of Talcott Parsons (1960, 172 ff.). Etzioni speaks
of the need for a set of "core values." These seem to be rather specific to
American society (or nation-state), which he then holds up as a model for the
world. Communitarians such as Bellah, Wolfe, and Selznick are deeply committed to the maintenance of a "civil society" in which moral discourse finds legiti-

mate expression. Etzioni's (1993) attack against "political corruption" can be interpreted as an effort to shore up a viable civil society.

Although I have fundamental disagreements with the communitarians, I find common ground with them on a number of matters. They are, as noted above, to be commended for revitalizing moral discourse in American sociology. I also share the communitarians' misgivings with contemporary individualism. Many forms of present-day individualism deny the social nature of human nature. Given my own use of a modified Meadian framework, I perceive even stark forms of individualism as requiring social support for their expression. In challenging the concept of the "autonomous individual," the communitarians are able to reintroduce the issues of altruism and trust into sociological discourse. So, too, their focus on the civil society as a basis for a democratic order cannot be dismissed lightly.[2] Even more specific contributions emerge from their writings. The notion of a "community of memory," used by some communitarians (Bellah et al. 1985; Bell 1993), has wide-ranging theoretical and empirical ramifications for those who study the community. How historical memories are constituted and sustained bears directly on the nature of how members of a community define themselves.[3] Still, my objective is not to elaborate on these matters but to evaluate critically the communitarian framework and, in the process, to suggest an alternative orientation toward morals. To achieve this goal, I will first clarify basic conceptual issues.

### Human Rights and Ethics: A Conceptual Clarification

Up to now I have employed the concept of "morals" to encompass both the ethicist and the human rights traditions. It is time to disentangle these two perspectives, at least to some degree. In ideal-typical terms, the ethicist framework begins with duties, and one attains rights by carrying out duties and responsibilities to the "community." In contrast, in the human rights tradition a person has "basic rights," and duties or responsibilities shore these up. Clearly, there are a variety of ethical traditions in sociology. We have already mentioned the communitarian, utilitarian, and liberal perspectives. However, sociologists (and other social scientists) introduce other ethical orientations, often in a confounding manner, into their theory and research. They may, for instance, adhere to some form of ethical relativism or, particularly, some form of "system commitment."

Ethical relativism has been widely debated, but the notion of system commitment as a moral framework is seldom, if ever, analyzed by social or moral theorists. Nonetheless, ideas such as the "national interest" or "loyalty to the nation-state" have been widely acknowledged by social scientists. So, too, persons may be committed to such subsystems as the army or to particular corporate entities. From a sociological vantage point, the wide-ranging ramifications of system commitment must be incorporated into moral theorizing.

As for utilitarianism, it has, in recent decades, been championed by a number of sociological theorists and, implicitly, by numerous researchers. It finds expression in exchange or rational choice theory and, in a more practical sense, in cost/benefit analysis—as applied even to the technical soundness of researchers' endeavors in academic settings. Institutional review boards, after all, are often called upon to make judgments in accordance with some form of utilitarianism.

Utilitarians typically espouse individual self-interest or the maximization of utilities, and one adds these up to determine the greatest good for the greatest number. However, utilitarians, from the days of Adam Smith and Jeremy Bentham, have also adhered to a form of system commitment. After all, the state, which sustains law and order, provides the umbrella under which individual preferences are pursued. Even the staunchest advocates of the market system recognize the need for an army and a criminal justice system.

The moral foundations of utilitarianism are more readily grasped than those of contemporary liberalism, particularly the "welfare liberalism" that has emerged in the United States in past decades. One reason for this situation is the diverse interpretations of contemporary liberalism. Another is that surprisingly few scholars have examined both the theory and the practice of modern-day liberalism. Insofar as sociology is concerned, Gouldner (1970) advanced our understanding of the moral premises of Parsons's version of welfare liberalism. But my analysis takes me in a different direction.

I begin by distinguishing, as did the political theorist C.B. Macpherson (1973), between two main strands of individualism embedded in liberalism. First, present-day liberals (including Parsons), for all their criticism of utilitarianism, have accepted the need for utility maximization in the economic sphere. Second, liberals have also supported the "realization of human potentiality" that Macpherson emphasized. This form of individualism can, in turn, be divided into two branches. One involves the maximization of human potential along utilitarian lines. This is what Bellah et al. (1985) call "expressive individualism." A second involves a conception of "basic liberties" (such as "free speech"). Still, at their base, these two types of individualism presuppose the existence of "autonomous individuals."

But there is more to liberalism than the conception of individualism. Liberals, like utilitarians, are also committed to the nation-state, albeit in a different way. On the one hand, they call upon the state to sustain neutrality regarding the moral good, but, on the other hand, the state also becomes a legitimate vehicle for attaining social justice in the economic realm (or even in other spheres).

At this point it should be apparent that communitarians stand in opposition to the individualism of both utilitarians and liberals. They are committed to a common good that emerges from participation in communal life. We now insert the issue of rights into the debate among communitarians, liberals, and utilitarians. Not surprisingly, each of these ethical traditions has a different conception of rights. The utilitarians have been highly critical of the concept of "rights," especially that which emerged from the French Revolution (compare Waldron 1987). In contrast, twentieth-century liberals have been supportive of advancing "social rights" or "civil rights" within a nation-state framework. In turn, the communitarians, while not agreeing with the utilitarians, have been sharply critical of liberals for overemphasizing rights and failing to emphasize duties and responsibilities to the family and the larger community.

Perhaps the most articulate representative of the rights tradition within modern-day liberalism has been the legal theorist Ronald Dworkin (1977). While drawing on constructive features of his work, I nonetheless distance myself from many of his formulations. Dworkin theorizes about rights in highly individualistic terms, and he focuses too narrowly on "legal decision making." Moreover, his conceptualization of rights is narrowly circumscribed by the Anglo-Saxon, especially American, sociocultural heritage. The human rights framework differs markedly from Dworkin's social (or civil) rights orientation. Consequently, I am intent on addressing human rights in a global, not just societal, framework. A conception of human rights is more general, and more fundamental, than a conception of social or civil rights.

My theoretical perspective runs counter, in a number of respects, to that voiced by communitarians, liberals, and utilitarians. Yet, even Bellah and his associates, I submit, acknowledge the issue with which I am grappling. In *The Good Society* (1991, 279–83), they introduce the concept of "higher law." What can this higher law be other than an appeal to a form of natural rights or, in more contemporary terms, a human rights framework? Clearly, such a standard transcends the societal or nation-state setting.

### A Sketch of a Sociology of Human Rights

The human rights framework emerged in the aftermath of World War II, notably in the steps taken after the war to construct a global moral order.[4] I am far from saying that universal human rights principles are firmly in place. Still, the steps toward their construction, however flawed, cannot be brushed aside. We are not talking about rights that are system-specific, but rights that offer at least a minimal set of universal standards for human conduct.

The Nuremberg trials and the United Nations Universal Declaration of Human Rights are landmarks in thinking about human rights. The Nuremberg trials have been roundly criticized in a number of quarters. The victors imposed justice on the vanquished after the fact. Although reservations about these trials should be carefully weighed, we cannot overlook the fact that the concept "crimes against humanity" was, in a real sense, invented at Nuremberg. Since then this principle has been invoked by some elements of the world community to judge the actions of a variety of nation-states in the treatment of its members (or outsiders). In addition to the notion of "crimes against humanity," the trials of the Nazi doctors led to the formulation of the Nuremberg Code regarding experimentation on human beings (Annas and Grodin 1992). This code has affected the manner in which some social research is conducted.

The United Nations Universal Declaration of Human Rights was also a product of the Holocaust. This declaration, which some scholars suggest has antecedents in the natural law doctrine, was a compromise between members of the Western powers and members of the then Eastern (or Communist) bloc. Expressing concern for universal individual rights, on the one hand, and various collective rights, on the other, it has spawned the International Covenant of Economic, Social and Cultural Rights as well as the International Covenant on Civil and Political Rights. It also led to the construction of the UN Commission on Human Rights and the European Court on Human Rights. The Helsinki Process, which culminated in the Helsinki Final Act (HFA) (1975), is of special relevance. "The Solidarity movement in Poland, the Charter 77 in Czechoslovakia, and the Helsinki Watch committees in the Soviet Union all trace their genesis to the HFA" (Buergenthal 1992, 256).

More generally, political leaders, scholars, and various citizen groups have appealed to the Nuremberg trials and the Universal Declaration when calling attention to the mass killings by the state apparatus in far-flung corners of the globe. The actions of the Khmer Rouge in Cambodia came to be regarded rather widely as a case of politicide or, some say, genocide (Kiernan 1993). Although not one-sided, the Serbian efforts at "ethnic cleansing," particularly with respect to the Bosnian Muslims, will likely haunt Europe and other nations for years to come. So, too, the repression in East Timor by Indonesia and the repression in Argentina and Chile during the 1970s and early 1980s received considerable attention in the world press. It is informative that when military leaders in Argentina and Chile stepped down, they were sensitive to the possibility of Nuremberg-like charges against them. In the case of Argentina, a trial was held, and key generals were convicted—even if later set free (Andersen 1993). In short, Nuremberg has become a potential precedent for sanctions against the instigators of mass killings. Beyond this, when Nelson Mandela visited the United States he spoke of both civil and human rights in appealing for international support to dismantle racial repression in South Africa.

Although no consensus on universal human rights is in place, we are not discussing mere idealized abstractions. Genocide, politicide and racial repression are being judged by moral standards that are not system-specific.[5] The morality of human rights challenges rather frontally the premise of nation-state sovereignty—the principle that a nation-state can control and treat its citizens as it sees fit (a form of relativism that is implicit in the writings of many sociologists).

In this context, 1994 marks a watershed of sorts in the history of the American Sociological Association (ASA), for a number of thematic or special sessions were organized around the issue of genocide and politicide. This is the first time that a president of the ASA, in this instance, William Gamson, has made these issues central to the agenda of the annual meetings. Coincidentally, human rights was the organizing theme of the meetings of the American Anthropological Association in 1994.

When confronting mass killings of citizens by elements of the state apparatus, sociologists perforce adopt, implicitly or explicitly, a moral standard in their research. On the one hand, they can (as would radical social constructionists) adhere to a form of relativism and assume that the power structure of each nation-state can manipulate its citizens as it sees fit. On the other hand, they can rely on some minimal standard of universal human rights when interpreting data on genocide and politicide.

Until now sociologists have largely left human rights theory and research to legal and political scholars. But how might sociologists proceed to come to terms with human rights? Here I set forth, in highly schematic terms, one course of action. It rests on the premise that any theory of human rights must be grounded in a theory of human nature (compare Donnelly 1993).

Most conceptions of human nature are grossly inadequate for any sound theory of human rights. For example, Kant's effort to found morality on the categorical imperative involves an essentially asocial conception of human beings. So, too, the biopsychological theory undergirding utilitarianism, be it of Bentham or of rational choice, provides us with no guidance. Just as Bentham scorned the idea of rights, so, too, contemporary utilitarians are, with rare exceptions, unsympathetic to a theory of human rights. Nor do I believe that one can anchor an adequate theory of human rights in the supposition that all humans share common emotions. Hatred, unfortunately, is widespread among human beings. In addition, Habermas, among others, defines the fundamental nature of human nature in terms of language, but such a conception is inadequate for a theory of human rights. For one thing, language per se cannot provide the basis for demonstrating how reasoned debate, which Habermas advocates, can transcend the social and cultural fissures within and among societies.

A highly modified version of the theoretical formulations of George Herbert Mead (or those of John Dewey to a lesser extent) offers the greatest possibility of anchoring human rights in what it means to be human. Mead, after all, recognized the social nature of the social self and the social mind (while Dewey stressed intelligence). Although sociologists have focused on the social self, it is the social mind that is most distinctively human (Mead 1934).[6]

The social mind is characterized by its reflectivity, which involves thinking about thinking. Language is a precondition for reflectivity, but reflectivity involves far more than language. It is only through reflectivity that humans are able to engage in the complex "social calculations" that make human life possible.[7] It is, after all, through the social mind that one comes to define oneself. The looking-glass self is possible only because of reflectivity, as persons engage in complex social calculations in the process of taking the roles of others and viewing themselves as others see them. Physical capabilities and language are necessary ingredients for reflectivity, but they cannot be equated with reflectivity.

Reflectivity exists, to some extent, in all social and cultural orders. Anthropologists and sociologists are often captivated by differences when they compare and contrast social orders, but they cannot forget that underlying the differences are human commonalities—and reflectivity is the most fundamental. The creation of new technologies and a wide range of organizational and cultural arrangements is predicated, at least in part, on the ability of humans to reflect on their own thoughts and actions. Furthermore, Strathern (1993) and Gellner (1985), among anthropologists, have observed that field-workers, despite their failings, have been able to take the role of "divergent Others," and thereby to describe social and cultural patterns in vastly different settings. By being able to understand others, in however fragile a manner, anthropologists and their respondents also overcome some of their own differences. They are able to accomplish this because of their shared capacity to reflect about social and cultural arrangements.

Reflectivity provides us with a universal grounding for human rights. It makes possible an emphasis on universalism while simultaneously recognizing, and ultimately respecting, a considerable range of social and cultural differences. For instance, Habermas (1990) rightly emphasizes universality with regard to the formulation of a moral order, but he has yet to grapple with the social world beyond a Western setting (compare Dews 1992). Human rights may have emerged in the West, but they push us outside the West. They impel us to come to terms with divergent Others, in theory and practice. Through the maintenance (and advancement) of human rights, human dignity becomes feasible. Several advantages accrue from thinking about human dignity in these terms.

First, if we take the social mind and reflectivity as a point of departure for the study of what it means to be human, we must recognize, both theoretically and empirically, that human beings exist and thrive only through interaction with others. Interdependence and social reciprocity are necessary ingredients for the creation and sustenance of reflective human agents. The views regarding autonomous individuals advanced by utilitarians, contemporary liberals, or postmodernists are untenable. These orientations fail to acknowledge that the concept of the "autonomous individual," which each takes as a given, emerges from interaction with others. The ability to think, to engage in reflective thought, occurs within some kind of sociocultural matrix.

Second, if one recognizes the centrality of interdependence and reciprocity in the formation of the social mind, we can, in Meadian terms, comprehend how the collectivity (particularly contemporary organizations) shapes the nature of one's reflectivity and how the reflectivity of human agents may reshape the nature of the collectivity.

Third, if we conceive of the social mind as the core feature of human nature, we can confront the manner in which reflectivity is sustained and how it is suppressed. To begin with, reflectivity cannot be sustained without physical security and basic subsistence (compare Shue 1980). Also, some organizational forms provide the basis for thinking about thinking, whereas other types of organizational structures may severely limit a person's capacity to reflect on oneself and take the role of others. Concomitantly, because of their reflectivity, human agents are in a position to create new organizational forms that provide the needed support for a human rights framework.

Fourth, by recognizing reflectivity as an essential feature of human nature, one must ultimately consider just how persons often are able, or can be enabled, to take the roles of multiple divergent Others. Most analysis of role taking is framed within rather narrow societal, or even subsocietal, confines. Such a perspective is out of keeping with any effort to formulate a cross-national moral order.

Taking the role of divergent Others eventually leads us to view ourselves as others see us. Equal concern and respect for one another as human beings is a minimal condition for the maintenance of human rights. Such a principle lays the foundation for interacting effectively with persons who are unlike ourselves. Although moral debates within social or cultural systems continue to be valuable, we must also recognize the need for external checks on this form of reasoning. Any human rights perspective worthy of the name looks to standards that are trans-societal in nature. Thus, any sociological theory of human rights must be founded on principles that allow us to communicate with those of differing persuasions and to discuss our common plight and aspirations as human beings. Our common fate is predicated on sustaining human reflectivity.

## Human Rights and the Major Trends of Our Time

Heretofore I have considered the debates among communitarians, liberals, and utilitarians and have sketched out how we might ground human rights sociologically. Before I return to an evaluation of the communitarian agenda, using human rights as a takeoff point, I must first analyze the empirical issues, both societally and globally, that lie beyond the grasp of contemporary moral theory. Any meaningful sociological contribution to moral reasoning must interweave moral analysis with an understanding of the empirical conditions.

Numerous global pathologies are worthy of consideration. However, I focus first on the growth of large-scale organizations and second on fragmentation according to race and ethnicity. Communitarians speak of the responsibilities and duties of individuals, but, with the exception of scholars such as Selznick (1993), they seldom discuss the responsibilities and duties of organizations. And communitarians have little to say about the heightened racial and ethnic divisions in the modern world.

### The Nature of Organizations in the Modern World

Can we and should we evaluate the morality of large-scale organizations? Policy makers and social scientists have done so and will continue to do so. Most research on genocide and politicide rests on the premise that state power has been (or is being) misused for socially harmful purposes. It was not enough to try the Nazi leadership at Nuremberg; the destruction of the Nazi Gestapo was in keeping with the moral agenda of the trials. Also, few among us would question the assertion that Nikita Khrushchev acted morally when he dismantled the organizational apparatus that undergirded the former Soviet Gulag. And slowly the organizational structure that has been the backbone of apartheid in South Africa is being reconstituted.

In analyzing organizations today, we observe the centralization of power nationally and globally. In the United States the military-industrial complex, although downsizing, is still with us, and the criminal justice system, particularly the prison-industrial complex, is ever more visible. In addition, mergers of corporations continue apace. That centralization will continue to evolve in the medical-industrial sphere is highly likely. Still, we have little or no grasp of the social and moral complications of this overall process.

On the international front we are spectators at the construction of a European Union. More dramatic still are the large-scale corporate organizations that span nation-states. In somewhat descending order of their power, they include finance capital, the educational/scientific complex, the mass media and information structures, and the organizations that produce and distribute agricultural products and manufactured goods. I return to these below.

But what is it about bureaucratic organizations that raises such a challenge to communitarians (and other moral theorists)? The logic of bureaucratic organizations, as it plays out in its ideal form, not only serves the cause of modernity but also poses a serious danger to human beings in the modern world. Although Weber was deeply troubled by the "iron cage," the imperatives of bureaucratic structures are more fundamental than Weber acknowledged (1978). Through his analysis of the lifeworld, Habermas (1987), for one, has sought to overcome Weber's pessimism. However, Habermas has yet to comprehend the actual practices of bureaucratic organizations, and he has studiously avoided examining the impact of large-scale organizations on the economically and politically disadvantaged members of Third World nations.

In order to update Weber's framework and address some of the issues raised by Habermas, I briefly outline a conception of bureaucracy that is more in keeping with contemporary reality. I begin, in a general sense, with Weber's characterization of bureaucracy. It is typified, for instance, by hierarchy of authority, a division of labor (or specialization within and among organizations), and a conception of rationality that emphasizes the selection of the most efficient means to attain a given end. Formal rationality, or efficiency, is in turn associated with the process of standardization or routinization and with the selection of personnel on the basis of universalistic, rather than particularistic, criteria.

Given his level of analysis, Weber sidestepped at least three issues: the relationship between bureaucratic organizations and human agents; hierarchy, discretion, and responsibility; and the broader implications of secrecy. I consider these, however briefly.

*Organizations and Human Agents.* Anthony Giddens (1984) has made a sustained effort, in his *The Constitution of Society,* to integrate social structure and human agents. He speaks of social structure as both constraining and enabling, and he rests his case for human agency on a version of "ego psychology." Still, Giddens neglects salient elements of organizations. Bureaucratic organizations exist in a dialectic relationship with human agency. Organizations are more than mere "reifications" of the actors: They shape the nature of interaction among human agents. Thus, specialization and hierarchy in modern universities channel the social interaction of academics within and among departments. Although organizations cannot exist without human agents, they also have a reality apart from the latter (Vaughan and Sjoberg 1984).

In addition, Mead's conception of human agency, defined primarily by the "social mind," must be incorporated into an analysis of bureaucratic organizations. This means that one must look closely at how large-scale structures facilitate and constrain reflectivity. Some organizational structures, such as those related to the sciences, support some form of reflectivity. Concomitantly, the constraints of bureaucracy loom large, particularly for those below. The Nazi case underlines, in extreme form, how reflectivity can be suppressed, as "ordinary men," all in a day's work, carried out mass killings. The leadership was also blinded by tunnel vision because of a commitment to maintenance of a system based on beliefs in Aryan racial superiority.

*Hierarchy, Discretion, and Responsibility.* In more concrete terms, the matter of reflectivity is deeply affected by the hierarchical nature of bureaucratic systems. As we move up the social ladder in large organizations, the leaders have far greater discretion than members below. Not that those below do not interpret rules, but they do so within very narrow terms. Those in positions of privilege and power are far less bound by formal rules than those below. Moreover, we find a pattern of blamability being delegated under the guise of responsibility. Persons functioning in large organizations soon recognize, if they step back only momentarily, that they will be blamed by those above if they act on their own. Blaming those below is built into the nature of both corporate and governmental organizations as they seek to sustain a hierarchy of authority and maintain efficiency (compare Thompson 1961).

*Secrecy.* Weber briefly discusses organizational secrecy but does not consider its broader ramifications. When I speak of secrecy I do more than hark back to the distinction between formal and informal arrangements, for secrecy systems cut across these social realms. Formal secrecy systems, for instance, are a way of life in governmental and corporate structures. Nor is all secrecy immoral. Privacy, for instance, can be viewed as keeping information from organizations and seems essential if a democratic order is to be sustained. Nonetheless, secrecy is one effective means for system maintenance and managerial control; it provides managers with a monopoly of various kinds of information. But this type of secrecy system also leads those below to create a hidden side to protect themselves against managerial manipulation and control. More generally, bureaucratic organizations, both corporate and governmental, foster secret arrangements in order to protect themselves against competition from others in their organizational field.

Secrecy has been the bedrock of totalitarian and authoritarian systems, but it also permeates organizations in democratic orders. Governmental secrecy, as evidenced by Watergate and Iran-Contra, is well known. But we should not overlook secrecy arrangements within the corporate sector. These seem to have multiplied in ways still unknown to scholars, as transnational corporations, which span national state boundaries, come to have a life of their own. The BCCI scandal, I suspect, represents only the tip of the iceberg with respect to international secrecy systems in the corporate sector.

*Bureaucracy and Social Triage*

I have elaborated on neglected features of bureaucracy in order to come to terms more fully with modern-day organizations. In general liberals have supported governmental structures and been skeptical of corporate ones, and utilitarians (the modern-day conservatives) have been skeptical of state intervention (save for law and order) and taken a benign, often supportive, view of the corporate apparatus. In these matters the communitarians seem closer to the liberals than to the utilitarians.

Both corporate and governmental sectors require critical attention. Unlike a few years ago, we are aware today of the enormous failings of centralized bureaucratic planning, especially in the economic sphere. The collapse of the former Soviet Union and the Eastern bloc has restructured the nature of economic, political, and social debate throughout the world.

Yet the capitalism that has triumphed is not the capitalism of Adam Smith or Ricardo, or even Marx. It is the "bureaucratic capitalism" of Weber. Parsons (1937), in *The Structure of Social Action,* understood well Weber's conceptual breakthrough. Parsons spoke of "capitalistic bureaucracy," or what I term "bureaucratic capitalism." Still, to this day, the larger social and moral ramifications of bureaucratic capitalism await attention. In *The Handbook of Economic Sociology* (Smelser and Swedberg 1994), some social scientists examine elements of this social arrangement, but no one addresses bureaucratic capitalism head-on.

Weber perceived formal rationality as undermining substantive rationality. However, Weber's analysis did not go far enough. Within the framework of bureaucratic capitalism, formal rationality seems ready to undermine itself. For one thing, built into bureaucratic capitalism, for all its emphasis on universalism, is a form of social triage.[8] From the perspective of the privileged sectors of bureaucratic structures, it is efficient to sacrifice the "unworthy poor."

Efficiency is the hallmark of large-scale organizations. This leads not only to an emphasis on profits but also to an expansion of markets and spheres of influence (Fligstein 1990). We can re-examine Wilson's (1987) *The Truly Disadvantaged* with this in mind. In the process we find that it is inefficient to assist the truly disadvantaged. If we upgrade poor African Americans' education and skills, they still may not have a place in a highly scientific/technological order wherein automation reduces the need for a sizable labor force. From the standpoint of utilitarianism, or modern rational choice theory, it makes little sense to invest in ghettos or barrios—or to assist the homeless. It is more cost effective, or efficient, to let the poor die young.

Other illustrations will clarify my reasoning. The banking system increasingly excludes or disfavors those below. Persons with a small amount in their checking account typically pay more for the privilege of banking; and the small saver is a nuisance. Under these circumstances the least privileged cannot become a sound credit risk, for they are excluded from participating in a central organization in U.S. society.

In the governmental arena, we find in recent decades cost/benefit analysis often serves as a standard for evaluating programs. Given this utilitarian moral imperative, organizations "cream off" those most likely to succeed. Thus, programs that are committed to improving job skills have engaged in selective recruitment in order to ensure that their objectives will be attained.

Still, our focus must be on bureaucratic capitalism in a global context. Although bureaucratic capitalism is the dominant force worldwide, both proponents of modernization theory and proponents of world system theory downplay or ignore its existence. Yet, the process of social triage associated with bureaucratic capitalism on a global scale is increasingly evident. Transnational corporations do little to upgrade poor developing nations. The plight of the countries in Africa in particular stands out.[9] Viewed more generally, the gap is growing between rich and poor nations. In relative terms, the poor are becoming poorer. In addition, the gap between the rich and the poor in less developed societies is accelerating. Only those persons who have a foothold, or toehold, in transnational organizations are in a position to prosper; those who do not must fend for themselves.

A somewhat closer look at the functioning of transnational bureaucratic capitalism is in order.[10] While differences can be readily discerned among the transnational structures based primarily in Europe, Japan, and the United States, the logic on which they function has much in common.

The most powerful bureaucratic organizations are those associated with finance capital, including the International Monetary Fund (IMF), the World Bank, and the large banking enterprises of the First World. One gains some insight into how finance capital deals with the dispossessed by considering the debt structure in developing nations. Devlin's *Debt and Crisis in Latin America* (1989) serves as a useful case study. One finds that during the 1970s the nations in Latin America "overborrowed." However, the banks aggressively sought out borrowers, as the banking systems were constructing their own demand. When the economic crisis of the 1980s came to a head, the poor nations were called on to carry the cost of the debt. Because the banks had political and economic clout, they fared quite well. As a consequence, resources have been transferred from developing to highly developed nations.[11]

I can do little more than mention the educational/scientific complex and the bureaucratic organizations associated with the mass media. Their role in social triage is more indirect than that of finance capital. Nonetheless, educational/scientific structures (though loosely coupled) continue to support the marginalization of the dispossessed within a global framework by training the managers, scientists, and technical experts that staff modern-day organizations. Moreover, scientific laboratories are a driving force behind technological change. From one perspective, scientists are the central players in facilitating the "creative destruction" by capitalism that Joseph Schumpeter (1950) so admired.

What is important to recognize is that the infrastructure associated with the educational/scientific complex can be supported only by elite industrial nations. The bottom layer of the developing world, such as the nations in Africa, is almost totally marginalized with respect to modern scientific efforts. These nations already suffer from a "book famine," and as the "information superhighway" becomes central to modern educational/scientific activities, the poorest nations seem destined to fall still further behind advanced industrial ones. Only a minuscule sector of developing nations will be linked to global educational structures.

The centralization of the mass media is more readily documented, but the implications of this process are subject to considerable debate ("Power of the Media in the Global System" 1993). I side with those who perceive the global mass media as spurring consumerism and fostering certain types of standardization. In addition, the increased centralization of power within the mass media, while creating countervailing forces, seems destined to make it more difficult for dissenting voices, especially by the dispossessed, to receive a hearing. This will further marginalize the truly disadvantaged in the global arena.

When we consider the production and distribution of goods (and services), social triage once again comes into sharp focus. For example, as transnational organizations control agro-food systems, farmers in many developing nations are being encouraged to produce cash crops that can be sold to those who hold positions of privilege in global bureaucratic structures (compare Reynolds et al. 1993). These cash crops, in turn, are replacing the production of staples for the local populace. In the process, the organizational structures, and those who command positions within them, can lay claim to being efficient, but at the expense of the poor within the world economy.[12]

Up to this point I have suggested how bureaucratic capitalism has been exploiting the disadvantaged in the global system. If we focus not just on people but on the environment, the problems associated with bureaucratic capitalism are compounded. Centralized planning economies failed miserably to cope with the environment (Feshbach and Friendly 1992), but that should not dissuade us from exposing the failures of bureaucratic capitalism in this realm. The threat of an environmental crisis is upon us.[13] This includes the dumping of toxic wastes in poor nations, deforestation on a worldwide basis, pollution of the oceans, and the destruction of arable lands.

Although new technologies have come to substitute for depleted resources or have even enhanced the environment, some environmental issues seem intractable to resolution within the framework of global bureaucratic capitalism. I mention two. First, efficiency is defined within a short time frame, and many environmental problems require a long-term approach (Berger 1992). Consequently, the managers of modern bureaucracies cannot adequately address the pollution of the oceans or the matter of toxic wastes. To do so requires that they think not only in terms of years but in terms of decades or even centuries, reasoning that is foreign to managers schooled in the efficiency principle. Second, the rationalization process, reflected in standardized procedures, has enhanced efficiency in the production of automobiles, clothing, and other consumer goods. However, standardized practices when applied, for example, to the cultivation of agricultural lands can foster environmental destruction. Soil capacity is often highly variable, even within a relatively small region. Therefore, standardized agricultural practices can be exceedingly harmful to soil capacity (compare Herring 1990).

But how does bureaucratic capitalism relate to our overall argument? Formal rationality, with its emphasis on efficiency, lies at the core of modern bureaucratic organizations. This comes to be judged not only by profits but also by the development of powerful organizational structures that coordinate diverse specialists and fend off competitors.

As transnational bureaucratic capitalism has come into its own, so has a form of social triage—the sacrifice of the most politically and economically disadvantaged. This process is then justified in one of several ways. First, those in positions of power and authority delegate blamability under the guise of responsibility. They judge those who fail as socially and morally incompetent or unworthy. Second, those who attain power and authority are imbued with a sense of system commitment. They strive to maintain or advance a particular bureaucratic system that is constantly threatened by real or potential competitors. One strategic means for keeping challengers at bay is through elaborate secrecy systems. If one doubts this, one has only to observe how difficult it is to decode the internal workings of powerful banking enterprises.[14]

Within the framework of bureaucratic capitalism, not only people but also the environment can become expendable. A full-scale analysis could demonstrate how the formal rationality of transnational bureaucratic capitalism, if left unchecked, can intensify, rather than diminish, the growing environmental crisis.

While one can admire many of the accomplishments of bureaucratic capitalism, its failings cannot be overlooked. Transnational structures have outgrown public accountability at local and national levels, creating a moral crisis on a worldwide scale. If the issues associated with social triage or the environment are to be addressed, more is needed than an emphasis on the duties and responsibilities of leadership. A restructuring of bureaucratic capitalism seems to be required. Put differently, if transnational corporations are to be held morally accountable, if they are to be reconstituted in accordance with some universal moral principles, then a human rights framework must be brought to the fore.

### Race and Ethnicity

I turn for a moment from bureaucratic organizations to race and ethnicity.[15] Evidence continues to mount that racial and ethnic tensions and divisions are increasing, not decreasing, around the world (compare Davis 1994). This fragmentation countervails, to a considerable degree, the centralization of organizations. The nation-state, which continues as a powerful social unit, is having its foundations eroded by both centralization and fragmentation.

I have emphasized that the human rights framework emerged as a result of the Holocaust. Yet, we continue to grapple with a set of standards by which to hold the perpetrators of genocidal massacres accountable, but it is not just the mass killings that command attention. Only a general acceptance of a set of universal principles based on human rights seems likely to permit persons of differing ethnic and racial backgrounds to come to terms with one another.

Racial and ethnic fragmentation may be found in every region of the world. The United States is far from resolving its racial and ethnic difficulties. England, France, and Germany face growing racial and ethnic divisions resulting from the immigration of peoples from various sectors of the globe. Latin America suffers from far greater racial and ethnic tensions than was supposed just a few decades ago. Conflicts in the Middle East are well known, though the situation of the Kurdish people (who live in Iraq and Turkey) is only dimly perceived. In South Asia, one can single out the strife between the Sinhalese and Tamils in Sri Lanka.

The end of the Cold War has brought to center stage racial and ethnic relations in Eastern Europe and the former Soviet Union.[16] The complex ethnic divisions in Eastern Europe are dramatized by the devastation in the former Yugoslavia. The situation in the former Soviet Union is fraught with potential dangers. Race and ethnic relations in Central Asia are particularly instructive. We have learned about the resistance of Turkic groups, notably the Uzbeks, to Soviet rule and how Mikhail Gorbachev, though a visionary, was severely limited in his understanding of these peoples (Critchlow 1991). Now after the breakup of the Soviet system the potential for race and ethnic strife has not lessened. Russians who moved to the Central Asian republics suddenly became an ethnic minority whose fate is subject not only to the Turkic peoples who control these new states and also to ongoing political struggles within Russia.

Although I offer no grand theoretical synthesis, a case can be made for a linkage between the bureaucratic process, observed earlier, and this racial and ethnic fragmentation. Three interrelated patterns can be delineated. First, power groups utilize, purposively or otherwise, organizations to keep racial and ethnic groups in their place. Second, the discrimination against minorities by those who control organizational power fosters racial and ethnic identity. A heightened focus on racial and ethnic identity offers people a partial buffer against bureaucratic domination. Third, the elites of various racial and ethnic groups break away from nation-states in order to construct direct linkages with global bureaucratic organizations.

With respect to the bureaucratic control of minorities, we have only to look to the United States. Although racial and ethnic minorities have climbed into powerful organizations (or onto the edges thereof), the bureaucratic organizations, dominated by Anglos, employ organizational power to keep minorities in their place. Data are accumulating that discrimination in housing, for instance, has been a widespread means of keeping minorities segregated (Massey and Denton 1993). More narrowly, economically disadvantaged racial and ethnic groups are unable to escape ghettos or barrios, and thus they are denied equal access to educational and economic opportunities.

Of compelling import is the growth of the prison-industrial complex in many nations in the West. The United States today can lay claim to the largest prison complex, on a per capita basis, in the world. In the process large segments of the black and Hispanic poor are being warehoused. "The potentially dangerous population is taken away and placed under complete control as raw material for parts of the very same industrial complex which made them superfluous and idle outside the walls" (Christie 1993, 116).

Economic restructuring, which has accompanied the growth of global bureaucratic capitalism, has triggered a large-scale effort by industrial societies to cope with "undesirables" who are economically expendable. The resulting prison-industrial complex may well have a law and order, as well as an economic, rationale. But this complex poses serious difficulties for social and moral theorists who perceive the United States or West European nations as beacons for democracy.[17]

Although bureaucratic organizations sustain privilege vis-à-vis racial and ethnic minorities, they are also being challenged by the latter. One source of opposition is the maintenance of counter social and cultural traditions that provide minorities with a social identity apart from the dominant order. Racial and ethnic minorities may also confront more directly those who command organizational power. Some racial and ethnic riots can be viewed in this light. So, too, the rebellion by Indians in Chiapas, Mexico, offers a rather stark illustration of resistance to the bureaucratization process. The leadership seems quite conscious of their opposition to discrimination by national and global structures that have kept them in a politically and economically disadvantaged position. Whatever the outcome of the rebellion in Chiapas, the world community knows that Mexico is far from providing social justice for its Indian minority.

Closely interrelated with the resurgence of racial and ethnic identity by those being discriminated against is the process whereby elites of these minority groups find it advantageous to break away from nation-states in order to build direct ties to worldwide bureaucratic structures. Thus, the privileged sector of Croatian society, by separating itself from Serbian-dominated Belgrade, is now in a position to cut deals directly with the European Union or other transnational organizations. A similar process seems to have been in place in many regions of the former Soviet Union—in Ukraine, Central Asia, and the Baltic states. This separatism is fueled, in many instances, by ethnonationalism.

The heightened divisions along racial and ethnic grounds must assume center place in any analysis of moral issues. More important still, the human rights perspective offers the greatest possibility for building the basis for reasoned moral discourse across the growing differences within and among societies.

## Conclusions and Implications

The empirical realities of the rise of transnational bureaucratic organizations and the divisions according to race and ethnicity serve as a backdrop, or foundation, for evaluating communitarianism. Like the communitarians, I also question the unbridled individualism that is championed by large sectors of U.S. society. Given my neo-Meadian orientation, I cannot perceive how potentialities of the social mind and its reflectivity can be realized without some kind of community being in place. Yet, I see a pressing need for communitarians (as well as liberals and especially utilitarians) to adopt a human rights framework. This is essential if we are to cope with issues in U.S. society, to say nothing of those in the larger global setting. There are several reasons for advancing a human rights orientation.

First, although duties and responsibilities to others are fundamental for a just and democratic social order, the communitarian conception of duties and responsibilities is flawed. The communitarians view these from the perspective of the privileged rather than from that of the underprivileged. The underprivileged lack the social and organizational resources to carry out the principles as enunciated by the privileged. For example, the burgeoning prison-industrial complex is making ex-convicts a major component of many urban centers in the United States. Yet, they will be unable to carry out the duties and responsibilities to their families and the broader community the communitarians espouse. One does not have to be a devotee of labeling theory to recognize that the more powerful sectors of society stigmatize ex-cons in ways that make it impossible for them to carry out duties and obligations that the privileged take for granted. In addition, the duties and responsibilities that most communitarians have in mind tend to stop at the American shoreline. But do not Americans have duties and responsibilities to the poor in the Third World? If we place "the community" within a global setting, would not, for example, some reduction of extreme consumerism be in order?

Second, except for Selznick, the communitarians have little to say about the duties, responsibilities, or obligations of powerful organizations.[18] Bellah et al. (1991) speak of the "tyranny of the market," and Etzioni (1988) insists on the moral dimension of economic activities. But they have not taken the step of examining "the market" in the context of global bureaucratic capitalism. Like other communitarians, they appear to be oblivious to transnational corporations which deeply affect not just the social and moral fabric of U.S. society but also the lives of people worldwide. The impact of bureaucratic capitalism on the Third World peoples cannot forever be disregarded in serious moral discourse. In addition, the communitarians have had little to say about the abuse of state power. Ultimately, they will need to confront the prison-industrial complex, to say nothing of genocide and politicide in far-flung corners of the world.

Third, Etzioni, Bellah, and Selznick, among others, skirt the issue of race and ethnic relations, nationally and globally.[19] In a world increasingly fractured by racial and ethnic divisions, communitarians have faltered in constructing moral principles that can transcend these continuing cleavages within U.S. society, as well as those that haunt humankind in the international realm. The concept of community evokes an imagery of exclusion, not inclusion—of us against them.

It is these limitations in communitarianism (as well as in other ethicist orientations) that lead me to advocate a human rights perspective. A universal human rights framework—one that calls for equal concern and respect for human beings—has much to recommend it.

1. If we are to speak adequately about genocide, politicide, or atrocities, we must be able to invoke a set of universal standards. Unless one is prepared to mount a moral defense of national sovereignty as the ultimate good, some general human rights framework becomes essential in order to investigate (and evaluate) killings of human collectivities on the global scene.

2. We stand in need of a global standard, or set of standards, as a check on the moral debates that are typically framed in system-specific terms. We need to view ourselves in relation to others and examine how others perceive us. To do otherwise is to adopt a questionable form of American exceptionalism.

3. We stand in need of a human rights framework that will provide a set of standards (or principles) for evaluating the activities of powerful, notably transnational, organizations. It is not enough to emphasize the duties and responsibilities of human agents. We must take account of the duties and responsibilities of organizations. Organizations, either state or corporate, can be faulted for many of the moral issues of our day. In extreme situations we have been quite ready to acknowledge that organizations must be restructured

or replaced. But we are often unwilling to generalize this principle, particularly as it relates to organizational structures that many moral theorists, including communitarians, have come to take for granted. Earlier I spoke of system commitment as a moral category. It follows that the nature and kind of organizations to which people are committed must be critically evaluated, and a set of universal human rights seems to be most applicable for doing so.

4. We stand in need of a universal set of human rights in order to facilitate discourse (and understanding) across racial and ethnic lines, not only within the United States but also globally. At the same time, any adequate human rights framework will require the construction of new organizational forms that will promote reflectivity. Yet, without a commitment to human rights—without, for instance, equal concern and respect for fellow human beings—there is little likelihood of transcending, or resolving, the ever-growing divisions along race and ethnic lines, thereby staving off the wanton destruction of various human groups.

I live under no illusions that human beings will be able to construct a viable moral order based on human rights. Nonetheless, a human rights framework is no mirage, for elements of this perspective exist, albeit in a fragile and fragmented form. The effort to build a viable moral order on a global scale is a worthy endeavor if we value human beings as such.

## Notes

1. The literature on the communitarian and liberal debate has become extensive. See, for example, Mulhall and Swift (1992) and Avineri and de-Shalit (1992).

2. The linkages of communitarianism to, for instance, theorizing about "citizenship" (Kymlicka and Norman 1994) and "civil society" (Cohen and Arato 1992) deserve to be spelled out—but not here.

3. The concept of "community of memory" is closely intertwined with that of "historical memory," and as such shapes the identity and policies of peoples within nation-states. See, for example, Rousso (1991).

4. For recent works on human rights see, for example, Claude and Weston (1992), Eide et al. (1992), Kent (1993), and Shute and Hurley (1993). The last volume mentioned includes chapters by John Rawls, Steven Lukes, Catherine MacKinnon, and others.

5. Fein (1993) provides a useful guide to the controversies regarding the meaning of genocide and related concepts. I distinguish between genocide and politicide and even between genocide and genocidal massacres. I reserve the concept genocide to the systematic destruction of collectivities in which race or ethnic issues play a significant role. An instance of genocidal massacre occurred in Guatemala and is carefully described by Falla (1994).

6. In light of my modified Meadian orientation, I find that the social mind can only emerge in the process of social interaction. I readily acknowledge the existence of individualism and creative human agents. Yet, how and why one thinks as one does is predicated on interaction with others in organizational settings. A Meadian conception of the social mind differs considerably from that of the mind advanced by cognitive psychologists and

philosophers whose views typically are founded on individuals as isolated entities. Empirically, this latter perspective is untenable (compare Vaughan and Sjoberg 1984).

7. "Social calculations" refers to complex reasoning processes that involve, for example, the use of various "logical forms"—analogy, classification (including typification), dialectical reasoning, deductive logic, and so on. They also include the imputation of meanings to social actions. These social calculations, which are little understood, come into play as persons engage in "taking the role of others."

8. The relationship of bureaucracy to social triage was first discussed by Sjoberg, Vaughan, and Williams (1984).

9. Articles and book reviews in *Africa Today* provide an informative guide to political and economic conditions on that continent.

10. For works on transnational corporations, see, for example, Barnet and Cavanagh (1994), Harrison (1994), Reich (1991), Wachtel (1990), and Cowhey and Aronson (1993).

11. Morgan (1979) provides convincing evidence regarding the manner in which transnational grain companies took advantage, through their secrecy systems, of poor nations by selling them "contaminated" grain. That agribusiness continues to exploit the less powerful has been brought up to date by Bonner and Bennett (1994) in their account of the selling of worthless seed to Ukraine.

12. My working thesis is that the contradictions of bureaucratic capitalism are likely to emerge, in rather heightened form, in Eastern Europe and the former Soviet Union. It is evident that centralized planning was a disaster. However, the effort to restore a market economy through "shock therapy" or the "big bang" will provide a formidable test for bureaucratic capitalism. Economists such as Jeffrey Sachs (1993), who have been ardent champions of the market for Eastern Europe, do not grasp that their model of capitalism has little relationship to the realities of bureaucratic capitalism. Thus the disjunction between the ideal and the real has the potential for creating serious instabilities.

13. I have consulted only a small segment of the enormous literature on the environment. With respect to Southeast Asia, see, for example, Broad and Cavanagh (1994) and Dauvergne (1993/94), and with respect to Asia more generally, see Howard (1994) and Smil (1993). For the former Soviet Union, see Feshbach and Friendly (1992). A somewhat more general account is contained in Rich (1994).

14. Banking systems are by no means alone in their secretiveness. Extensive news accounts in June 1994, detail how American tobacco companies employed secrecy systems in order to construct demand, as well as supply, for their product.

15. I am all too cognizant that I should consider fragmentation along gender lines. However, I have yet to formulate, in an adequate manner, just how gender divisions are related to race and ethnicity and, more particularly, to transnational bureaucratic organizations.

16. For an overview of the disintegration of Yugoslavia, see Denitch (1994). Unfortunately, his analysis of the Bosnian Muslims is far too thin. Also see Draper (1993) for data on the collapse of the former Czechoslovakia. With respect to the former Soviet Union I have read the *Central Asian Survey* and the *Central Asia Monitor,* as well as the *New York Times,* the *New York Review,* and *The Economist.*

17. Along with the prison-industrial complex, the moral dimensions of a "surveillance society" beg for attention, (see for example, Lyon 1994).

18. Frazer and Lacey (1993) take both liberals and communitarians to task for ignoring power. I agree, but I go further by calling on moral theorists to confront powerful large-scale organizations.

19. Some moral theorists are beginning to grapple with race and ethnicity, with cultural particularity, in the context of universalism. See, for example, Taylor (1992) and Gutmann (1993).

# References

Andersen, Martin E. 1993. *Dossier Secrets: Argentina's Desaparecidas and the Myth of the "Dirty War."* Boulder, CO: Westview Press.

Annas, George A., and Grodin, Michael A., eds. 1992. *The Nazi Doctors and the Nuremberg Code.* New York: Oxford University Press.

Avineri, Shlomo, and de-Shalit, Avner, eds. 1992. *Communitarianism and Individualism.* New York: Oxford University Press.

Barnet, Richard J., and Cavanagh, John. 1994. *Global Dreams: Imperial Corporations and the New World Order.* New York: Simon and Schuster.

Bell, Daniel. 1993. *Communitarianism and Its Critics.* New York: Oxford University Press.

Bellah, Robert N.; Madsen, Richard; Sullivan, William M.; Swidler, Ann; and Tipton, Steven M. 1985. *Habits of the Heart.* Berkeley: University of California Press.

————. 1991. *The Good Society.* New York: Alfred A. Knopf.

Berger, Johannes. 1992. "The Future of Capitalism." In *Social Change and Modernity,* eds. Hans Haferkamp and Neil J. Smelser, 237–55. Berkeley: University of California Press.

Bonner, Raymond, and Bennett, James. 1994. "A Bitter Harvest for Ukraine from an American Seed Deal." *New York Times* (June 19): 1, A7.

Broad, Robin, and Cavanagh, John. 1993. *Plundering Paradise.* Berkeley: University of California Press.

Buergenthal, Thomas. 1992. "The Helsinki Process: Birth of a Human Rights System." In Claude and Weston, 1992, 256–68.

Christie, Nils. 1993. *Crime Control as Industry: Towards GULAGS, Western Style?* New York: Routledge.

Claude, Richard Pierre, and Weston, Burns H., eds. 1992. *Human Rights in the World Community.* 2d ed. Philadelphia: University of Pennsylvania Press.

Cohen, Jean L., and Arato, Andrew. 1992. *Civil Society and Political Theory.* Cambridge, MA: MIT Press.

Cowhey, Peter F., and Aronson, Jonathan D. 1993. *Managing the World Economy.* New York: Council on Foreign Relations Press.

Critchlow, James. 1991. *Nationalism in Uzbekistan.* Boulder, CO: Westview Press.

Daubergne, Peter. 1993/94. "The Politics of Deforestation in Indonesia." *Pacific Affairs* 66 (Winter): 497–518.

Davis, Bob. 1994. "Global Paradox: Growth of Trade Binds Nations, but It Also Can Spur Separatism." *Wall Street Journal* (June 20): 1, A4.

Denitch, Bogdan. 1994. *Ethnic Nationalism: The Tragic Death of Yugoslavia.* Minneapolis: University of Minnesota Press.

Devlin, Robert. 1989. *Debt and Crisis in Latin America.* Princeton, NJ: Princeton University Press.

Dews, Peter, ed. 1992. *Autonomy and Solidarity: Interviews with Jürgen Habermas.* Rev. ed. London: Verso.

Donnelly, Jack. 1993. *International Human Rights.* Boulder, CO: Westview Press.

Draper, Theodore. 1993. "The End of Czechoslovakia." *New York Review* 40: 20–26.

Dworkin, Ronald. 1977. *Taking Rights Seriously.* Cambridge, MA: Harvard University Press.

Eide, Asbjorn; Alfredsson, Gudmundur; Melander, Göran; Adam Rehof, Lars; and Rosas, Allan. 1992. *The Universal Declaration of Human Rights: A Commentary.* Oslo: Scandinavian University Press.

Etzioni, Amitai. 1988. *The Moral Dimension.* New York: Free Press.

————. 1991. *A Responsive Society.* San Francisco: Jossey-Bass.

————. 1993. *The Spirit of Community: The Reinvention of American Society.* New York: Simon and Schuster.

Falla, Ricardo. 1994. *Massacres in the Jungles: Incán, Guatemala, 1975–1982.* Boulder, CO: Westview Press.

Favell, Adrian. 1993. "James Coleman: Social Theorist and Moral Philosopher?" *American Journal of Sociology* 99 (November): 590–613.

Fein, Helen. 1993. *Genocide: A Sociological Perspective.* Newbury Park, CA: Sage.

Feshbach, Murray, and Friendly, Alfred, Jr. 1992. *Ecocide in the USSR.* New York: Basic Books.

Fligstein, Neil. 1990. *The Transformation of Corporate Control.* Cambridge, MA: Harvard University Press.

Frazer, Elizabeth, and Lacey, Nicola. 1993. *The Politics of Community: A Feminist Critique of the Liberal-Communitarian Debate.* Toronto: University of Toronto Press.

Gellner, Ernest. 1985. *Relativism and the Social Sciences.* Cambridge: Cambridge University Press.

Giddens, Anthony. 1984. *The Constitution of Society.* Berkeley: University of California Press.

Glendon, Mary Ann. 1991. *Rights Talk.* New York: Free Press.

Gouldner, Alvin W. 1970. *The Coming Crisis of Western Sociology.* New York: Basic Books.

Gutmann, Amy. 1993. "The Challenge of Multiculturalism in Political Ethics." *Philosophy and Public Affairs* 22 (Summer): 171–206.

Habermas, Jürgen. 1987. *The Theory of Communicative Action, Lifeworld and System: A Critique of Functionalist Reason.* Boston: Beacon Press.

————. 1990. *Moral Consciousness and Communicative Action.* Cambridge, MA: MIT Press.

Harrison, Bennett. 1994. *Lean and Mean.* New York: Basic Books.

Herring, Ronald J. 1990. "Resurrecting the Commons." *Items.* 44 (December): 64–68.

Howard, Michael, ed. 1994. *Asia's Environmental Crisis.* Boulder, CO: Westview Press.

Jones, Robert Alun. 1994. "The Positive Science of Ethics in France: German Influences on *De la division du travail social.*" *Sociological Forum* 9 (March): 37–58.

Kent, Ann. 1993. *Between Freedom and Subsistence: China and Human Rights.* New York: Oxford University Press.

Kiernan, Ben, ed. 1993. *Genocide and Democracy in Cambodia.* New Haven, CT: Yale University Southeast Asia Studies, no. 41.

Kymlicka, Will, and Norman, Wayne. 1994. "Return of the Citizen: A Survey of Recent Work on Citizenship Theory." *Ethics* 104 (January): 352–86.

Lyon, David. 1994. *The Electronic Eye: The Rise of Surveillance Society.* Minneapolis: University of Minnesota Press.

Macpherson, C.B. 1973. *Democratic Theory.* Oxford: Oxford University Press.

Massey, Douglas S., and Denton, Nancy A. 1993. *American Apartheid.* Cambridge, MA: Harvard University Press.

Mead, George Herbert. 1934. *Mind, Self and Society.* Chicago: University of Chicago Press.

Mills, C. Wright. 1959. *The Sociological Imagination.* New York: Oxford University Press.

Morgan, Dan. 1979. *Merchants of Grain.* New York: Viking Press.

Mulhall, Stephen, and Swift, Adam. 1992. *Liberals and Communitarians.* Oxford: Blackwell.

Parsons, Talcott. 1937. *The Structure of Social Action.* New York: McGraw-Hill.

————. 1960. *Structure and Process in Modern Societies.* New York: Free Press.

Popenoe, David. 1993. "American Family Decline, 1960–1990: A Review and Appraisal." *Journal of Marriage and the Family* 55 (August): 527–41.

"Power of the Media in the Global System." Special Issue. 1993. *Journal of International Affairs* 47 (Summer).

Rawls, John. 1971. *A Theory of Justice.* Cambridge, MA: Harvard University Press.

Reich, Robert B. 1991. *The Work of Nations.* New York: Alfred A. Knopf.

"The Responsive Communitarian Platform: Rights and Responsibilities." 1991/92. *Responsive Community* 2: 4–20.

Reynolds, Laura T.; Mayre, David; McMichael, Philip; Carro-Figueroa, Vivana; and Buttell, Frederick H. 1993. "The 'New' Internationalization of Agriculture: A Reformulation." *World Development* 21: 1101–21.

Rich, Bruce. 1994. *Mortgaging the Bank: The World Bank, Environmental Impoverishment and the Crisis of Development.* Boston: Beacon Press.

Rousso, Henry. 1991. *The Vichy Syndrome: History and Memory in France Since 1944.* Cambridge, MA: Harvard University Press.

Sachs, Jeffrey. 1993. *Poland's Jump to the Market Economy.* Cambridge, MA: MIT Press.

Schumpeter, Joseph A. 1950. *Capitalism, Socialism and Democracy.* Rev. ed. New York: Harper and Row.

Selznick, Philip. 1993. *The Moral Commonwealth.* Berkeley: University of California Press.

Shue, Henry. 1980. *Basic Rights.* Princeton, NJ: Princeton University Press.

Shute, Stephen, and Hurley, Susan, eds. 1993. *On Human Rights.* New York: Basic Books.

Sjoberg, Gideon; Vaughan, Ted R.; and Williams, Norma. 1984. "Bureaucracy as a Moral Issue." *Journal of Applied Behavioral Science* 20: 441–53.

Smelser, Neil J. 1992. "The Rational Choice Perspective." *Rationality and Society* 4 (October): 381–410.

Smelser, Neil J., and Swedberg, Richard, eds. 1994. *The Handbook of Economic Sociology.* Princeton, NJ: Princeton University Press.

Smil, Vaclav. 1993. *China's Environmental Crisis.* Armonk, NY: M.E. Sharpe.

Sorokin, Pitirim A., and Lunden, Walter. 1959. *Power and Morality.* New York: Porter Sargent.

Stacey, Judith. 1993. "Good Riddance to 'The Family': A Response to David Popenoe," *Journal of Marriage and the Family* 55 (August): 545–47.

Strathern, Andrew. 1993. *Landmarks: Reflections on Anthropology.* Kent, OH: Kent State University Press.

Taylor, Charles. 1992. *Multiculturalism and "The Politics of Recognition."* Princeton, NJ: Princeton University Press.

Thompson, Victor A. 1961. *Modern Organizations.* New York: Alfred A. Knopf.

Vaughan, Ted R., and Sjoberg, Gideon. 1984. "The Individual and Bureaucracy: An Alternative Meadian Interpretation." *Journal of Applied Behavioral Science* 20: 57–69.

Wachtel, Howard. 1990. *The Money Mandarins.* Rev. ed. Armonk, NY: M.E. Sharpe.

Waldron, Jeremy, ed. 1987. *'Nonsense Upon Stilts': Bentham, Burke and Marx on the Rights of Man.* New York: Methuen.

Weber, Max. 1978. *Economy and Society.* 2 vols. Berkeley: University of California Press.

Wilson, William Julius. 1987. *The Truly Disadvantaged.* Chicago: University of Chicago Press.

# Index

International Covenant of Economic,
Social and Cultural Rights, 279
International Monetary Fund (IMF), 286
Italy, labor-management relations in,
194*n.5*, 194*n.7*
Iyengar, Shanto, 59, 66

**J**

Jackall, Robert, 213
Jacob, Herbert, 170
Jaggar, Alison M., 227, 231, 232, 234
James, Selma, 231
Japan
abortion in, 180
labor-management relations in, 184,
185
pornography in, 178
Jefferson, Thomas, 269*n.15*
Jessel, David, 174
Joas, Hans, 7, 35-48
Job evaluation, 221-227, 232
Johnson, Miriam M., 173
Jones, Robert Alun, 274
Just, Marion R., 56, 57, 58, 65

**K**

Kahneman, Daniel, 21
*Kahn v. Sprouse*, 111*n.30*
Kanter, R.M., 28, 213
Kanter, Rosabeth M., 211
Kaplan, A.G., 172
Katz, Elihu, 52, 57, 58, 62, 66, 67
Katz, Paul A., 238*n.1*
*Keech v. Sandford*, 101
Keller, Catherine, 234
Keller, Evelyn Fox, 234
Kelley, 187
Kellner, Douglas, 64, 66
Kellogg, Susan, 173
Kelly, Michael, 71*n.11*
Keynes, John Maynard, 251, 255
Khrushchev, Nikita, 283
Kiernan, Ben, 279
Killingsworth, Mark R., 221, 229
Kinder, Donald R., 66

Kitson, Gay C., 179
Kittay, Eva Feder, 235
Knight, Frank, 270*n.18*
Kolb, Deborah M., 205
Kotter, John P., 213
Kraus, Sidney, 57
Kuhn, Thomas S., 19, 20

**L**

Labor force. *See* Workers
Labor law, 187, 188-190, 229
Labor unions, 10, 186, 187, 191,
192-193
Ladd, Everett C., Jr., 62, 68-69
Laissez-faire liberalism, 228, 237, 254,
270*n.18*
Lamont, Michele, 247, 252, 268*n.4*
Lang, Gladys and Kurt, 52, 66, 68
Language, social context of, 196-201,
212
Lasch, Christopher, 245, 251, 253, 255,
256, 271*n.36*
Law
contract, 104, 106, 108, 109-110
fiduciary obligation and, 99-110, 154,
270*n.28*
higher, 278
labor, 187, 188-190, 229
as normative framework, 126
positional interests and, 160*n.32*
property, 105
trust, 107-108
Lazarsfeld, Paul F., 57, 66, 67
*Legitimation Crisis* (Habermas), 149
Lehman, Edward W., 7-8, 51-70, 53, 54,
68, 70, 71*n.6*
Lehman, Ethna, 7-8, 51-70
Lester, Marilyn, 58, 59, 71*n.8*
Lewin, Kurt, 8, 94*n.4*
Liberal complacency, 136, 146-147,
152, 255, 258, 260
Liberalism
159*n.26*, 227
feminist, 227-230, 234, 237
individualism and, 277-278
laissez-faire, 228, 237, 254

# Contributors

**Richard Coughlin,** professor of sociology, University of New Mexico, is studying domestic and comparative social policy, public opinion, and social change in industrialized societies. He is the author of *Ideology, Public Opinion and Welfare Policy* (1980) and the editor of *Reforming Welfare* (1989) and *Morality, Rationality and Efficiency* (1991).

**Deborah DeMott,** professor of law, Duke University, is the author of *Fiduciary Obligation, Agency and Partnership: Duties in Ongoing Business Relationships* (1991) and *Shareholder Derivative Actions* (1987).

**Paula England,** professor of sociology, University of Arizona, is the coauthor (with George Farkas) of *Households, Employment, and Gender* (1986) and the author of *Comparable Worth: Theories and Evidence* (1992). She is also currently the editor of the *American Sociological Review*.

**Uta Gerhardt,** professor of sociology, Institut für Soziologie, Ruprecht-Karls-Universitat, Heidelberg, Germany, has taught at the University of London and the University of California at Berkeley. She is the author of *Rollenanalyse als Kritische Soziologie* (1971), *Ideas About Illness* (1989), and *Talcott Parsons on National Socialism* (1993).

**Hans Joas,** professor of sociology, John F. Kennedy-Institut for Nordamerikastudien, Freie Universitat, Berlin, Germany, is the author of *G.H. Mead: A Contemporary Re-examination of His Thought* (1985), *Social Action and Human Nature* (1989), *Pragmatism and Social Theory* (1993), and *The Creativity of Action* (forthcoming).

**Edward Lehman,** professor and chair of sociology, New York University, is the author of *The Viable Polity* (1992), *Political Society* (1977), and *Coordinating Health Care: Explorations in Interorganizational Relations* (1975) and the coeditor (with Amitai Etzioni) of *A Sociological Reader in Complex Organizations*, 3d ed. (1980).

**Ethna Lehman,** instructor of sociology, New York University, is a freelance sociologist in New York City.

**Linda Markowitz,** Ph.D. candidate, Department of Sociology, University of Arizona, is completing her dissertation on union organizing and is a student editor of *Contemporary Sociology.*

**Calvin Morrill,** associate professor of sociology, University of Arizona, studies the structural and cultural foundations of social control using ethnographic, experimental, and network methods. He is the author of *The Executive Way: Conflict Management in Corporations* (forthcoming) and is developing a study of law and informal dispute resolution on the United States–Mexico border.

**David Popenoe,** Social Science Dean of Arts and Sciences, professor of sociology, Rutgers University, is the author of *Disturbing the Nest: Family Change and Decline in Modern Societies* (1988). He is also cochair of the Council on Families in America, a nonpartisan, interdisciplinary group of scholars and family experts concerned about family and child well-being.

**David Sciulli,** associate professor of sociology, Texas A&M University, is completing a short history of corporate law in the United States using a neoinstitutionalist approach and is also studying sociological approaches to the professions since the 1930s. He is the author of *Theory of Societal Constitutionalism: Foundations of a Non-Marxist Critical Theory* (1992) and *The End of Corporate Governance* (forthcoming).

**Gideon Sjoberg,** professor of sociology, University of Texas at Austin, is working on a sociological theory of human rights, bureaucracy, and methodology. He is the author of *The Preindustrial City* (1965) and the coauthor (with Roger Nett) of *A Methodology for Social Research* (1968).

**Wolfgang Streeck,** professor of sociology and industrial relations, University of Wisconsin, was senior research fellow, Wissenschaftszentrum, Berlin, and fellow at the Institute for Advanced Study, Berlin. He has held visiting appointments at the European University Institute, Florence; the University of Warwick; and the Center for Advanced Studies in the Social Sciences, Madrid. He is the author of *Social Institutions and Economic Performance* (1992), the coauthor (with David G. Mayes and Wolfgang Hager) of *Public Interest and Market Pressures* (1992), and the coeditor (with J. Rogers Hollingsworth and Philippe C. Schmitter) of *Governing Capitalist Economies* (1994).

**Göran Therborn,** professor of sociology, Sociologiska institutionen, Gotesborg Universitet, Goteborg, Sweden, is the author most recently of *European Modernity and Beyond: The Trajectory of European Societies, 1945–2000* (1995).

For Product Safety Concerns and Information please contact our EU
representative  GPSR@taylorandfrancis.com
Taylor & Francis Verlag GmbH, Kaufingerstraße 24, 80331 München, Germany

www.ingramcontent.com/pod-product-compliance
Ingram Content Group UK Ltd.
Pitfield, Milton Keynes, MK11 3LW, UK
UKHW021113180425
457613UK00005B/68